Alex W Inker
Artist

I warmly thank Virginia for letting me borrow her characters,
I thank Fred and his editing crew at Sarbacane for supporting this adaptation,
A heartfelt thank you to Stephen and Montana for returning it to its mothertongue,
I thank my family, my children and my friends for their endless support.

Alex W Inker is a young author from the North of France, and a graduate of the Saint Luc Institute in Brussels.
He is the author of 5 graphic novels that have garnered critical acclaim.
All 5 of them center around characters on the margins of society.

Photo by Antoine Vanbelle

Virginia Reeves
Author

Many thanks to Alex for his vivid, fresh, and honest artwork. Also many thanks to the amazing
people at Stock, Sarbacane and, Fanfare / Ponent Mon, and to Carine Chichereau for the original
English-to-French translation and Montana Kane for bringing it back to English.
I'm honored by the care you've taken with my work.

Virginia Reeves is a graduate of the Michener Center for Writers at the University of Texas at Austin. Her debut novel,
'Work Like Any Other', was longlisted for the Man Booker Prize and the Center for Fiction's First Novel Prize.
Her second novel, The Behavior of Love', was released in 2019. Virginia teaches writing, literature, and communications
at Helena College. She lives with her husband, daughters, and three-legged rescue pit bull in Montana.

Montana Kane
Translator

Virginia Reeves wrote a great novel, which Alex W Inker adapted into a great graphic novel in French,
which Stephen and Amiram from Fanfare / Ponent Mon were smart enough to acquire,
and which I was lucky enough to translate. Thanks, guys!
Favorite part: researching colorful Southern expressions.

Montana Kane grew up reading French and Belgian comic books
in France and Morocco. She has translated over 180 graphic novels and won
a Will Eisner Award in 2019 for 'Brazen' by Pénélope Bagieu (First Second).

© 2020, Éditions Sarbacane, Paris (www.editions-sarbacane.com)
For the original novel *Work Like Any Other*: Copyright © 2016 by Virginia Reeves

© Ponent Mon Ltd, 2021 for the English language edition.

www.ponentmon.com

Translated by: Montana Kane
Layout: RG e Hijas S.C.P.
ISBN: 978-1-912097-45-6
Printed and bound in European Union

ALEX W. INKER

WORK LIKE ANY OTHER

AFTER THE NOVEL BY VIRGINIA REEVES

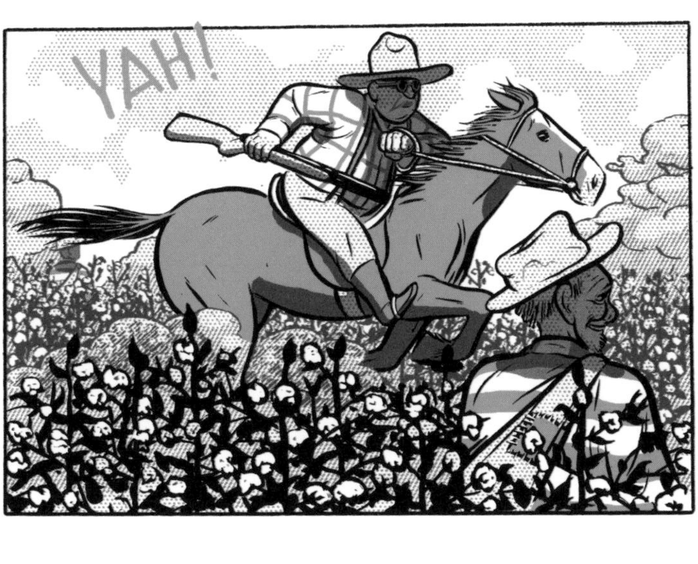
YAH!

FANFARE · PONENT MON

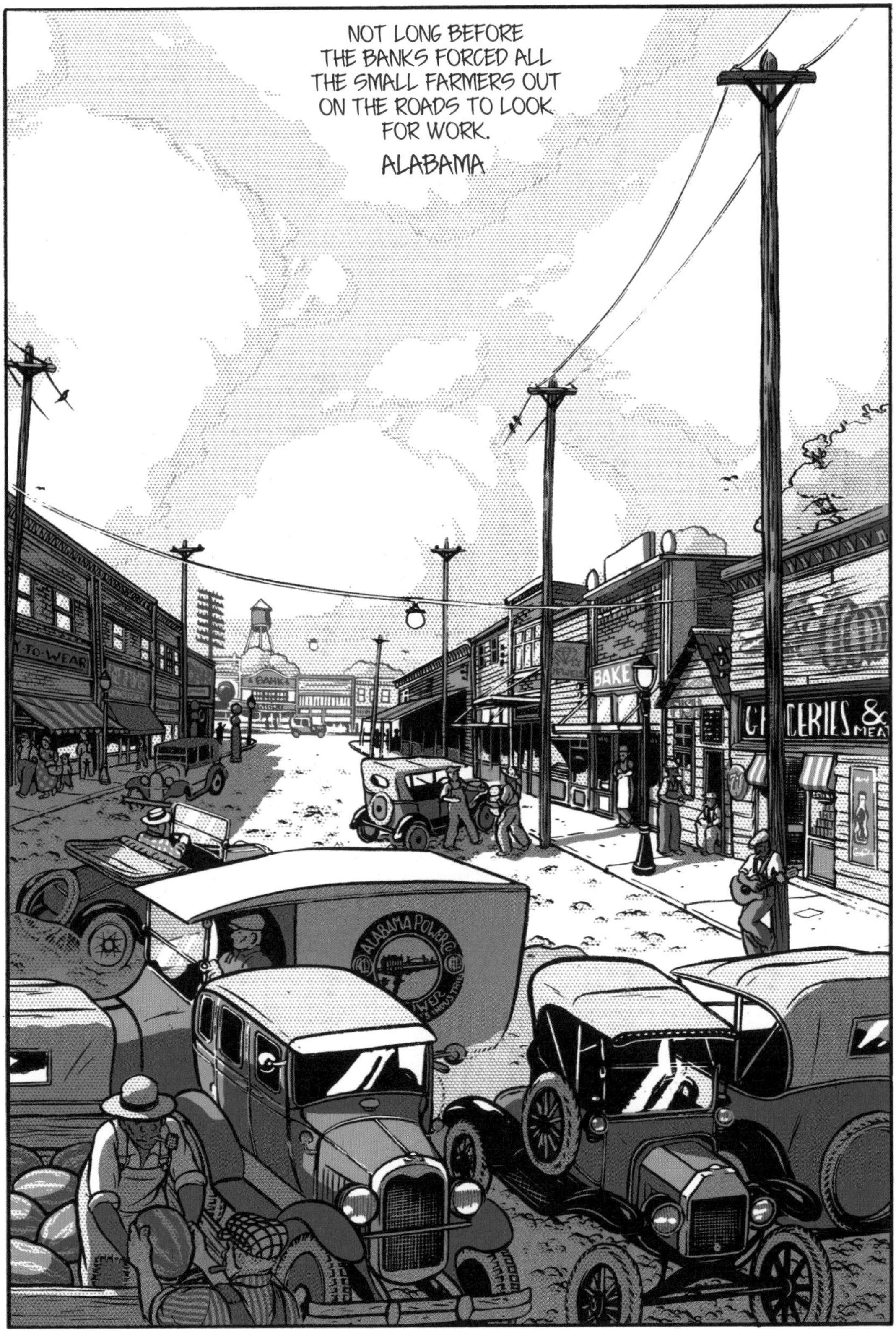
NOT LONG BEFORE THE BANKS FORCED ALL THE SMALL FARMERS OUT ON THE ROADS TO LOOK FOR WORK.
ALABAMA
BAKE
BANK
GROCERIES &
MEAT
ALABAMA POWER CO.

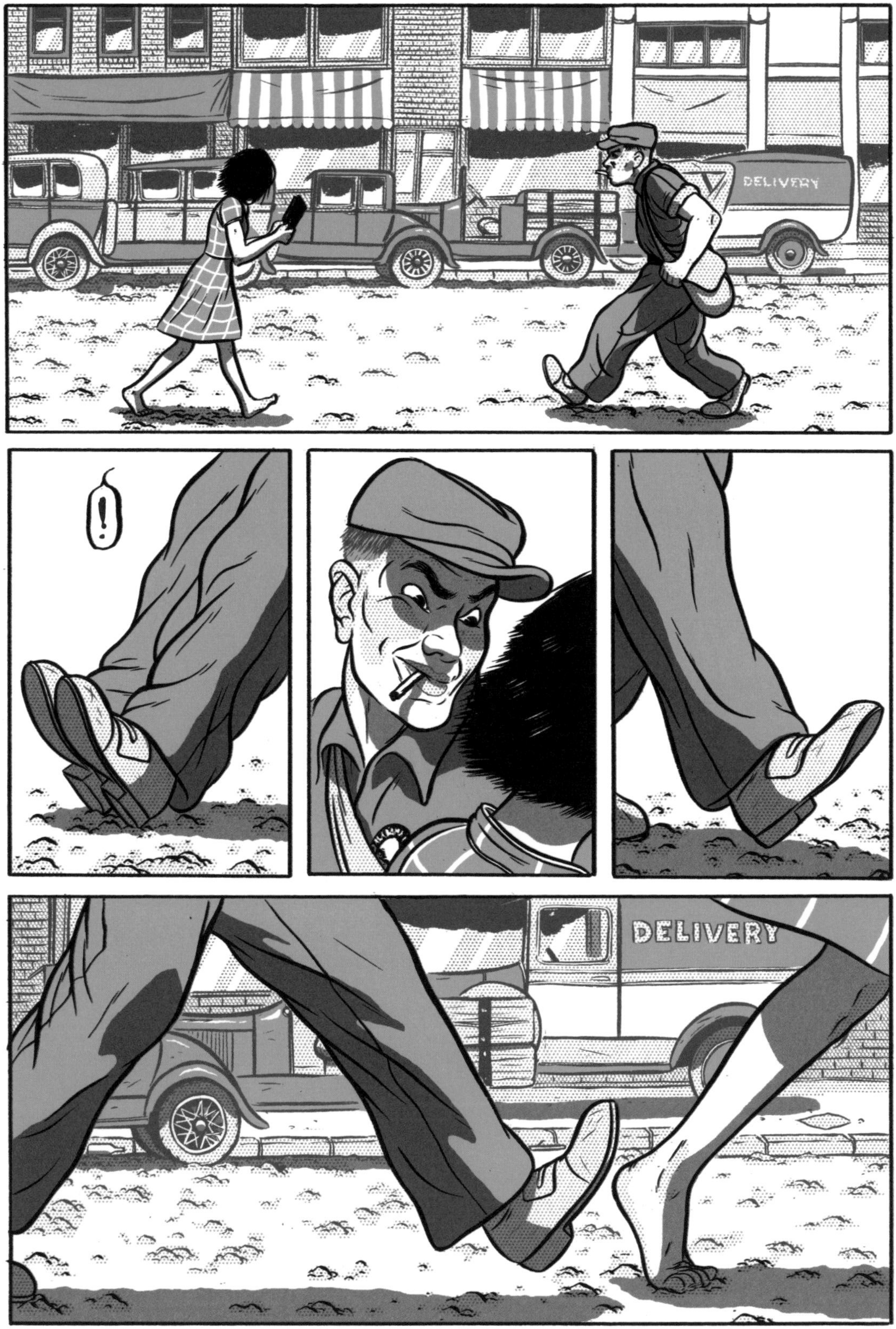
DELIVERY
!
DELIVERY

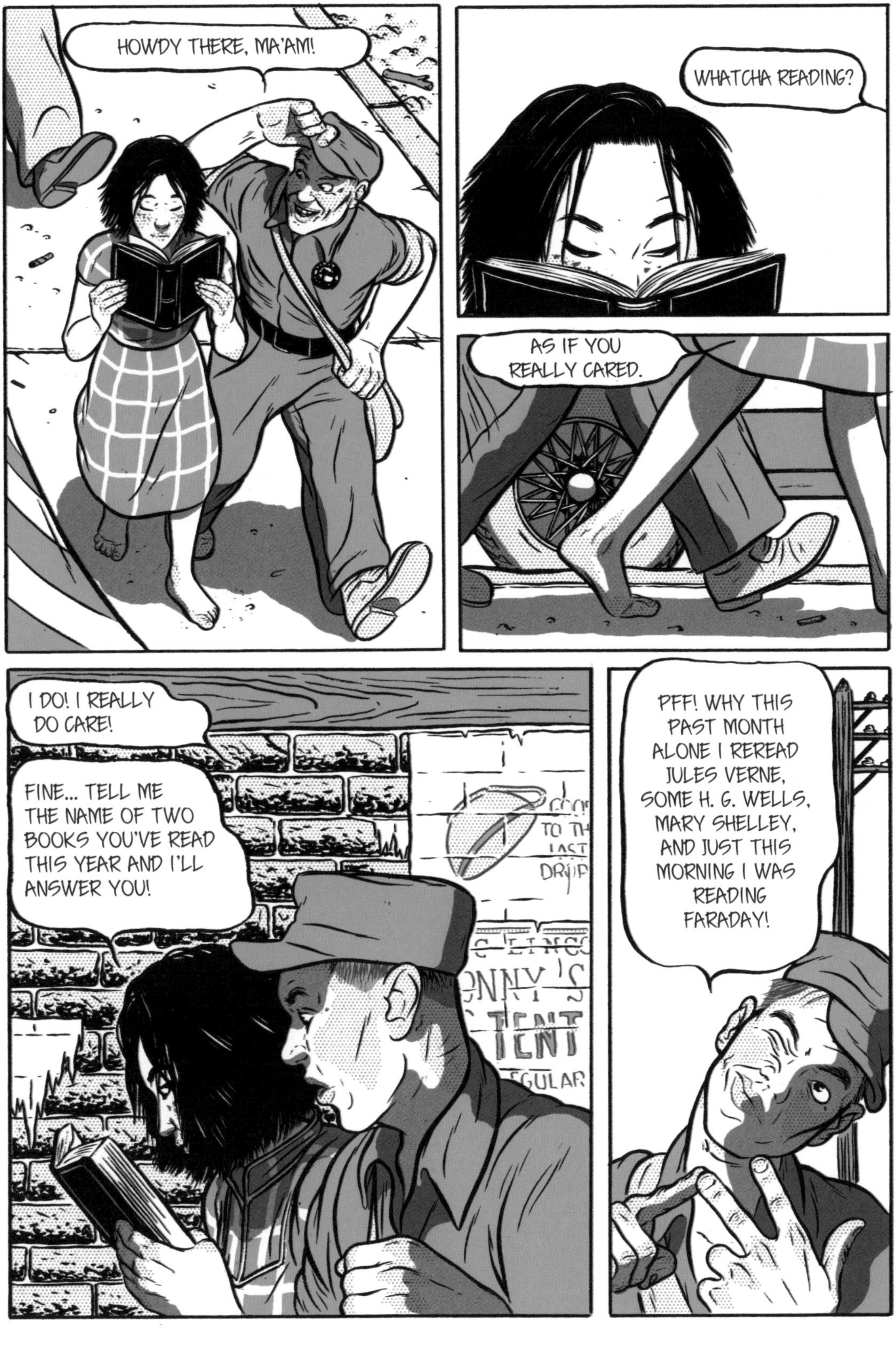
HOWDY THERE, MA'AM!
WHATCHA READING?
AS IF YOU REALLY CARED.
I DO! I REALLY DO CARE!
FINE... TELL ME THE NAME OF TWO BOOKS YOU'VE READ THIS YEAR AND I'LL ANSWER YOU!
PFF! WHY THIS PAST MONTH ALONE I REREAD JULES VERNE, SOME H. G. WELLS, MARY SHELLEY, AND JUST THIS MORNING I WAS READING FARADAY!

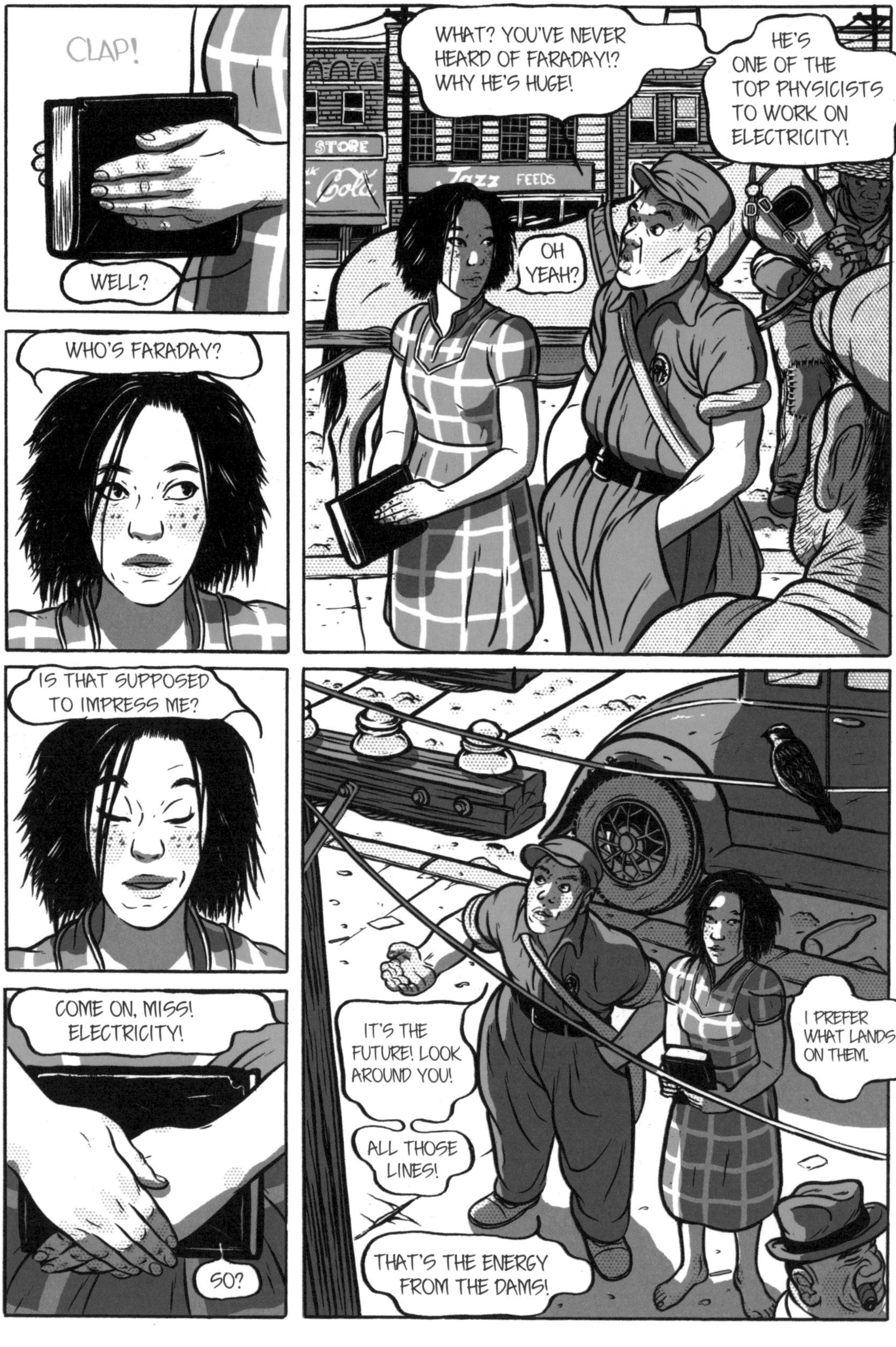
CLAP!
WELL?
WHAT? YOU'VE NEVER HEARD OF FARADAY!? WHY HE'S HUGE!
OH YEAH?
HE'S ONE OF THE TOP PHYSICISTS TO WORK ON ELECTRICITY!
STORE
Jazz FEEDS
WHO'S FARADAY?
IS THAT SUPPOSED TO IMPRESS ME?
COME ON, MISS! ELECTRICITY!
SO?
IT'S THE FUTURE! LOOK AROUND YOU!
ALL THOSE LINES!
THAT'S THE ENERGY FROM THE DAMS!
I PREFER WHAT LANDS ON THEM.

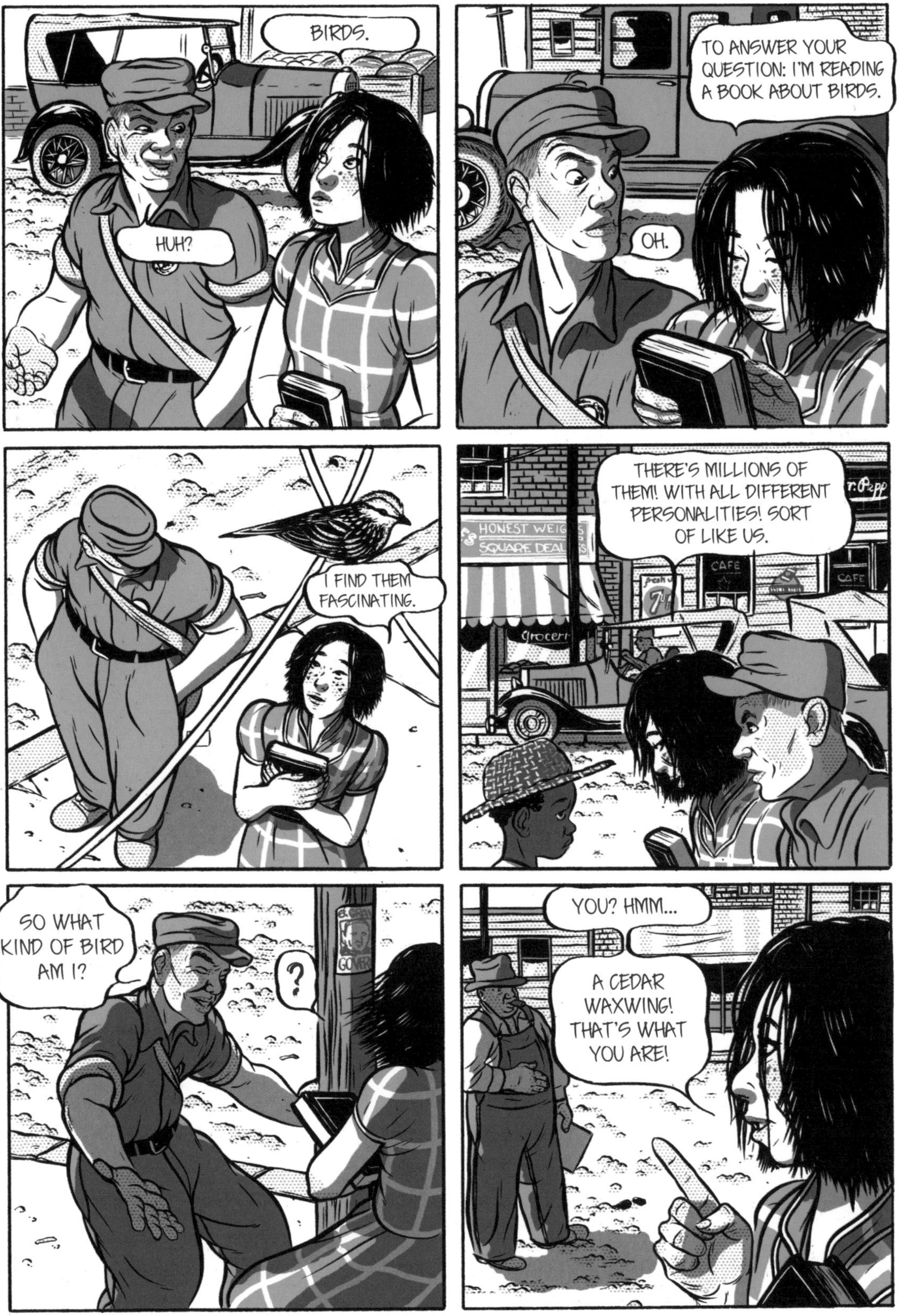
BIRDS.
HUH?
TO ANSWER YOUR QUESTION: I'M READING A BOOK ABOUT BIRDS.
OH.
I FIND THEM FASCINATING.
THERE'S MILLIONS OF THEM! WITH ALL DIFFERENT PERSONALITIES! SORT OF LIKE US.
HONEST WEIG
SQUARE DEAL
CAFE
grocer
SO WHAT KIND OF BIRD AM I?
?
YOU? HMM...
A CEDAR WAXWING! THAT'S WHAT YOU ARE!

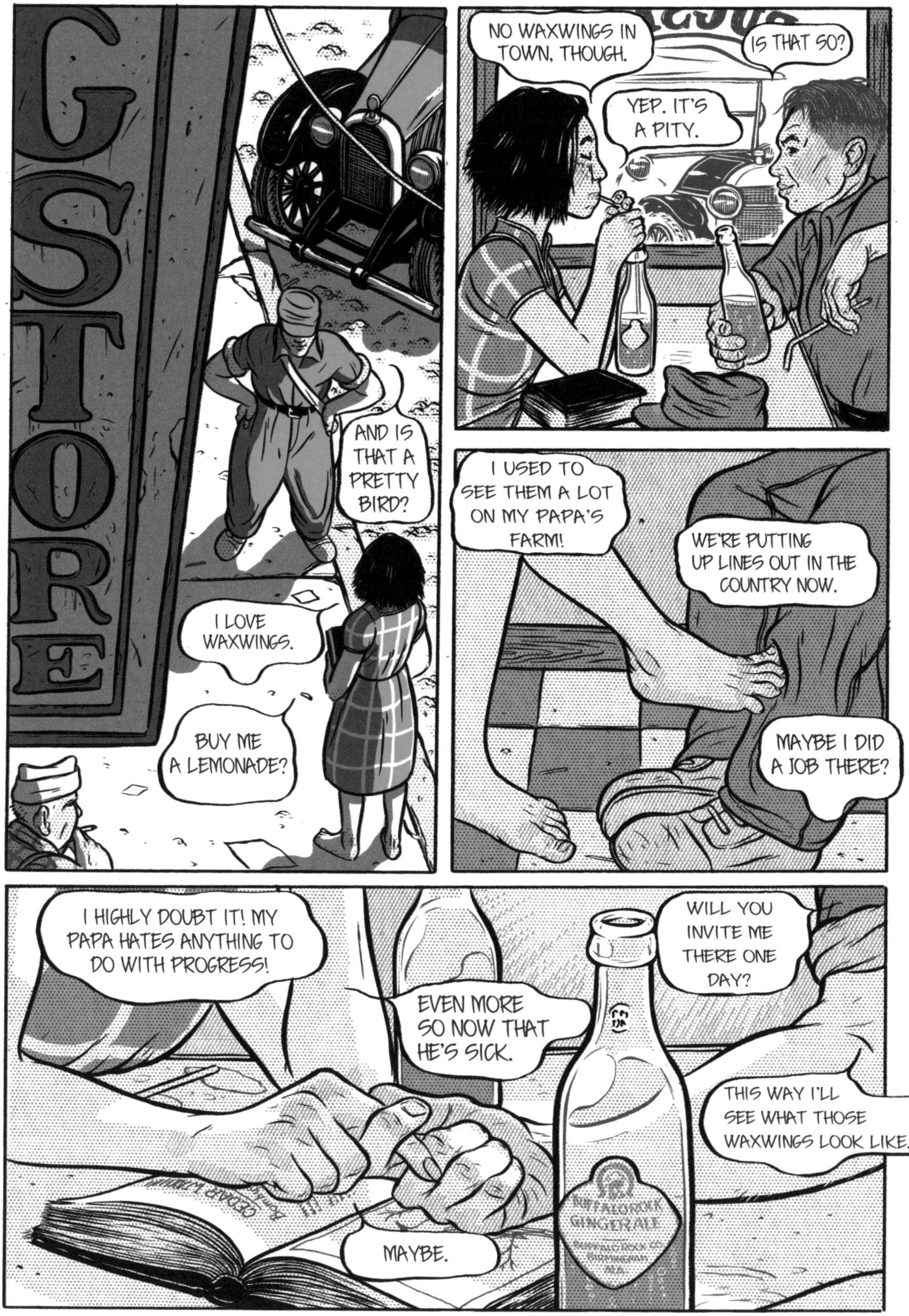
STORE
AND IS THAT A PRETTY BIRD?
I LOVE WAXWINGS.
BUY ME A LEMONADE?
NO WAXWINGS IN TOWN, THOUGH.
IS THAT SO?
YEP. IT'S A PITY.
I USED TO SEE THEM A LOT ON MY PAPA'S FARM!
WE'RE PUTTING UP LINES OUT IN THE COUNTRY NOW.
MAYBE I DID A JOB THERE?
I HIGHLY DOUBT IT! MY PAPA HATES ANYTHING TO DO WITH PROGRESS!
EVEN MORE SO NOW THAT HE'S SICK.
WILL YOU INVITE ME THERE ONE DAY?
THIS WAY I'LL SEE WHAT THOSE WAXWINGS LOOK LIKE.
MAYBE.

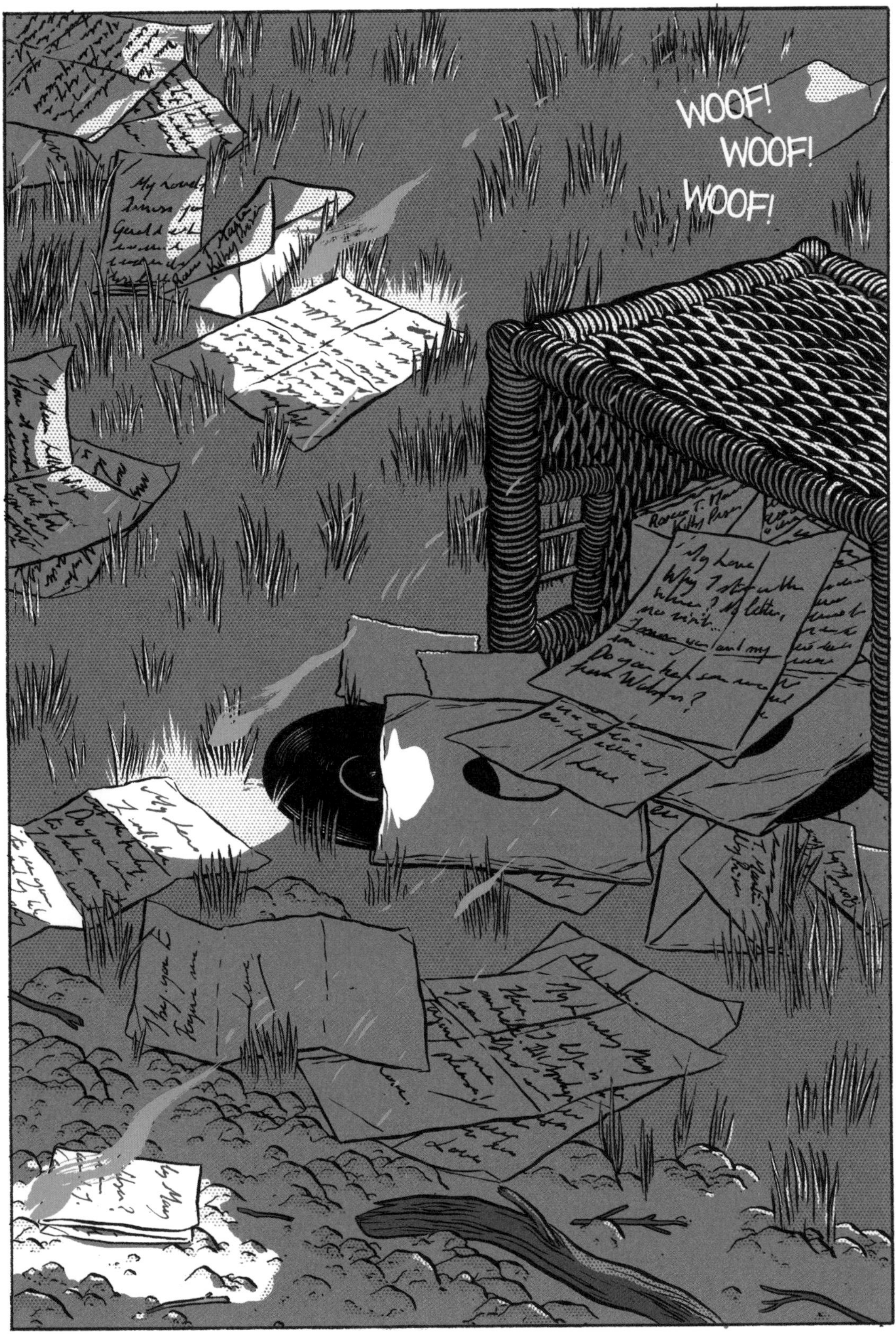
WOOF!
WOOF!
WOOF!

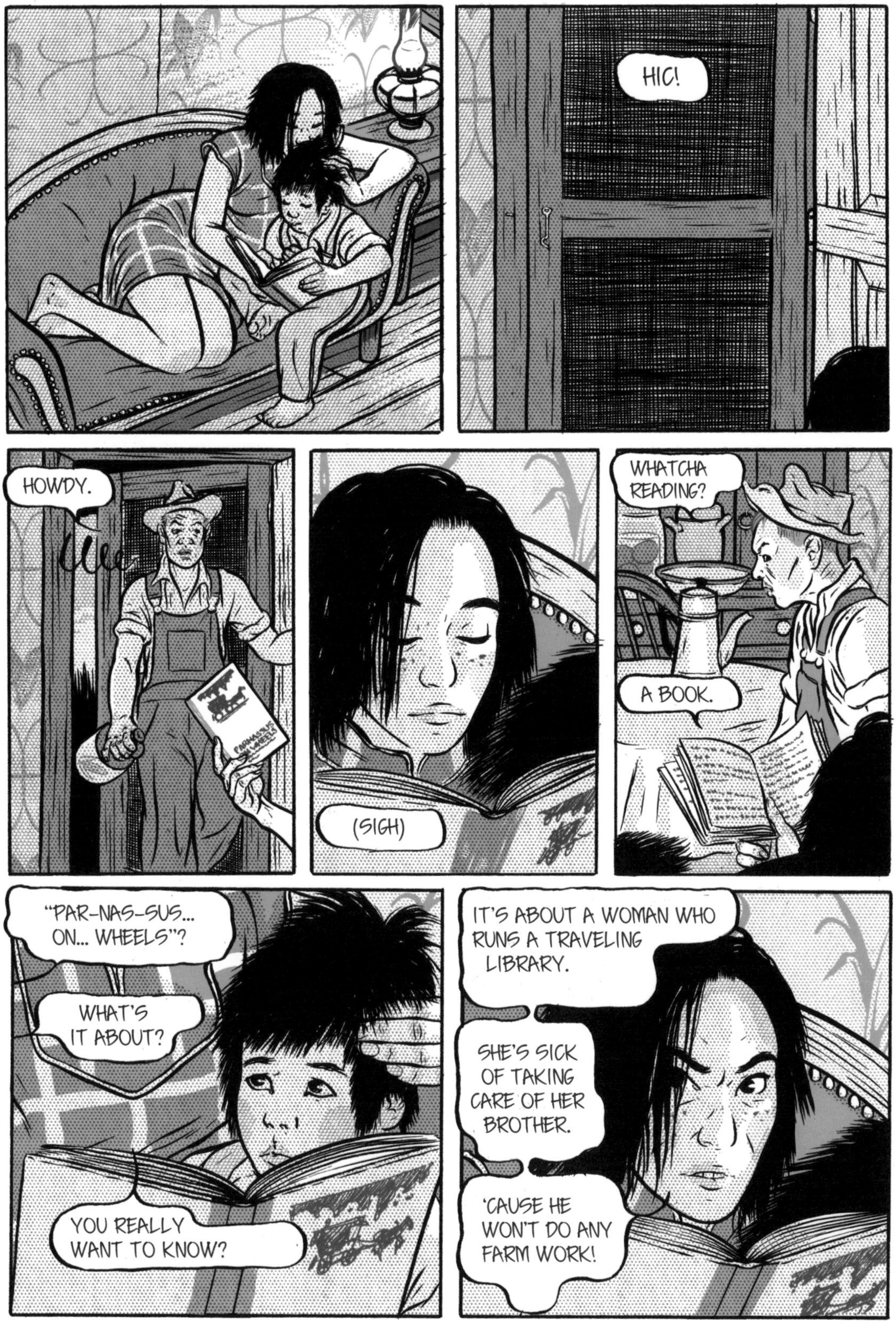
HIC!
HOWDY.
(SIGH)
WHATCHA READING?
A BOOK.
"PAR-NAS-SUS... ON... WHEELS"?
WHAT'S IT ABOUT?
YOU REALLY WANT TO KNOW?
IT'S ABOUT A WOMAN WHO RUNS A TRAVELING LIBRARY.
SHE'S SICK OF TAKING CARE OF HER BROTHER.
'CAUSE HE WON'T DO ANY FARM WORK!

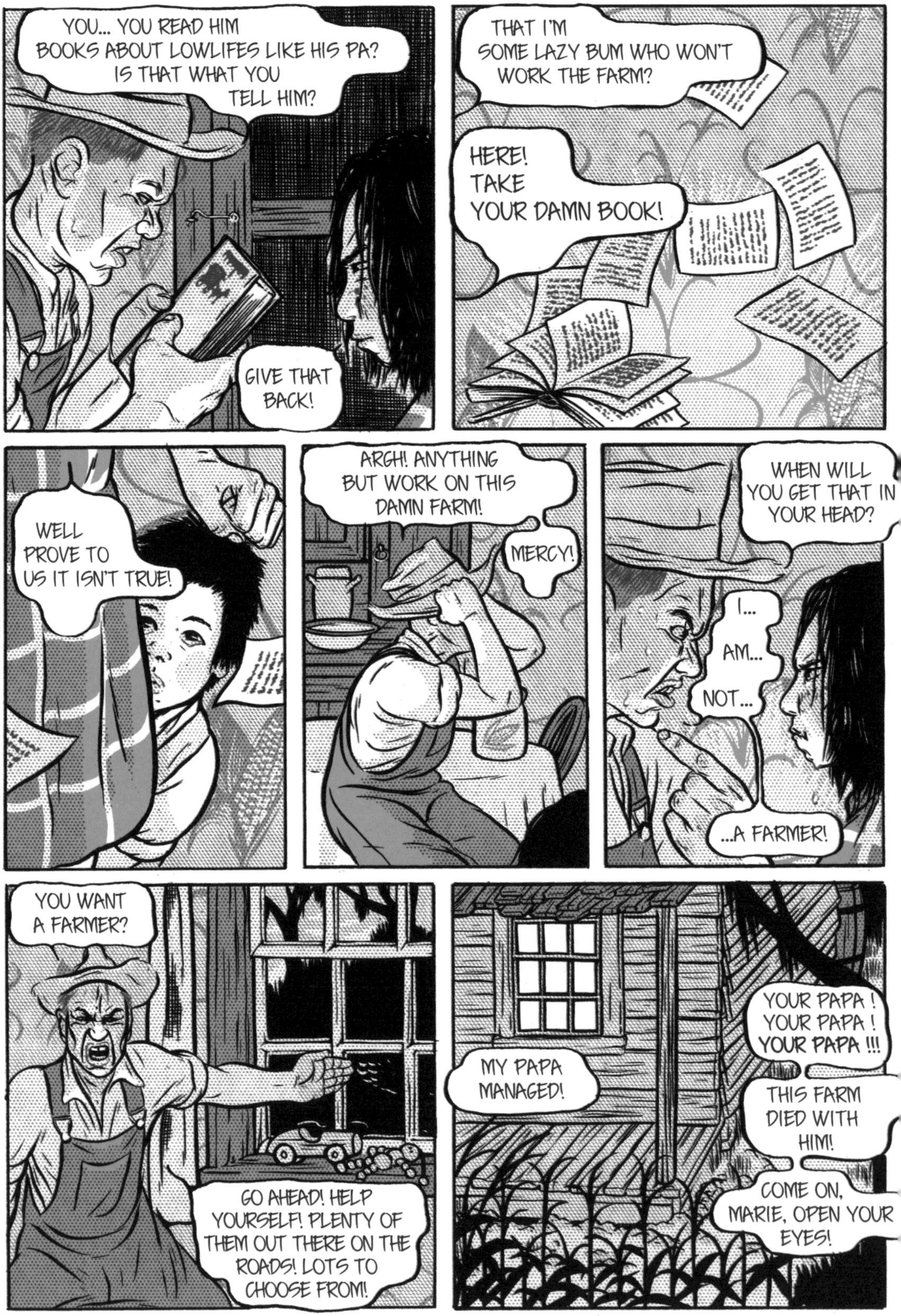
YOU... YOU READ HIM BOOKS ABOUT LOWLIFES LIKE HIS PA? IS THAT WHAT YOU TELL HIM?
GIVE THAT BACK!
THAT I'M SOME LAZY BUM WHO WON'T WORK THE FARM?
HERE! TAKE YOUR DAMN BOOK!
WELL PROVE TO US IT ISN'T TRUE!
ARGH! ANYTHING BUT WORK ON THIS DAMN FARM!
MERCY!
WHEN WILL YOU GET THAT IN YOUR HEAD?
I...
AM...
NOT...
...A FARMER!
YOU WANT A FARMER?
GO AHEAD! HELP YOURSELF! PLENTY OF THEM OUT THERE ON THE ROADS! LOTS TO CHOOSE FROM!
MY PAPA MANAGED!
YOUR PAPA ! YOUR PAPA ! YOUR PAPA !!!
THIS FARM DIED WITH HIM!
COME ON, MARIE, OPEN YOUR EYES!

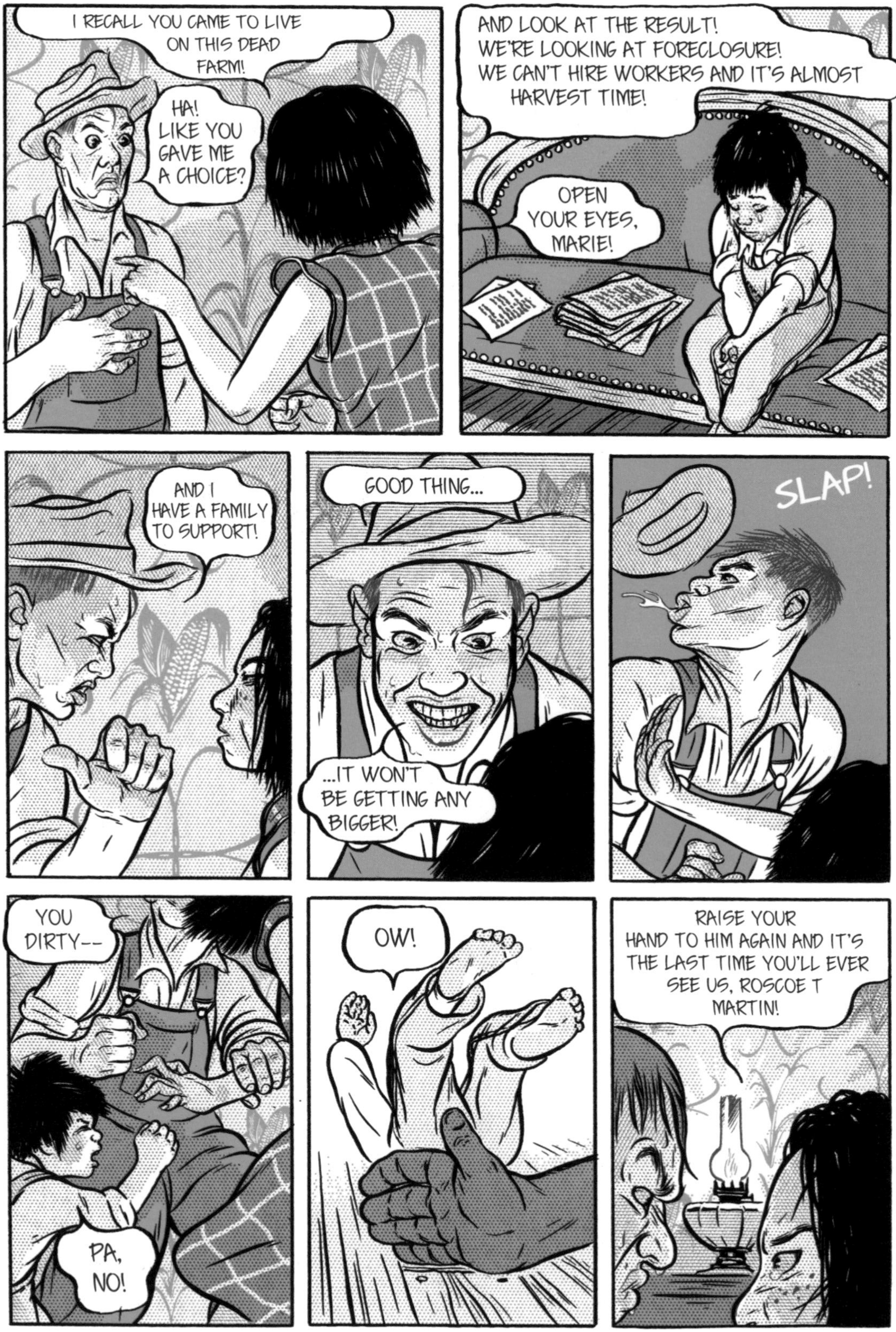
I RECALL YOU CAME TO LIVE ON THIS DEAD FARM!
HA! LIKE YOU GAVE ME A CHOICE?
AND LOOK AT THE RESULT! WE'RE LOOKING AT FORECLOSURE! WE CAN'T HIRE WORKERS AND IT'S ALMOST HARVEST TIME!
OPEN YOUR EYES, MARIE!
AND I HAVE A FAMILY TO SUPPORT!
GOOD THING...
...IT WON'T BE GETTING ANY BIGGER!
SLAP!
YOU DIRTY--
PA, NO!
OW!
RAISE YOUR HAND TO HIM AGAIN AND IT'S THE LAST TIME YOU'LL EVER SEE US, ROSCOE T MARTIN!

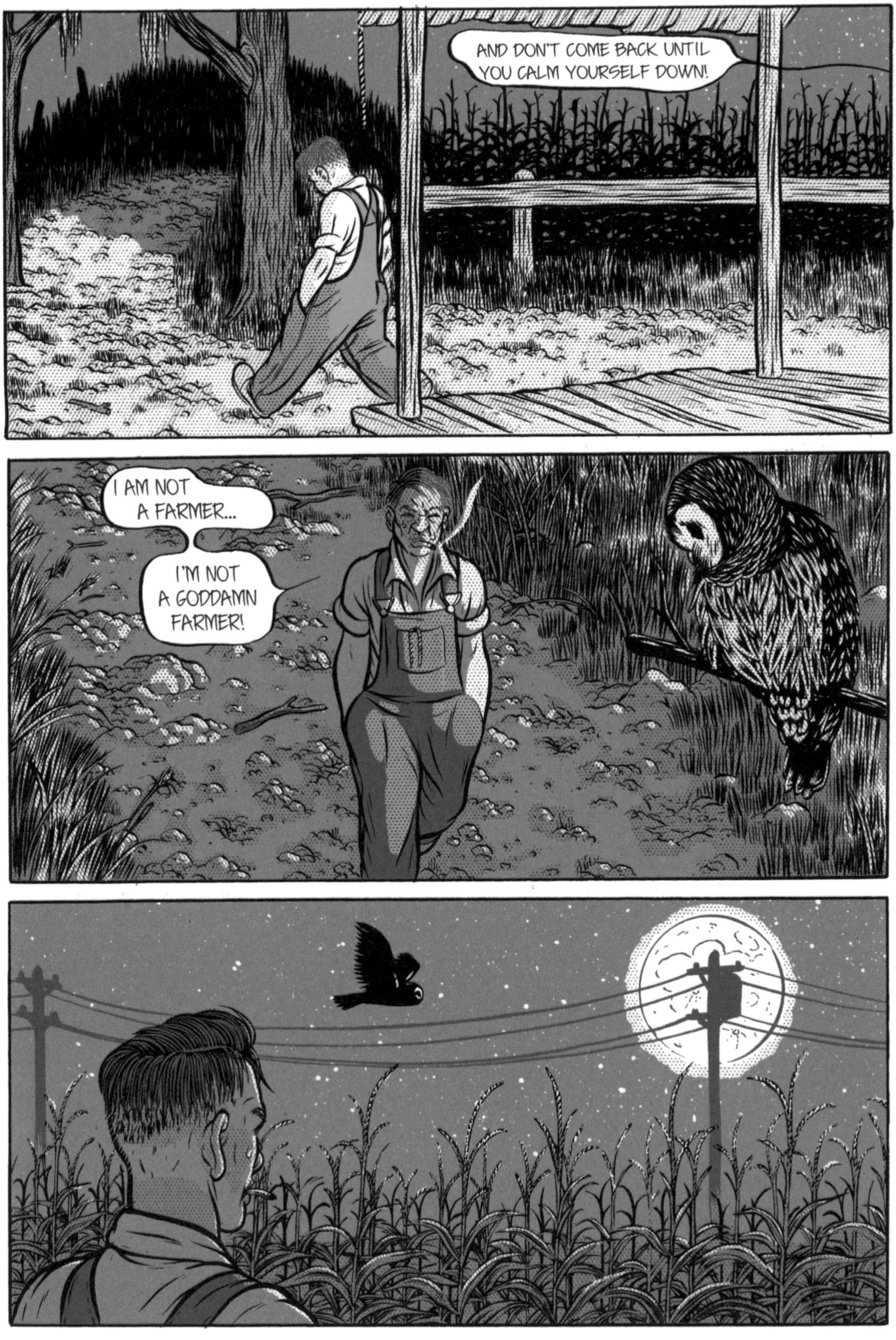
AND DON'T COME BACK UNTIL YOU CALM YOURSELF DOWN!
I AM NOT A FARMER...
I'M NOT A GODDAMN FARMER!

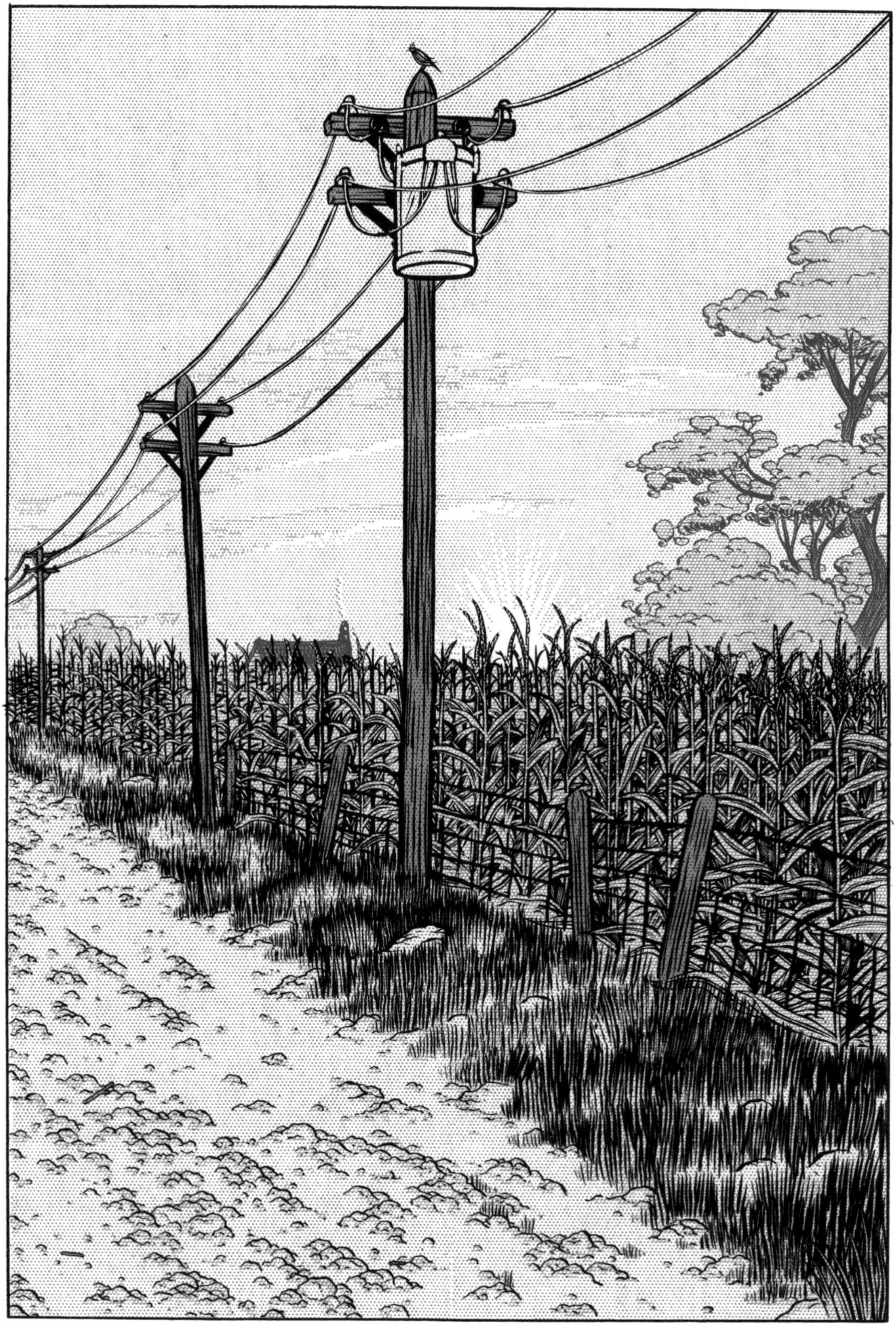

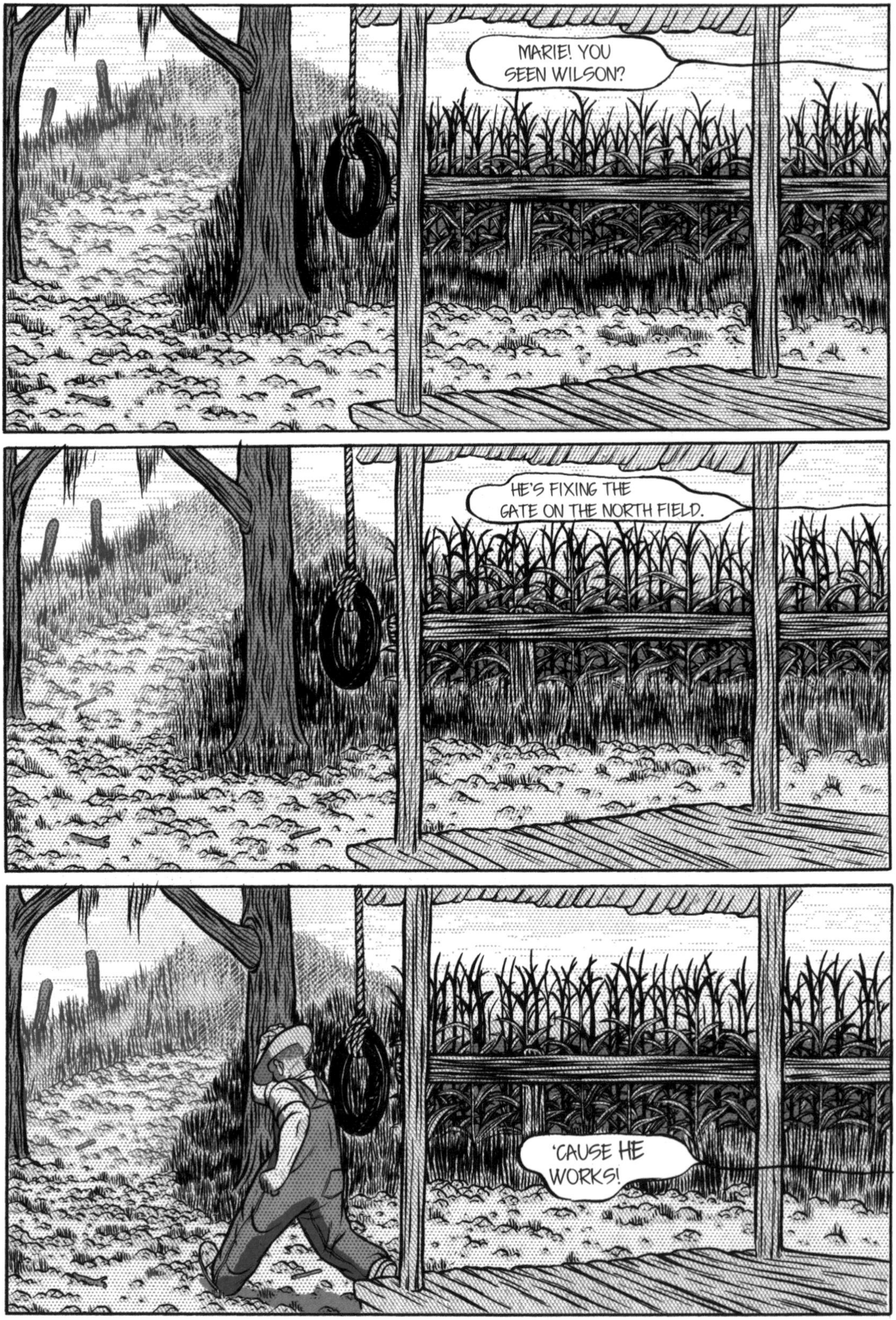
MARIE! YOU SEEN WILSON?
HE'S FIXING THE GATE ON THE NORTH FIELD.
'CAUSE HE WORKS!

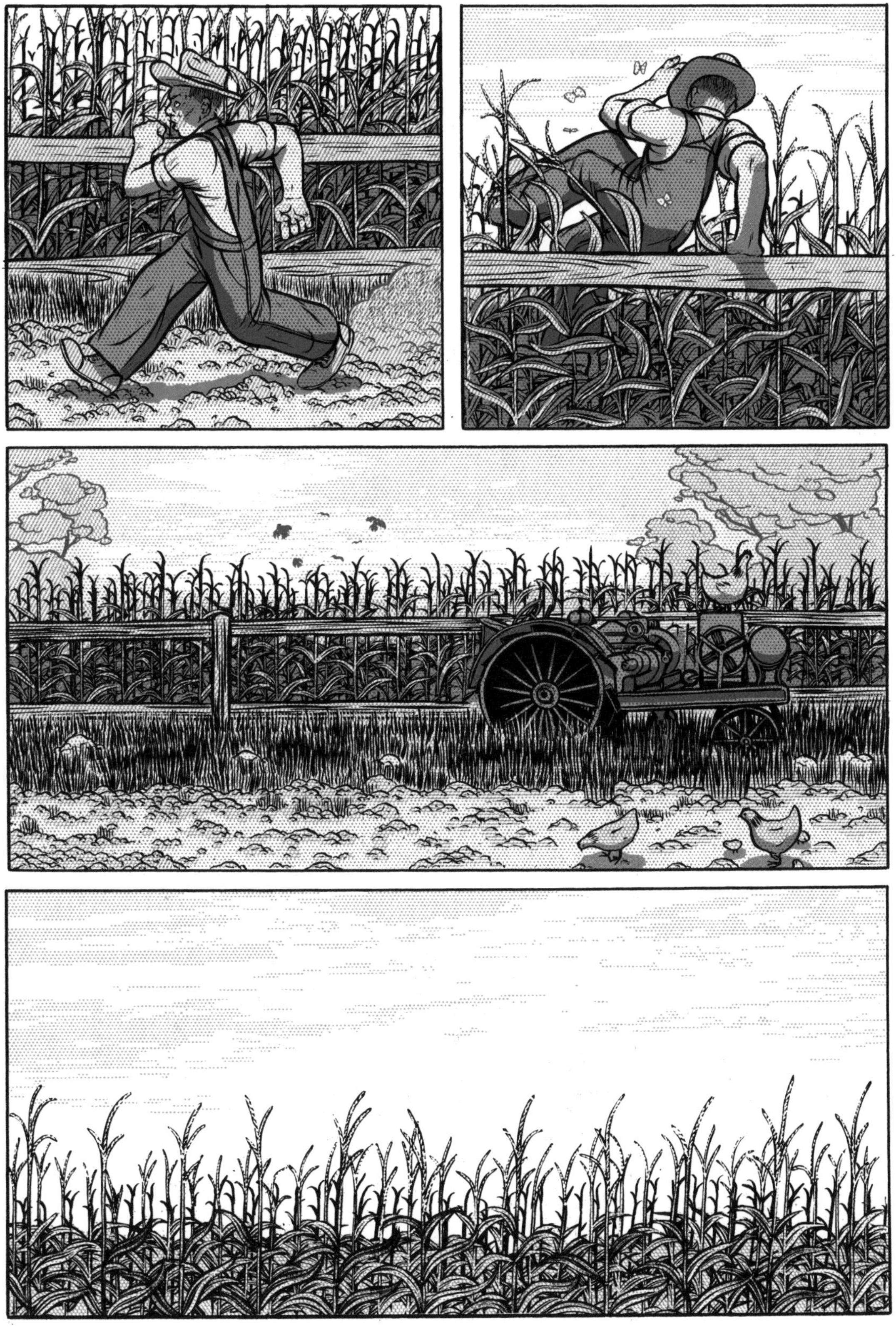

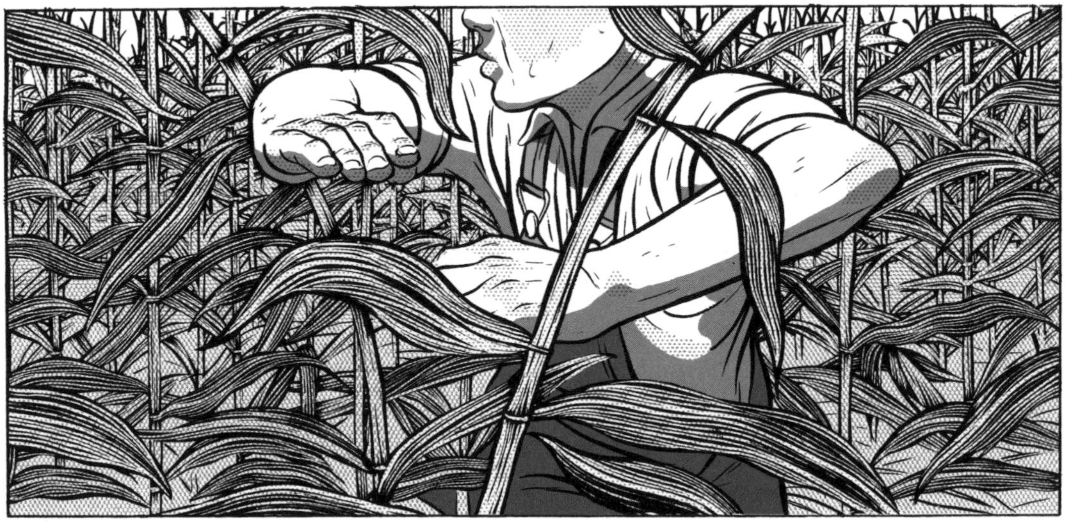

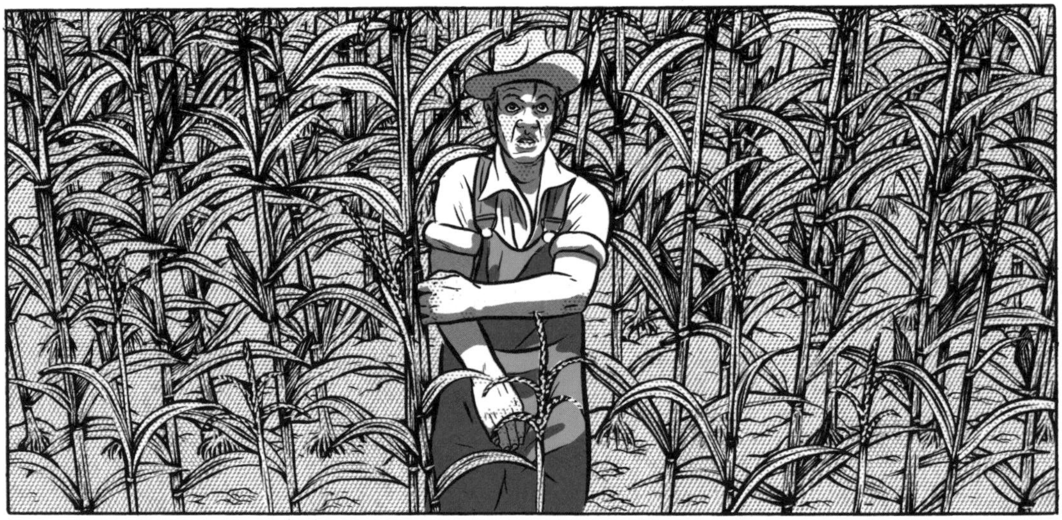

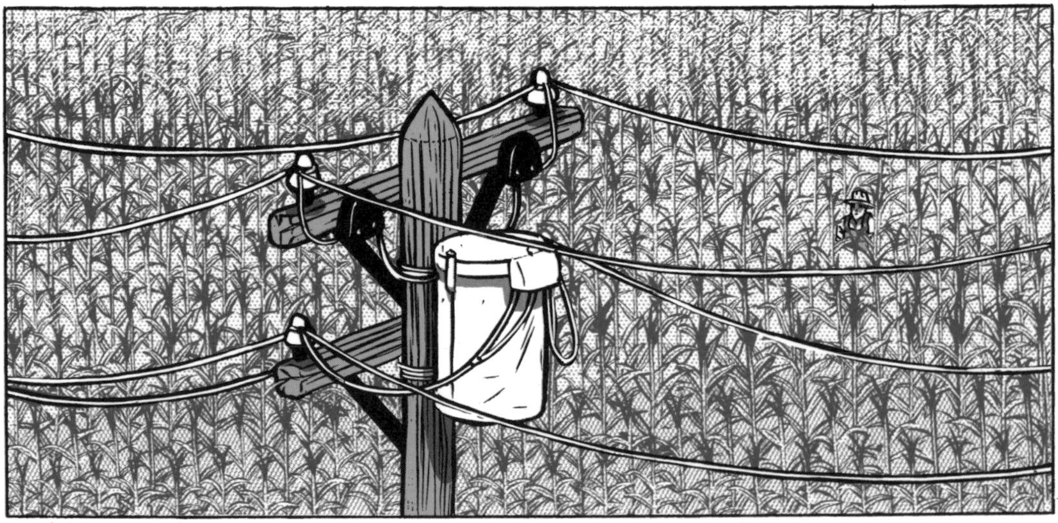

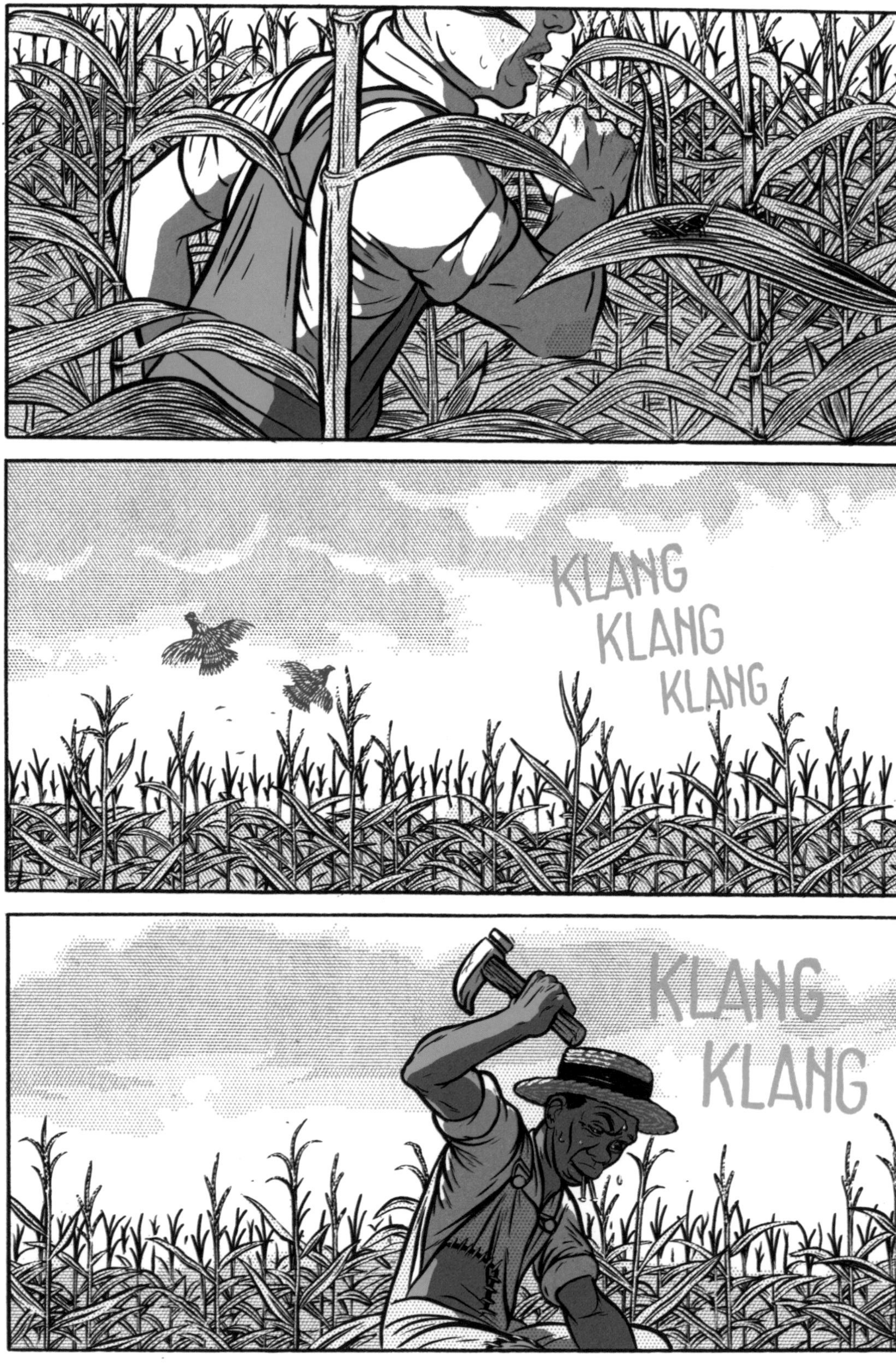
KLANG
KLANG
KLANG
KLANG
KLANG

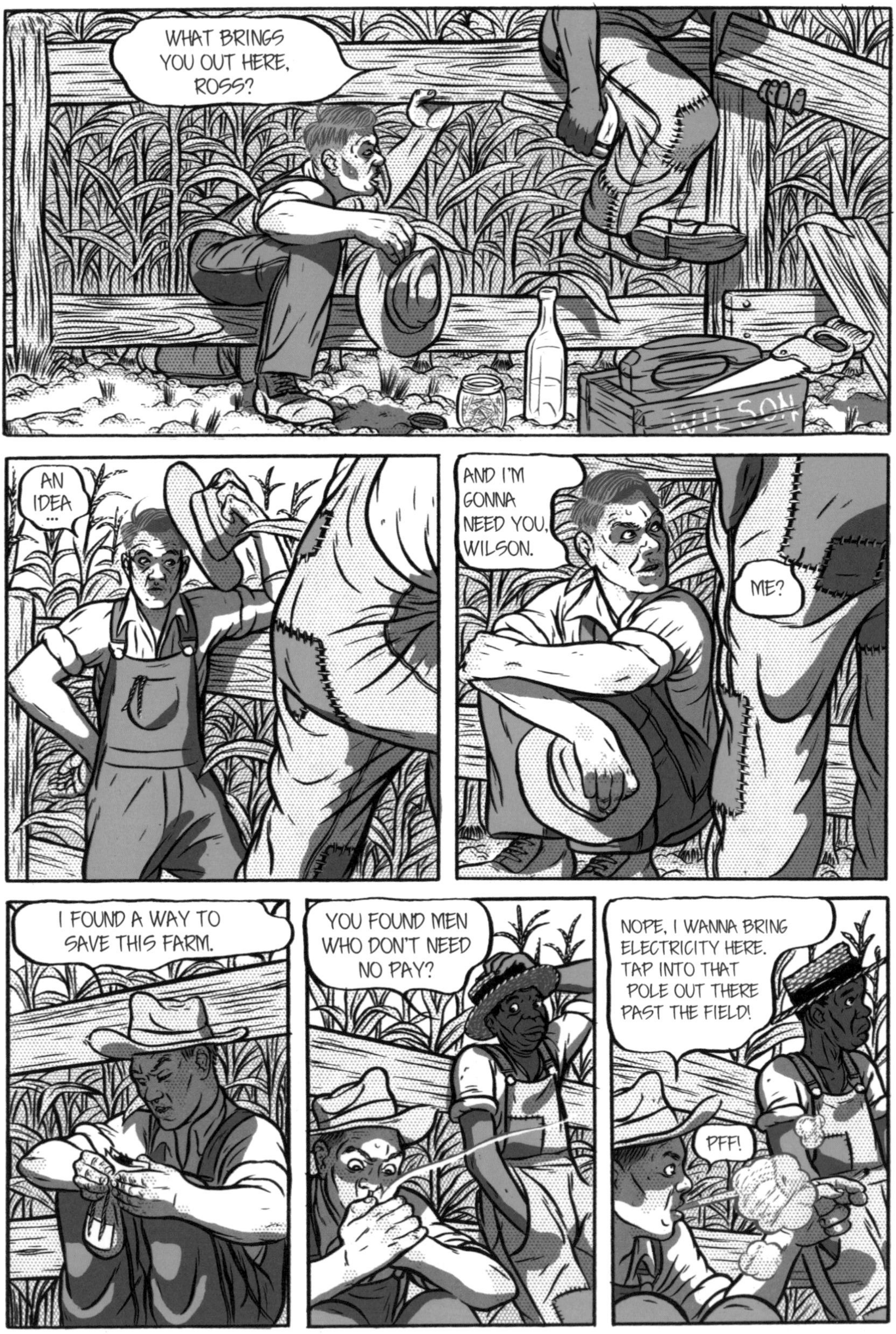
WHAT BRINGS YOU OUT HERE, ROSS?
WILSON
AN IDEA ...
AND I'M GONNA NEED YOU, WILSON.
ME?
I FOUND A WAY TO SAVE THIS FARM.
YOU FOUND MEN WHO DON'T NEED NO PAY?
NOPE, I WANNA BRING ELECTRICITY HERE. TAP INTO THAT POLE OUT THERE PAST THE FIELD!
PFF!

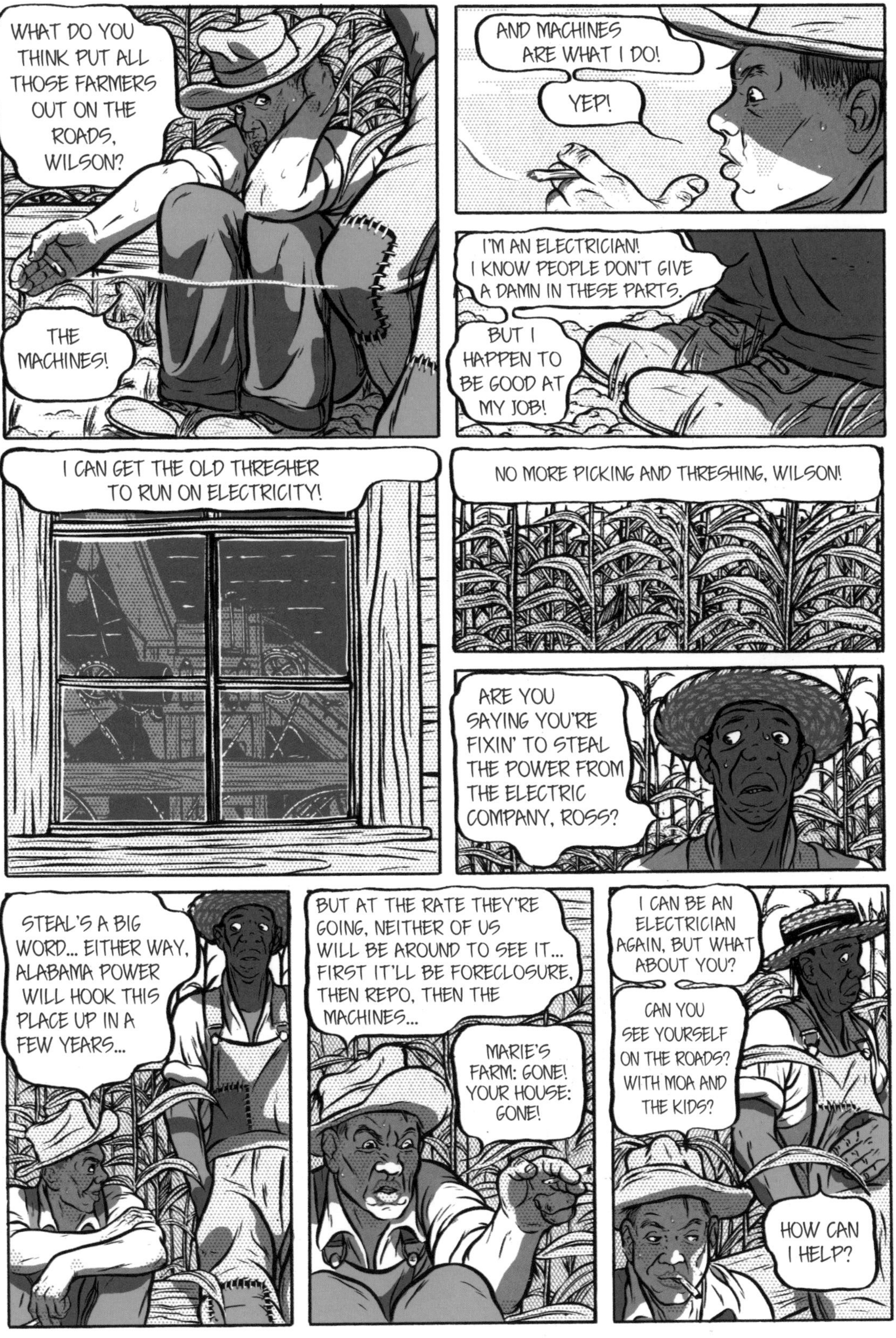
WHAT DO YOU THINK PUT ALL THOSE FARMERS OUT ON THE ROADS, WILSON?
THE MACHINES!
AND MACHINES ARE WHAT I DO!
YEP!
I'M AN ELECTRICIAN! I KNOW PEOPLE DON'T GIVE A DAMN IN THESE PARTS.
BUT I HAPPEN TO BE GOOD AT MY JOB!
I CAN GET THE OLD THRESHER TO RUN ON ELECTRICITY!
NO MORE PICKING AND THRESHING, WILSON!
ARE YOU SAYING YOU'RE FIXIN' TO STEAL THE POWER FROM THE ELECTRIC COMPANY, ROSS?
STEAL'S A BIG WORD... EITHER WAY, ALABAMA POWER WILL HOOK THIS PLACE UP IN A FEW YEARS...
BUT AT THE RATE THEY'RE GOING, NEITHER OF US WILL BE AROUND TO SEE IT... FIRST IT'LL BE FORECLOSURE, THEN REPO, THEN THE MACHINES...
MARIE'S FARM: GONE! YOUR HOUSE: GONE!
I CAN BE AN ELECTRICIAN AGAIN, BUT WHAT ABOUT YOU?
CAN YOU SEE YOURSELF ON THE ROADS? WITH MOA AND THE KIDS?
HOW CAN I HELP?

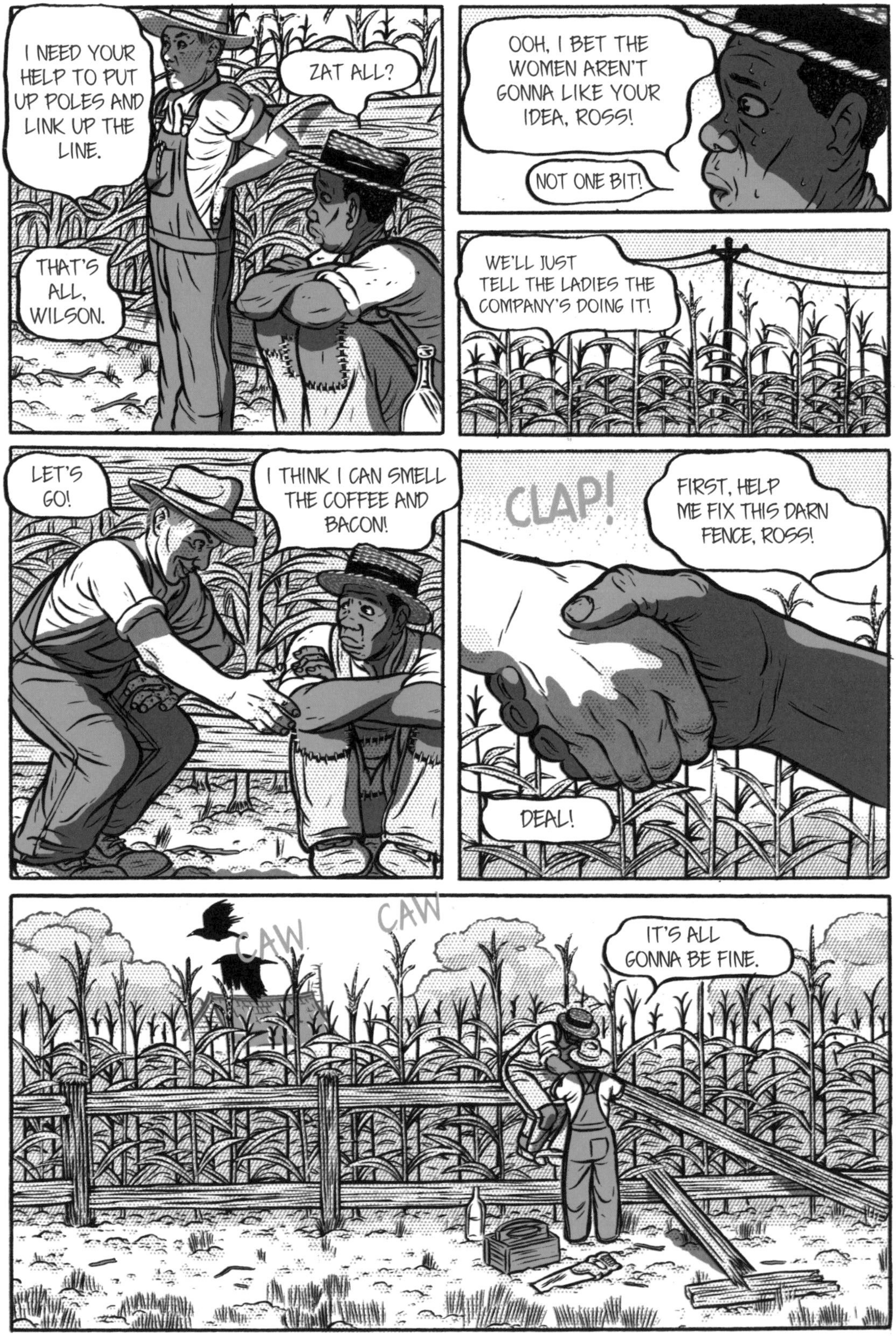
I NEED YOUR HELP TO PUT UP POLES AND LINK UP THE LINE.
ZAT ALL?
THAT'S ALL, WILSON.
OOH, I BET THE WOMEN AREN'T GONNA LIKE YOUR IDEA, ROSS!
NOT ONE BIT!
WE'LL JUST TELL THE LADIES THE COMPANY'S DOING IT!
LET'S GO!
I THINK I CAN SMELL THE COFFEE AND BACON!
CLAP!
FIRST, HELP ME FIX THIS DARN FENCE, ROSS!
DEAL!
CAW
CAW
IT'S ALL GONNA BE FINE.

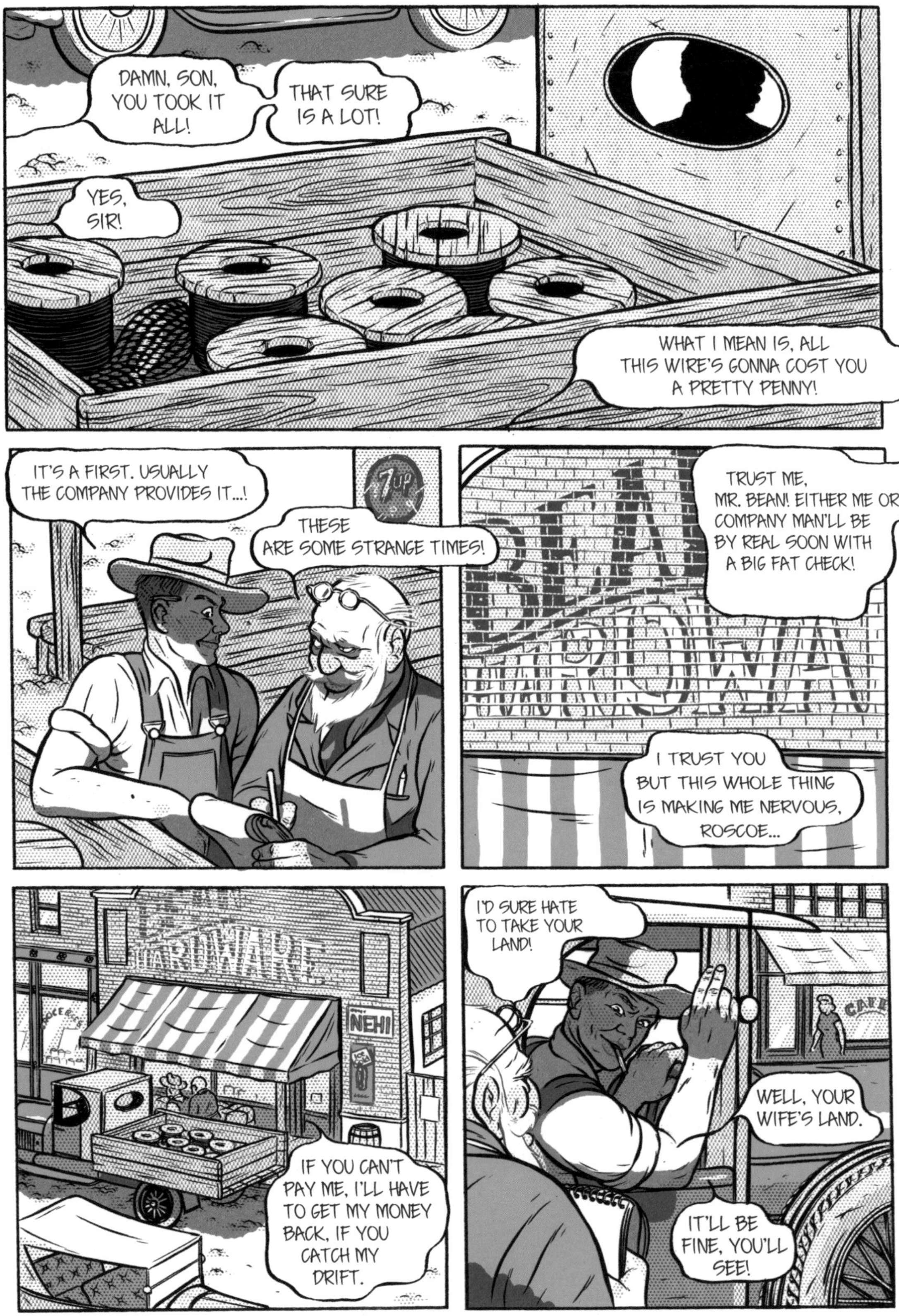
DAMN, SON, YOU TOOK IT ALL!
THAT SURE IS A LOT!
YES, SIR!
WHAT I MEAN IS, ALL THIS WIRE'S GONNA COST YOU A PRETTY PENNY!
IT'S A FIRST. USUALLY THE COMPANY PROVIDES IT...!
THESE ARE SOME STRANGE TIMES!
TRUST ME, MR. BEAN! EITHER ME OR A COMPANY MAN'LL BE BY REAL SOON WITH A BIG FAT CHECK!
I TRUST YOU BUT THIS WHOLE THING IS MAKING ME NERVOUS, ROSCOE...
HARDWARE
NEHI
IF YOU CAN'T PAY ME, I'LL HAVE TO GET MY MONEY BACK, IF YOU CATCH MY DRIFT.
I'D SURE HATE TO TAKE YOUR LAND!
WELL, YOUR WIFE'S LAND.
IT'LL BE FINE, YOU'LL SEE!

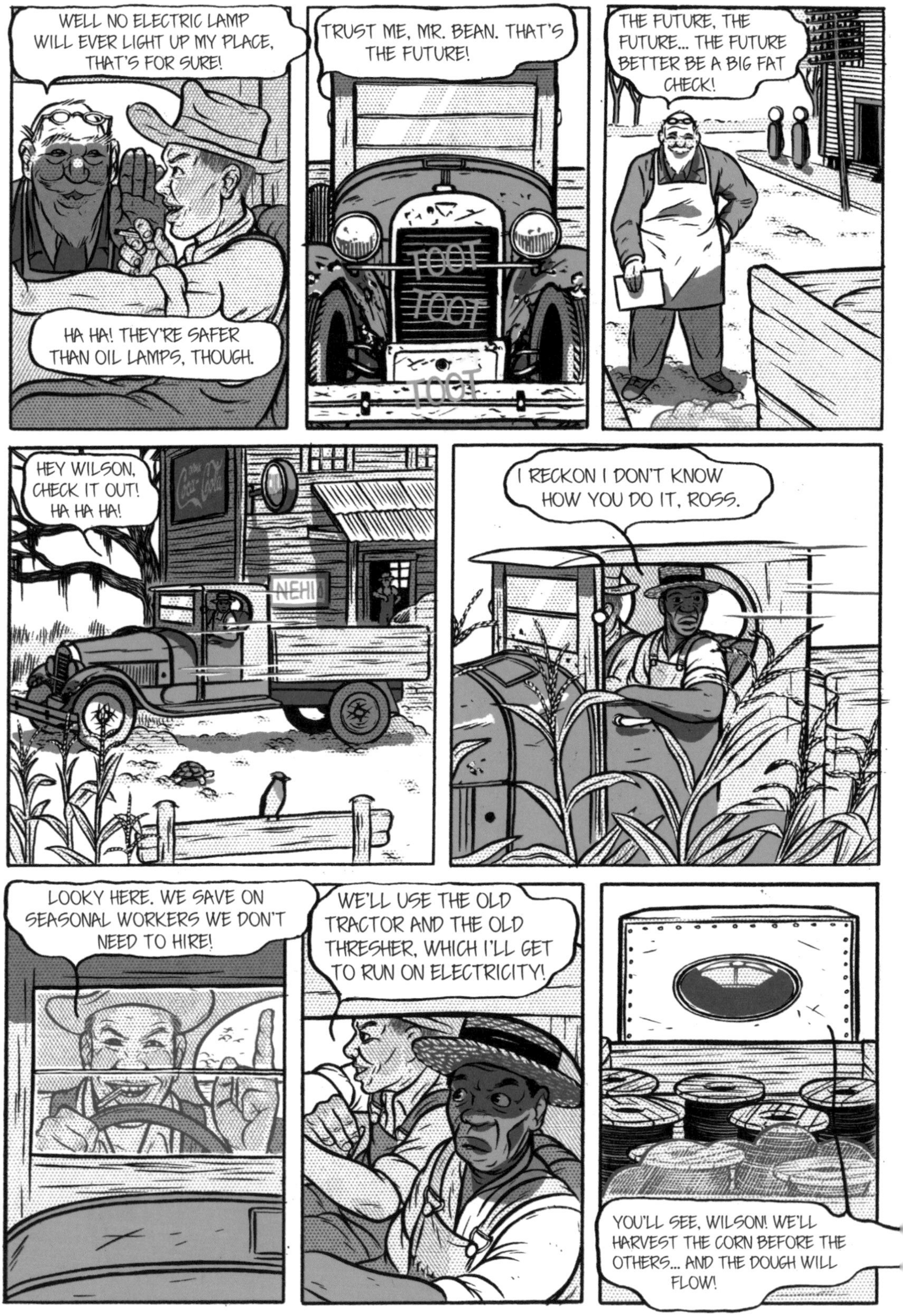
WELL NO ELECTRIC LAMP WILL EVER LIGHT UP MY PLACE, THAT'S FOR SURE!
HA HA! THEY'RE SAFER THAN OIL LAMPS, THOUGH.
TRUST ME, MR. BEAN. THAT'S THE FUTURE!
TOOT TOOT
TOOT
THE FUTURE, THE FUTURE... THE FUTURE BETTER BE A BIG FAT CHECK!
HEY WILSON, CHECK IT OUT! HA HA HA!
NEHI
I RECKON I DON'T KNOW HOW YOU DO IT, ROSS.
LOOKY HERE. WE SAVE ON SEASONAL WORKERS WE DON'T NEED TO HIRE!
WE'LL USE THE OLD TRACTOR AND THE OLD THRESHER, WHICH I'LL GET TO RUN ON ELECTRICITY!
YOU'LL SEE, WILSON! WE'LL HARVEST THE CORN BEFORE THE OTHERS... AND THE DOUGH WILL FLOW!

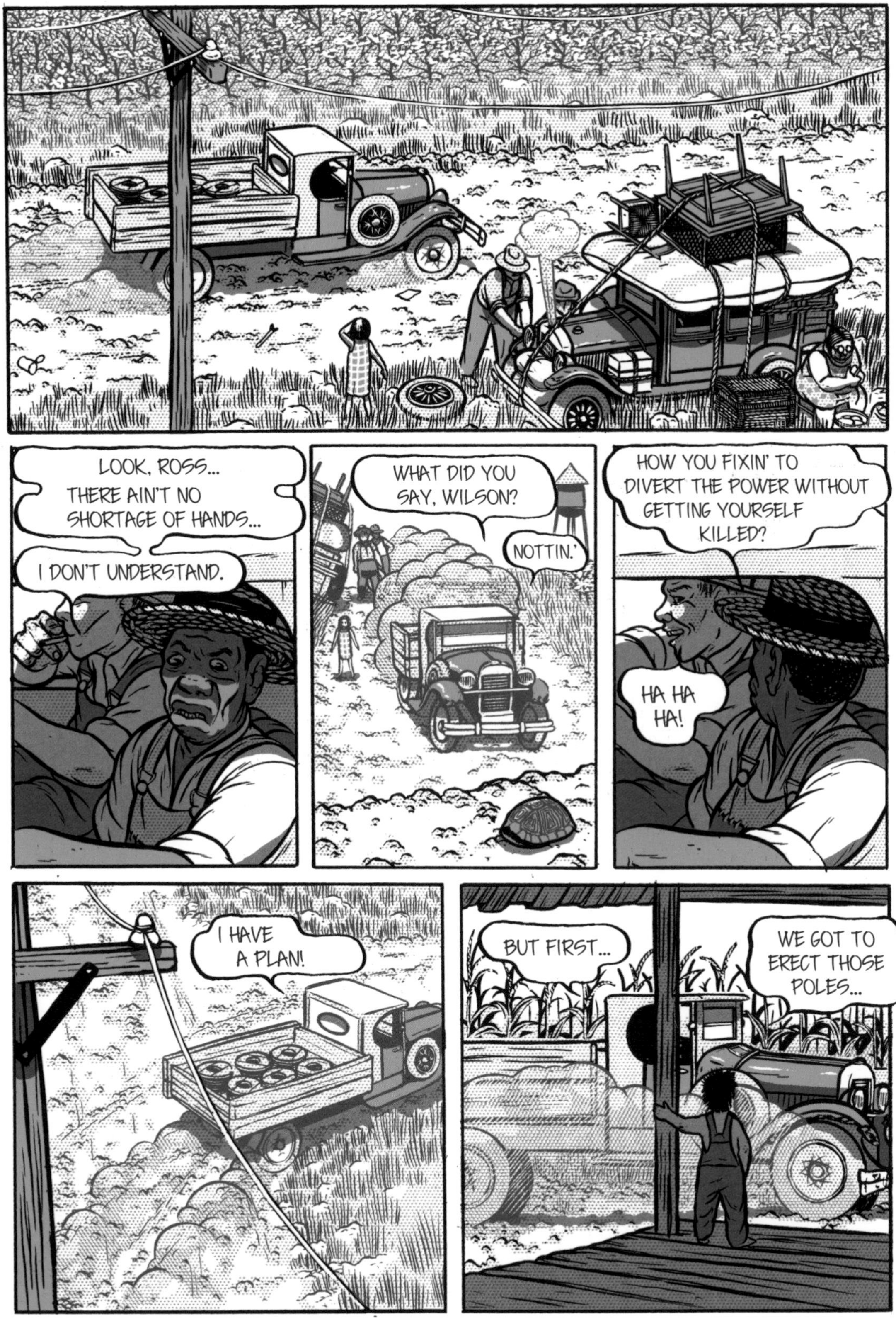
LOOK, ROSS...
THERE AIN'T NO SHORTAGE OF HANDS...
I DON'T UNDERSTAND.
WHAT DID YOU SAY, WILSON?
NOTTIN.'
HOW YOU FIXIN' TO DIVERT THE POWER WITHOUT GETTING YOURSELF KILLED?
HA HA HA!
I HAVE A PLAN!
BUT FIRST...
WE GOT TO ERECT THOSE POLES...

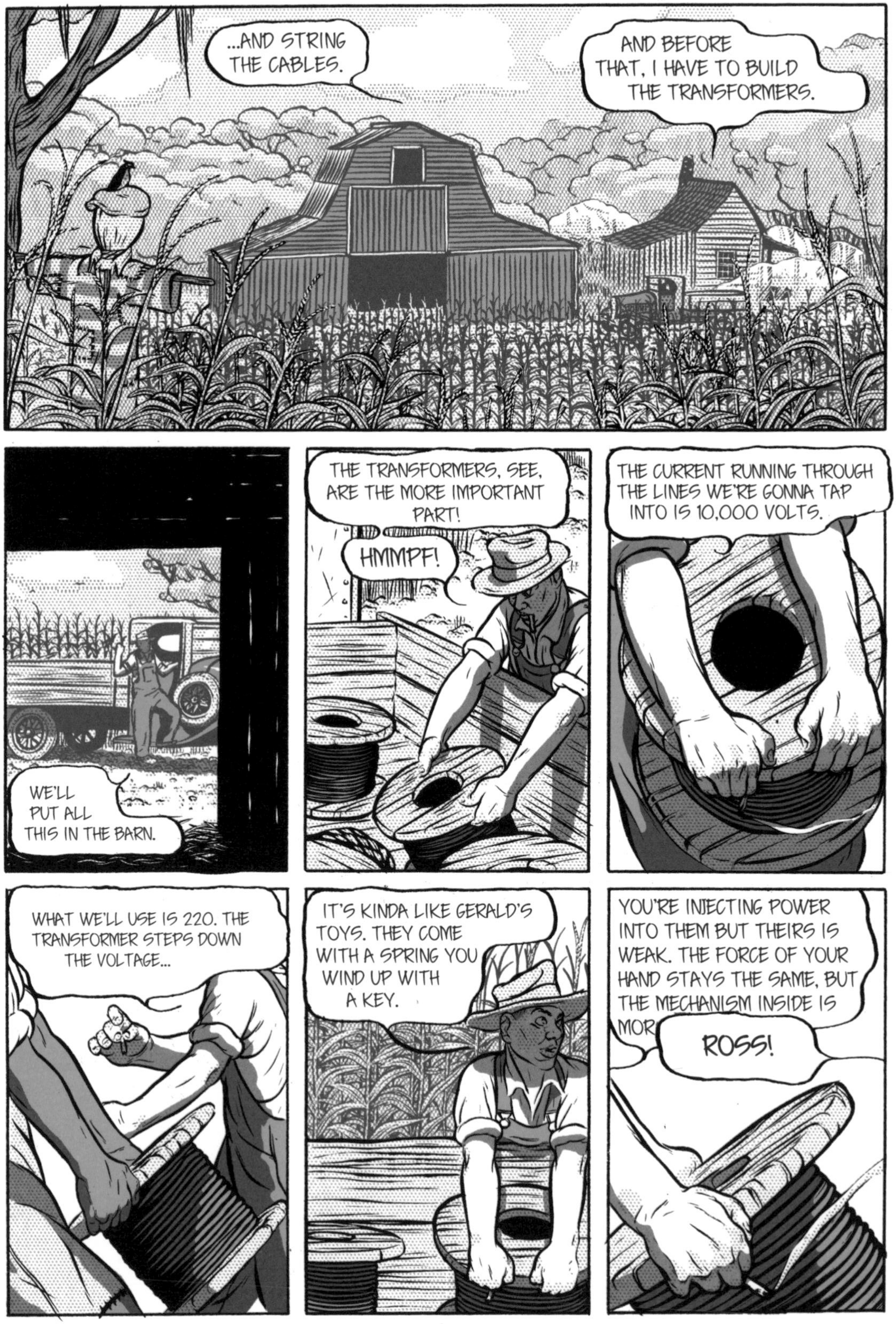
...AND STRING THE CABLES.
AND BEFORE THAT, I HAVE TO BUILD THE TRANSFORMERS.
WE'LL PUT ALL THIS IN THE BARN.
THE TRANSFORMERS, SEE, ARE THE MORE IMPORTANT PART!
HMMPF!
THE CURRENT RUNNING THROUGH THE LINES WE'RE GONNA TAP INTO IS 10,000 VOLTS.
WHAT WE'LL USE IS 220. THE TRANSFORMER STEPS DOWN THE VOLTAGE...
IT'S KINDA LIKE GERALD'S TOYS. THEY COME WITH A SPRING YOU WIND UP WITH A KEY.
YOU'RE INJECTING POWER INTO THEM BUT THEIRS IS WEAK. THE FORCE OF YOUR HAND STAYS THE SAME, BUT THE MECHANISM INSIDE IS MOR
ROSS!

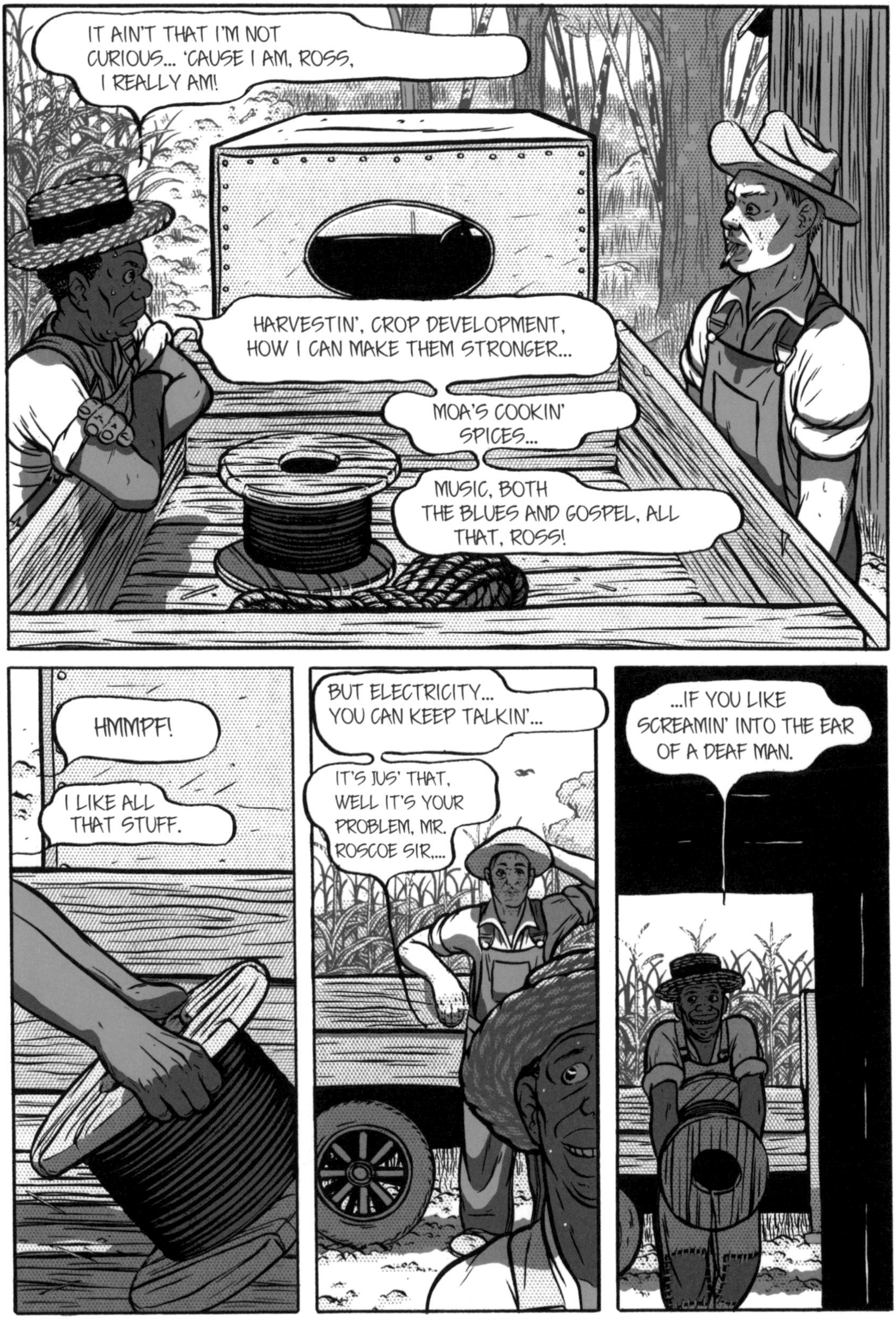
IT AIN'T THAT I'M NOT CURIOUS... 'CAUSE I AM, ROSS, I REALLY AM!
HARVESTIN', CROP DEVELOPMENT, HOW I CAN MAKE THEM STRONGER...
MOA'S COOKIN' SPICES...
MUSIC, BOTH THE BLUES AND GOSPEL, ALL THAT, ROSS!
HMMPF!
I LIKE ALL THAT STUFF.
BUT ELECTRICITY... YOU CAN KEEP TALKIN'...
IT'S JUS' THAT, WELL IT'S YOUR PROBLEM, MR. ROSCOE SIR,...
...IF YOU LIKE SCREAMIN' INTO THE EAR OF A DEAF MAN.

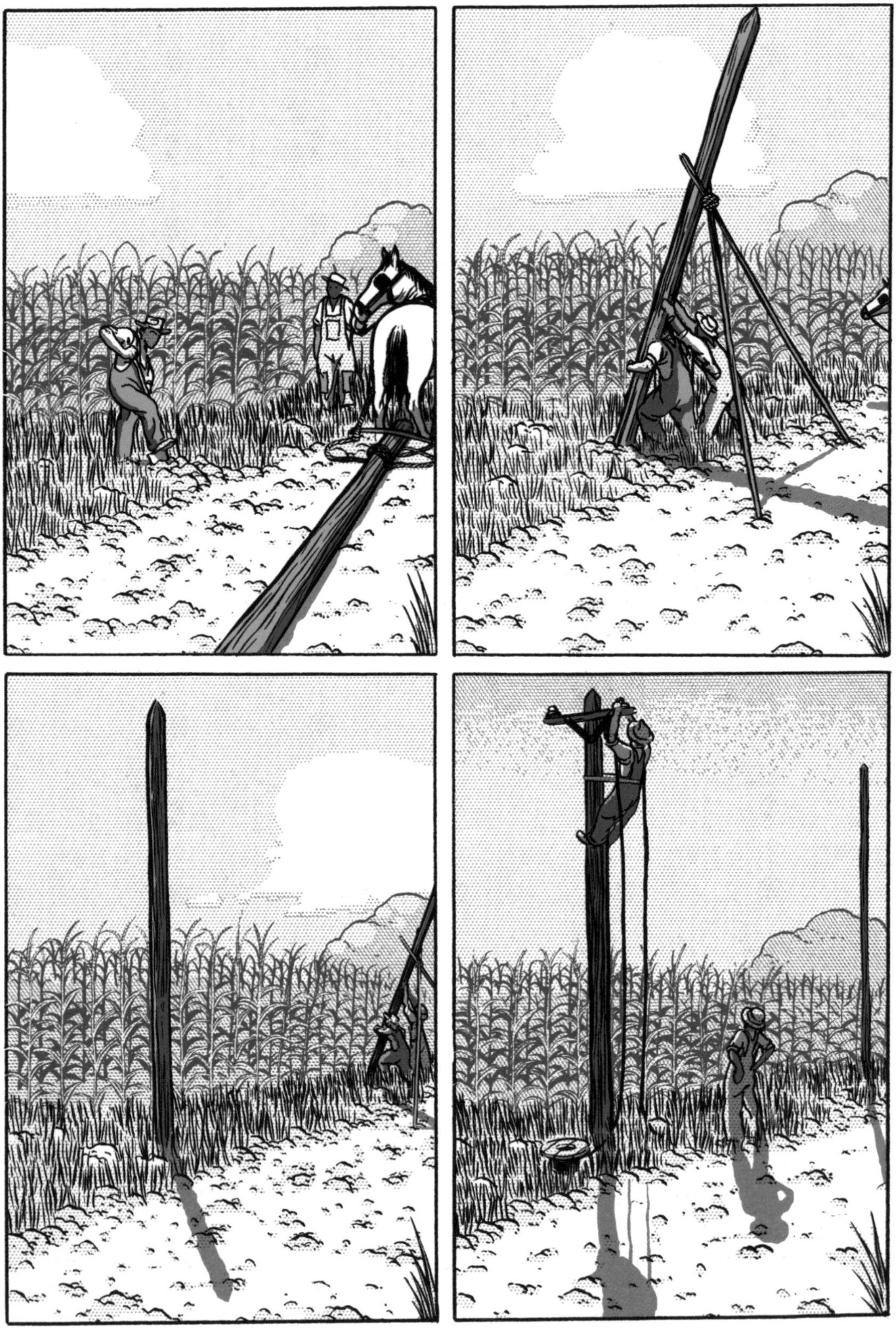

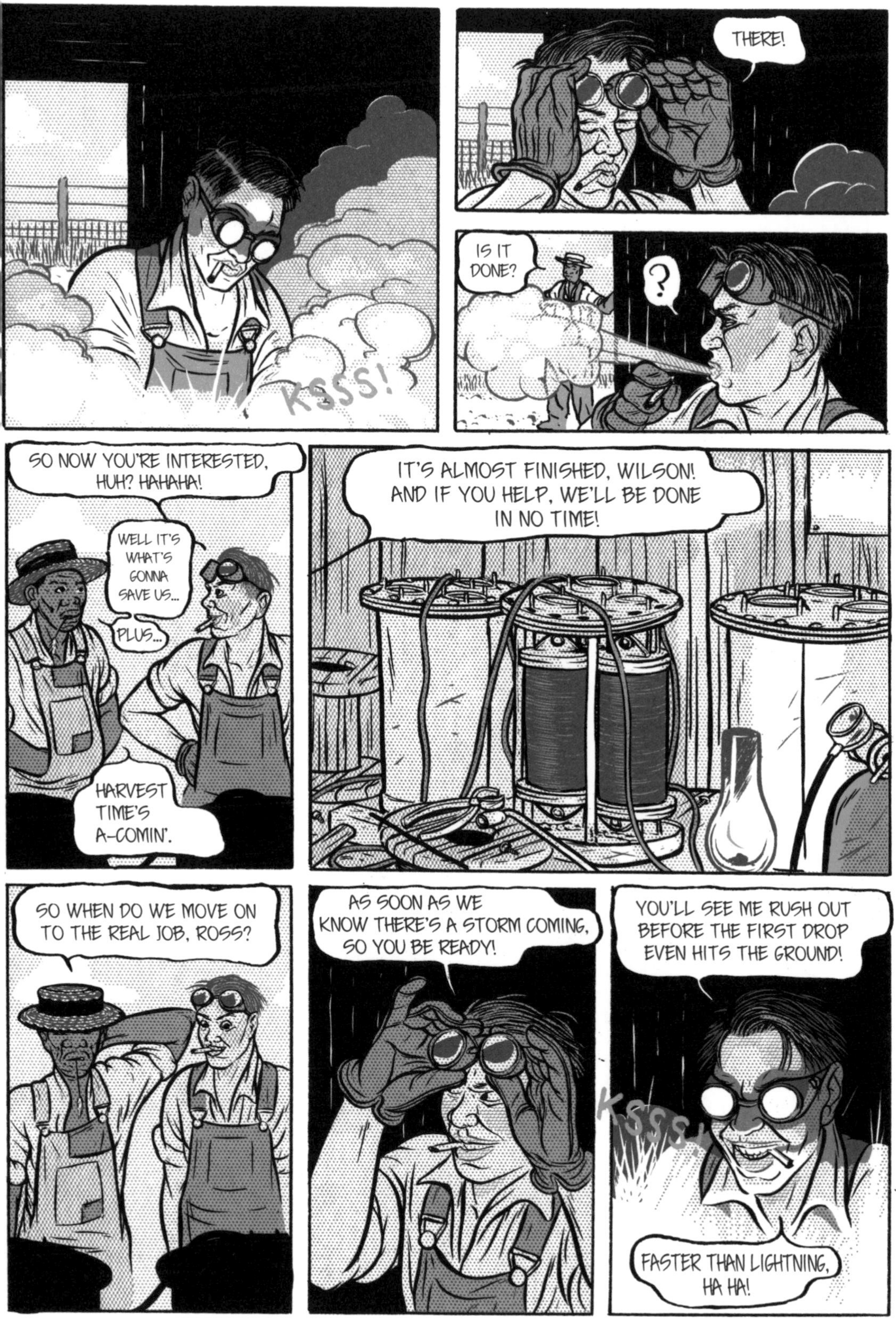
KSSS!
THERE!
IS IT DONE?
?
SO NOW YOU'RE INTERESTED, HUH? HAHAHA!
WELL IT'S WHAT'S GONNA SAVE US...
PLUS...
HARVEST TIME'S A-COMIN'.
IT'S ALMOST FINISHED, WILSON! AND IF YOU HELP, WE'LL BE DONE IN NO TIME!
SO WHEN DO WE MOVE ON TO THE REAL JOB, ROSS?
AS SOON AS WE KNOW THERE'S A STORM COMING, SO YOU BE READY!
YOU'LL SEE ME RUSH OUT BEFORE THE FIRST DROP EVEN HITS THE GROUND!
KSSS!
FASTER THAN LIGHTNING, HA HA!

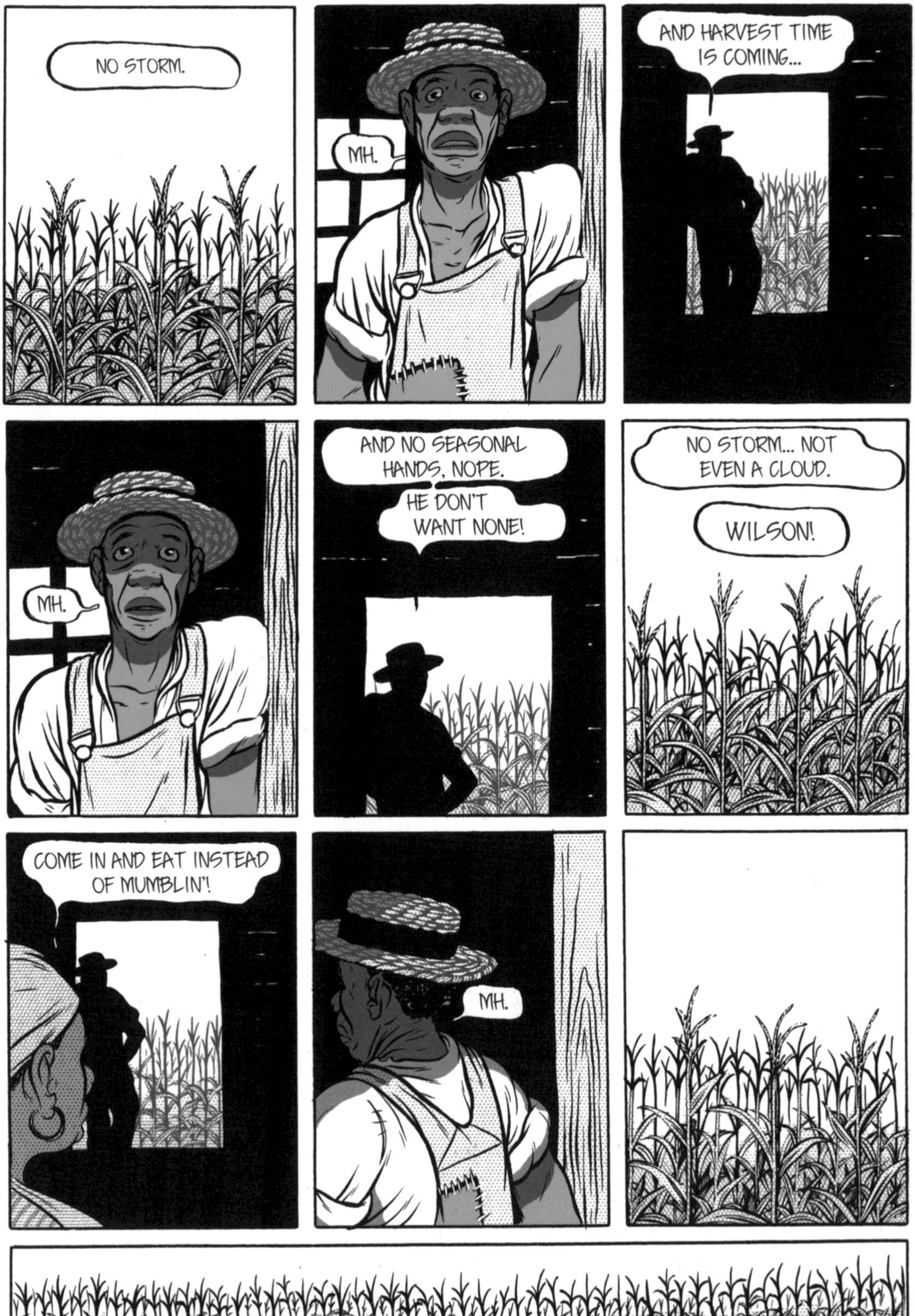
NO STORM.
MH.
AND HARVEST TIME IS COMING...
MH.
AND NO SEASONAL HANDS, NOPE.
HE DON'T WANT NONE!
NO STORM... NOT EVEN A CLOUD.
WILSON!
COME IN AND EAT INSTEAD OF MUMBLIN'!
MH.

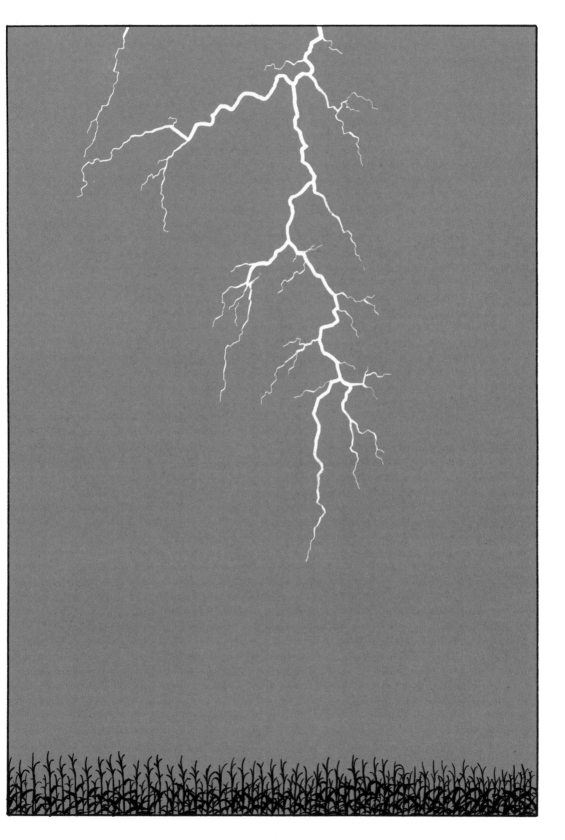

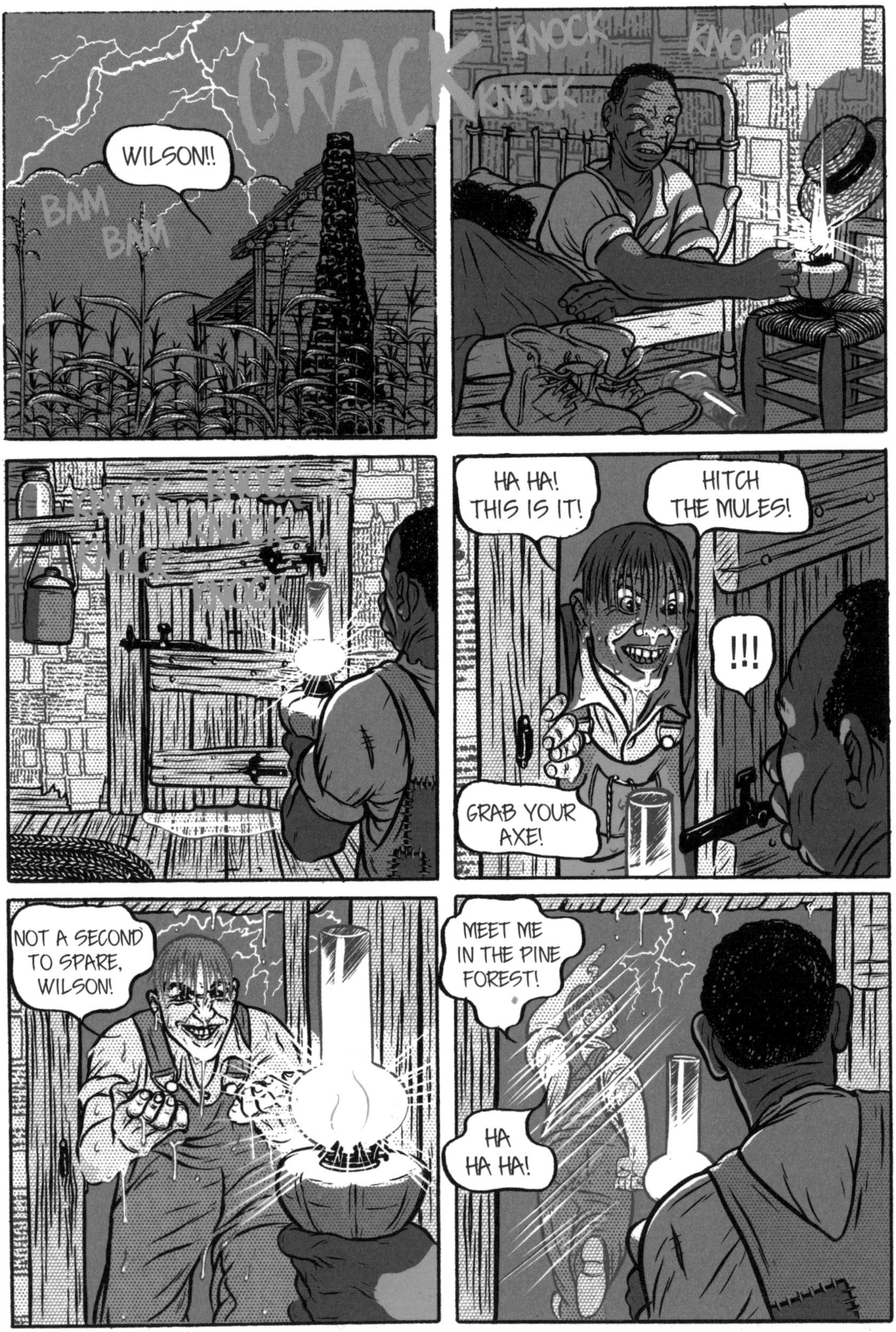
CRACK
WILSON!!
BAM
BAM
KNOCK
KNOCK
KNOCK
KNOCK
KNOCK
KNOCK
KNOCK
KNOCK
HA HA!
THIS IS IT!
HITCH
THE MULES!
!!!
GRAB YOUR
AXE!
NOT A SECOND
TO SPARE,
WILSON!
MEET ME
IN THE PINE
FOREST!
HA
HA HA!

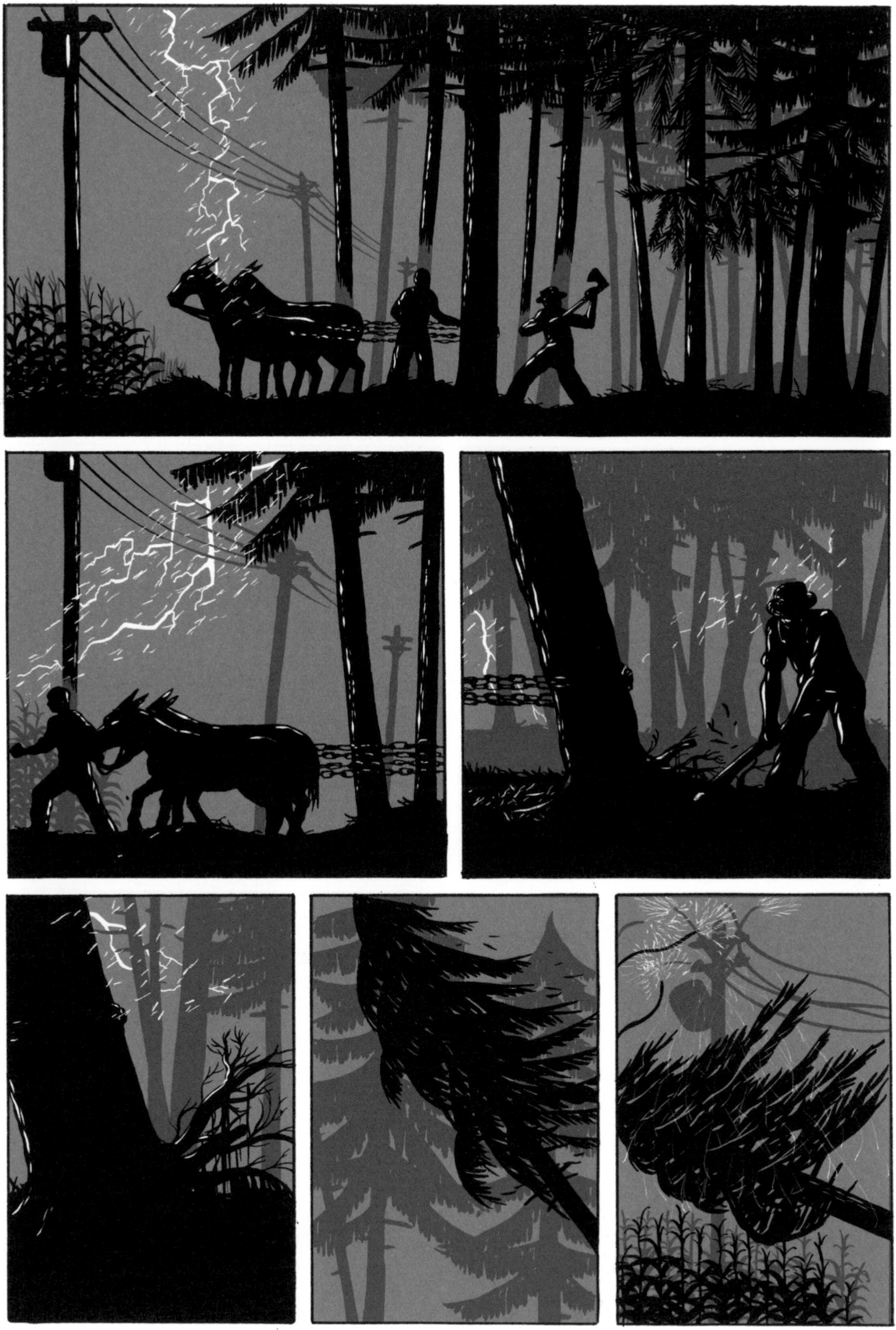

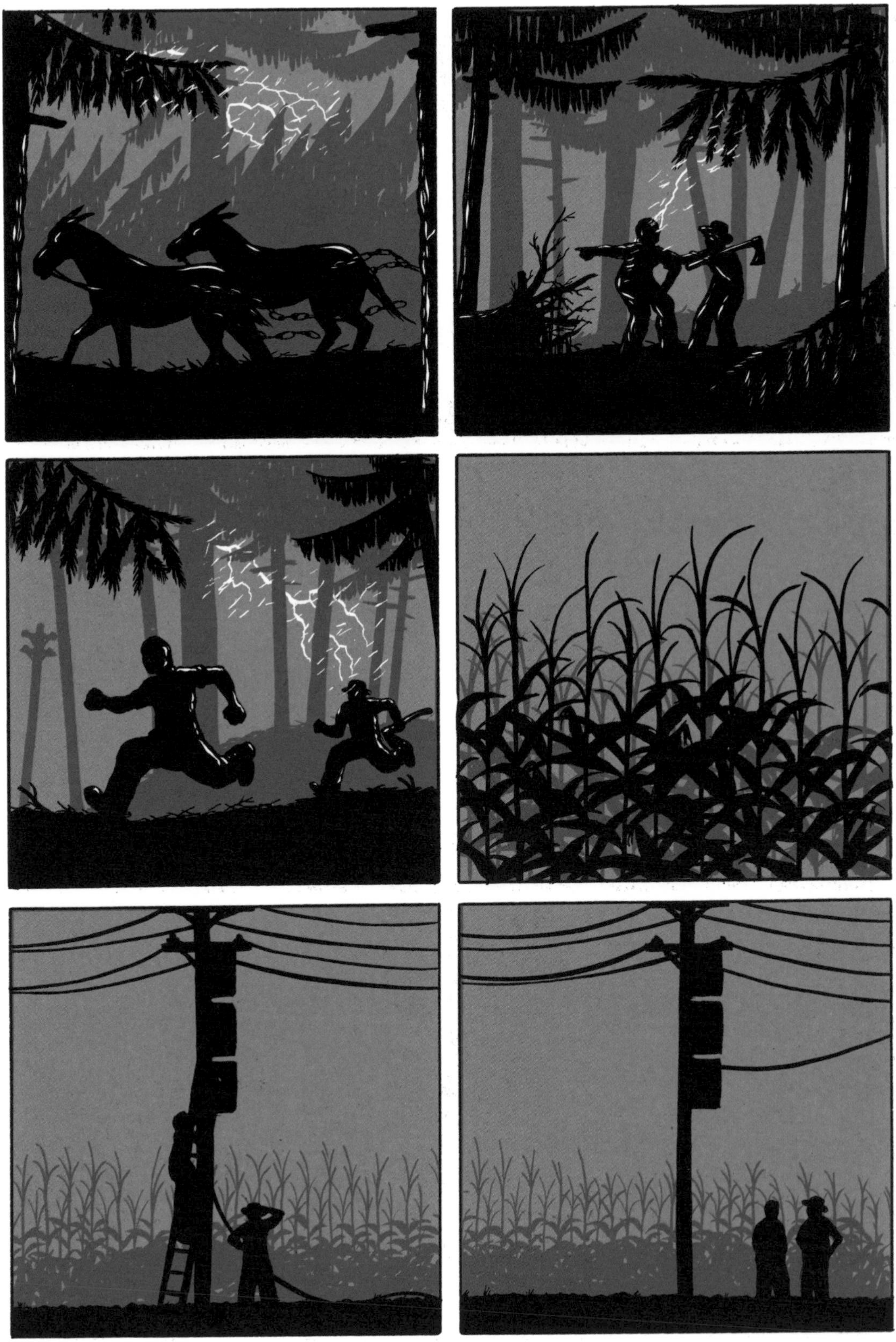

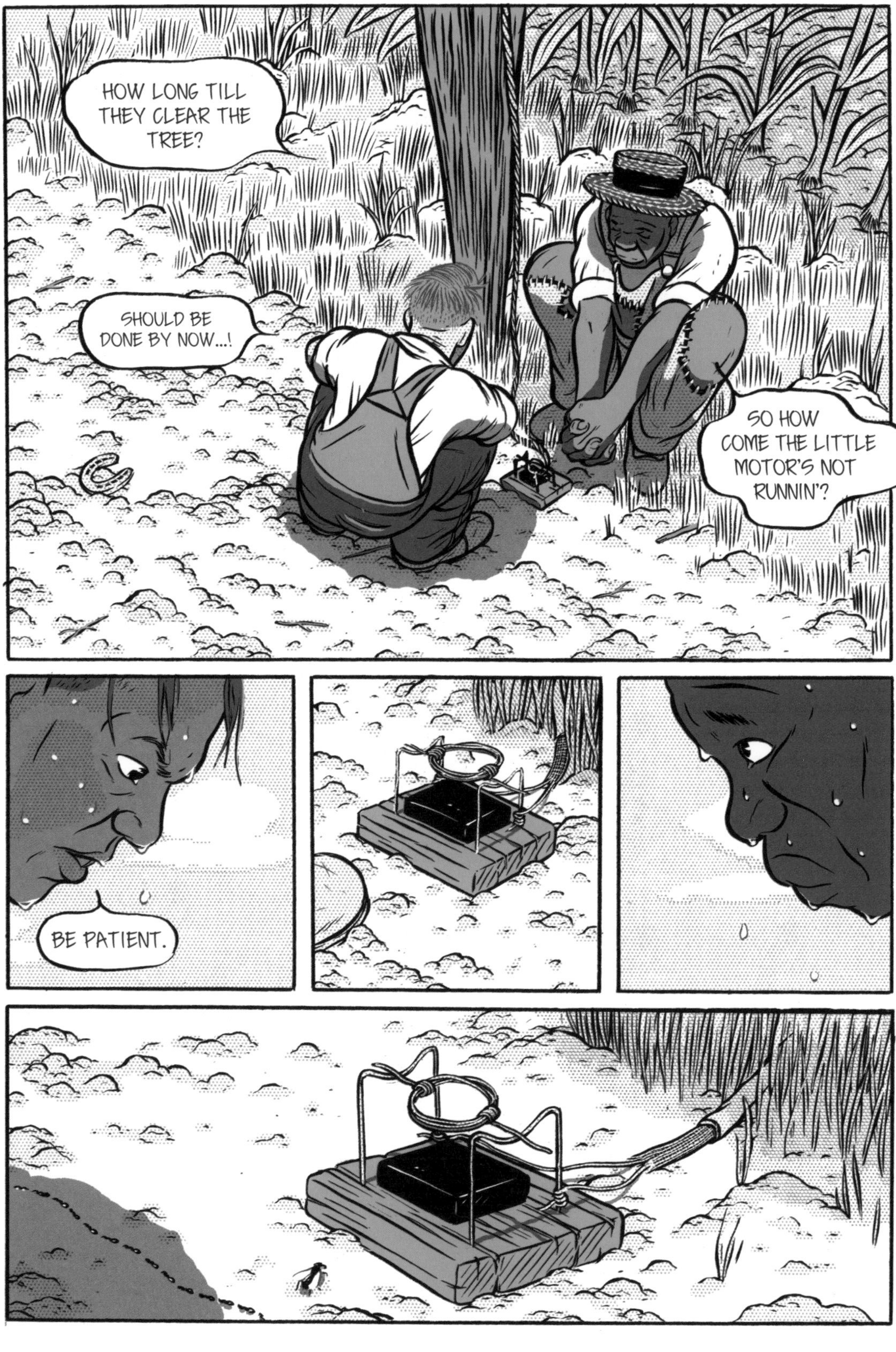
HOW LONG TILL THEY CLEAR THE TREE?
SHOULD BE DONE BY NOW...!
SO HOW COME THE LITTLE MOTOR'S NOT RUNNIN'?
BE PATIENT.

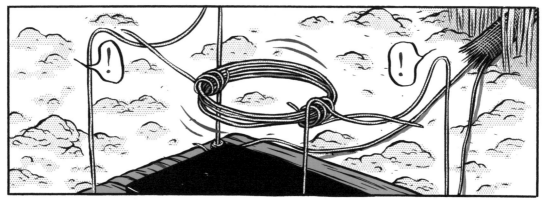

HEH HEH HEH!

BZZZ

HA HA HA!

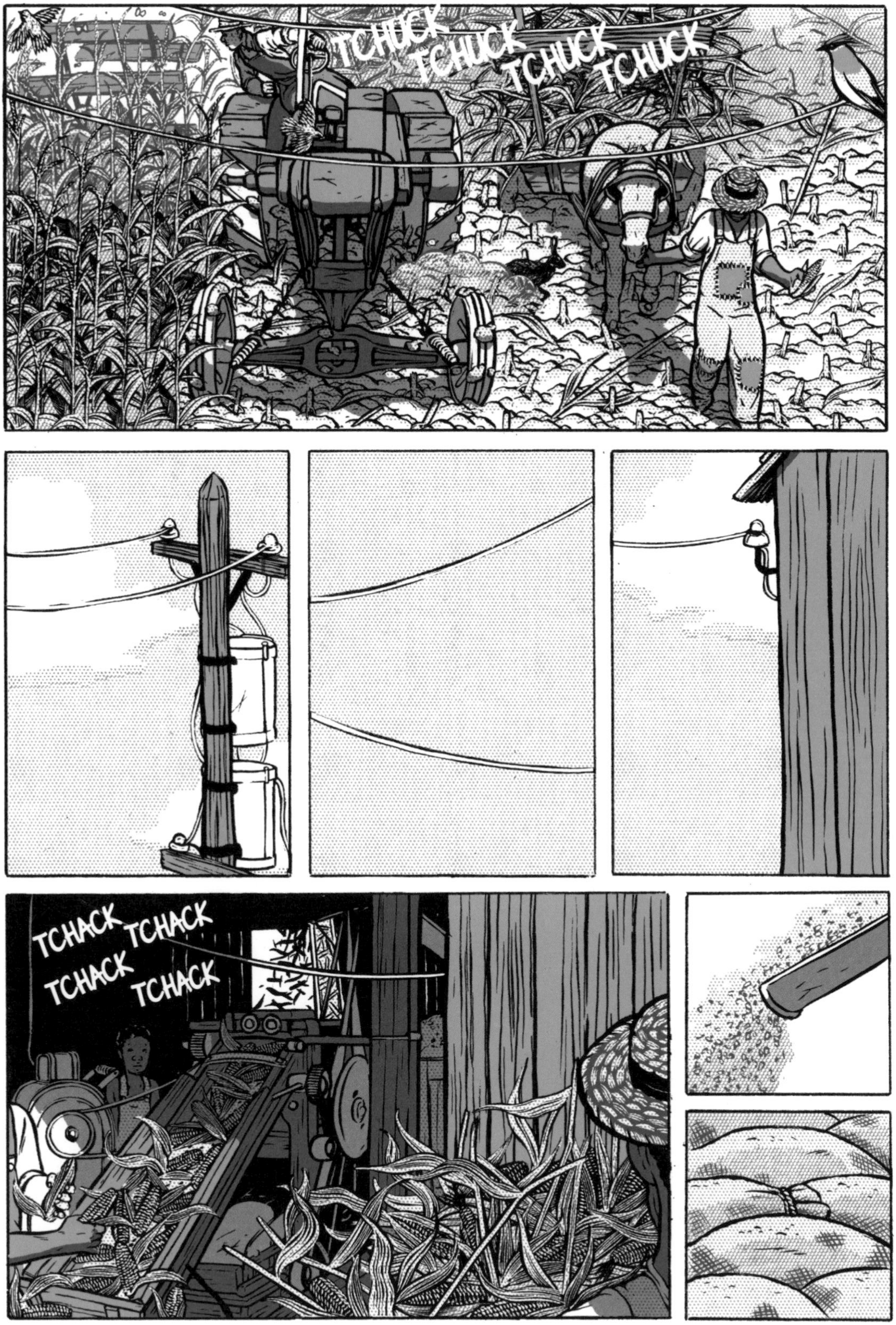
TCHUCK
TCHUCK
TCHUCK
TCHUCK
TCHACK
TCHACK
TCHACK
TCHACK

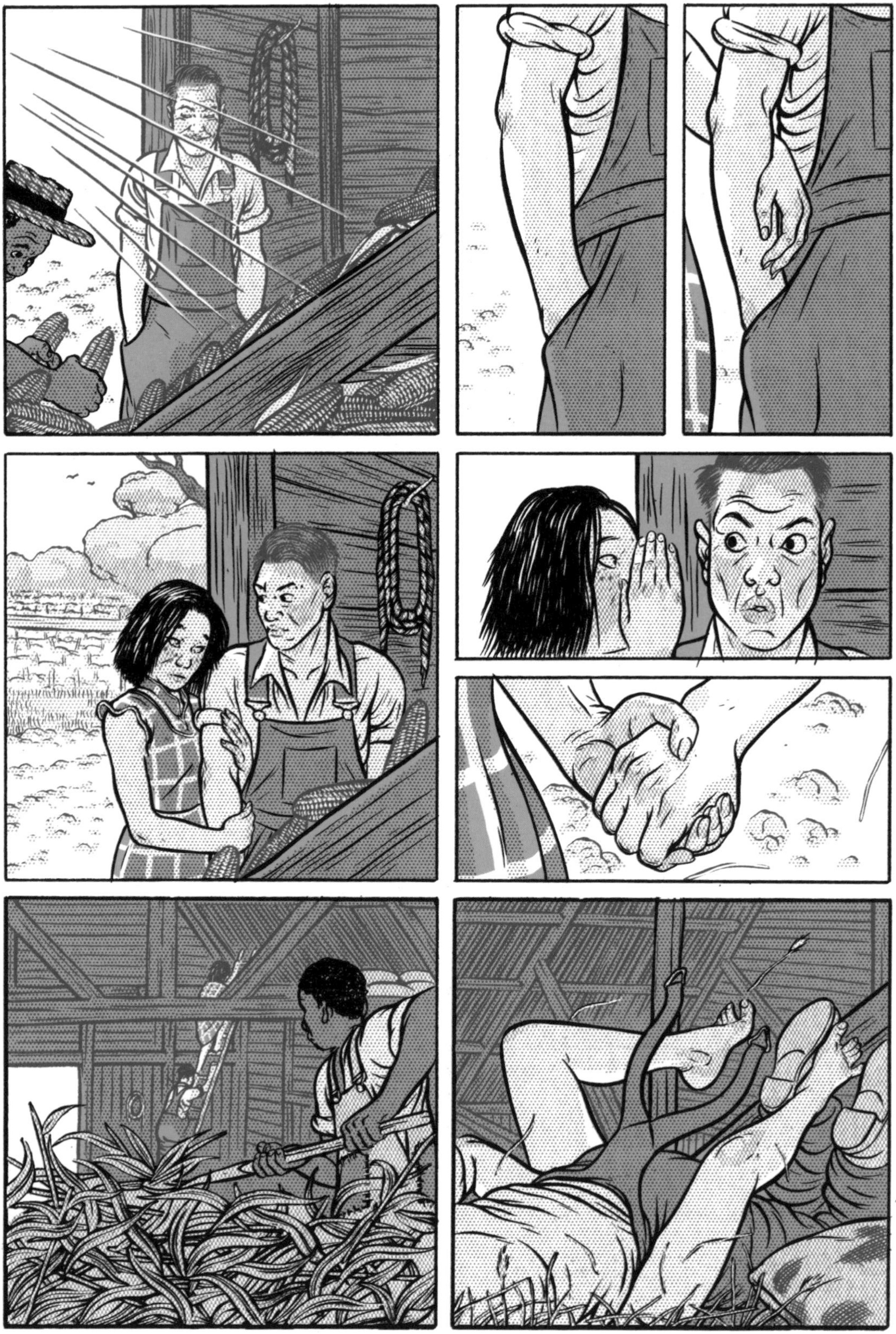

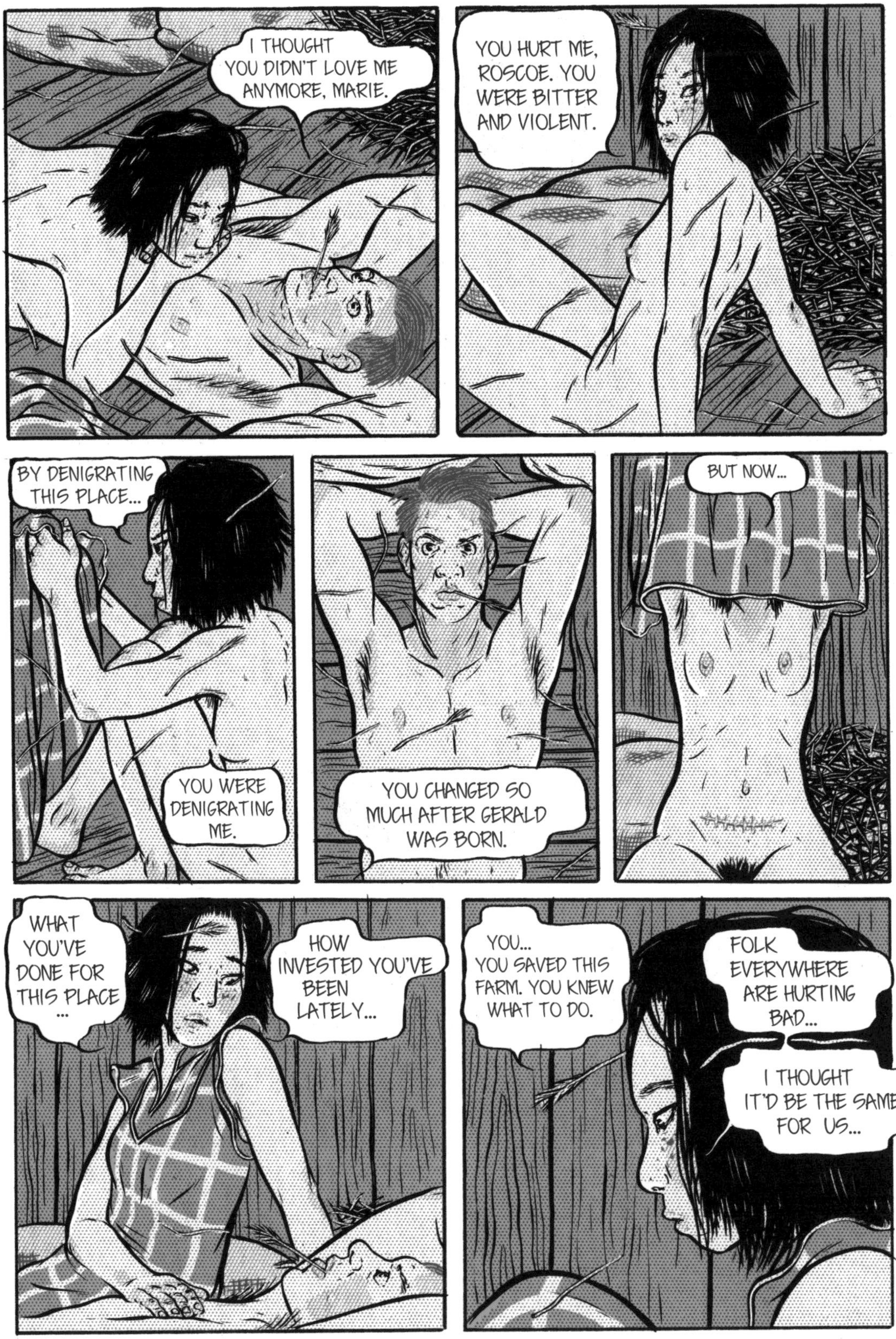
I THOUGHT YOU DIDN'T LOVE ME ANYMORE, MARIE.
YOU HURT ME, ROSCOE. YOU WERE BITTER AND VIOLENT.
BY DENIGRATING THIS PLACE...
YOU WERE DENIGRATING ME.
YOU CHANGED SO MUCH AFTER GERALD WAS BORN.
BUT NOW...
WHAT YOU'VE DONE FOR THIS PLACE ...
HOW INVESTED YOU'VE BEEN LATELY...
YOU... YOU SAVED THIS FARM. YOU KNEW WHAT TO DO.
FOLK EVERYWHERE ARE HURTING BAD...
I THOUGHT IT'D BE THE SAME FOR US...

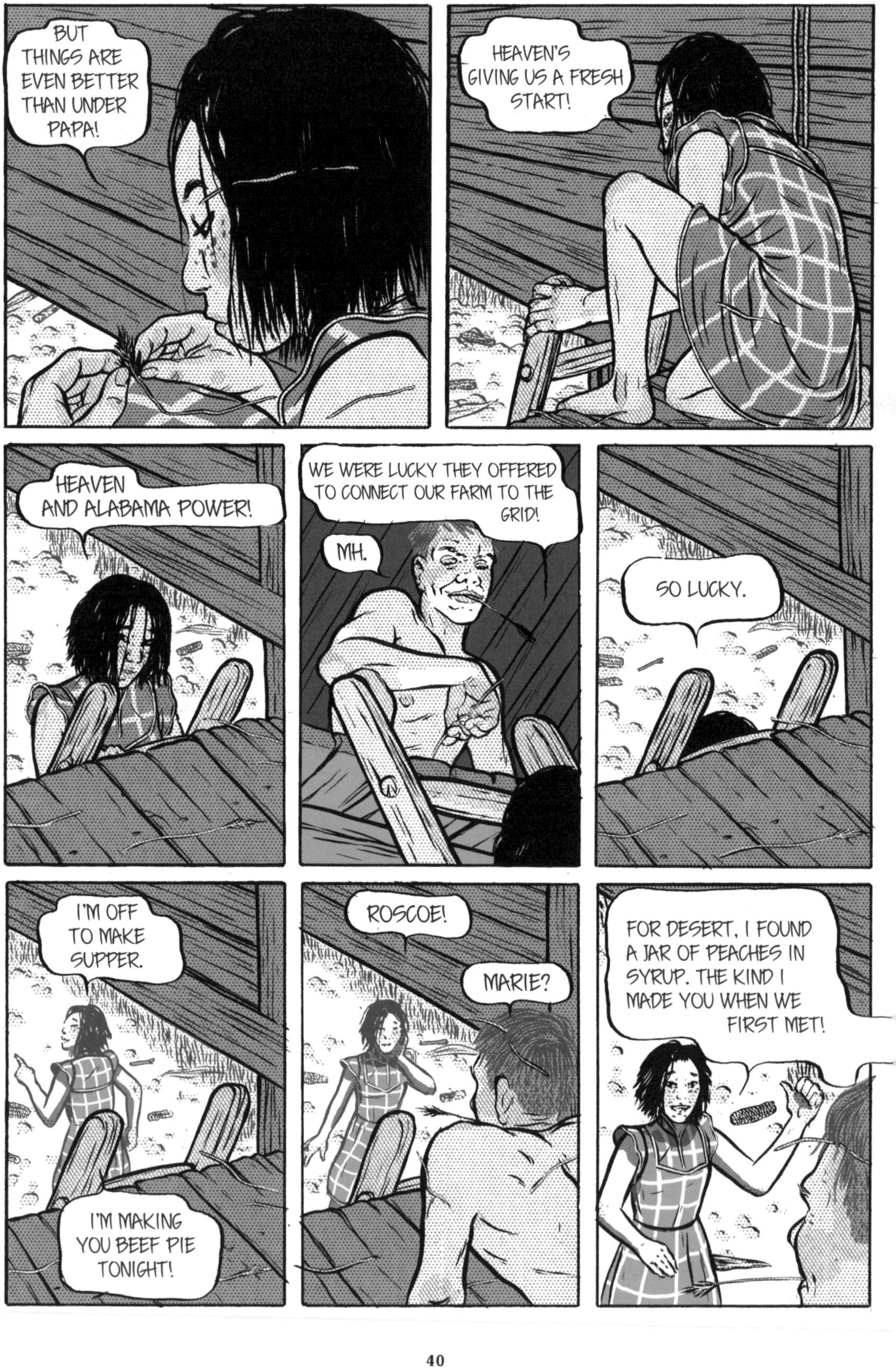
BUT THINGS ARE EVEN BETTER THAN UNDER PAPA!
HEAVEN'S GIVING US A FRESH START!
HEAVEN AND ALABAMA POWER!
WE WERE LUCKY THEY OFFERED TO CONNECT OUR FARM TO THE GRID!
MH.
SO LUCKY.
I'M OFF TO MAKE SUPPER.
I'M MAKING YOU BEEF PIE TONIGHT!
ROSCOE!
MARIE?
FOR DESERT, I FOUND A JAR OF PEACHES IN SYRUP. THE KIND I MADE YOU WHEN WE FIRST MET!

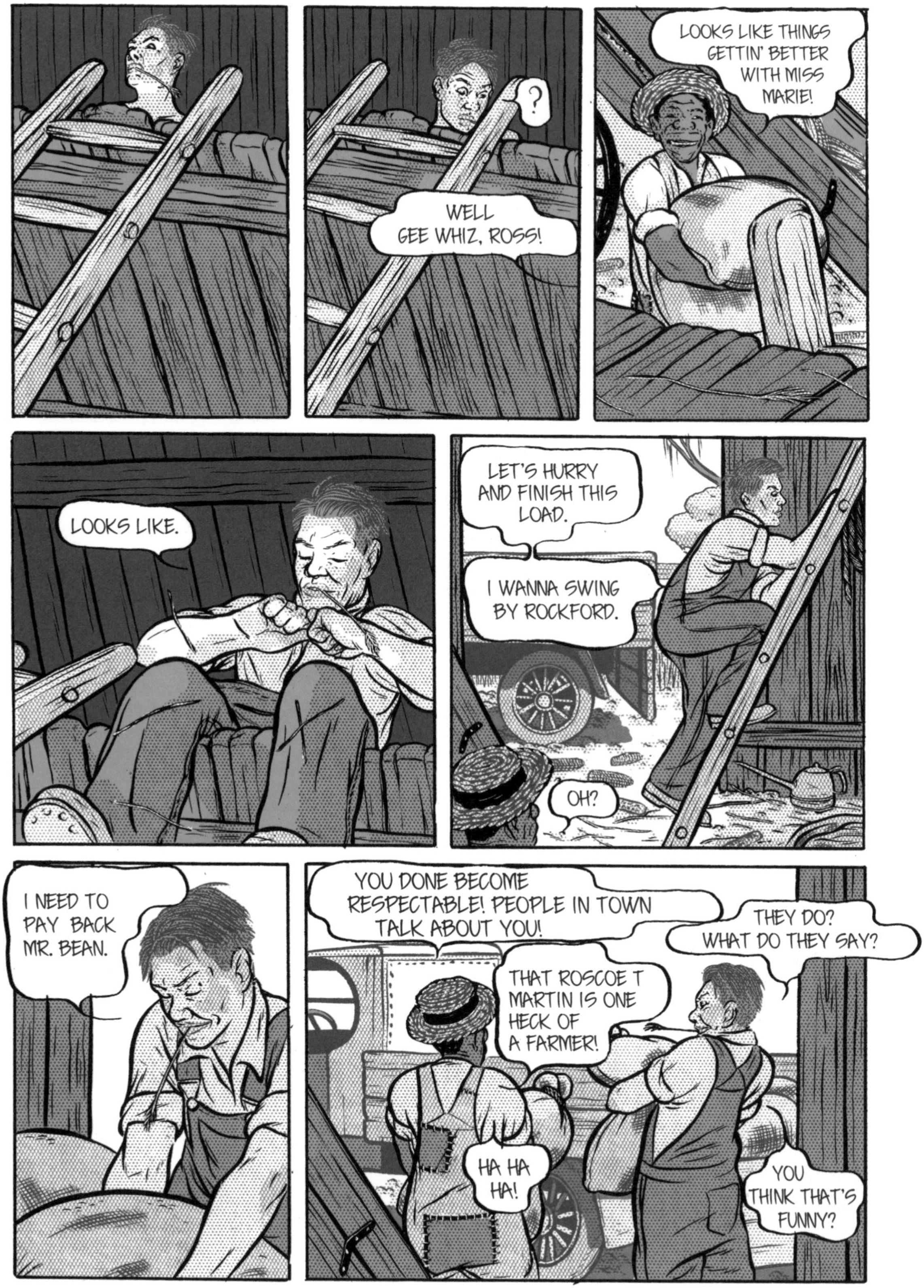
?
WELL GEE WHIZ, ROSS!
LOOKS LIKE THINGS GETTIN' BETTER WITH MISS MARIE!
LOOKS LIKE.
LET'S HURRY AND FINISH THIS LOAD.
I WANNA SWING BY ROCKFORD.
OH?
I NEED TO PAY BACK MR. BEAN.
YOU DONE BECOME RESPECTABLE! PEOPLE IN TOWN TALK ABOUT YOU!
THEY DO? WHAT DO THEY SAY?
THAT ROSCOE T MARTIN IS ONE HECK OF A FARMER!
HA HA HA!
YOU THINK THAT'S FUNNY?

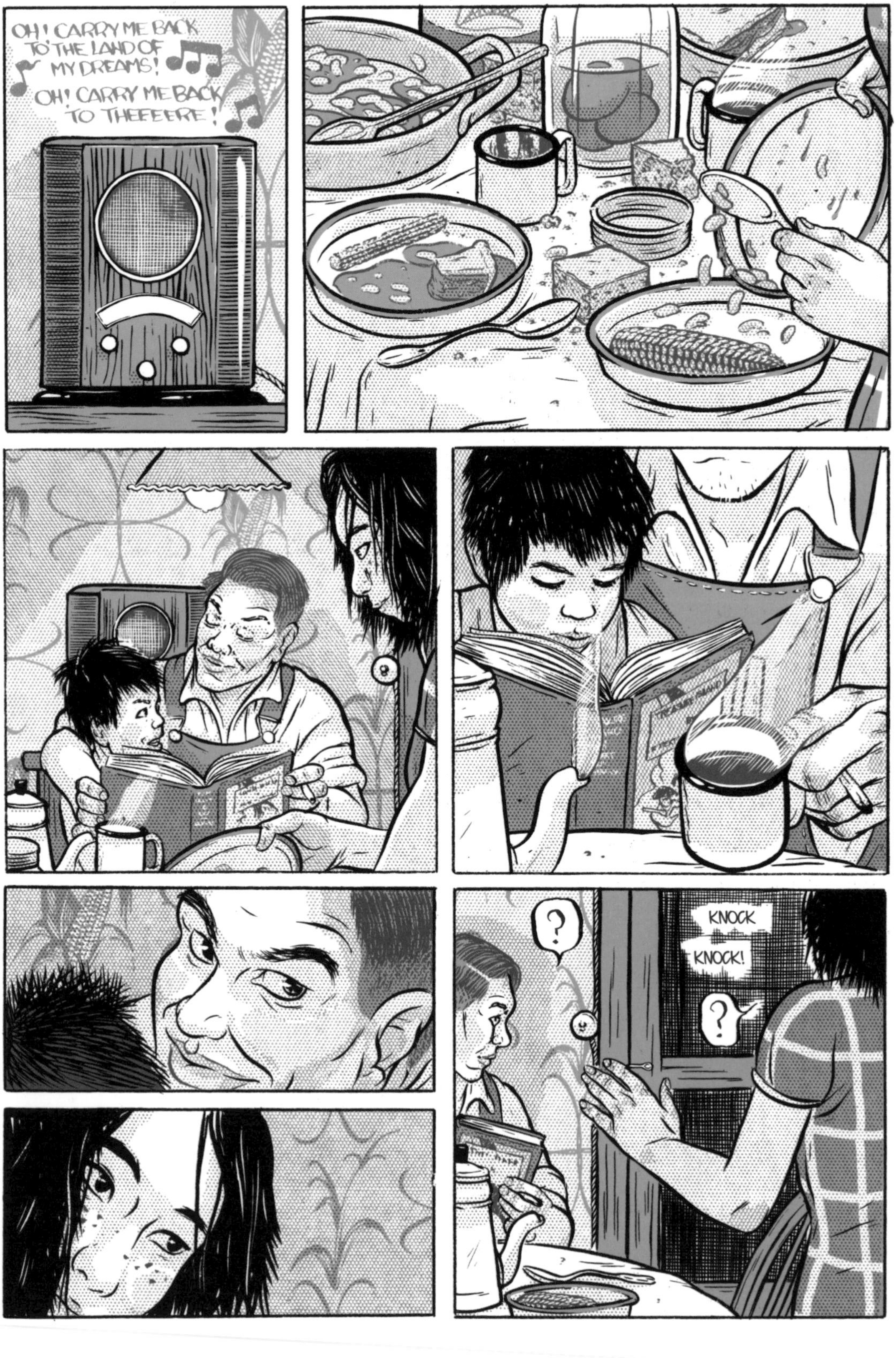
OH! CARRY ME BACK TO THE LAND OF MY DREAMS!
OH! CARRY ME BACK TO THEEEERE!
?
KNOCK
KNOCK!
?

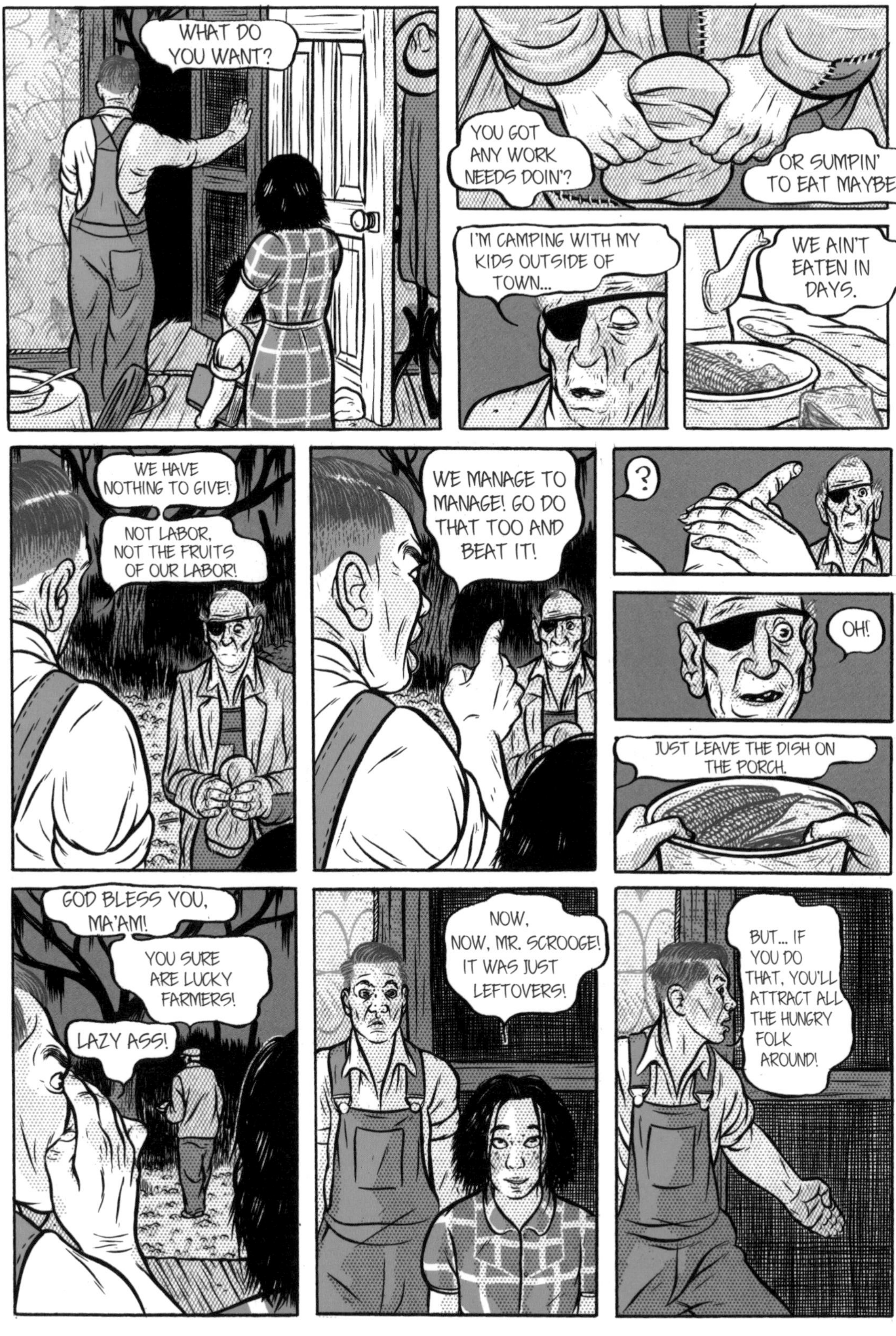
WHAT DO YOU WANT?
YOU GOT ANY WORK NEEDS DOIN'?
OR SUMPIN' TO EAT MAYBE?
I'M CAMPING WITH MY KIDS OUTSIDE OF TOWN...
WE AIN'T EATEN IN DAYS.
WE HAVE NOTHING TO GIVE!
NOT LABOR, NOT THE FRUITS OF OUR LABOR!
WE MANAGE TO MANAGE! GO DO THAT TOO AND BEAT IT!
?
OH!
JUST LEAVE THE DISH ON THE PORCH.
GOD BLESS YOU, MA'AM!
YOU SURE ARE LUCKY FARMERS!
LAZY ASS!
NOW, NOW, MR. SCROOGE! IT WAS JUST LEFTOVERS!
BUT... IF YOU DO THAT, YOU'LL ATTRACT ALL THE HUNGRY FOLK AROUND!

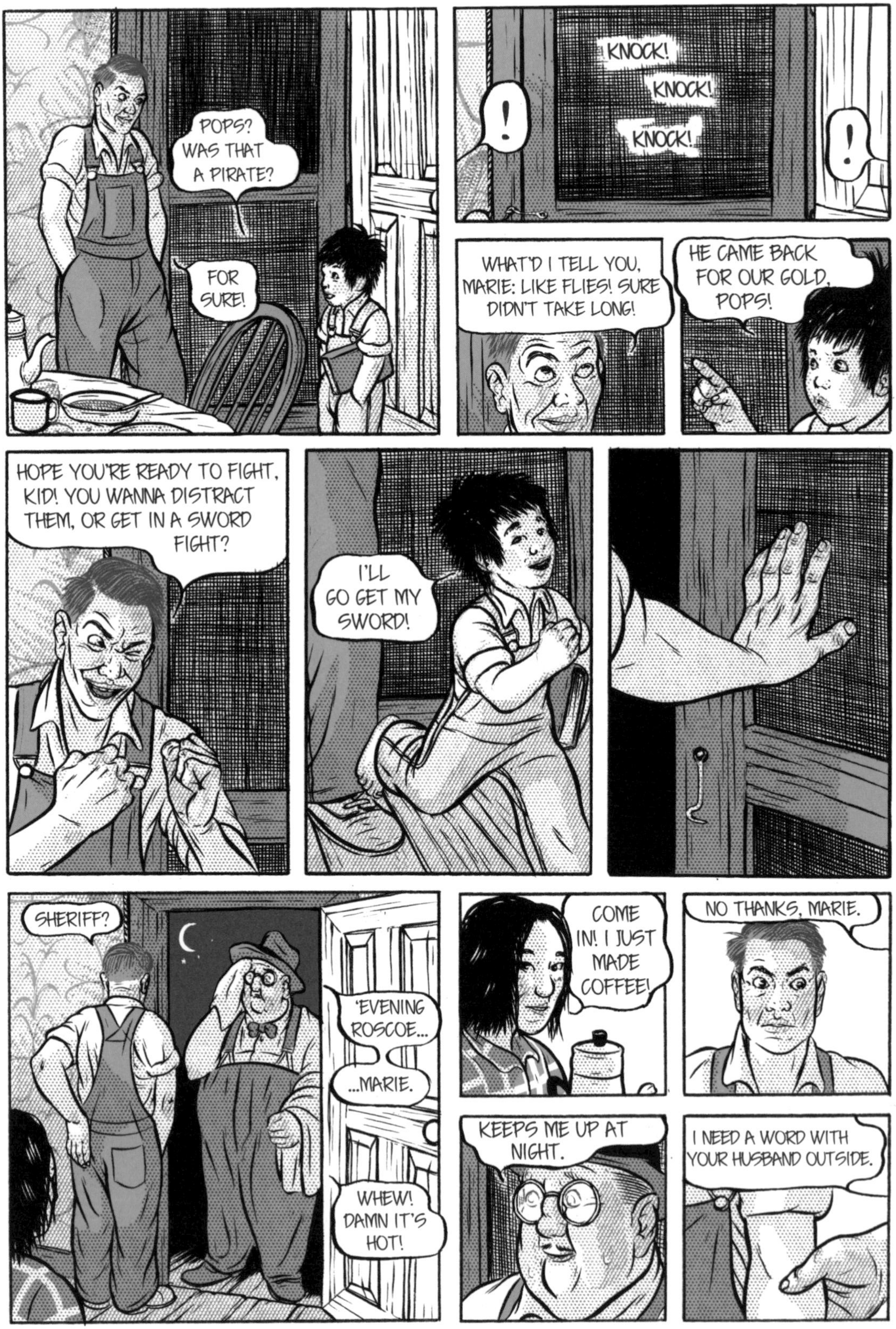
POPS? WAS THAT A PIRATE?
FOR SURE!
KNOCK! KNOCK! KNOCK!
!
!
WHAT'D I TELL YOU, MARIE: LIKE FLIES! SURE DIDN'T TAKE LONG!
HE CAME BACK FOR OUR GOLD, POPS!
HOPE YOU'RE READY TO FIGHT, KID! YOU WANNA DISTRACT THEM, OR GET IN A SWORD FIGHT?
I'LL GO GET MY SWORD!
SHERIFF?
'EVENING ROSCOE...
...MARIE.
WHEW! DAMN IT'S HOT!
COME IN! I JUST MADE COFFEE!
NO THANKS, MARIE.
KEEPS ME UP AT NIGHT.
I NEED A WORD WITH YOUR HUSBAND OUTSIDE.

DON'T YOU WORRY, AND FINISH READING TO GERALD.

I'LL BE BACK BEFORE YOU TWO TURN IN.

MARIE.

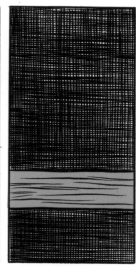

ANY IDEA WHY I'M HERE, SON?

THE ELECTRICITY?

WE DON'T TAKE MUCH.

WE'LL PAY FOR IT!

IT WAS TO SAVE THE FARM, SHERIFF.

THE ELECTRICITY, YES.

HMM.

FOR STARTERS.

I'M GONNA NEED YOU TO PUT OUT YOUR HANDS.

DIDN'T HAVE THE HEART TO CUFF YOU IN FRONT OF YOUR WIFE AND KID.

CUFF ME, SHERIFF? BUT...

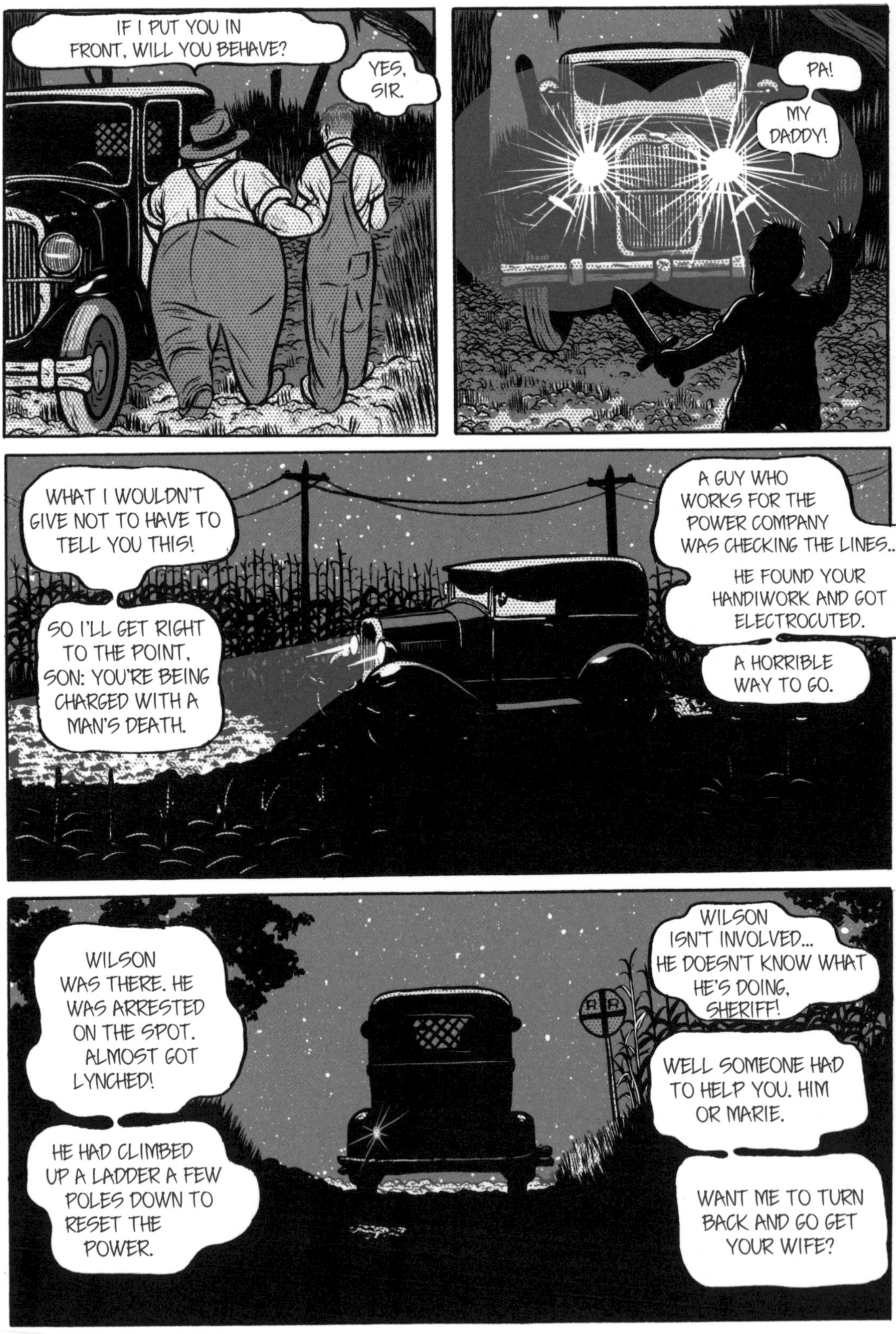
IF I PUT YOU IN FRONT, WILL YOU BEHAVE?
YES, SIR.
PA!
MY DADDY!
WHAT I WOULDN'T GIVE NOT TO HAVE TO TELL YOU THIS!
SO I'LL GET RIGHT TO THE POINT, SON: YOU'RE BEING CHARGED WITH A MAN'S DEATH.
A GUY WHO WORKS FOR THE POWER COMPANY WAS CHECKING THE LINES...
HE FOUND YOUR HANDIWORK AND GOT ELECTROCUTED.
A HORRIBLE WAY TO GO.
WILSON WAS THERE. HE WAS ARRESTED ON THE SPOT. ALMOST GOT LYNCHED!
HE HAD CLIMBED UP A LADDER A FEW POLES DOWN TO RESET THE POWER.
WILSON ISN'T INVOLVED... HE DOESN'T KNOW WHAT HE'S DOING, SHERIFF!
WELL SOMEONE HAD TO HELP YOU. HIM OR MARIE.
WANT ME TO TURN BACK AND GO GET YOUR WIFE?

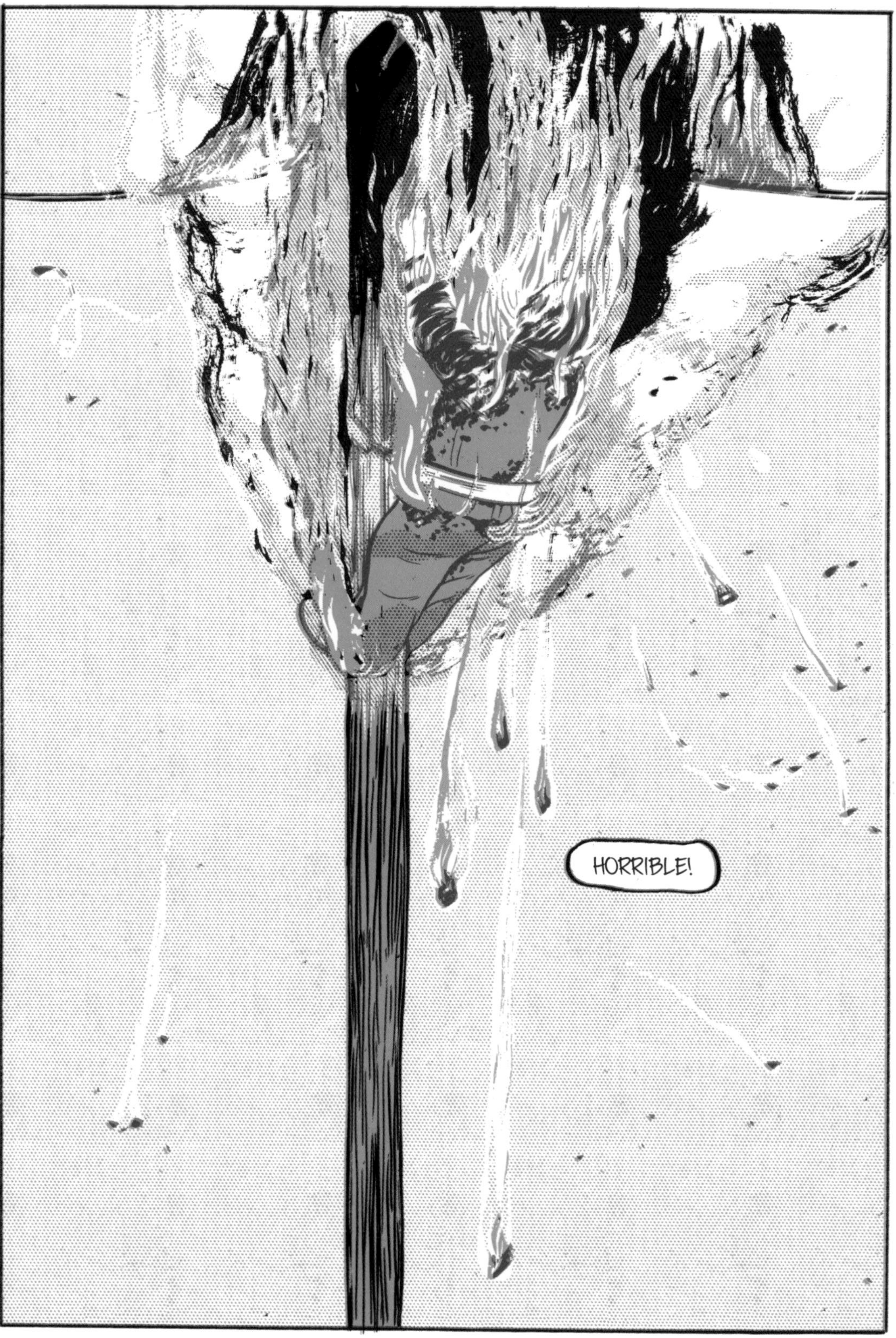
HORRIBLE!

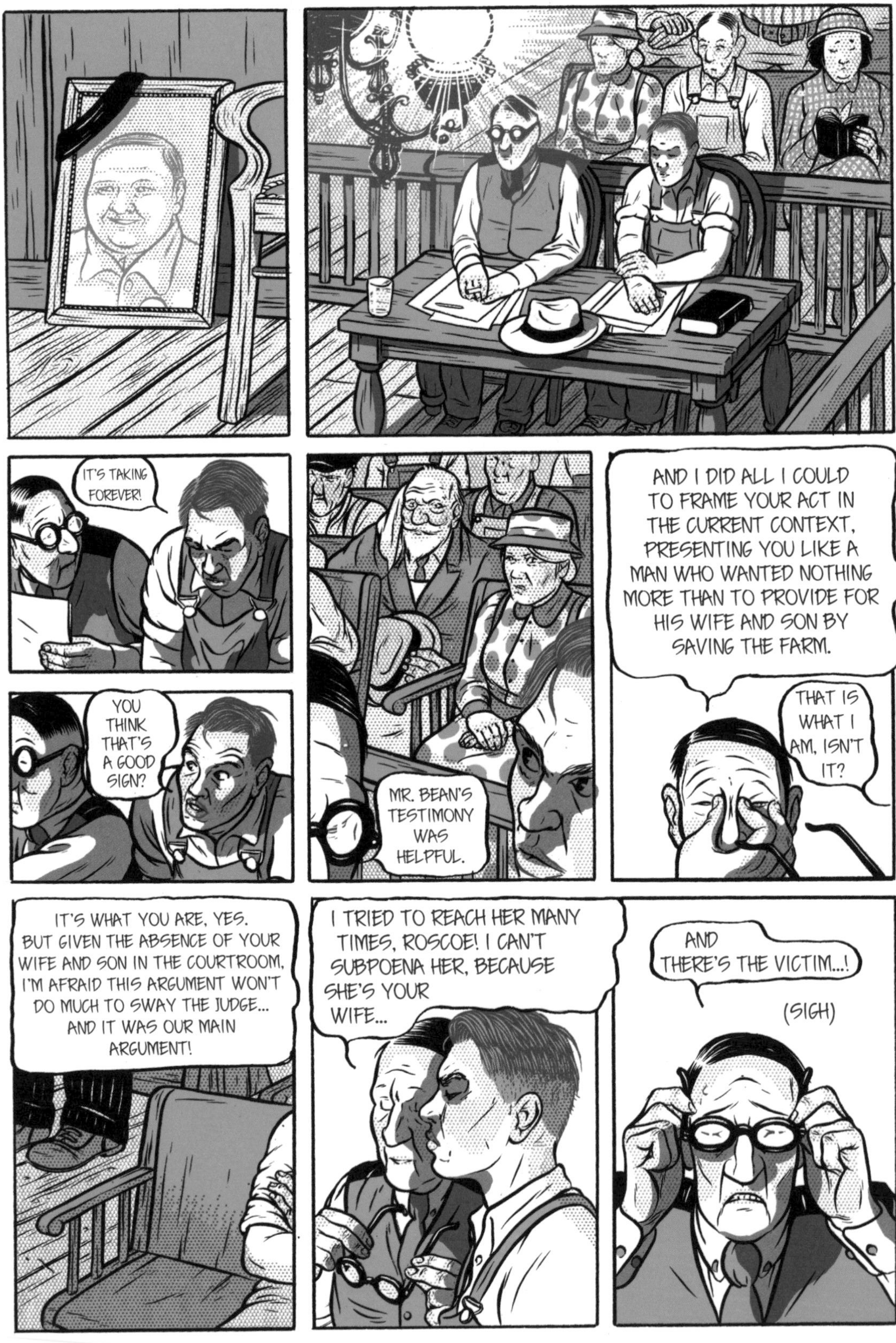
IT'S TAKING FOREVER!
YOU THINK THAT'S A GOOD SIGN?
MR. BEAN'S TESTIMONY WAS HELPFUL.
AND I DID ALL I COULD TO FRAME YOUR ACT IN THE CURRENT CONTEXT, PRESENTING YOU LIKE A MAN WHO WANTED NOTHING MORE THAN TO PROVIDE FOR HIS WIFE AND SON BY SAVING THE FARM.
THAT IS WHAT I AM, ISN'T IT?
IT'S WHAT YOU ARE, YES. BUT GIVEN THE ABSENCE OF YOUR WIFE AND SON IN THE COURTROOM, I'M AFRAID THIS ARGUMENT WON'T DO MUCH TO SWAY THE JUDGE... AND IT WAS OUR MAIN ARGUMENT!
I TRIED TO REACH HER MANY TIMES, ROSCOE! I CAN'T SUBPOENA HER, BECAUSE SHE'S YOUR WIFE...
AND THERE'S THE VICTIM...!
(SIGH)

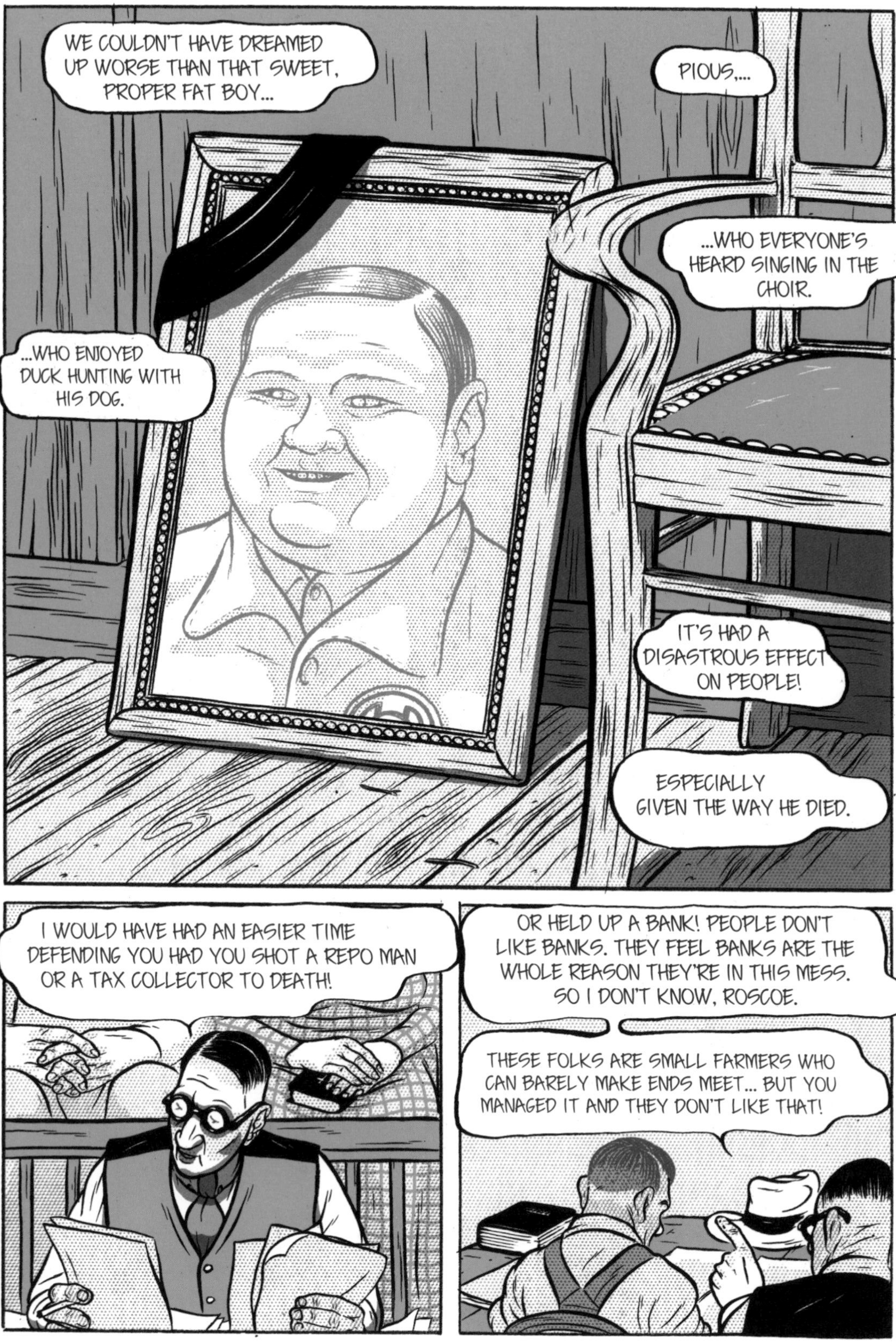
WE COULDN'T HAVE DREAMED UP WORSE THAN THAT SWEET, PROPER FAT BOY...
PIOUS,...
...WHO EVERYONE'S HEARD SINGING IN THE CHOIR.
...WHO ENJOYED DUCK HUNTING WITH HIS DOG.
IT'S HAD A DISASTROUS EFFECT ON PEOPLE!
ESPECIALLY GIVEN THE WAY HE DIED.
I WOULD HAVE HAD AN EASIER TIME DEFENDING YOU HAD YOU SHOT A REPO MAN OR A TAX COLLECTOR TO DEATH!
OR HELD UP A BANK! PEOPLE DON'T LIKE BANKS. THEY FEEL BANKS ARE THE WHOLE REASON THEY'RE IN THIS MESS. SO I DON'T KNOW, ROSCOE.
THESE FOLKS ARE SMALL FARMERS WHO CAN BARELY MAKE ENDS MEET... BUT YOU MANAGED IT AND THEY DON'T LIKE THAT!

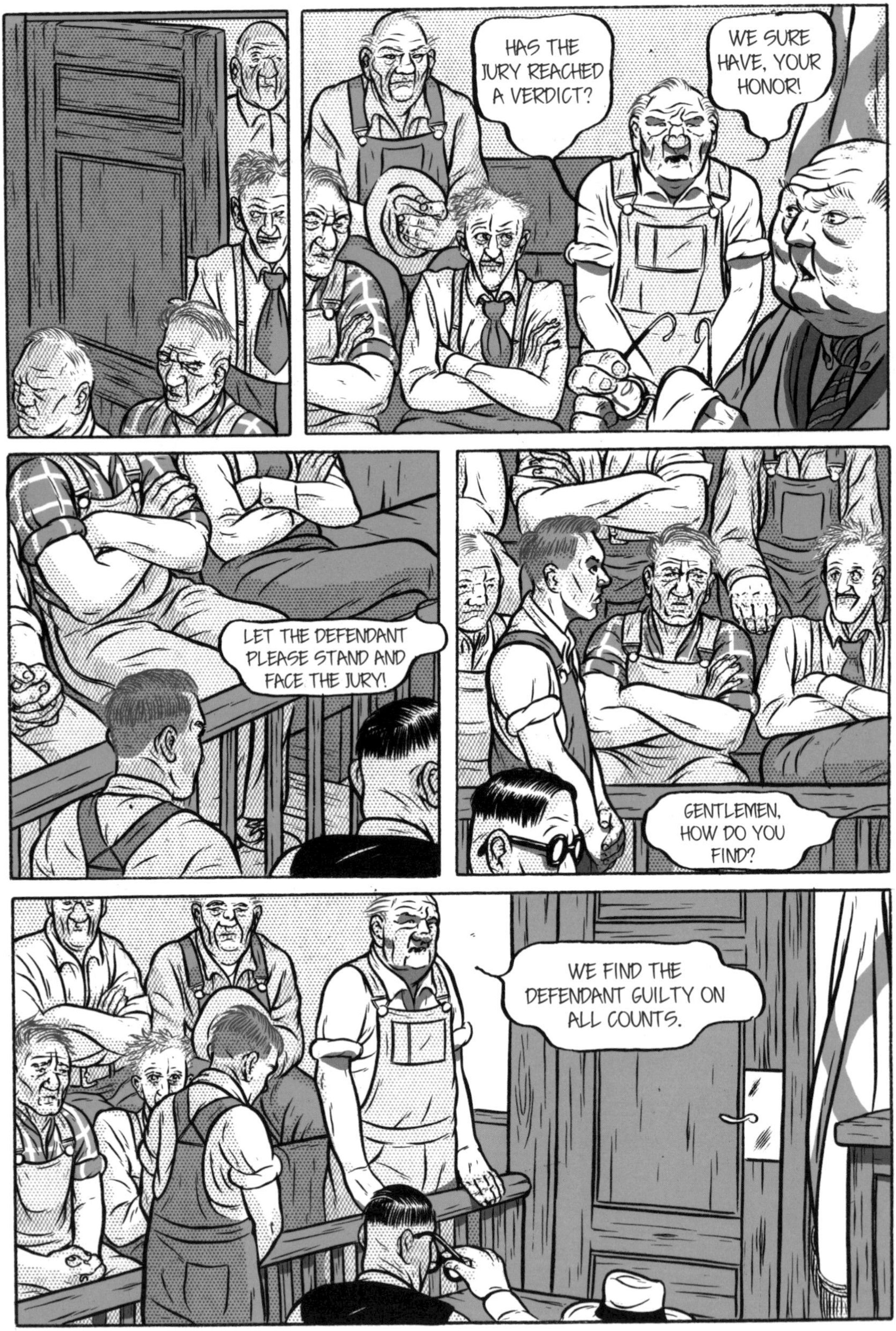
HAS THE JURY REACHED A VERDICT?
WE SURE HAVE, YOUR HONOR!
LET THE DEFENDANT PLEASE STAND AND FACE THE JURY!
GENTLEMEN, HOW DO YOU FIND?
WE FIND THE DEFENDANT GUILTY ON ALL COUNTS.

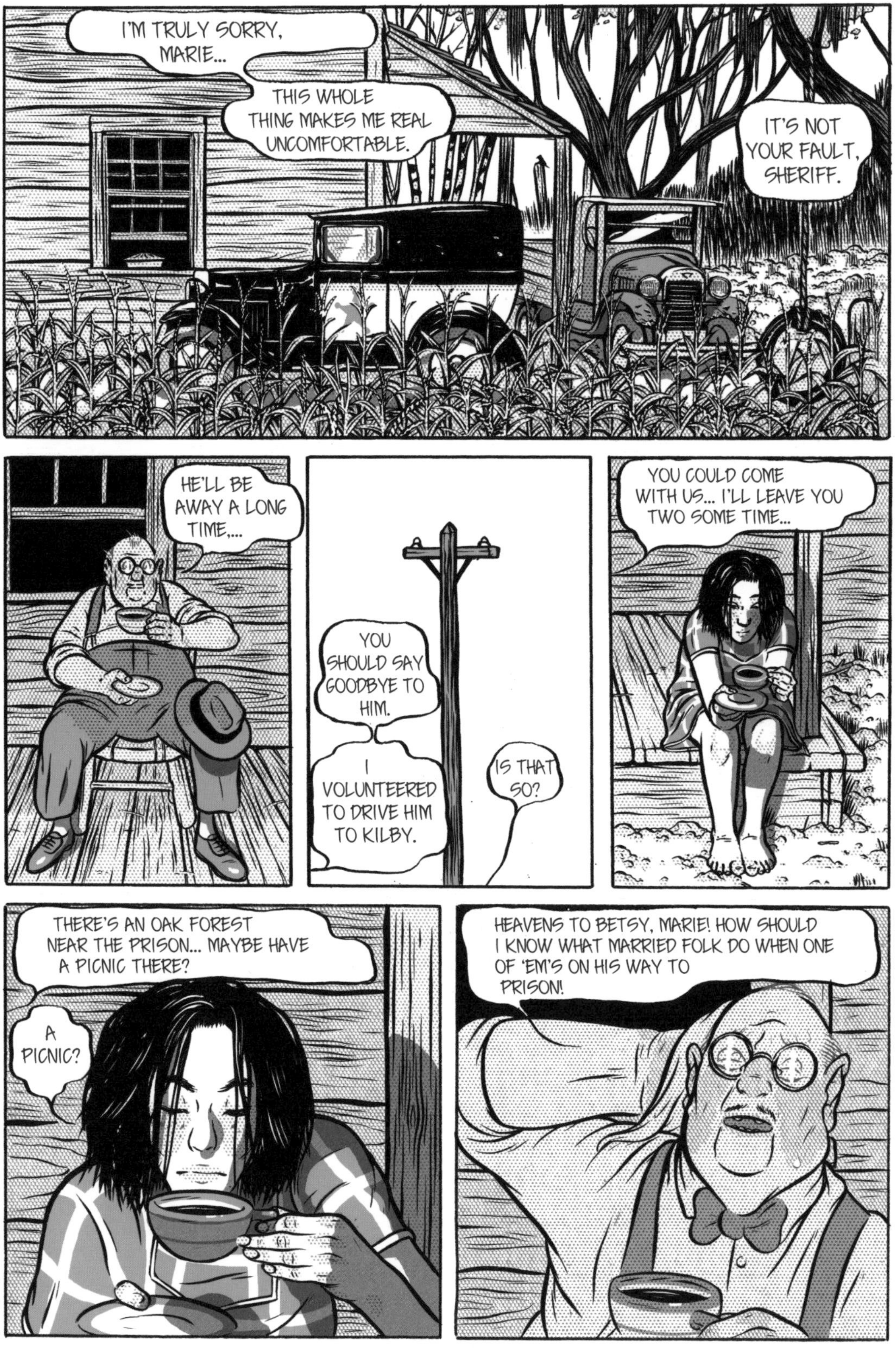
I'M TRULY SORRY, MARIE...
THIS WHOLE THING MAKES ME REAL UNCOMFORTABLE.
IT'S NOT YOUR FAULT, SHERIFF.
HE'LL BE AWAY A LONG TIME,...
YOU SHOULD SAY GOODBYE TO HIM.
I VOLUNTEERED TO DRIVE HIM TO KILBY.
IS THAT SO?
YOU COULD COME WITH US... I'LL LEAVE YOU TWO SOME TIME...
THERE'S AN OAK FOREST NEAR THE PRISON... MAYBE HAVE A PICNIC THERE?
A PICNIC?
HEAVENS TO BETSY, MARIE! HOW SHOULD I KNOW WHAT MARRIED FOLK DO WHEN ONE OF 'EM'S ON HIS WAY TO PRISON!

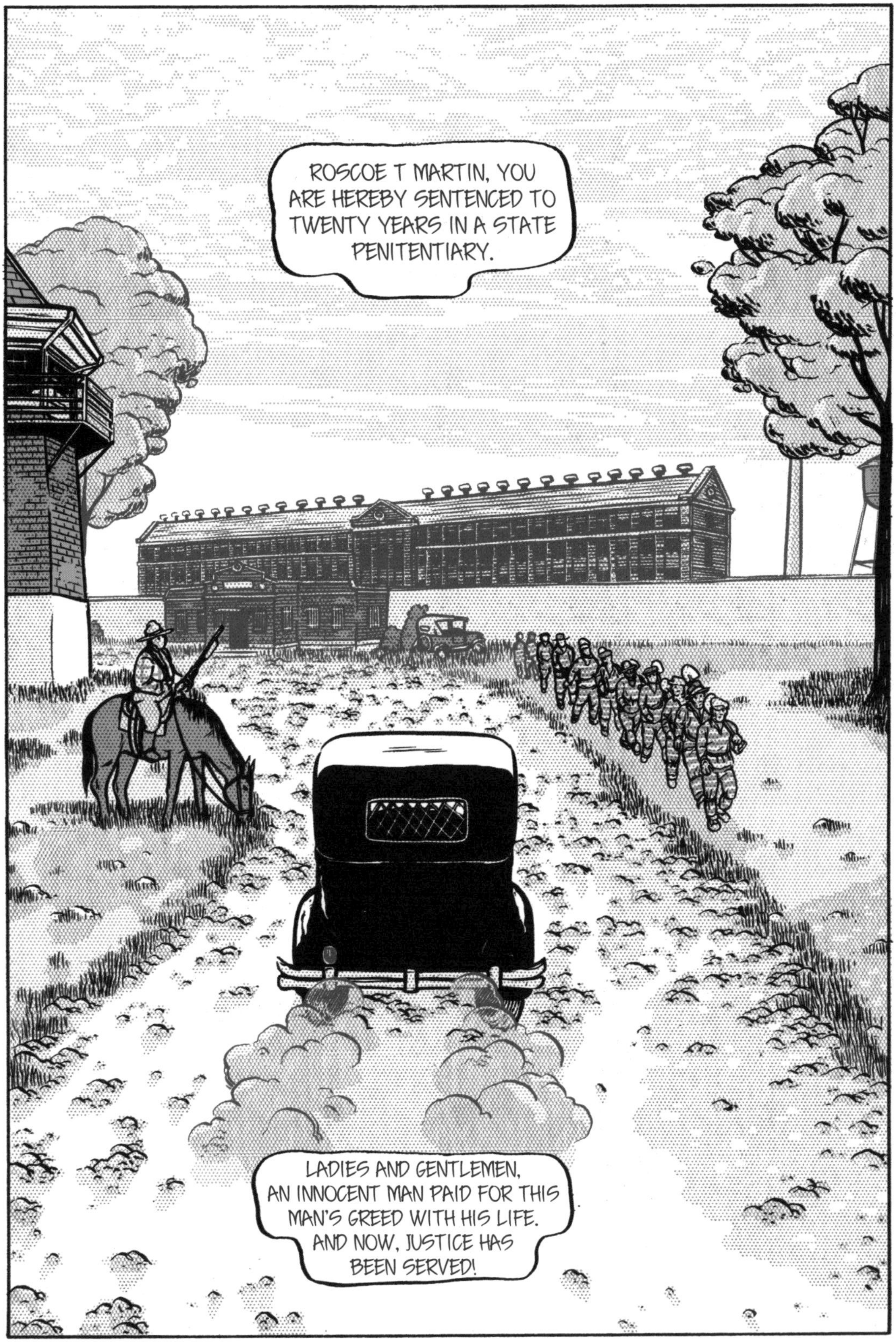
ROSCOE T MARTIN, YOU ARE HEREBY SENTENCED TO TWENTY YEARS IN A STATE PENITENTIARY.
LADIES AND GENTLEMEN, AN INNOCENT MAN PAID FOR THIS MAN'S GREED WITH HIS LIFE. AND NOW, JUSTICE HAS BEEN SERVED!

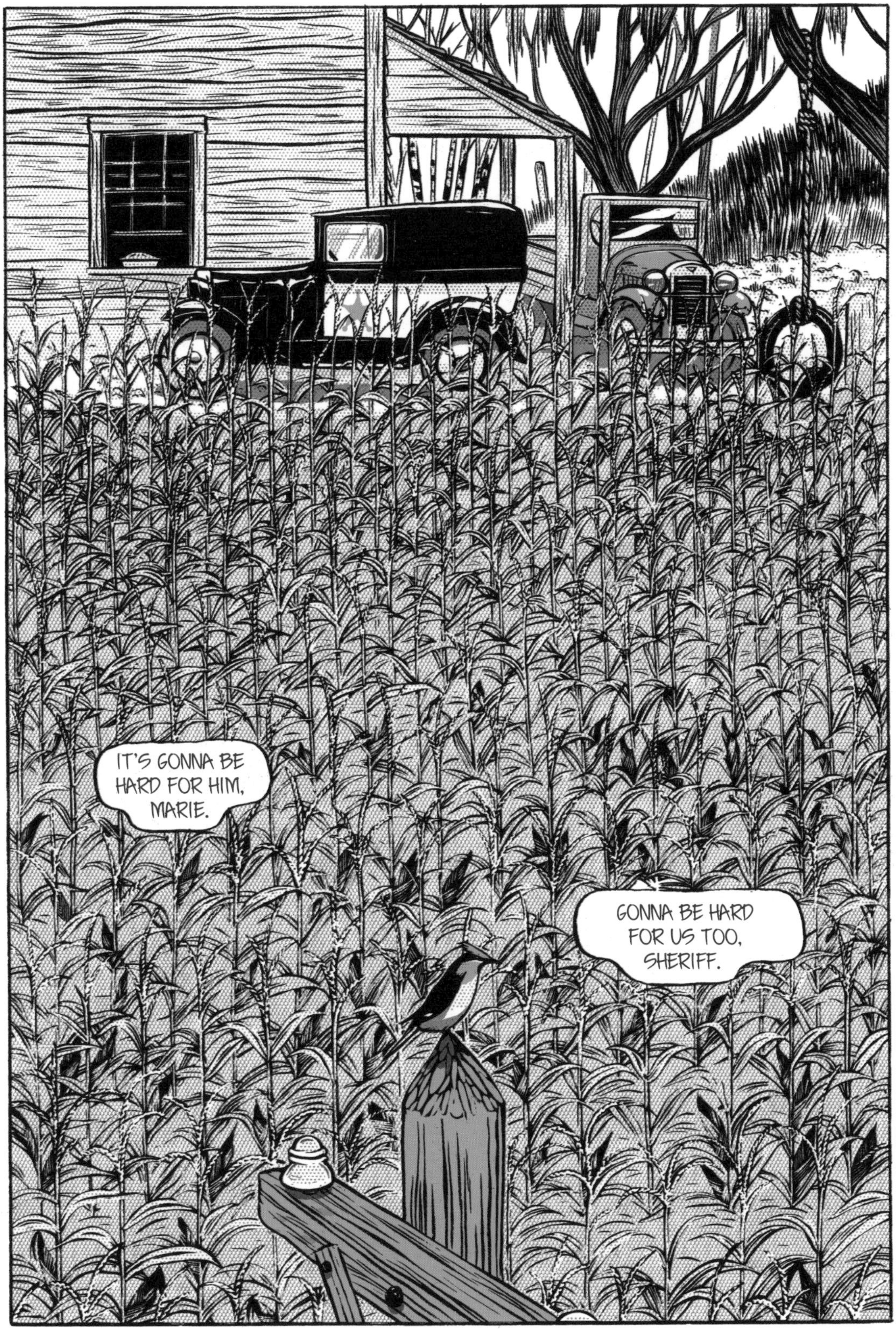
IT'S GONNA BE HARD FOR HIM, MARIE.
GONNA BE HARD FOR US TOO, SHERIFF.

ALL DONE, SIR.

HOLD ON! ?

WHAT'S THAT ON YOUR LIPS, MARTIN?

IS THAT MILK, HUH? !

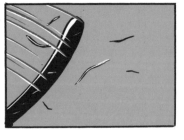

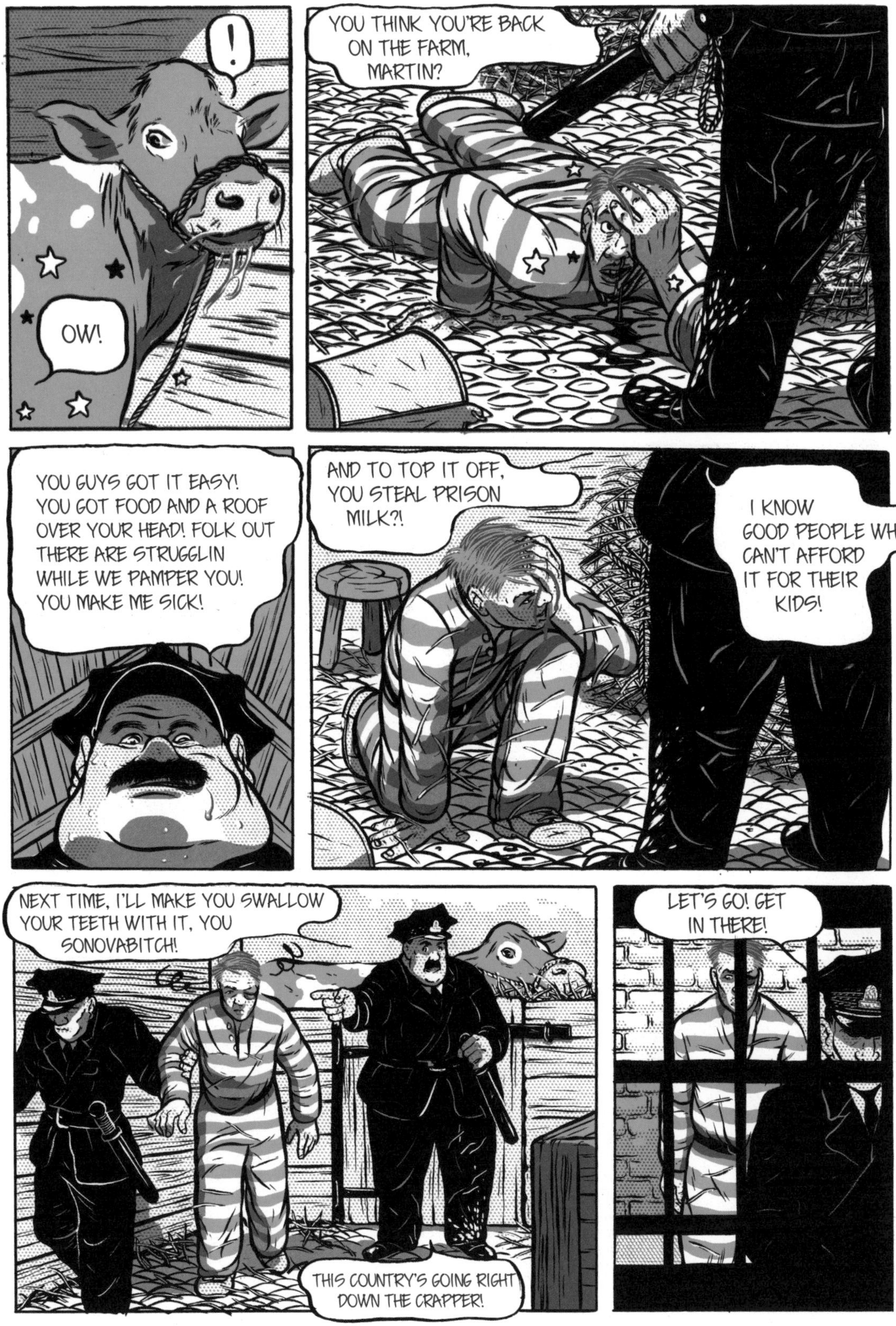

!
OW!
YOU THINK YOU'RE BACK ON THE FARM, MARTIN?
YOU GUYS GOT IT EASY! YOU GOT FOOD AND A ROOF OVER YOUR HEAD! FOLK OUT THERE ARE STRUGGLIN WHILE WE PAMPER YOU! YOU MAKE ME SICK!
AND TO TOP IT OFF, YOU STEAL PRISON MILK?!
I KNOW GOOD PEOPLE WHO CAN'T AFFORD IT FOR THEIR KIDS!
NEXT TIME, I'LL MAKE YOU SWALLOW YOUR TEETH WITH IT, YOU SONOVABITCH!
THIS COUNTRY'S GOING RIGHT DOWN THE CRAPPER!
LET'S GO! GET IN THERE!

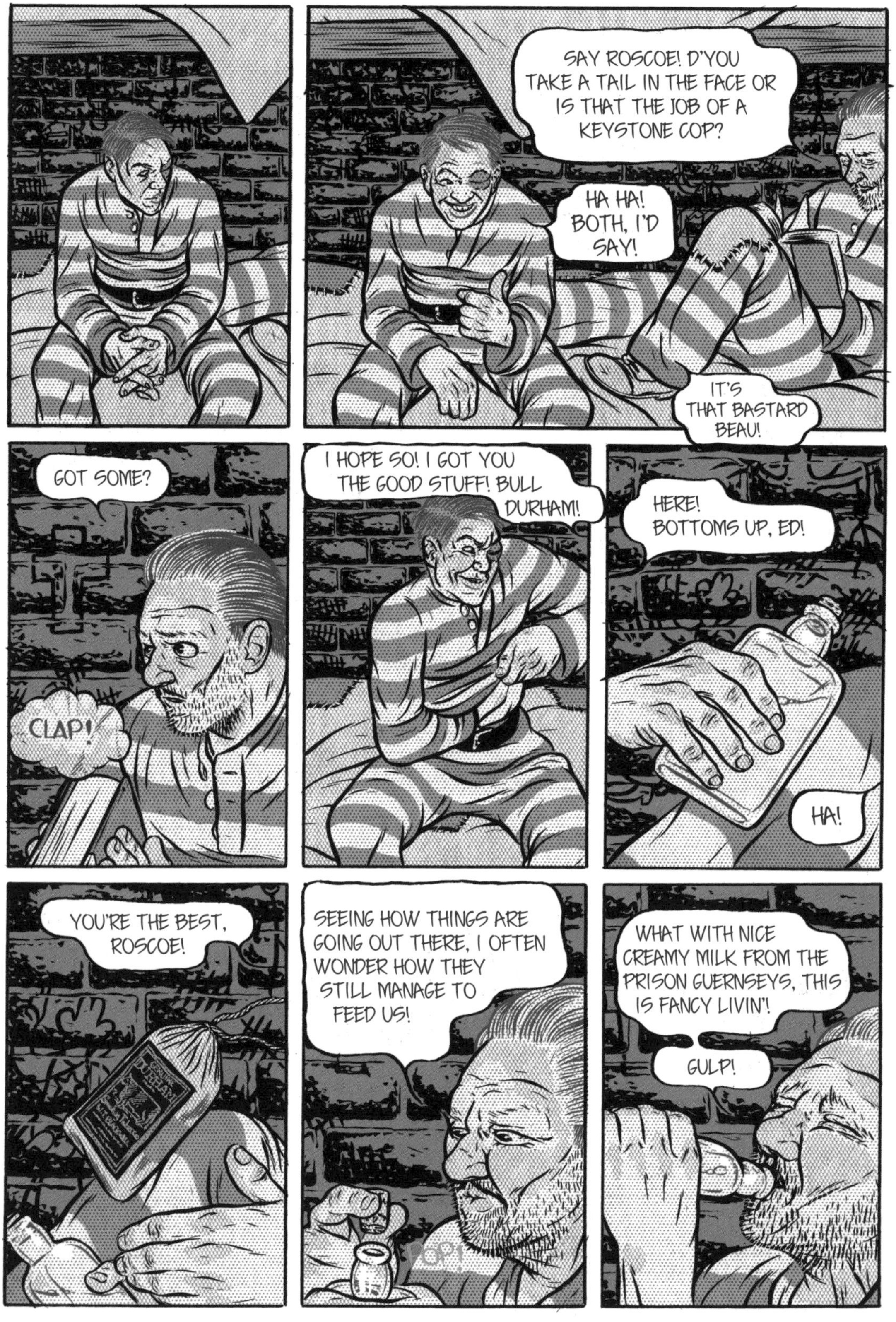
SAY ROSCOE! D'YOU TAKE A TAIL IN THE FACE OR IS THAT THE JOB OF A KEYSTONE COP?
HA HA! BOTH, I'D SAY!
IT'S THAT BASTARD BEAU!
GOT SOME?
CLAP!
I HOPE SO! I GOT YOU THE GOOD STUFF! BULL DURHAM!
HERE! BOTTOMS UP, ED!
HA!
YOU'RE THE BEST, ROSCOE!
SEEING HOW THINGS ARE GOING OUT THERE, I OFTEN WONDER HOW THEY STILL MANAGE TO FEED US!
POP!
WHAT WITH NICE CREAMY MILK FROM THE PRISON GUERNSEYS, THIS IS FANCY LIVIN'!
GULP!

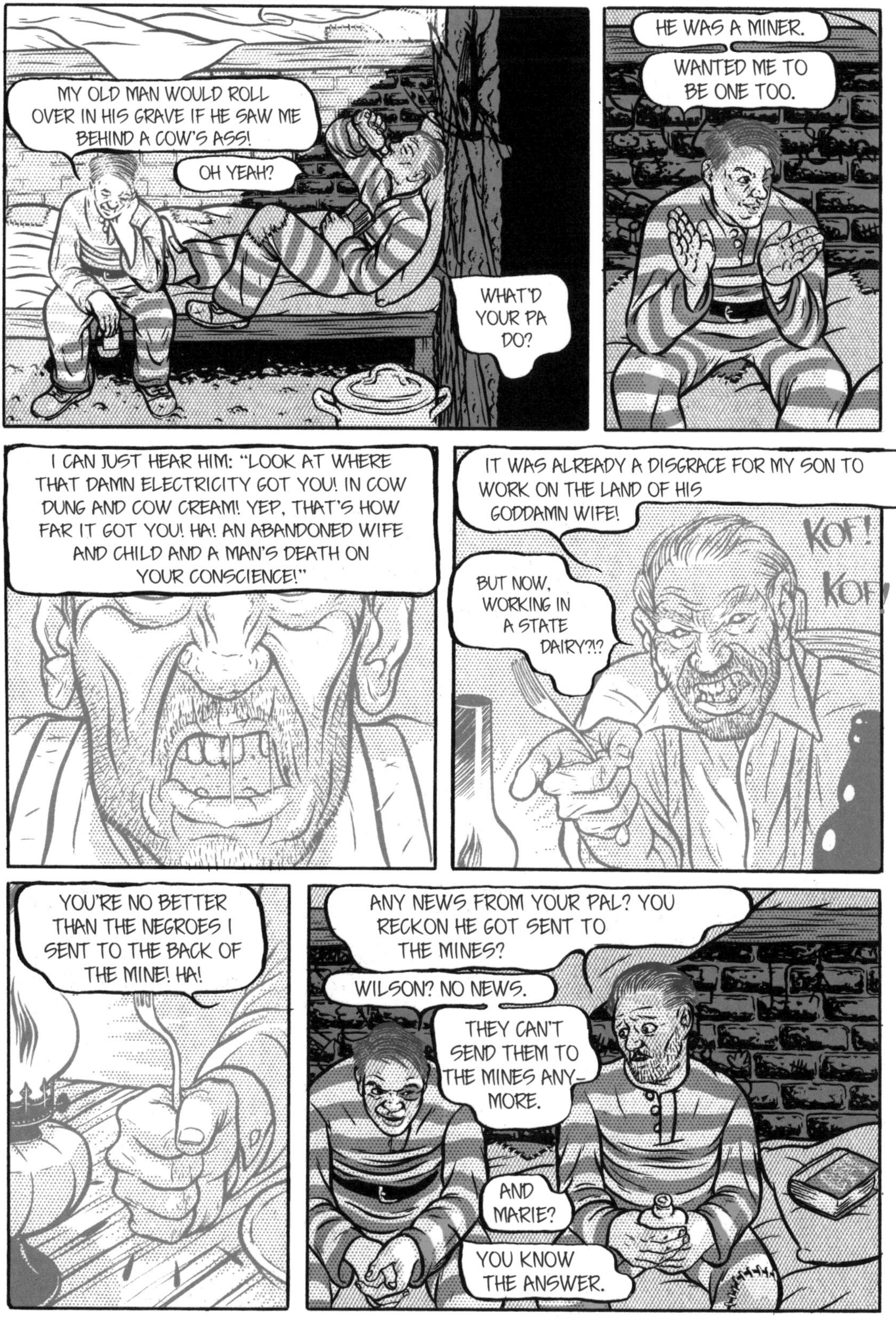
MY OLD MAN WOULD ROLL OVER IN HIS GRAVE IF HE SAW ME BEHIND A COW'S ASS!
OH YEAH?
WHAT'D YOUR PA DO?
HE WAS A MINER.
WANTED ME TO BE ONE TOO.
I CAN JUST HEAR HIM: "LOOK AT WHERE THAT DAMN ELECTRICITY GOT YOU! IN COW DUNG AND COW CREAM! YEP, THAT'S HOW FAR IT GOT YOU! HA! AN ABANDONED WIFE AND CHILD AND A MAN'S DEATH ON YOUR CONSCIENCE!"
IT WAS ALREADY A DISGRACE FOR MY SON TO WORK ON THE LAND OF HIS GODDAMN WIFE!
KOF!
BUT NOW, WORKING IN A STATE DAIRY?!?
YOU'RE NO BETTER THAN THE NEGROES I SENT TO THE BACK OF THE MINE! HA!
ANY NEWS FROM YOUR PAL? YOU RECKON HE GOT SENT TO THE MINES?
WILSON? NO NEWS.
THEY CAN'T SEND THEM TO THE MINES ANY-MORE.
AND MARIE?
YOU KNOW THE ANSWER.

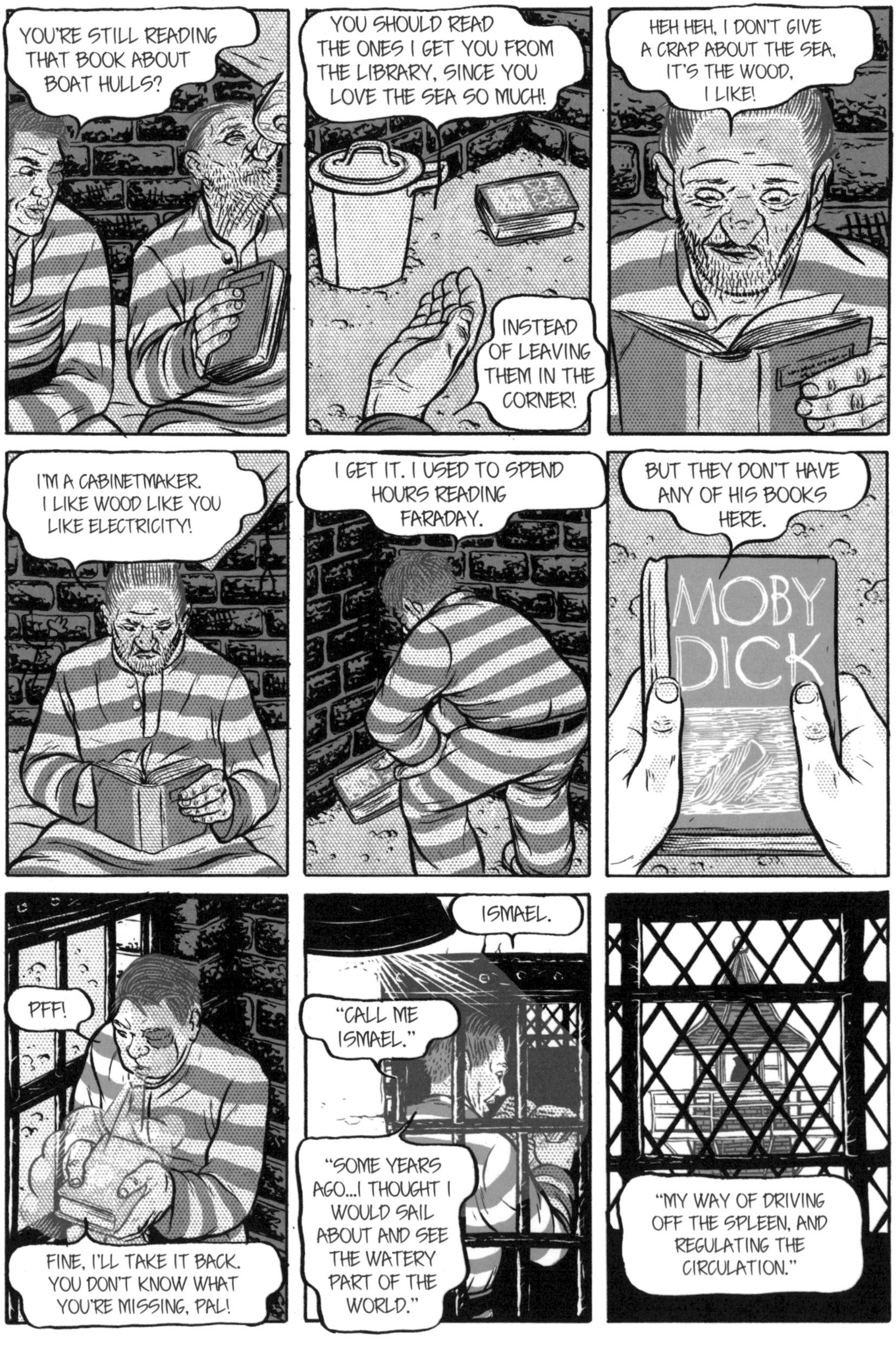
YOU'RE STILL READING THAT BOOK ABOUT BOAT HULLS?
YOU SHOULD READ THE ONES I GET YOU FROM THE LIBRARY, SINCE YOU LOVE THE SEA SO MUCH!
INSTEAD OF LEAVING THEM IN THE CORNER!
HEH HEH, I DON'T GIVE A CRAP ABOUT THE SEA, IT'S THE WOOD, I LIKE!
I'M A CABINETMAKER. I LIKE WOOD LIKE YOU LIKE ELECTRICITY!
I GET IT. I USED TO SPEND HOURS READING FARADAY.
BUT THEY DON'T HAVE ANY OF HIS BOOKS HERE.
MOBY DICK
PFF!
FINE, I'LL TAKE IT BACK. YOU DON'T KNOW WHAT YOU'RE MISSING, PAL!
ISMAEL.
"CALL ME ISMAEL."
"SOME YEARS AGO...I THOUGHT I WOULD SAIL ABOUT AND SEE THE WATERY PART OF THE WORLD."
"MY WAY OF DRIVING OFF THE SPLEEN, AND REGULATING THE CIRCULATION."

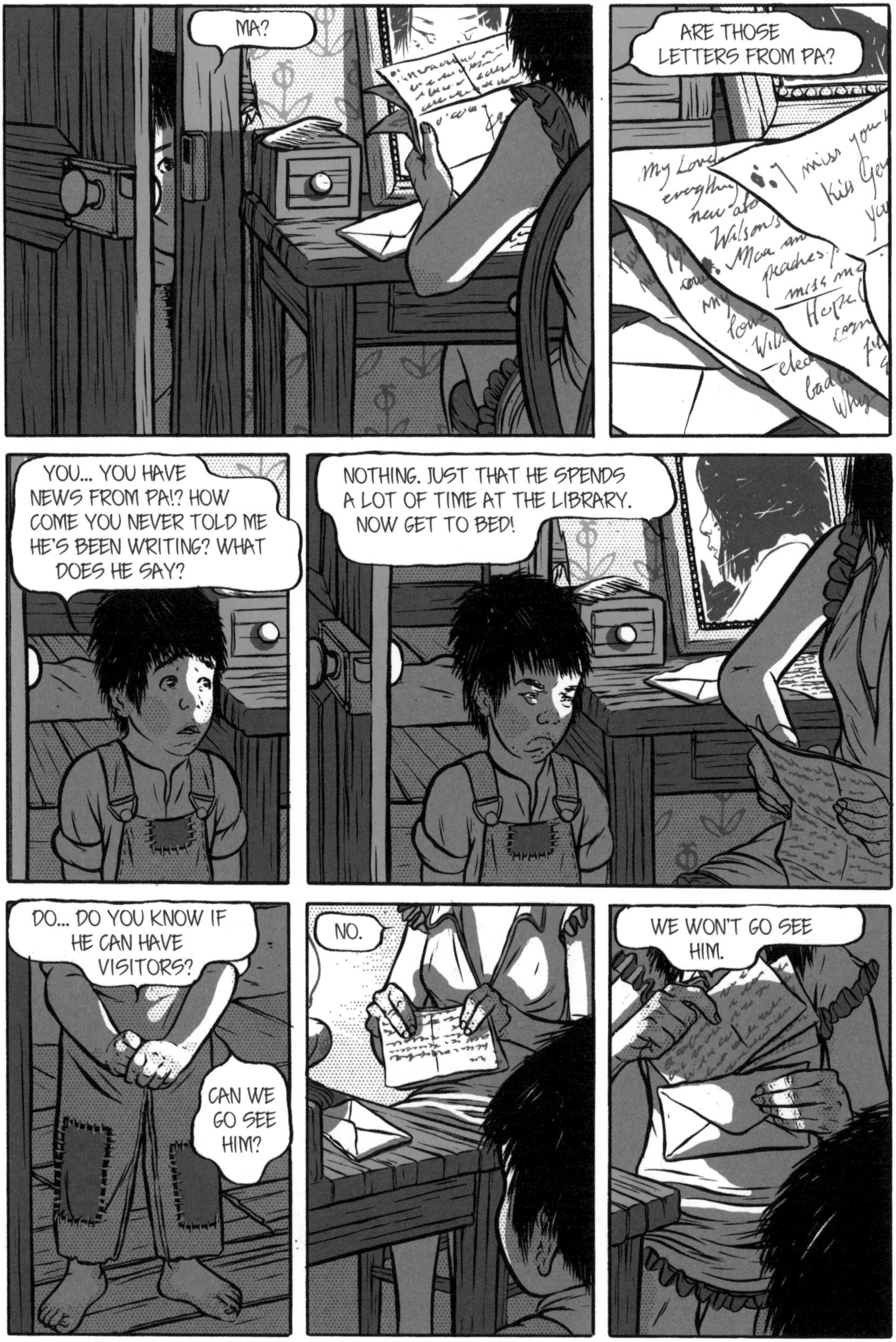
MA?
ARE THOSE LETTERS FROM PA?
YOU... YOU HAVE NEWS FROM PA!? HOW COME YOU NEVER TOLD ME HE'S BEEN WRITING? WHAT DOES HE SAY?
NOTHING. JUST THAT HE SPENDS A LOT OF TIME AT THE LIBRARY. NOW GET TO BED!
DO... DO YOU KNOW IF HE CAN HAVE VISITORS?
CAN WE GO SEE HIM?
NO.
WE WON'T GO SEE HIM.

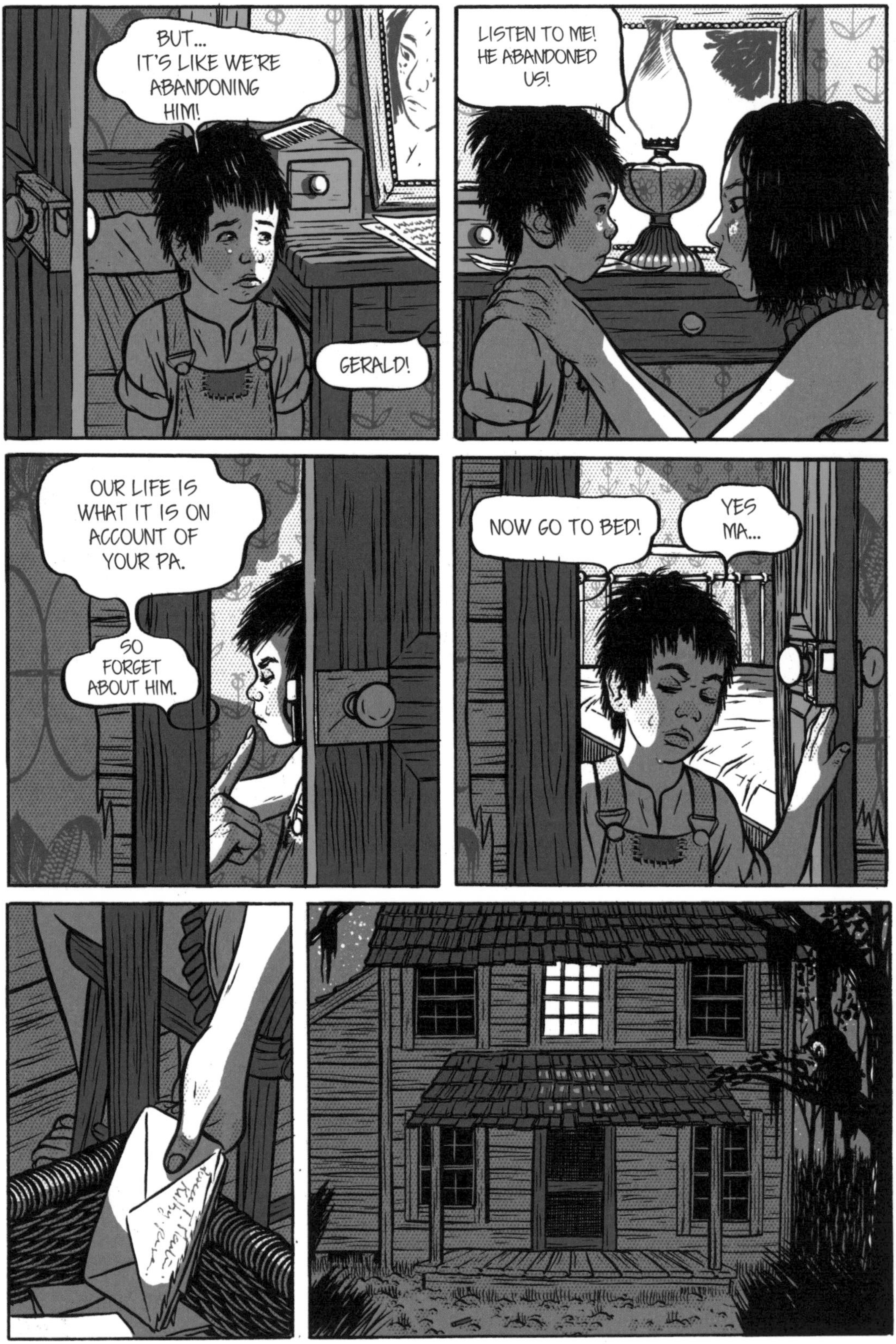
BUT... IT'S LIKE WE'RE ABANDONING HIM!
GERALD!
LISTEN TO ME! HE ABANDONED US!
OUR LIFE IS WHAT IT IS ON ACCOUNT OF YOUR PA.
SO FORGET ABOUT HIM.
NOW GO TO BED!
YES MA...

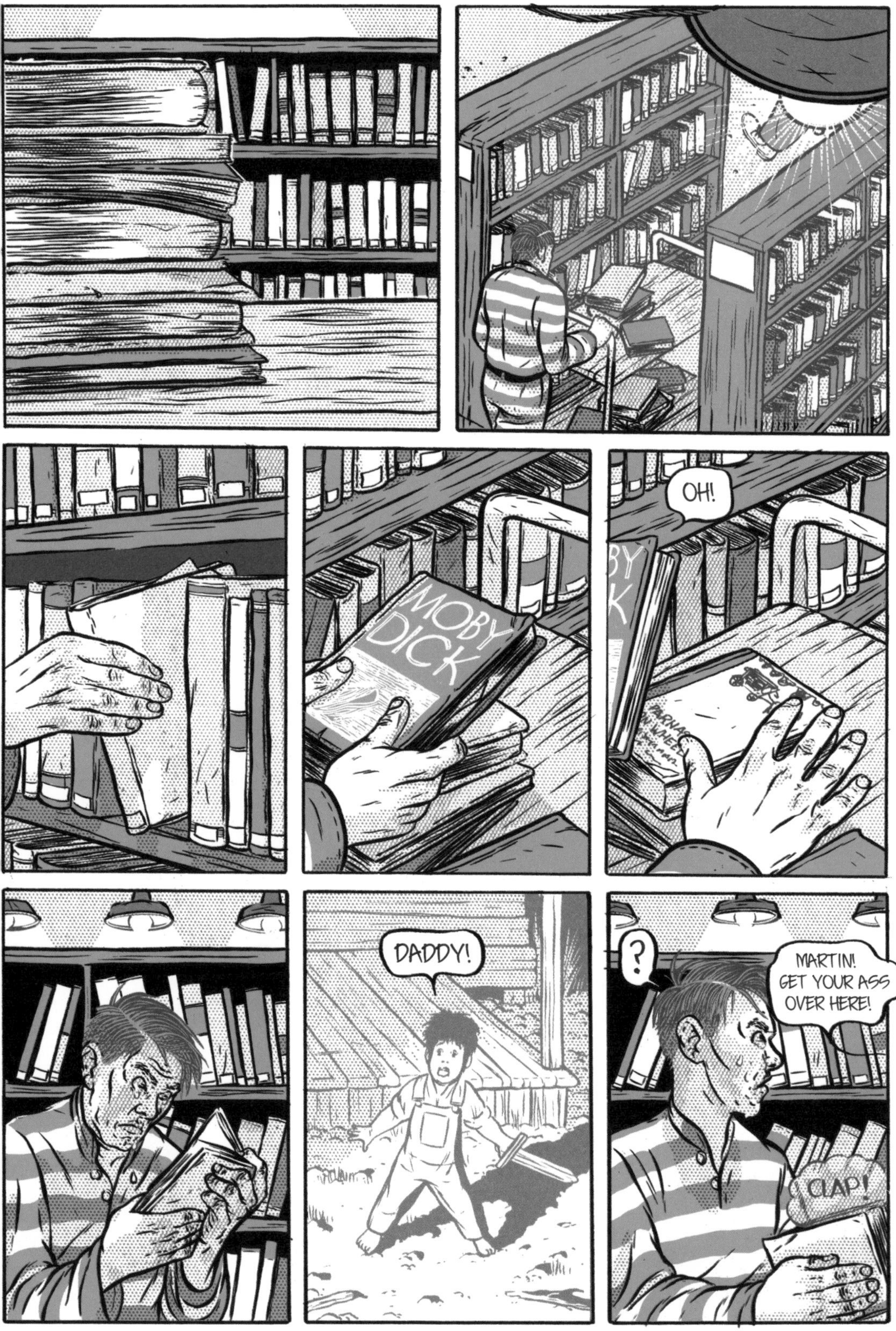
MOBY DICK
OH!
DADDY!
?
MARTIN! GET YOUR ASS OVER HERE!
CLAP!

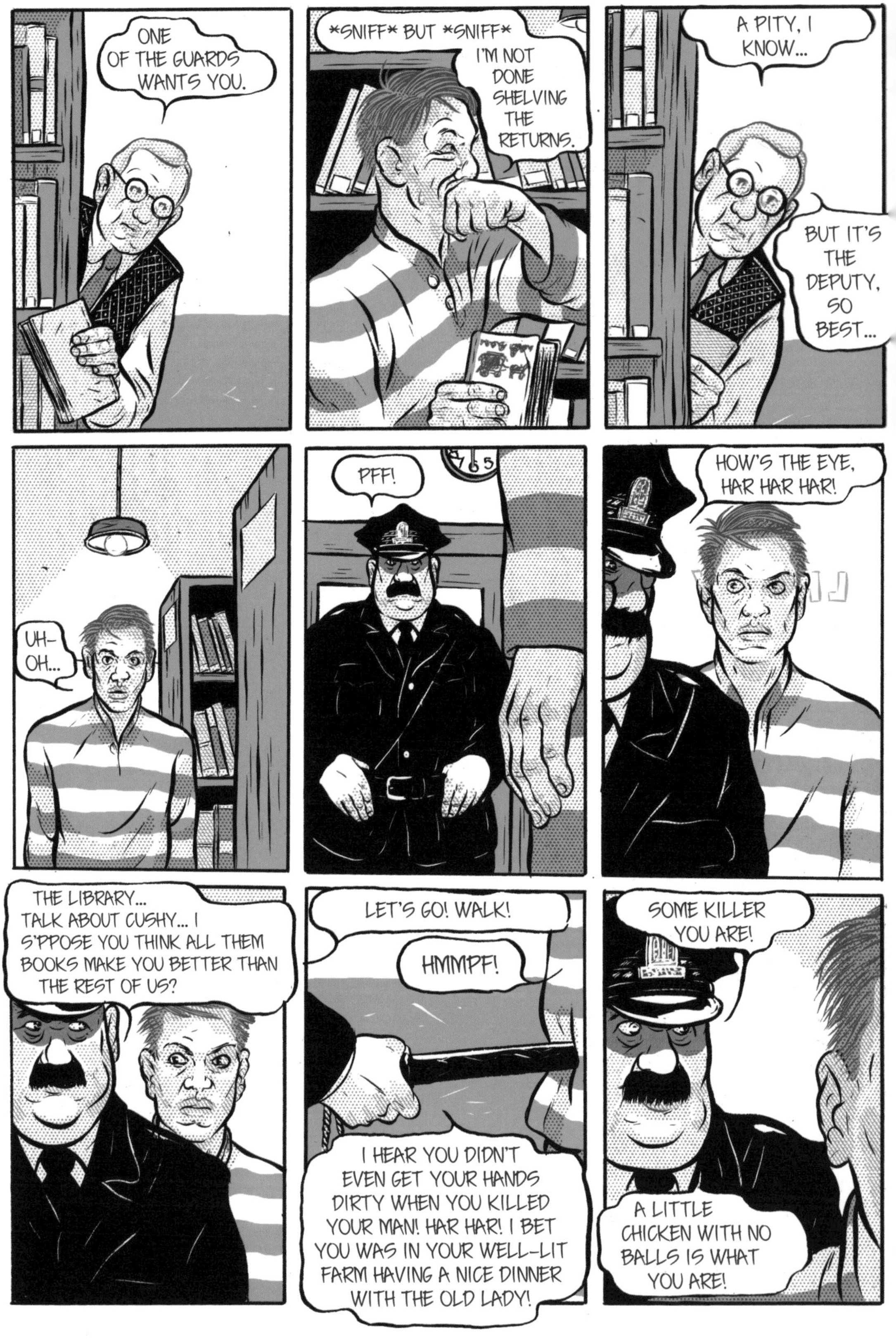
ONE OF THE GUARDS WANTS YOU.
SNIFF BUT *SNIFF*
I'M NOT DONE SHELVING THE RETURNS.
A PITY, I KNOW...
BUT IT'S THE DEPUTY, SO BEST...
UH-OH...
PFF!
HOW'S THE EYE, HAR HAR HAR!
THE LIBRARY... TALK ABOUT CUSHY... I S'PPOSE YOU THINK ALL THEM BOOKS MAKE YOU BETTER THAN THE REST OF US?
LET'S GO! WALK!
HMMPF!
I HEAR YOU DIDN'T EVEN GET YOUR HANDS DIRTY WHEN YOU KILLED YOUR MAN! HAR HAR! I BET YOU WAS IN YOUR WELL-LIT FARM HAVING A NICE DINNER WITH THE OLD LADY!
SOME KILLER YOU ARE!
A LITTLE CHICKEN WITH NO BALLS IS WHAT YOU ARE!

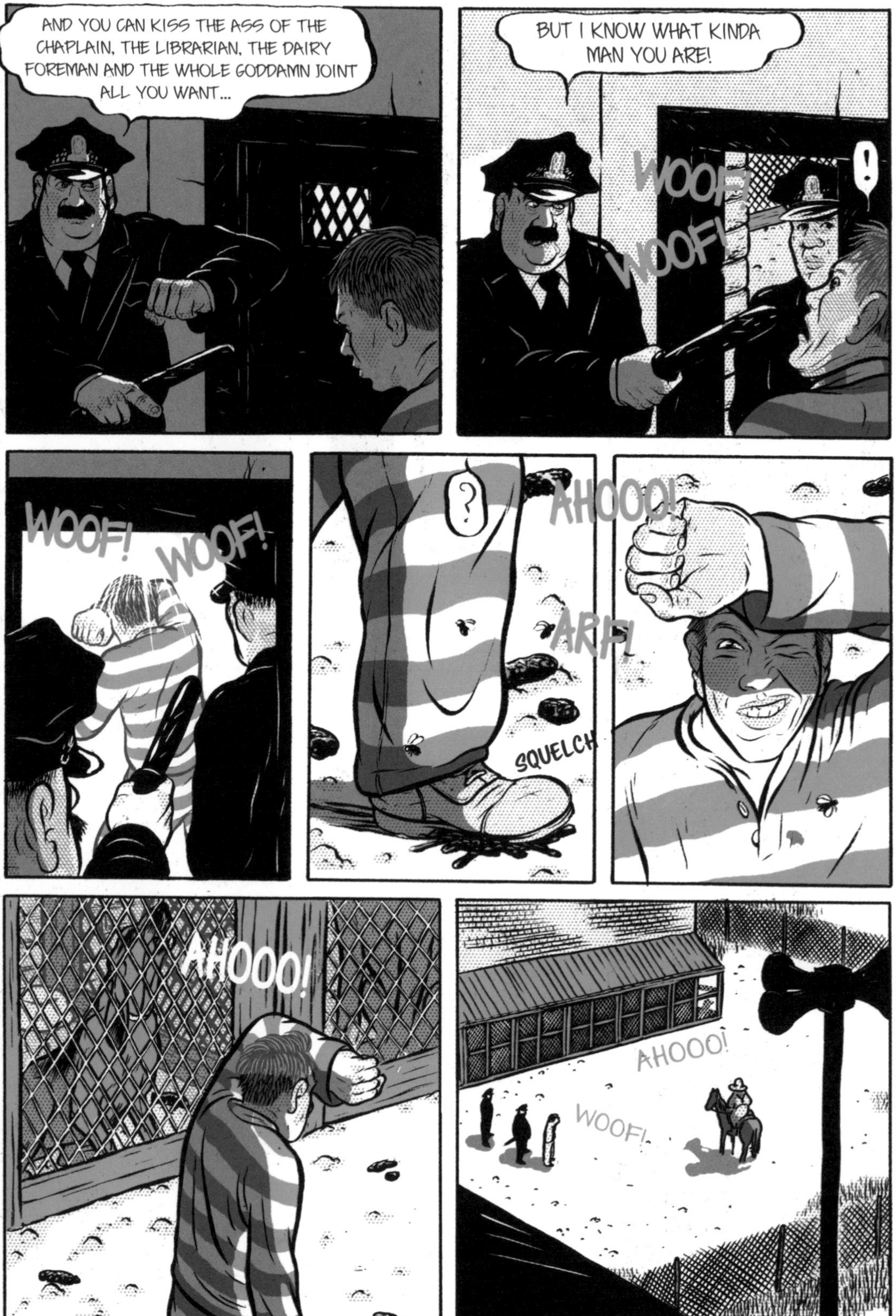
AND YOU CAN KISS THE ASS OF THE CHAPLAIN, THE LIBRARIAN, THE DAIRY FOREMAN AND THE WHOLE GODDAMN JOINT ALL YOU WANT...
BUT I KNOW WHAT KINDA MAN YOU ARE!
WOOF!
WOOF!
!
WOOF!
WOOF!
?
AHOOO!
SQUELCH
ARF!
AHOOO!
AHOOO!
WOOF!

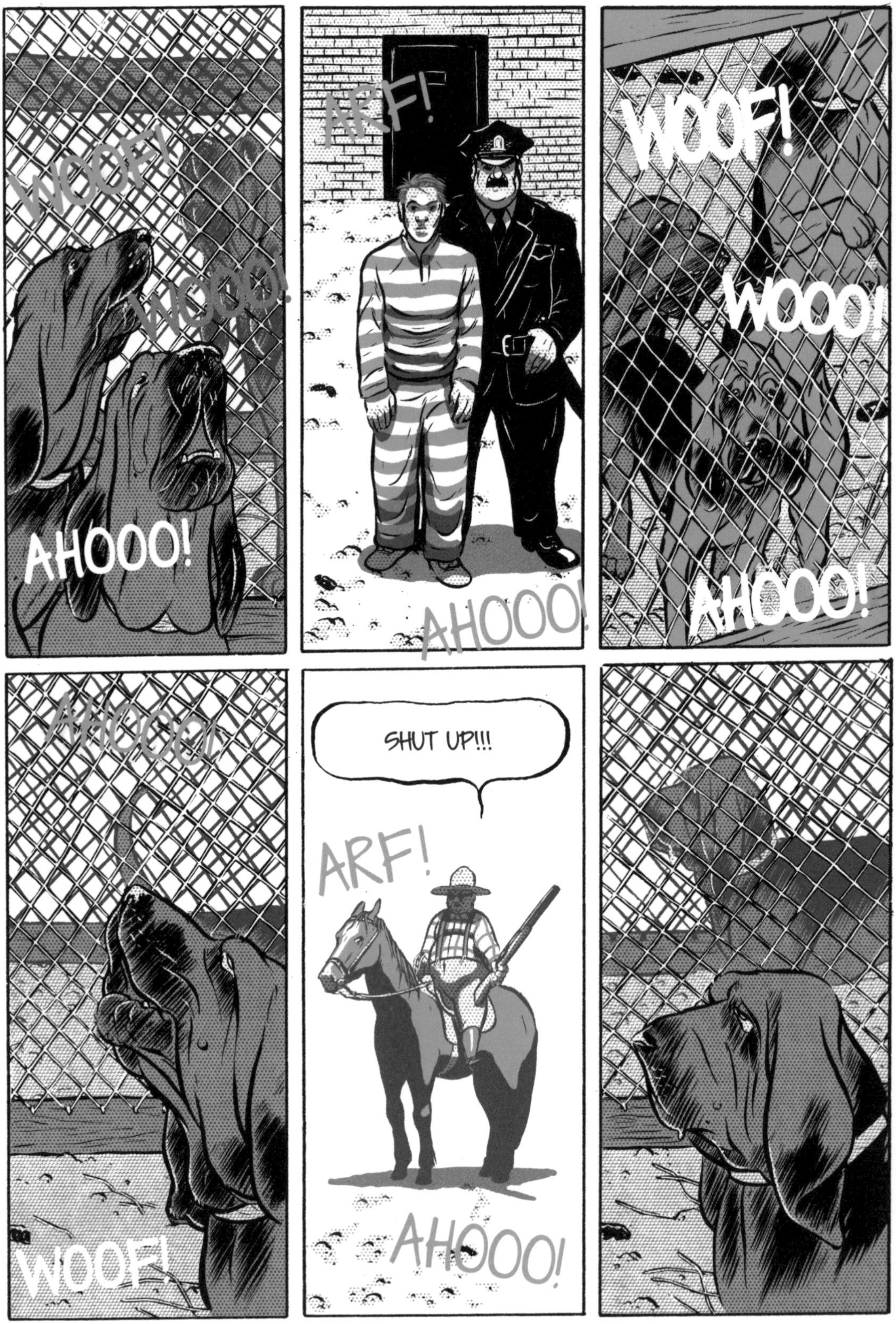
WOOF!
WOOO!
AHOOO!
ARF!
AHOOO!
WOOF!
WOOO!
AHOOO!
AHOOO!
WOOF!
SHUT UP!!!
ARF!
AHOOO!

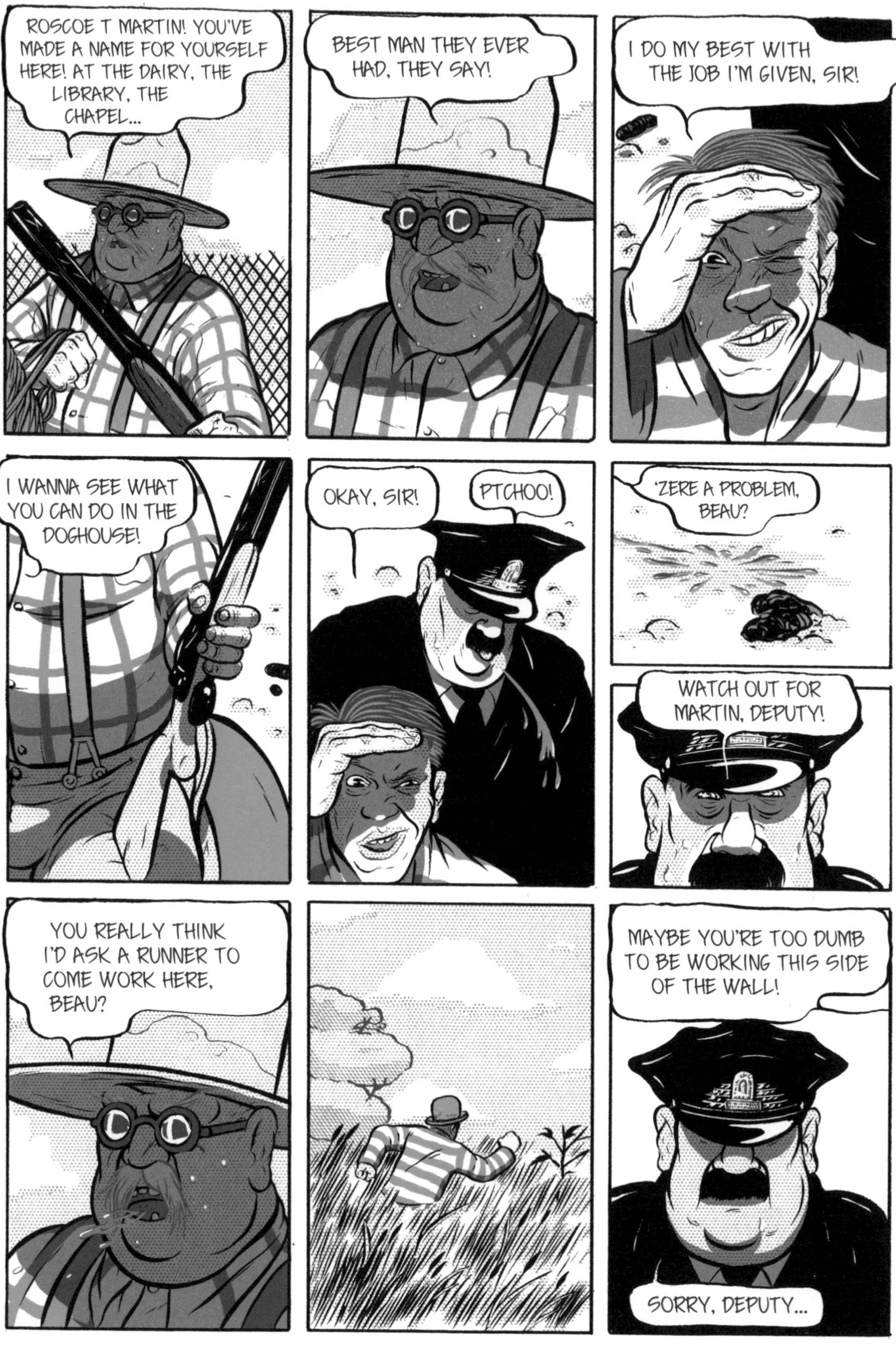
ROSCOE T MARTIN! YOU'VE MADE A NAME FOR YOURSELF HERE! AT THE DAIRY, THE LIBRARY, THE CHAPEL...
BEST MAN THEY EVER HAD, THEY SAY!
I DO MY BEST WITH THE JOB I'M GIVEN, SIR!
I WANNA SEE WHAT YOU CAN DO IN THE DOGHOUSE!
OKAY, SIR!
PTCHOO!
'ZERE A PROBLEM, BEAU?
WATCH OUT FOR MARTIN, DEPUTY!
YOU REALLY THINK I'D ASK A RUNNER TO COME WORK HERE, BEAU?
MAYBE YOU'RE TOO DUMB TO BE WORKING THIS SIDE OF THE WALL!
SORRY, DEPUTY...

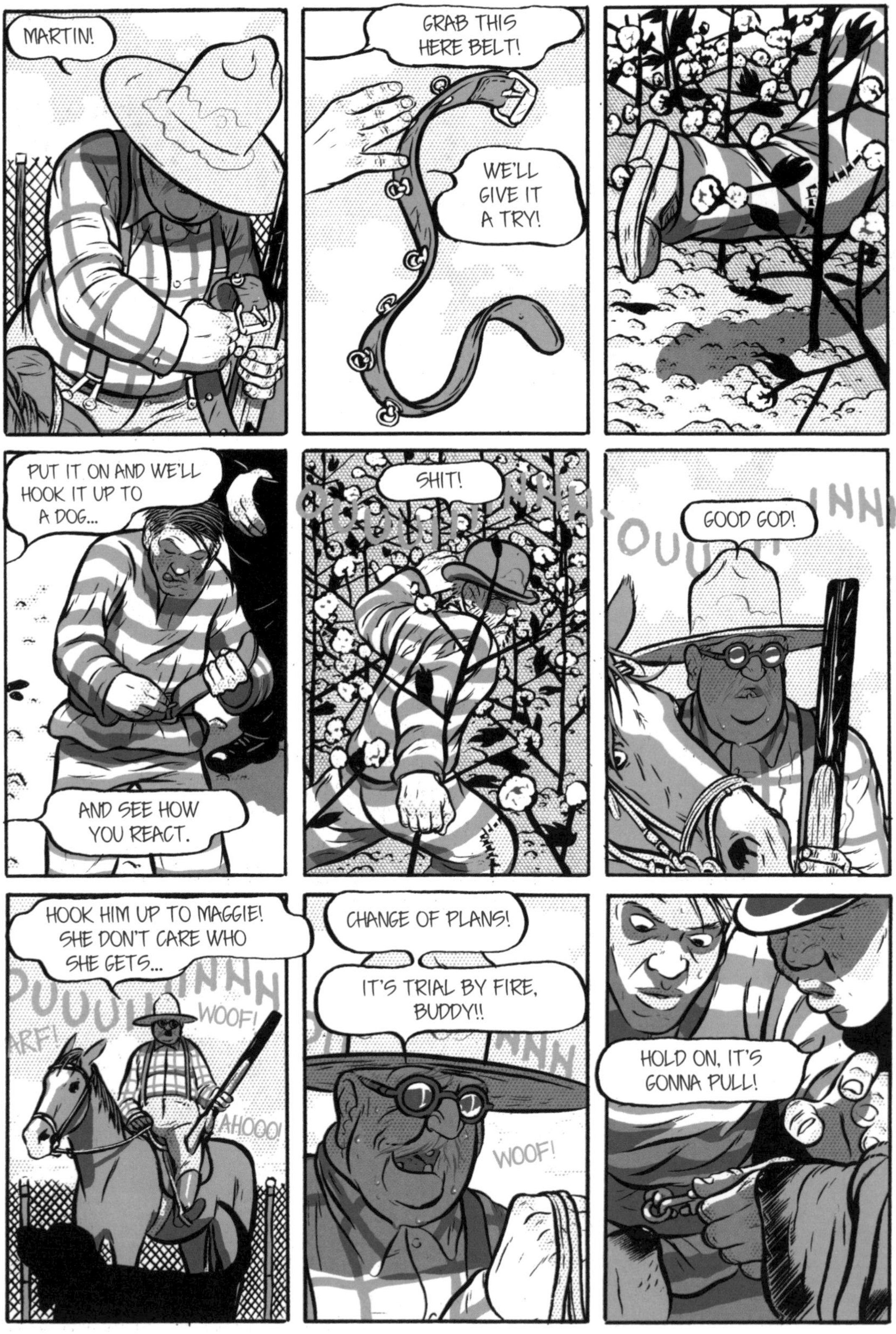
MARTIN!
GRAB THIS HERE BELT!
WE'LL GIVE IT A TRY!
PUT IT ON AND WE'LL HOOK IT UP TO A DOG...
AND SEE HOW YOU REACT.
SHIT!
GOOD GOD!
HOOK HIM UP TO MAGGIE! SHE DON'T CARE WHO SHE GETS...
WOOF!
ARF!
AHOOO!
CHANGE OF PLANS!
IT'S TRIAL BY FIRE, BUDDY!!
WOOF!
HOLD ON, IT'S GONNA PULL!

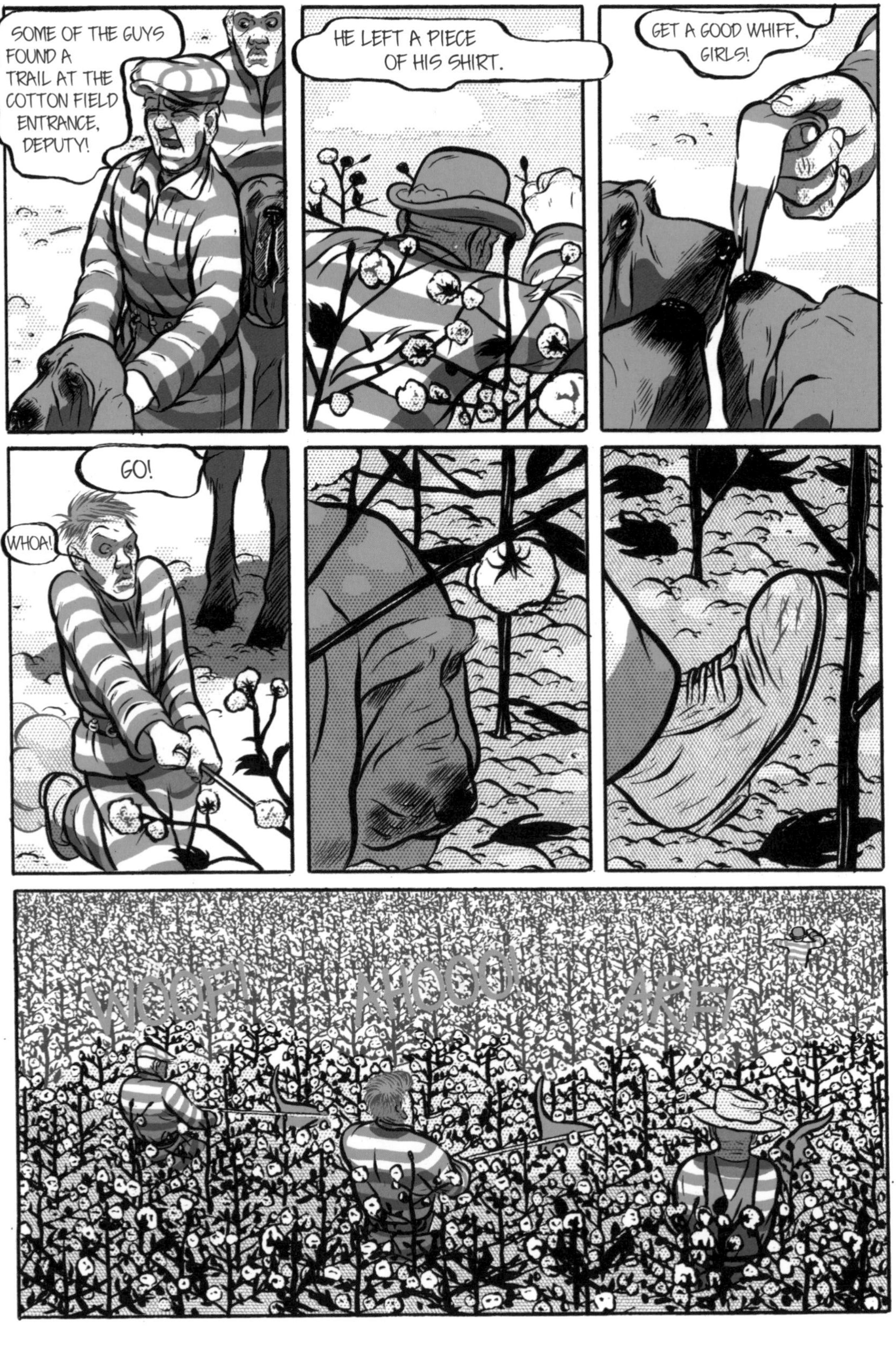
SOME OF THE GUYS FOUND A TRAIL AT THE COTTON FIELD ENTRANCE, DEPUTY!
HE LEFT A PIECE OF HIS SHIRT.
GET A GOOD WHIFF, GIRLS!
GO!
WHOA!
WOOF!
AHOOO!
ARF!

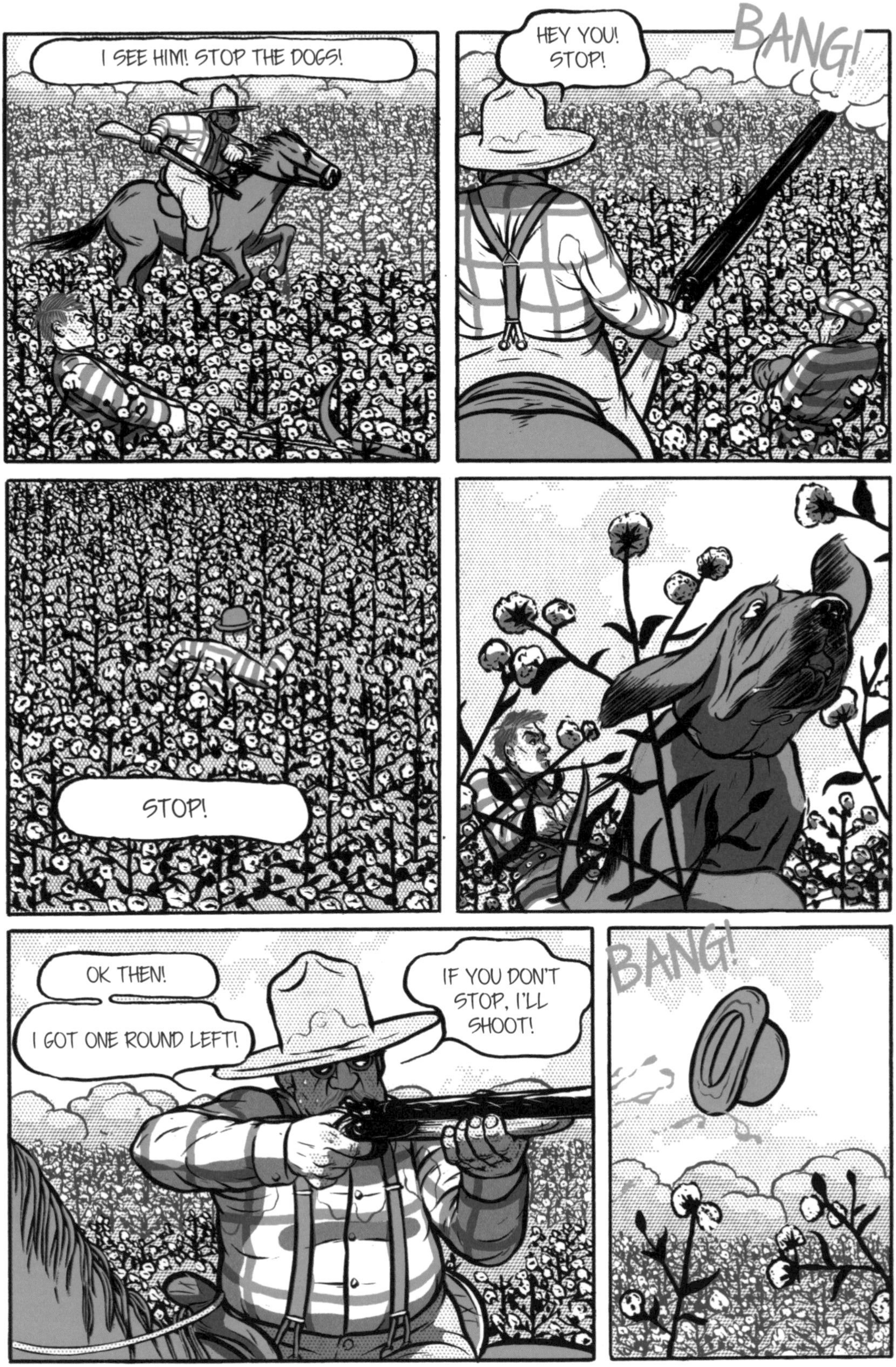
I SEE HIM! STOP THE DOGS!
HEY YOU! STOP!
BANG!
STOP!
OK THEN!
I GOT ONE ROUND LEFT!
IF YOU DON'T STOP, I'LL SHOOT!
BANG!

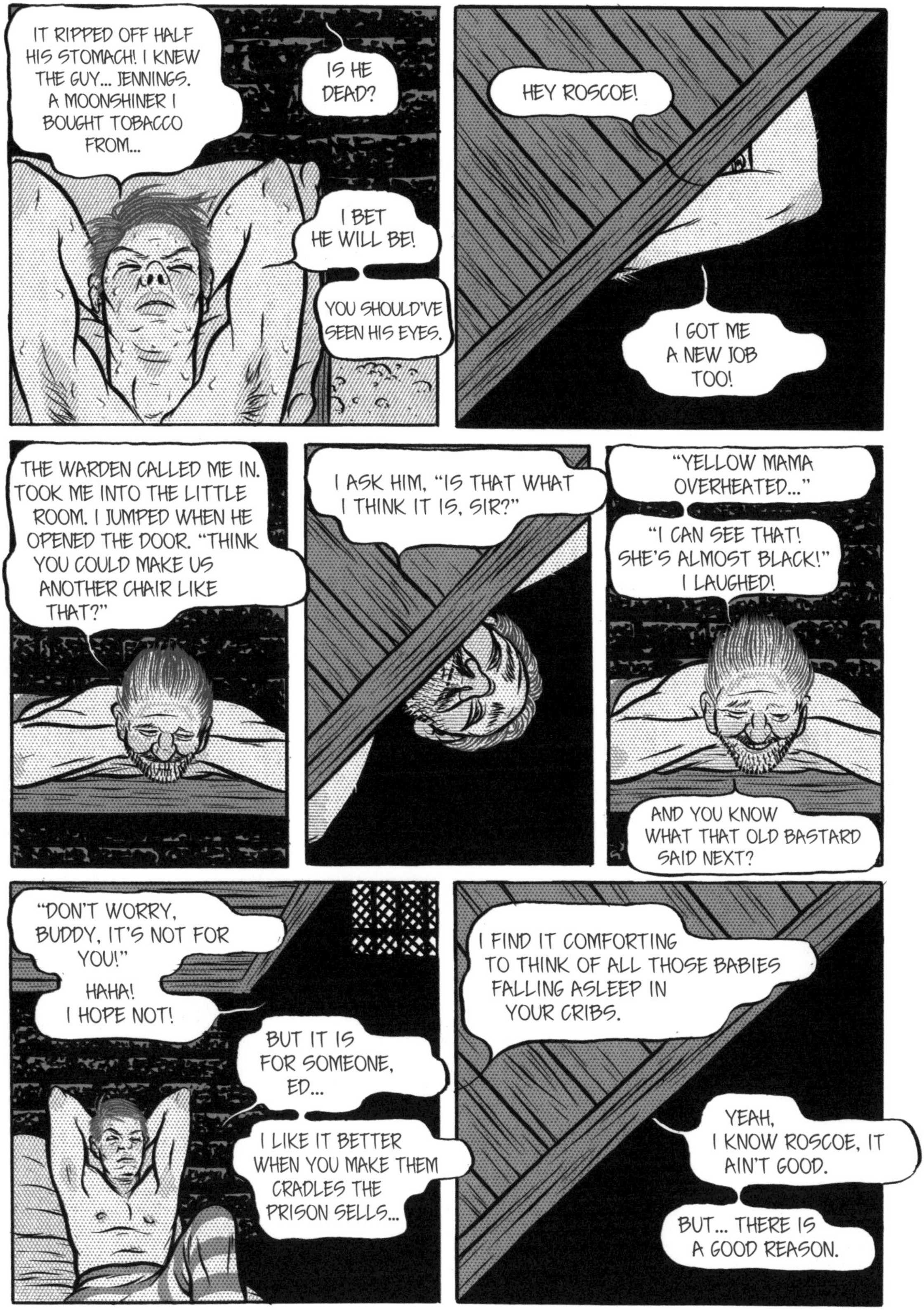
IT RIPPED OFF HALF HIS STOMACH! I KNEW THE GUY... JENNINGS. A MOONSHINER I BOUGHT TOBACCO FROM...
IS HE DEAD?
I BET HE WILL BE!
YOU SHOULD'VE SEEN HIS EYES.
HEY ROSCOE!
I GOT ME A NEW JOB TOO!
THE WARDEN CALLED ME IN. TOOK ME INTO THE LITTLE ROOM. I JUMPED WHEN HE OPENED THE DOOR. "THINK YOU COULD MAKE US ANOTHER CHAIR LIKE THAT?"
I ASK HIM, "IS THAT WHAT I THINK IT IS, SIR?"
"YELLOW MAMA OVERHEATED..."
"I CAN SEE THAT! SHE'S ALMOST BLACK!" I LAUGHED!
AND YOU KNOW WHAT THAT OLD BASTARD SAID NEXT?
"DON'T WORRY, BUDDY, IT'S NOT FOR YOU!"
HAHA! I HOPE NOT!
BUT IT IS FOR SOMEONE, ED...
I LIKE IT BETTER WHEN YOU MAKE THEM CRADLES THE PRISON SELLS...
I FIND IT COMFORTING TO THINK OF ALL THOSE BABIES FALLING ASLEEP IN YOUR CRIBS.
YEAH, I KNOW ROSCOE, IT AIN'T GOOD.
BUT... THERE IS A GOOD REASON.

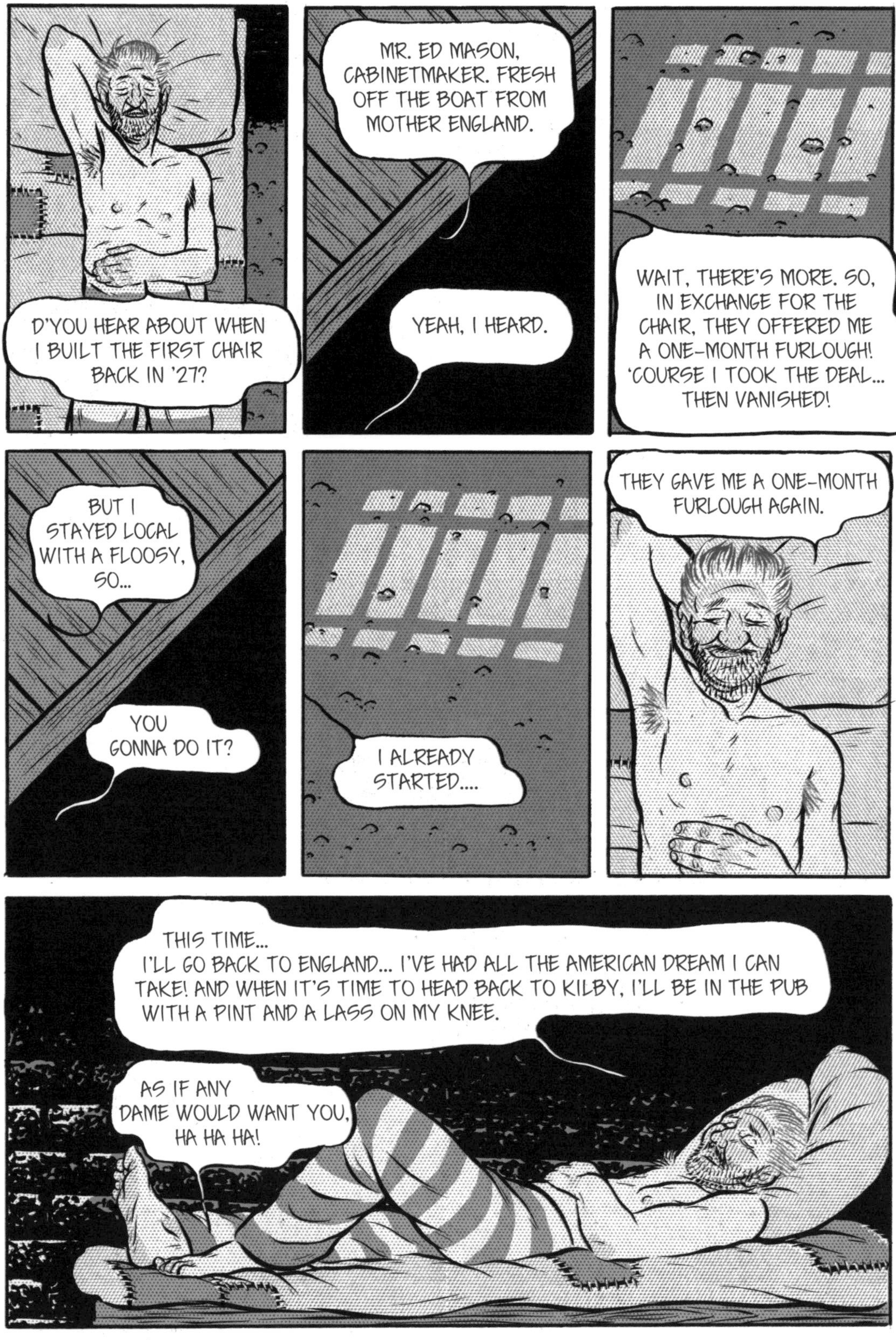
D'YOU HEAR ABOUT WHEN I BUILT THE FIRST CHAIR BACK IN '27?
MR. ED MASON, CABINETMAKER. FRESH OFF THE BOAT FROM MOTHER ENGLAND.
YEAH, I HEARD.
WAIT, THERE'S MORE. SO, IN EXCHANGE FOR THE CHAIR, THEY OFFERED ME A ONE-MONTH FURLOUGH! 'COURSE I TOOK THE DEAL... THEN VANISHED!
BUT I STAYED LOCAL WITH A FLOOSY, SO...
YOU GONNA DO IT?
I ALREADY STARTED....
THEY GAVE ME A ONE-MONTH FURLOUGH AGAIN.
THIS TIME... I'LL GO BACK TO ENGLAND... I'VE HAD ALL THE AMERICAN DREAM I CAN TAKE! AND WHEN IT'S TIME TO HEAD BACK TO KILBY, I'LL BE IN THE PUB WITH A PINT AND A LASS ON MY KNEE.
AS IF ANY DAME WOULD WANT YOU, HA HA HA!

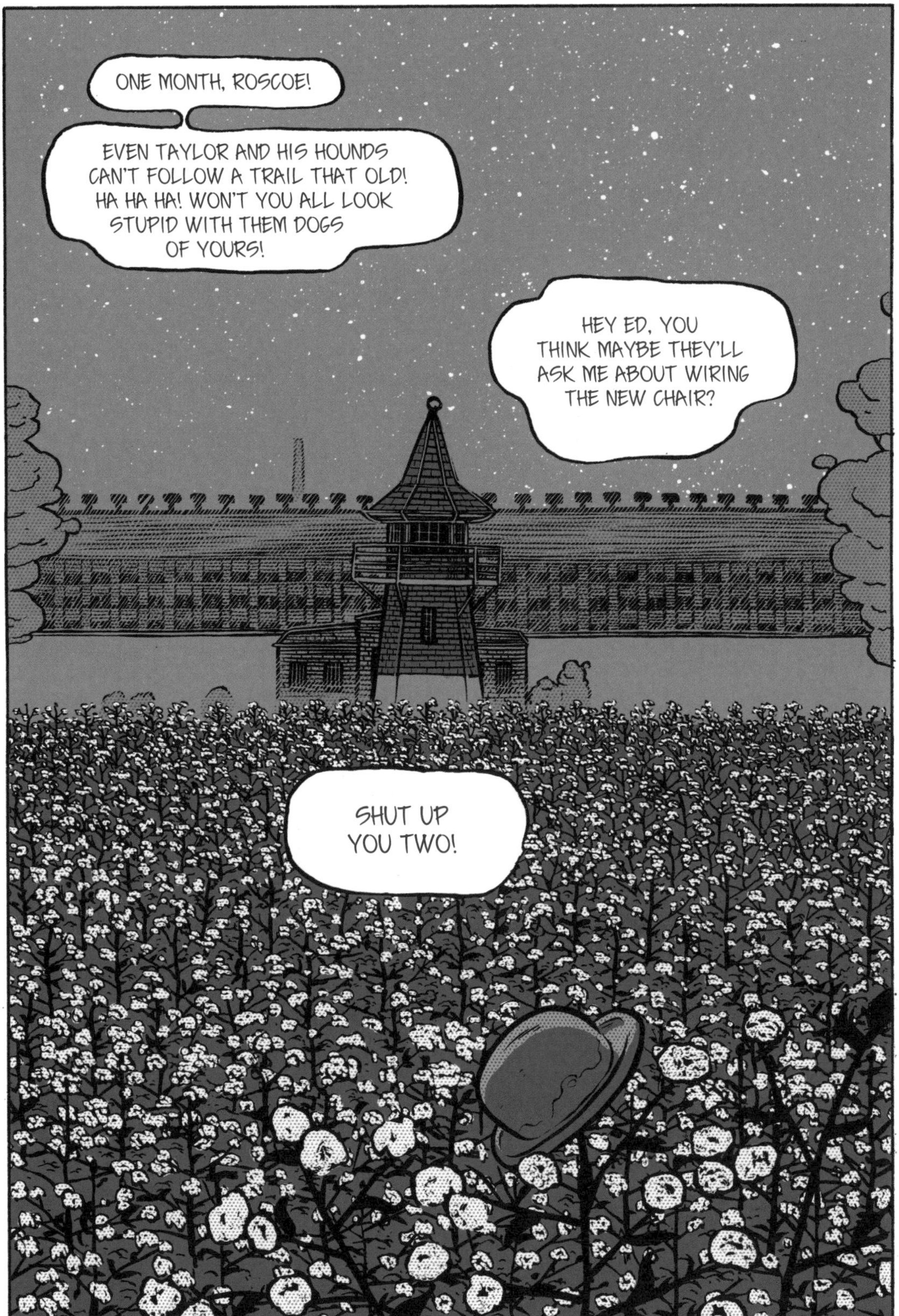
ONE MONTH, ROSCOE!
EVEN TAYLOR AND HIS HOUNDS CAN'T FOLLOW A TRAIL THAT OLD! HA HA HA! WON'T YOU ALL LOOK STUPID WITH THEM DOGS OF YOURS!
HEY ED, YOU THINK MAYBE THEY'LL ASK ME ABOUT WIRING THE NEW CHAIR?
SHUT UP YOU TWO!

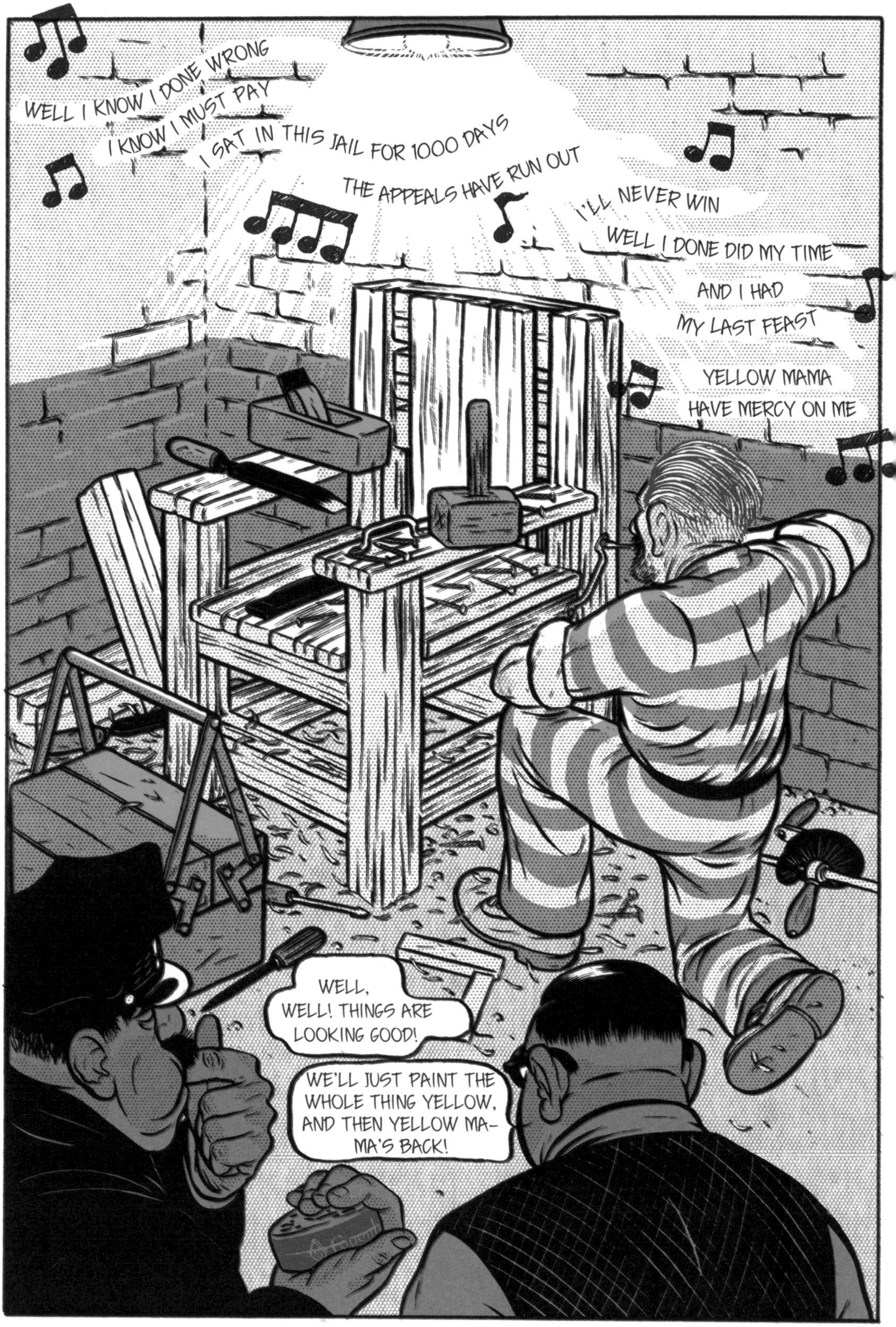
WELL I KNOW I DONE WRONG
I KNOW I MUST PAY
I SAT IN THIS JAIL FOR 1000 DAYS
THE APPEALS HAVE RUN OUT
I'LL NEVER WIN
WELL I DONE DID MY TIME
AND I HAD
MY LAST FEAST
YELLOW MAMA
HAVE MERCY ON ME
WELL, WELL! THINGS ARE LOOKING GOOD!
WE'LL JUST PAINT THE WHOLE THING YELLOW, AND THEN YELLOW MA-MA'S BACK!

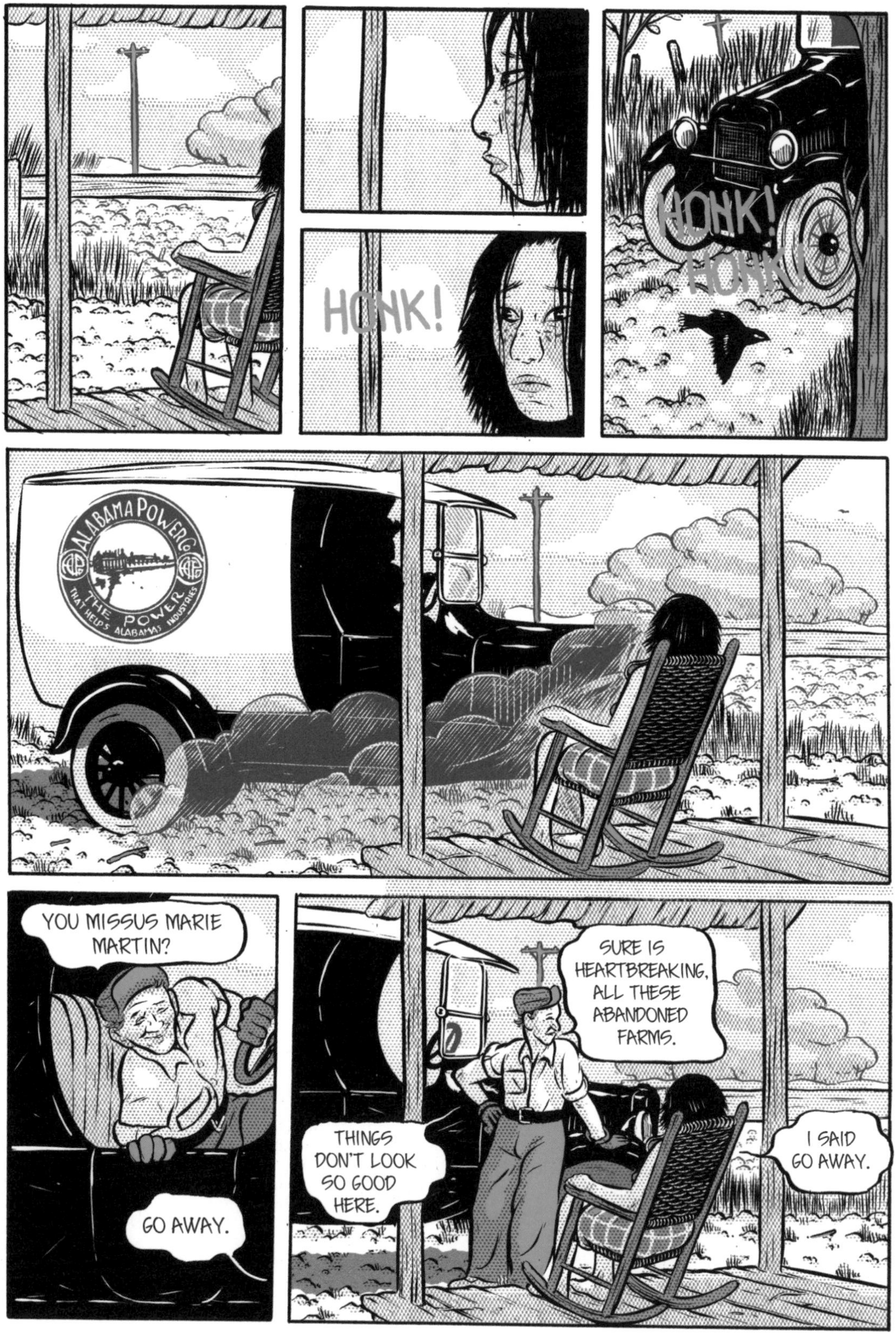

HONK!
HONK!
HONK!
ALABAMA POWER Co
THE POWER THAT HELPS ALABAMA'S INDUSTRIES
YOU MISSUS MARIE MARTIN?
GO AWAY.
SURE IS HEARTBREAKING, ALL THESE ABANDONED FARMS.
THINGS DON'T LOOK SO GOOD HERE.
I SAID GO AWAY.

WHAT DO YOU WANT? TO OFFER ME TO PUT THE POWER BACK ON?

THAT'S RIGHT, MA'AM!

WE'RE EXTENDING THE ELECTRIFI-CATION.

GO TO HELL.

FROM WHAT I HEAR, YOUR FARM IS ALL SET UP... VERY WELL SET UP! YOUR HUSBAND DID A GOOD JOB ON THAT.

WELL...

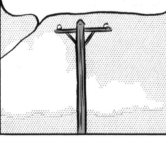

JUST IMAGINE WHAT ELECTRICITY COULD DO FOR THIS PLACE. WITH ALL THE WIRING YOUR HUSBAND ALREADY DID HERE, YOU MIGHT STILL BE ABLE TO SAVE YOUR FARM.

MAYBE YOU SHOULD TALK TO THE OTHER PEOPLE W WORK HERE.

I DON'T CARE FOR ELECTRICITY.

MARIE!

!

FINE.

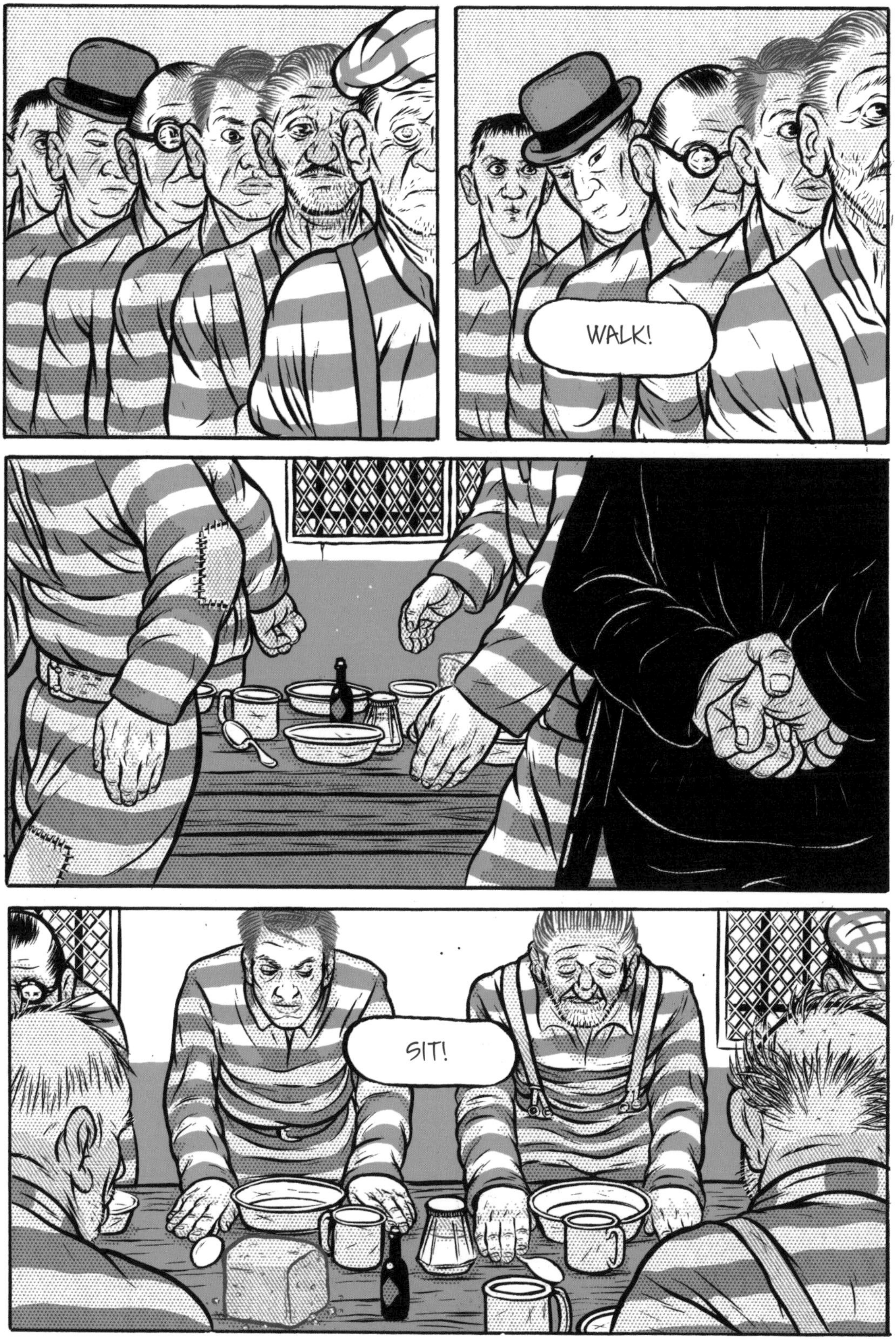
WALK!
SIT!

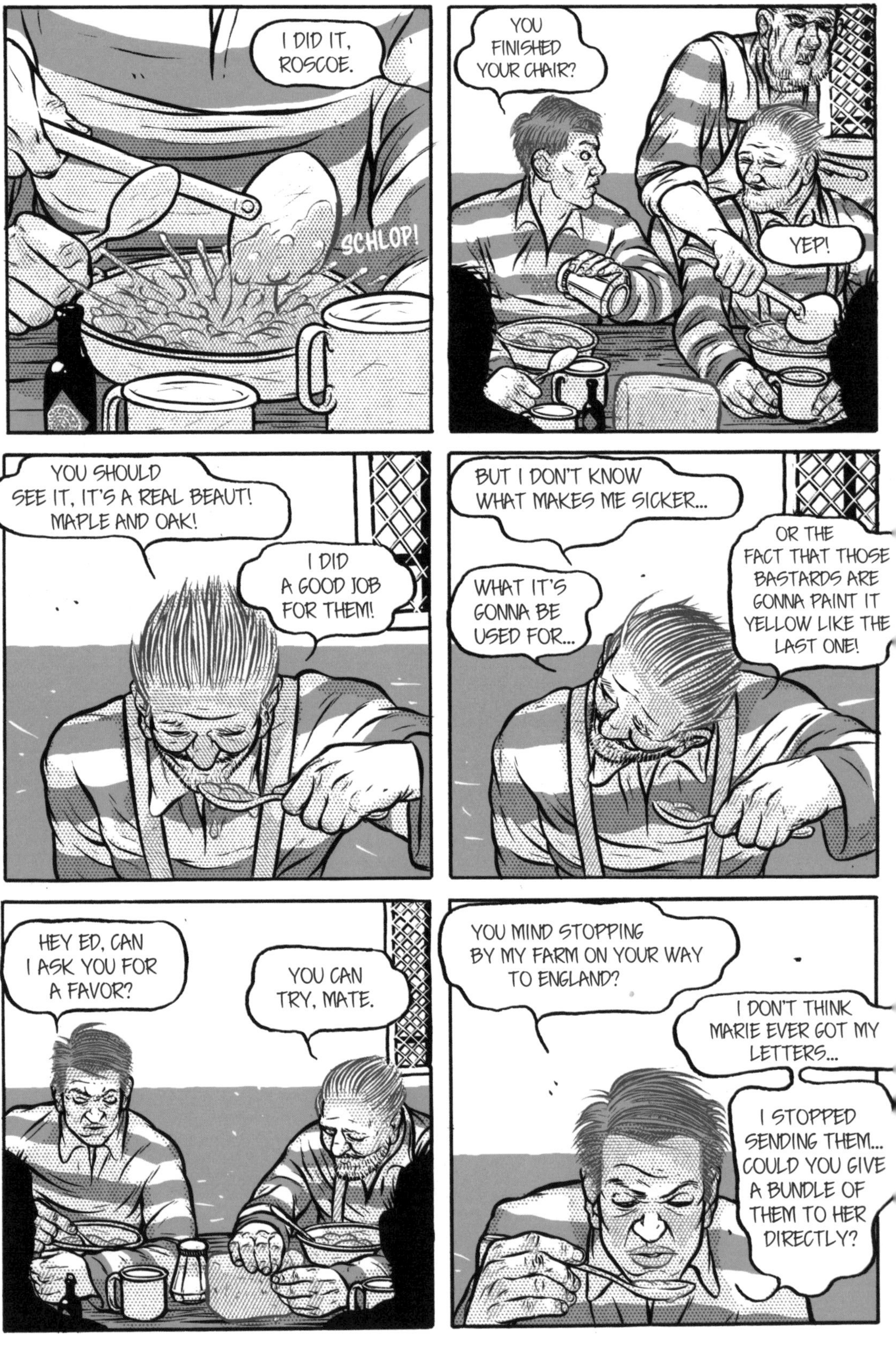
I DID IT, ROSCOE.
SCHLOP!
YOU FINISHED YOUR CHAIR?
YEP!
YOU SHOULD SEE IT, IT'S A REAL BEAUT! MAPLE AND OAK!
I DID A GOOD JOB FOR THEM!
BUT I DON'T KNOW WHAT MAKES ME SICKER...
WHAT IT'S GONNA BE USED FOR...
OR THE FACT THAT THOSE BASTARDS ARE GONNA PAINT IT YELLOW LIKE THE LAST ONE!
HEY ED, CAN I ASK YOU FOR A FAVOR?
YOU CAN TRY, MATE.
YOU MIND STOPPING BY MY FARM ON YOUR WAY TO ENGLAND?
I DON'T THINK MARIE EVER GOT MY LETTERS...
I STOPPED SENDING THEM... COULD YOU GIVE A BUNDLE OF THEM TO HER DIRECTLY?

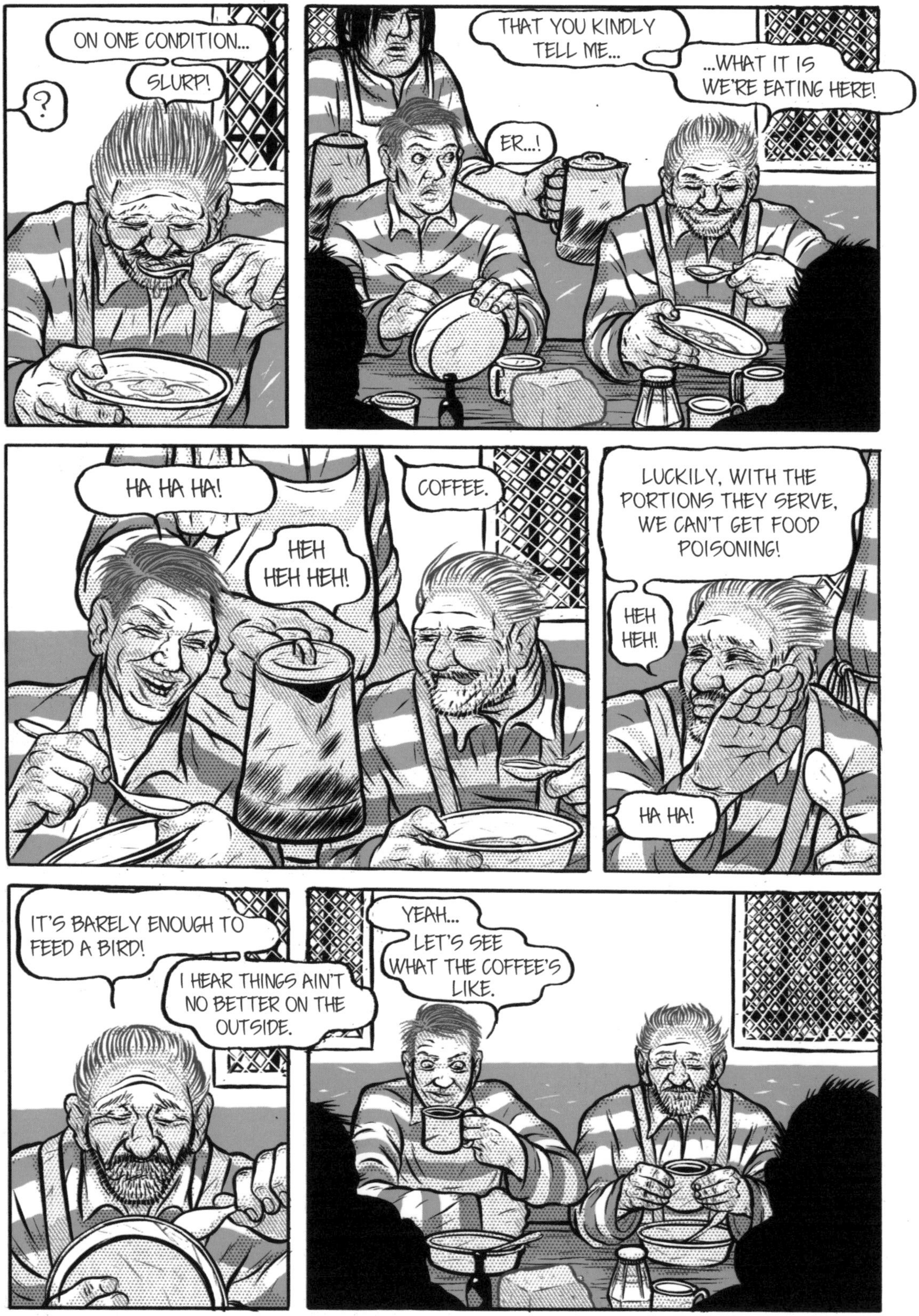
ON ONE CONDITION...
SLURP!
?
THAT YOU KINDLY TELL ME...
...WHAT IT IS WE'RE EATING HERE!
ER...!
HA HA HA!
COFFEE.
HEH HEH HEH!
LUCKILY, WITH THE PORTIONS THEY SERVE, WE CAN'T GET FOOD POISONING!
HEH HEH!
HA HA!
IT'S BARELY ENOUGH TO FEED A BIRD!
I HEAR THINGS AIN'T NO BETTER ON THE OUTSIDE.
YEAH... LET'S SEE WHAT THE COFFEE'S LIKE.

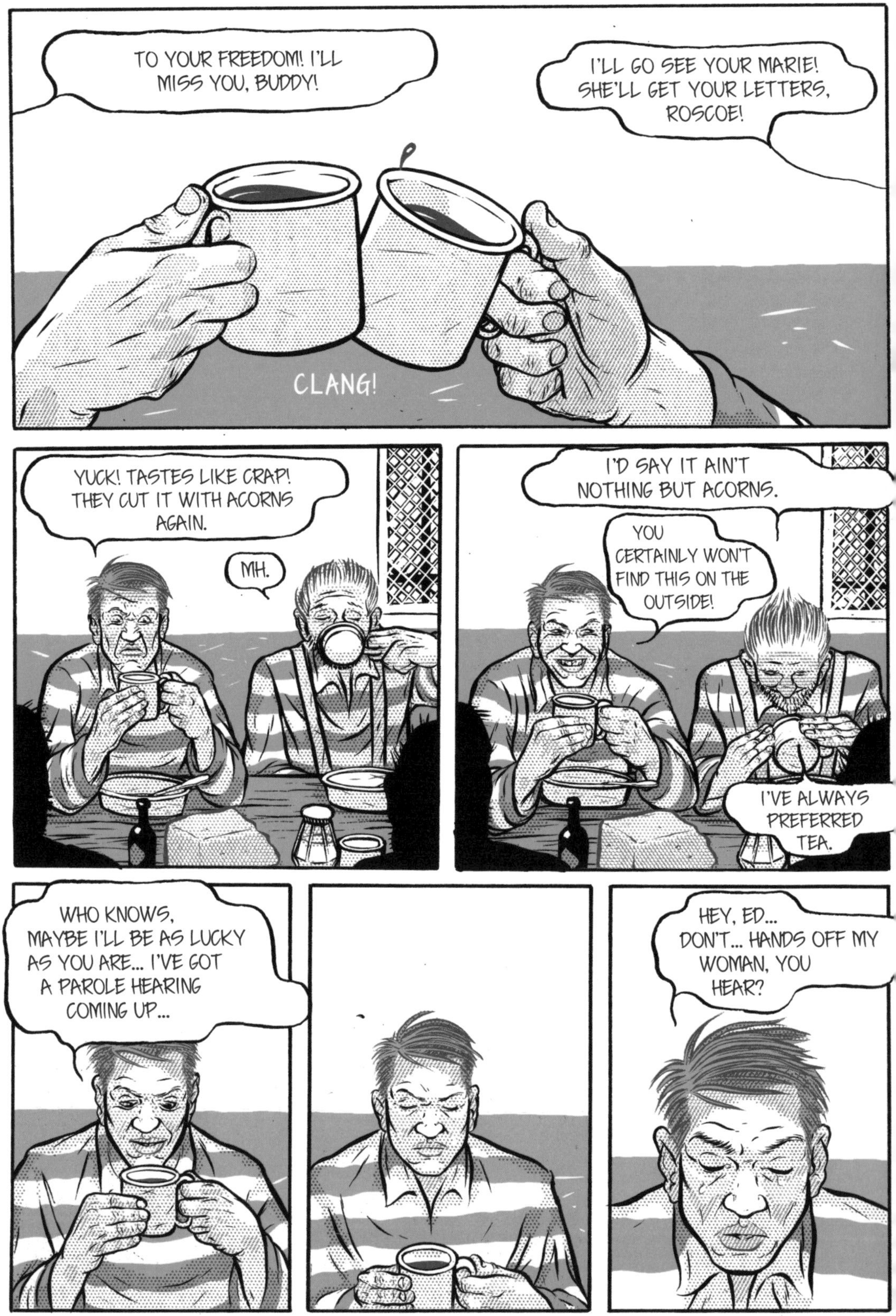
TO YOUR FREEDOM! I'LL MISS YOU, BUDDY!
I'LL GO SEE YOUR MARIE! SHE'LL GET YOUR LETTERS, ROSCOE!
CLANG!
YUCK! TASTES LIKE CRAP! THEY CUT IT WITH ACORNS AGAIN.
MH.
I'D SAY IT AIN'T NOTHING BUT ACORNS.
YOU CERTAINLY WON'T FIND THIS ON THE OUTSIDE!
I'VE ALWAYS PREFERRED TEA.
WHO KNOWS, MAYBE I'LL BE AS LUCKY AS YOU ARE... I'VE GOT A PAROLE HEARING COMING UP...
HEY, ED... DON'T... HANDS OFF MY WOMAN, YOU HEAR?

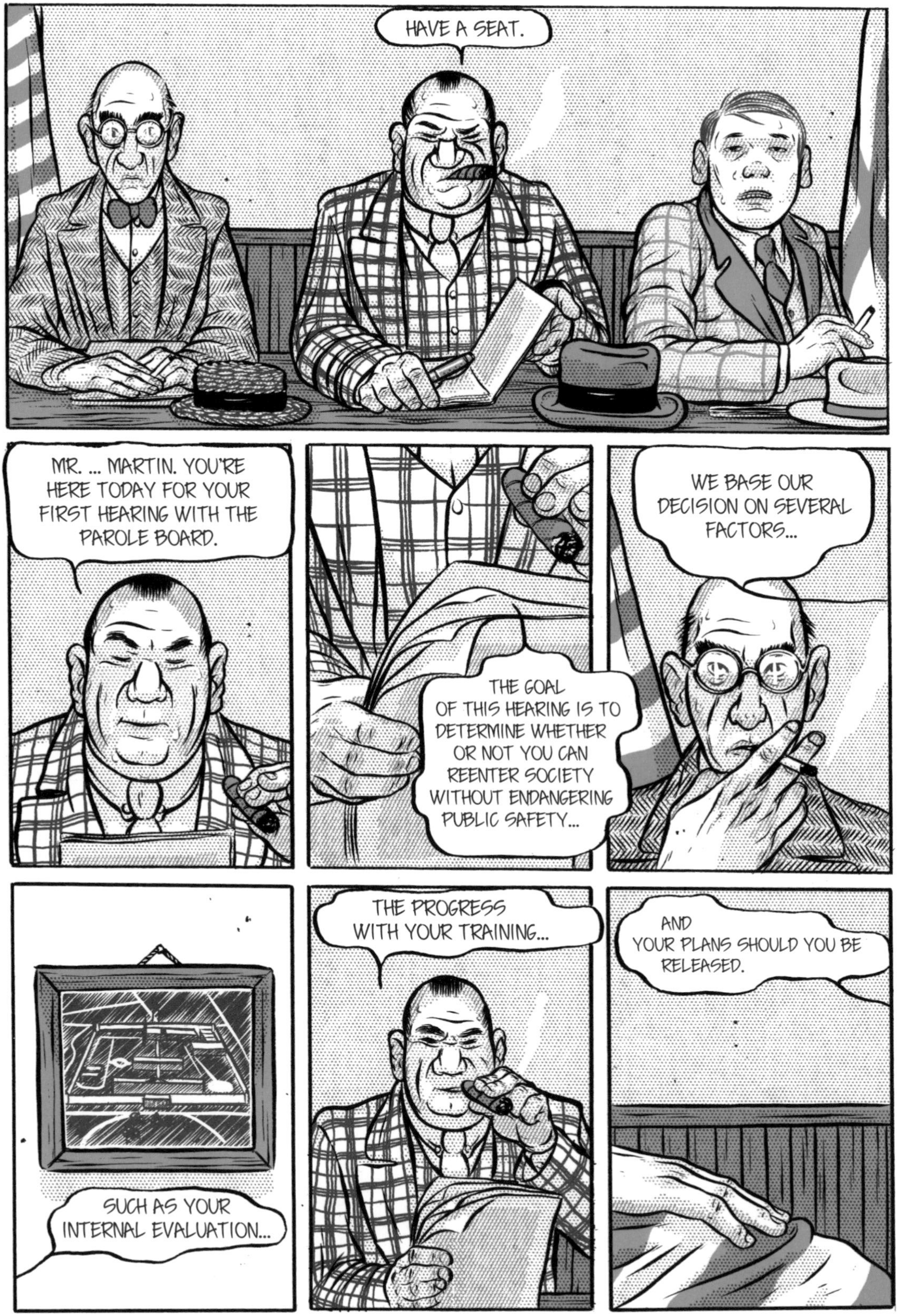
HAVE A SEAT.
MR. ... MARTIN. YOU'RE HERE TODAY FOR YOUR FIRST HEARING WITH THE PAROLE BOARD.
THE GOAL OF THIS HEARING IS TO DETERMINE WHETHER OR NOT YOU CAN REENTER SOCIETY WITHOUT ENDANGERING PUBLIC SAFETY...
WE BASE OUR DECISION ON SEVERAL FACTORS...
SUCH AS YOUR INTERNAL EVALUATION...
THE PROGRESS WITH YOUR TRAINING...
AND YOUR PLANS SHOULD YOU BE RELEASED.

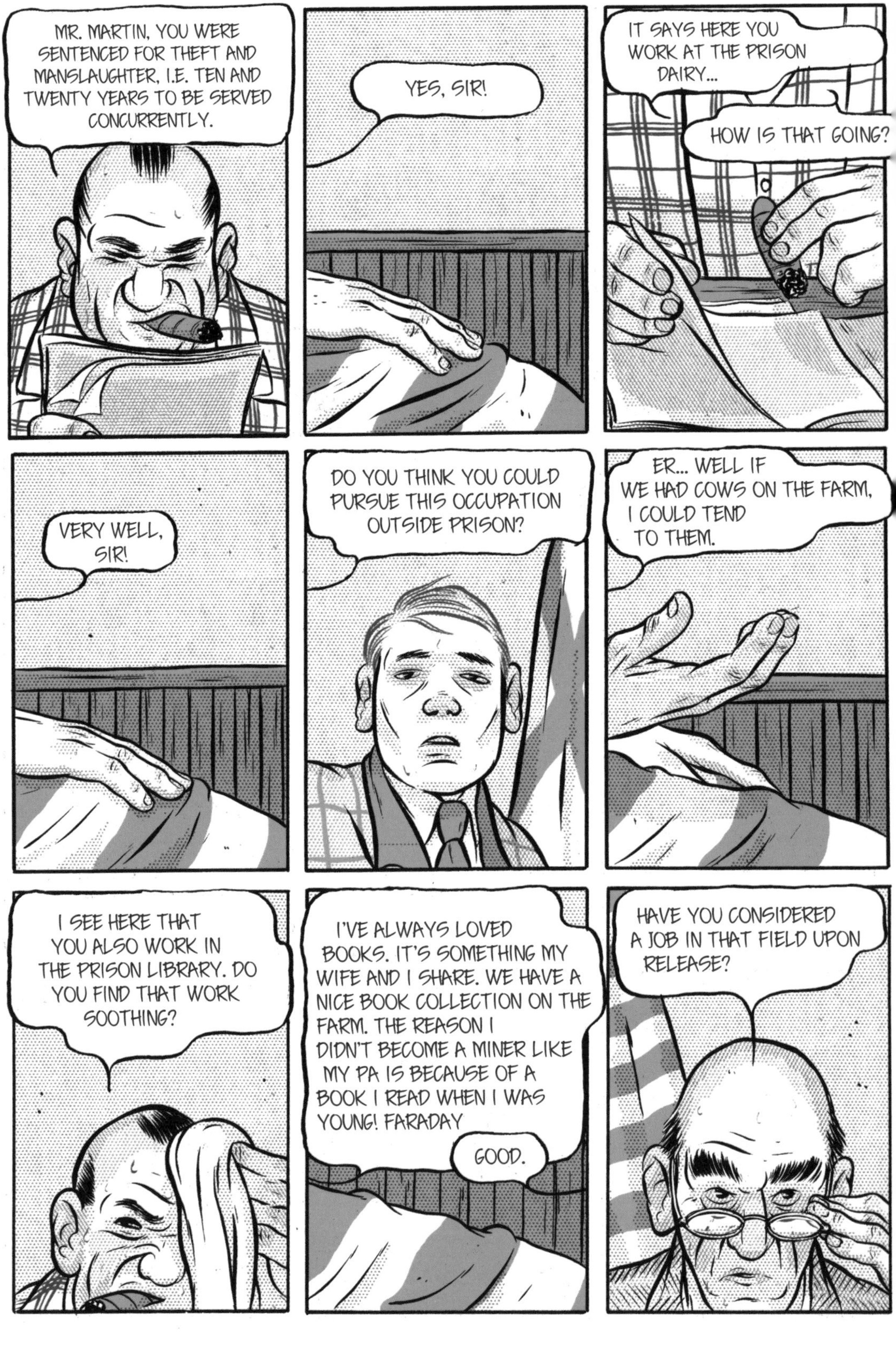
MR. MARTIN, YOU WERE SENTENCED FOR THEFT AND MANSLAUGHTER, I.E. TEN AND TWENTY YEARS TO BE SERVED CONCURRENTLY.
YES, SIR!
IT SAYS HERE YOU WORK AT THE PRISON DAIRY...
HOW IS THAT GOING?
VERY WELL, SIR!
DO YOU THINK YOU COULD PURSUE THIS OCCUPATION OUTSIDE PRISON?
ER... WELL IF WE HAD COWS ON THE FARM, I COULD TEND TO THEM.
I SEE HERE THAT YOU ALSO WORK IN THE PRISON LIBRARY. DO YOU FIND THAT WORK SOOTHING?
I'VE ALWAYS LOVED BOOKS. IT'S SOMETHING MY WIFE AND I SHARE. WE HAVE A NICE BOOK COLLECTION ON THE FARM. THE REASON I DIDN'T BECOME A MINER LIKE MY PA IS BECAUSE OF A BOOK I READ WHEN I WAS YOUNG! FARADAY
GOOD.
HAVE YOU CONSIDERED A JOB IN THAT FIELD UPON RELEASE?

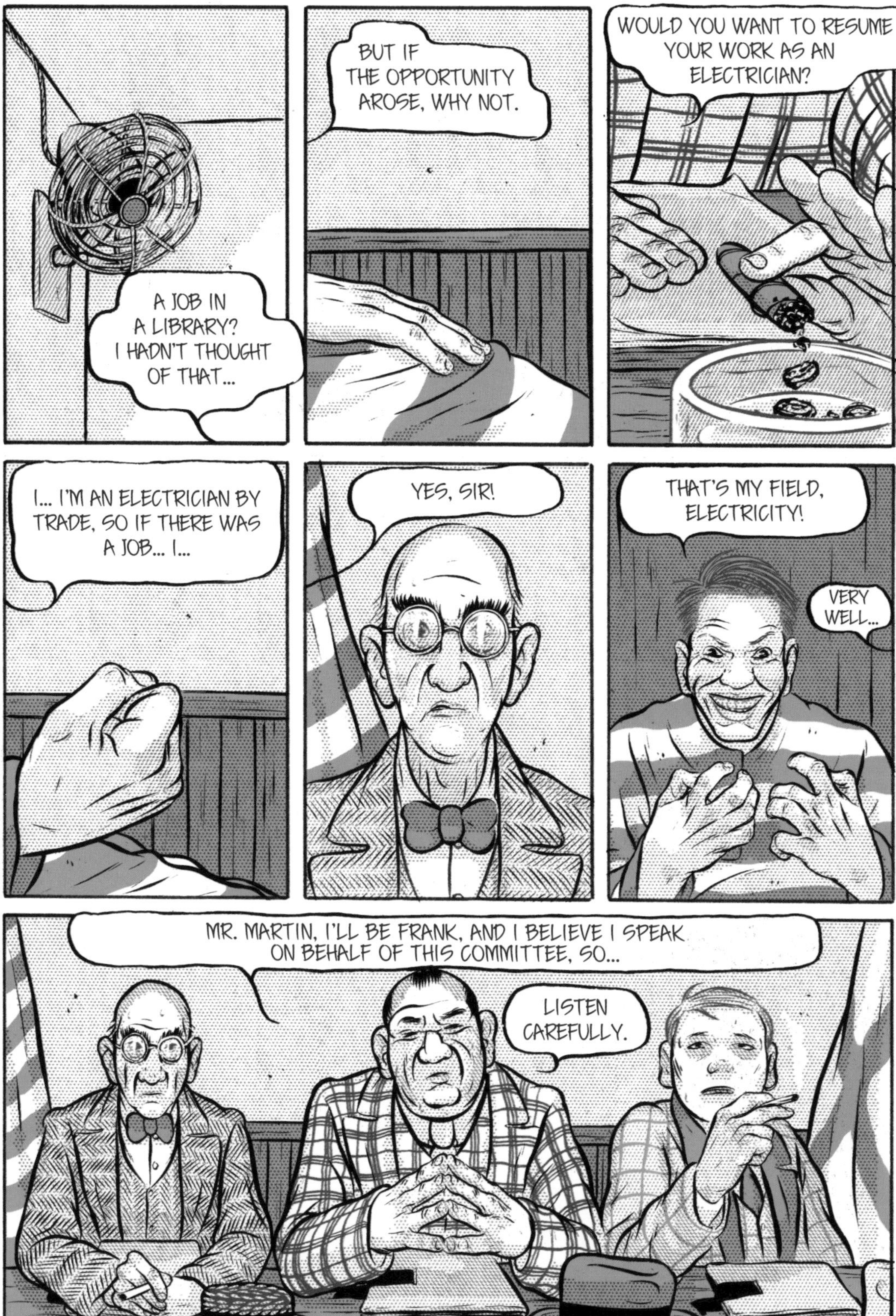
A JOB IN A LIBRARY? I HADN'T THOUGHT OF THAT...
BUT IF THE OPPORTUNITY AROSE, WHY NOT.
WOULD YOU WANT TO RESUME YOUR WORK AS AN ELECTRICIAN?
I... I'M AN ELECTRICIAN BY TRADE, SO IF THERE WAS A JOB... I...
YES, SIR!
THAT'S MY FIELD, ELECTRICITY!
VERY WELL...
MR. MARTIN, I'LL BE FRANK, AND I BELIEVE I SPEAK ON BEHALF OF THIS COMMITTEE, SO...
LISTEN CAREFULLY.

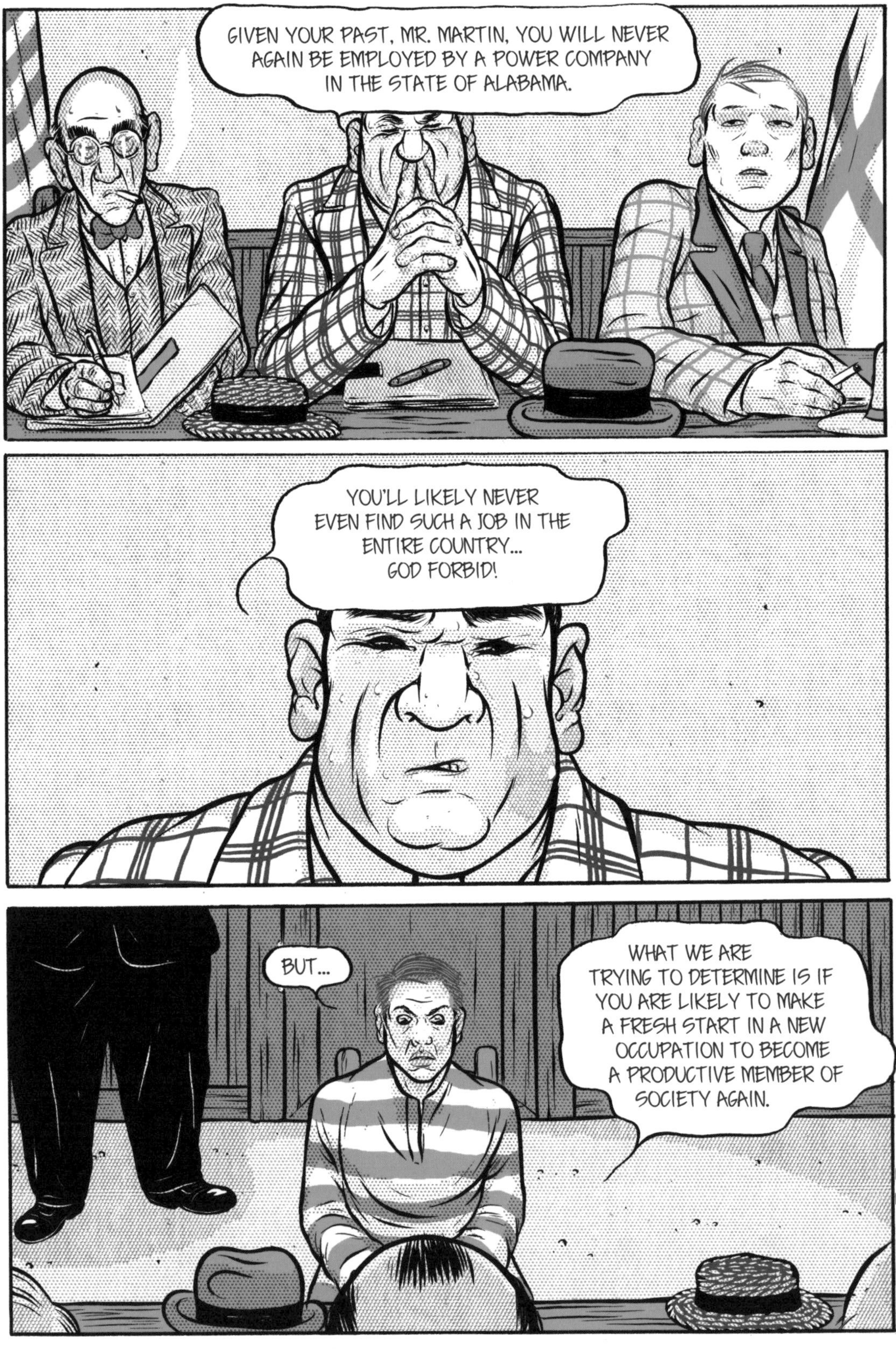
GIVEN YOUR PAST, MR. MARTIN, YOU WILL NEVER AGAIN BE EMPLOYED BY A POWER COMPANY IN THE STATE OF ALABAMA.
YOU'LL LIKELY NEVER EVEN FIND SUCH A JOB IN THE ENTIRE COUNTRY... GOD FORBID!
BUT...
WHAT WE ARE TRYING TO DETERMINE IS IF YOU ARE LIKELY TO MAKE A FRESH START IN A NEW OCCUPATION TO BECOME A PRODUCTIVE MEMBER OF SOCIETY AGAIN.

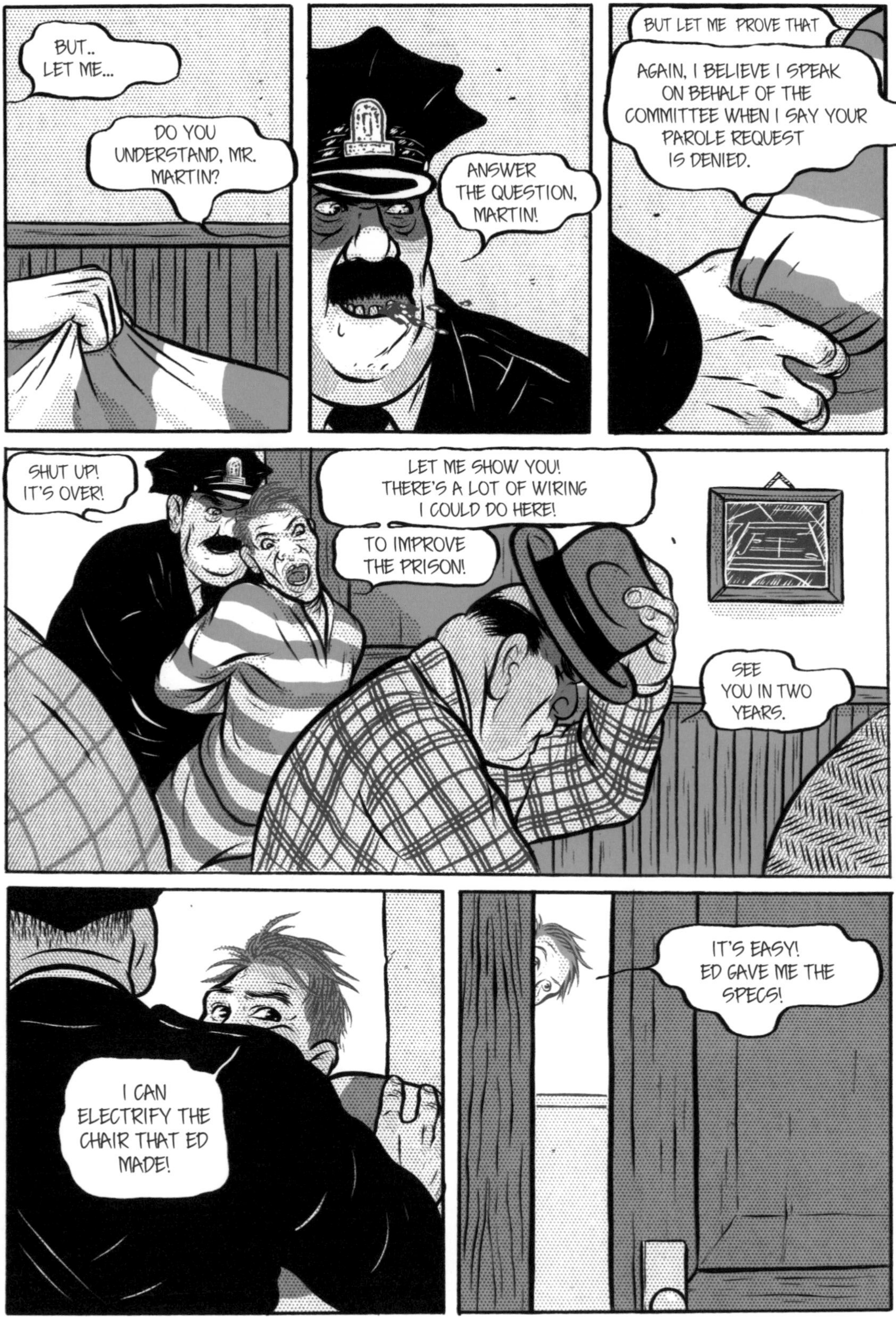
BUT..
LET ME...
DO YOU UNDERSTAND, MR. MARTIN?
ANSWER THE QUESTION, MARTIN!
BUT LET ME PROVE THAT
AGAIN, I BELIEVE I SPEAK ON BEHALF OF THE COMMITTEE WHEN I SAY YOUR PAROLE REQUEST IS DENIED.
SHUT UP! IT'S OVER!
LET ME SHOW YOU! THERE'S A LOT OF WIRING I COULD DO HERE!
TO IMPROVE THE PRISON!
SEE YOU IN TWO YEARS.
I CAN ELECTRIFY THE CHAIR THAT ED MADE!
IT'S EASY! ED GAVE ME THE SPECS!

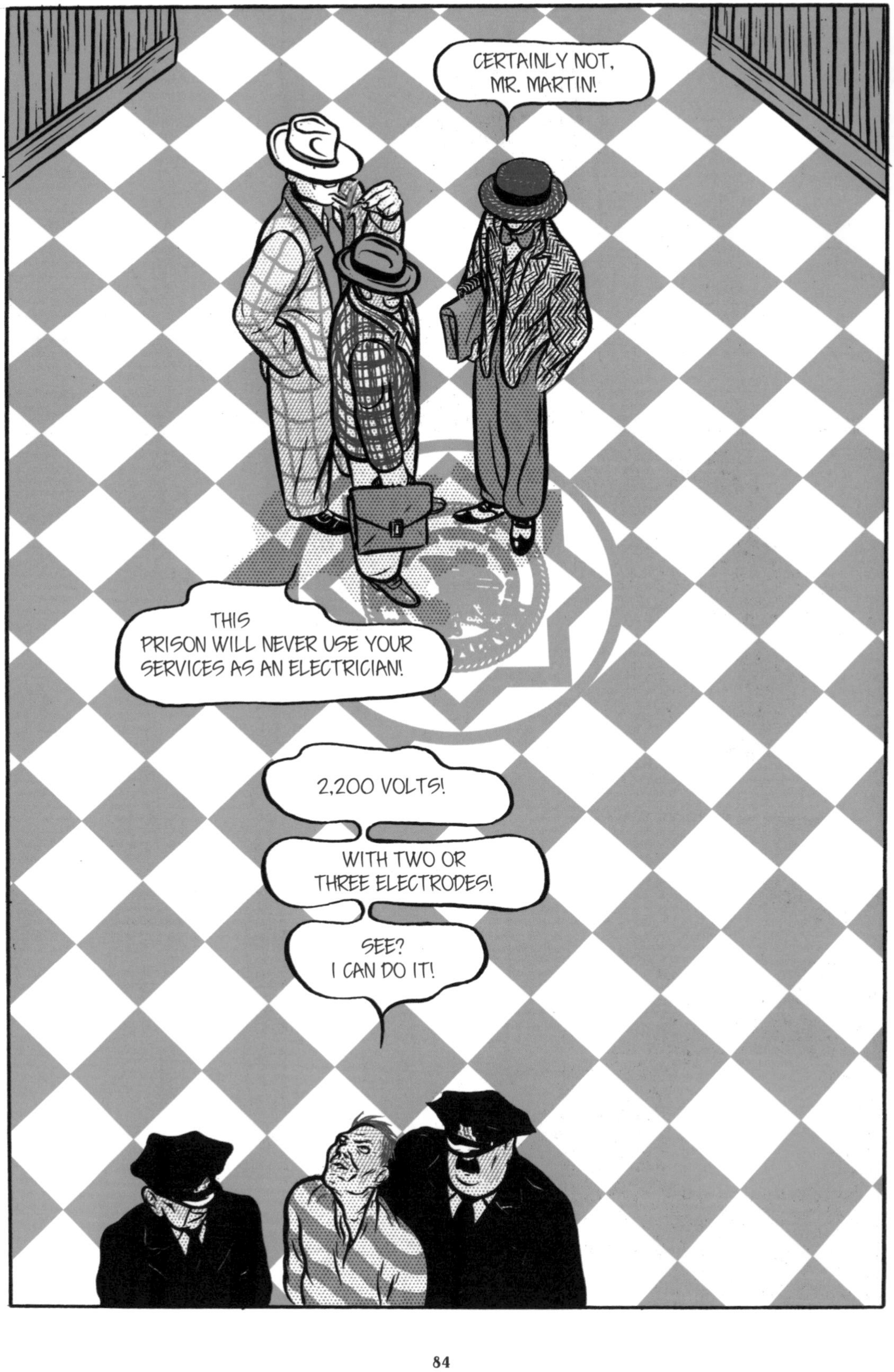
CERTAINLY NOT, MR. MARTIN!
THIS PRISON WILL NEVER USE YOUR SERVICES AS AN ELECTRICIAN!
2,200 VOLTS!
WITH TWO OR THREE ELECTRODES!
SEE? I CAN DO IT!

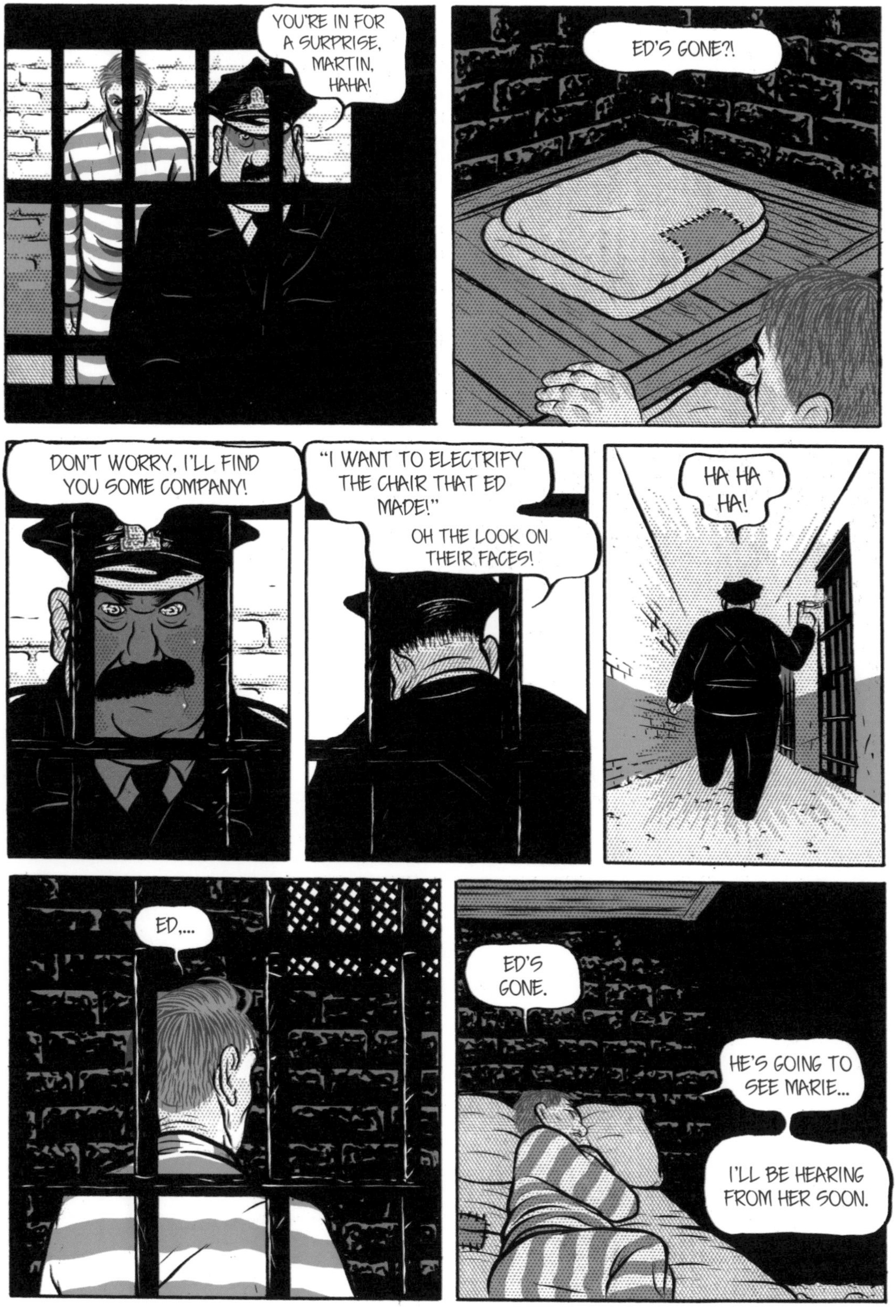
YOU'RE IN FOR A SURPRISE, MARTIN, HAHA!
ED'S GONE?!
DON'T WORRY, I'LL FIND YOU SOME COMPANY!
"I WANT TO ELECTRIFY THE CHAIR THAT ED MADE!"
OH THE LOOK ON THEIR FACES!
HA HA HA!
ED,...
ED'S GONE.
HE'S GOING TO SEE MARIE...
I'LL BE HEARING FROM HER SOON.

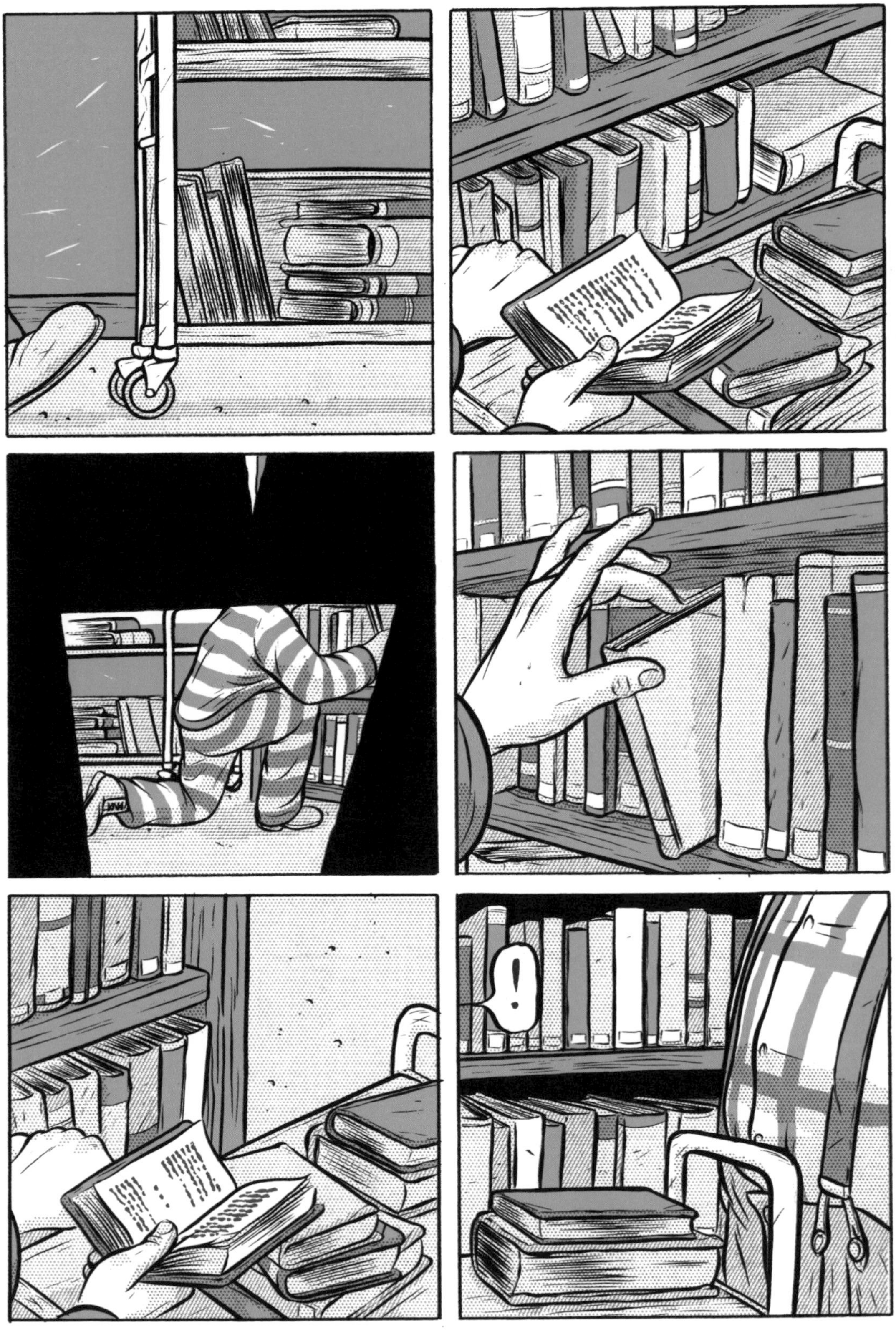
!

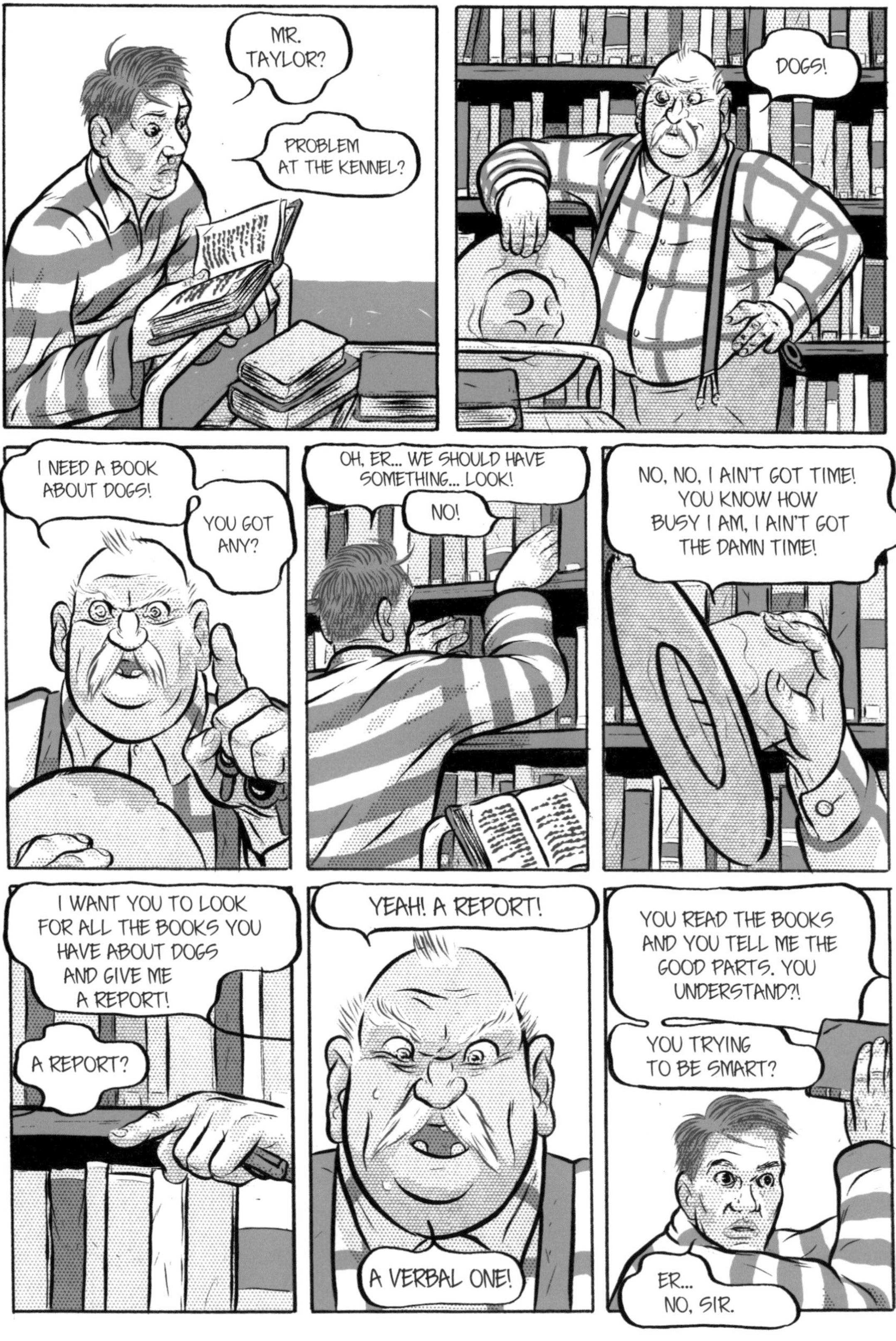
MR. TAYLOR?
PROBLEM AT THE KENNEL?
DOGS!
I NEED A BOOK ABOUT DOGS!
YOU GOT ANY?
OH, ER... WE SHOULD HAVE SOMETHING... LOOK!
NO!
NO, NO, I AIN'T GOT TIME! YOU KNOW HOW BUSY I AM, I AIN'T GOT THE DAMN TIME!
I WANT YOU TO LOOK FOR ALL THE BOOKS YOU HAVE ABOUT DOGS AND GIVE ME A REPORT!
A REPORT?
YEAH! A REPORT!
A VERBAL ONE!
YOU READ THE BOOKS AND YOU TELL ME THE GOOD PARTS. YOU UNDERSTAND?!
YOU TRYING TO BE SMART?
ER... NO, SIR.

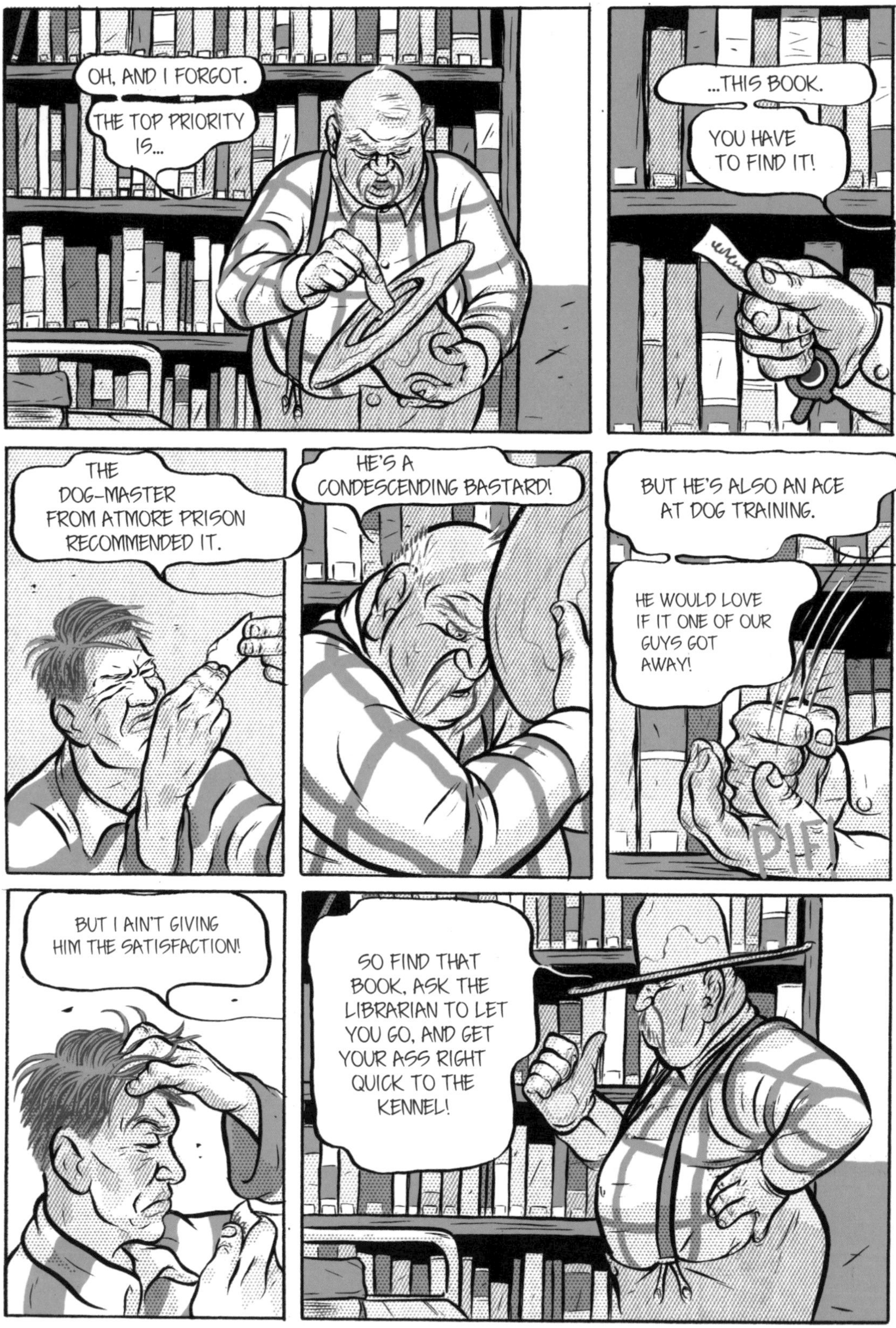
OH, AND I FORGOT.
THE TOP PRIORITY IS...
...THIS BOOK.
YOU HAVE TO FIND IT!
THE DOG-MASTER FROM ATMORE PRISON RECOMMENDED IT.
HE'S A CONDESCENDING BASTARD!
BUT HE'S ALSO AN ACE AT DOG TRAINING.
HE WOULD LOVE IF IT ONE OF OUR GUYS GOT AWAY!
PIF!
BUT I AIN'T GIVING HIM THE SATISFACTION!
SO FIND THAT BOOK, ASK THE LIBRARIAN TO LET YOU GO, AND GET YOUR ASS RIGHT QUICK TO THE KENNEL!

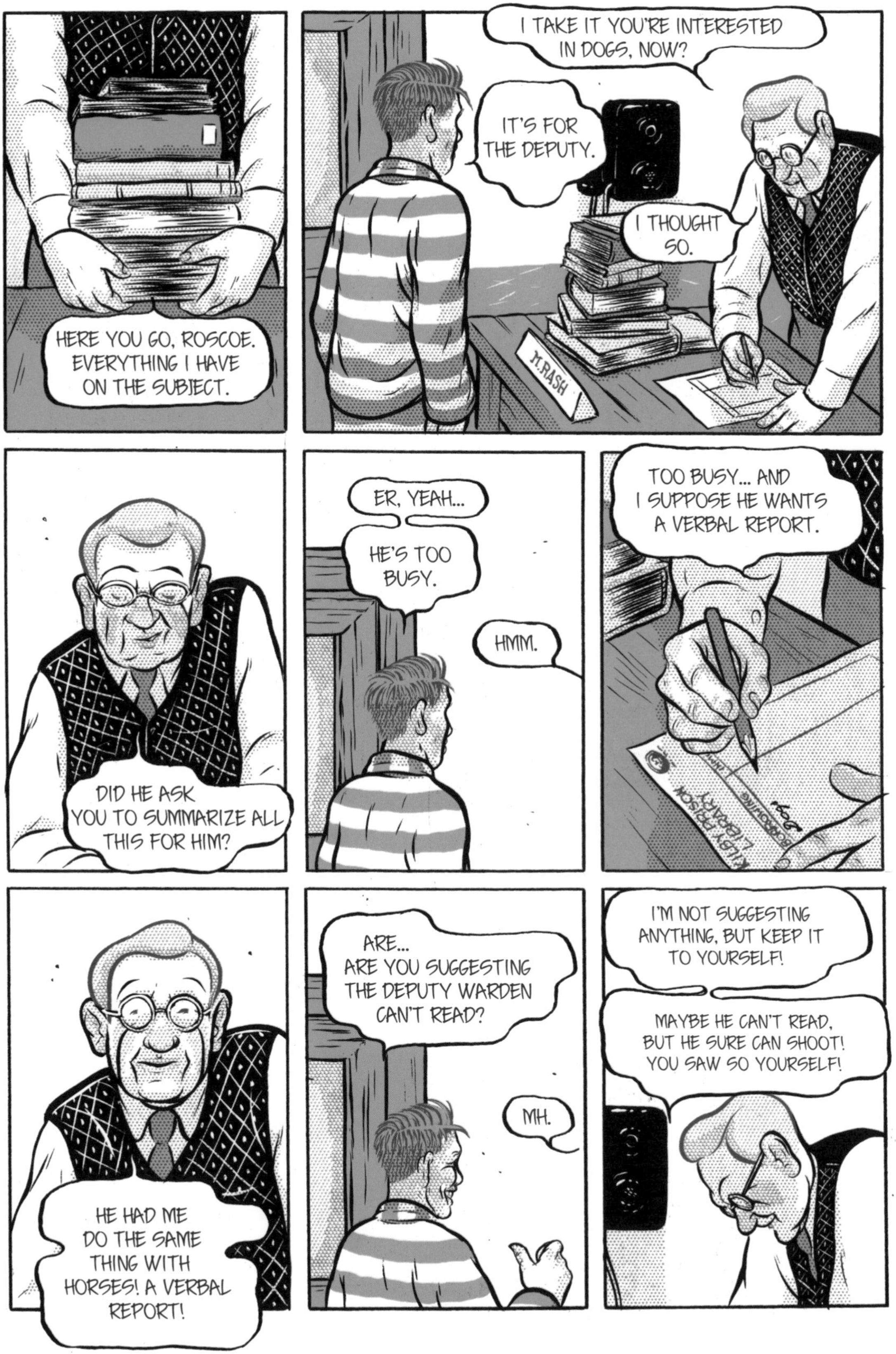
HERE YOU GO, ROSCOE. EVERYTHING I HAVE ON THE SUBJECT.
I TAKE IT YOU'RE INTERESTED IN DOGS, NOW?
IT'S FOR THE DEPUTY.
I THOUGHT SO.
M.RASH
DID HE ASK YOU TO SUMMARIZE ALL THIS FOR HIM?
ER, YEAH...
HE'S TOO BUSY.
HMM.
TOO BUSY... AND I SUPPOSE HE WANTS A VERBAL REPORT.
HE HAD ME DO THE SAME THING WITH HORSES! A VERBAL REPORT!
ARE... ARE YOU SUGGESTING THE DEPUTY WARDEN CAN'T READ?
MH.
I'M NOT SUGGESTING ANYTHING, BUT KEEP IT TO YOURSELF!
MAYBE HE CAN'T READ, BUT HE SURE CAN SHOOT! YOU SAW SO YOURSELF!

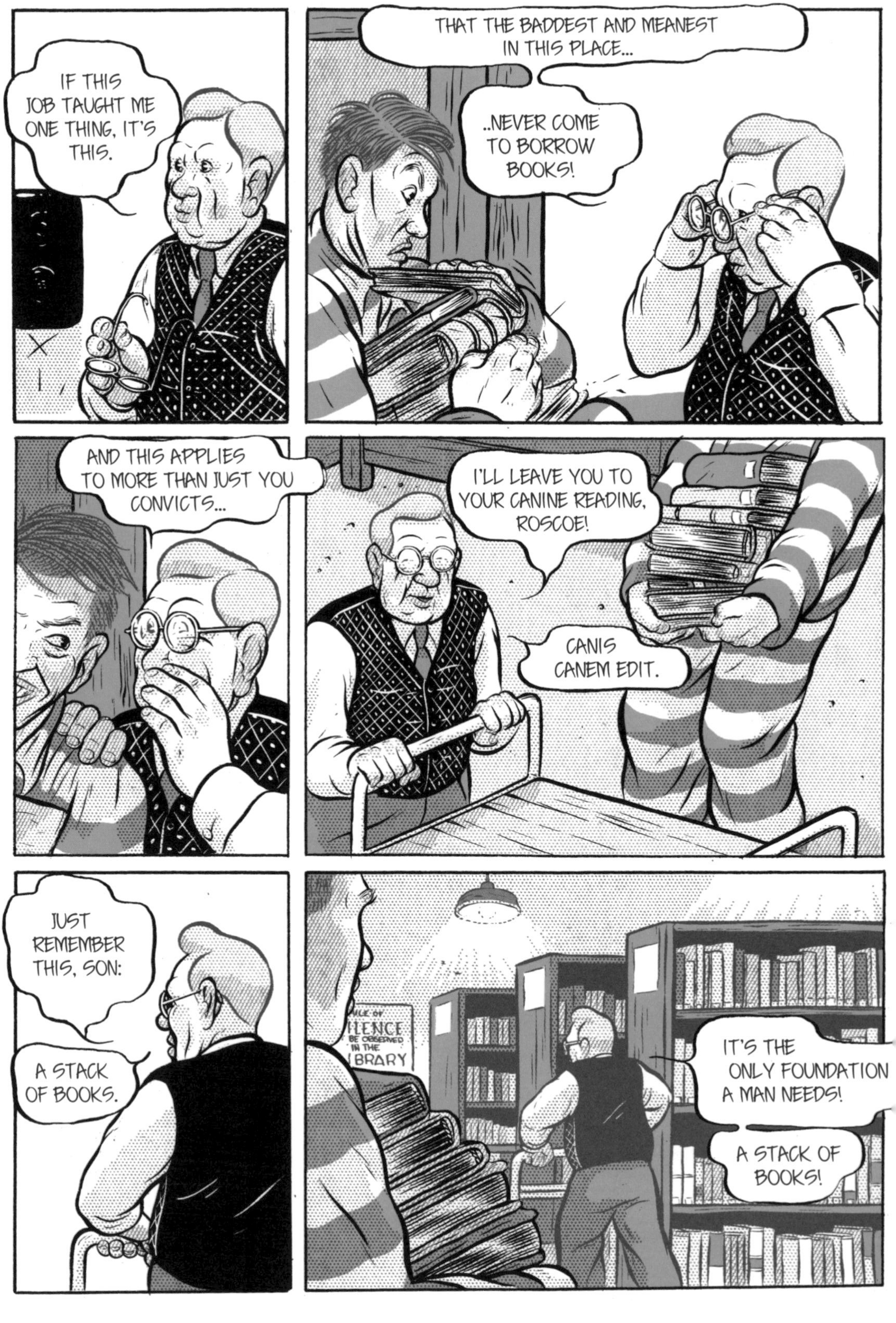
IF THIS JOB TAUGHT ME ONE THING, IT'S THIS.
THAT THE BADDEST AND MEANEST IN THIS PLACE...
..NEVER COME TO BORROW BOOKS!
AND THIS APPLIES TO MORE THAN JUST YOU CONVICTS...
I'LL LEAVE YOU TO YOUR CANINE READING, ROSCOE!
CANIS CANEM EDIT.
JUST REMEMBER THIS, SON:
A STACK OF BOOKS.
IT'S THE ONLY FOUNDATION A MAN NEEDS!
A STACK OF BOOKS!

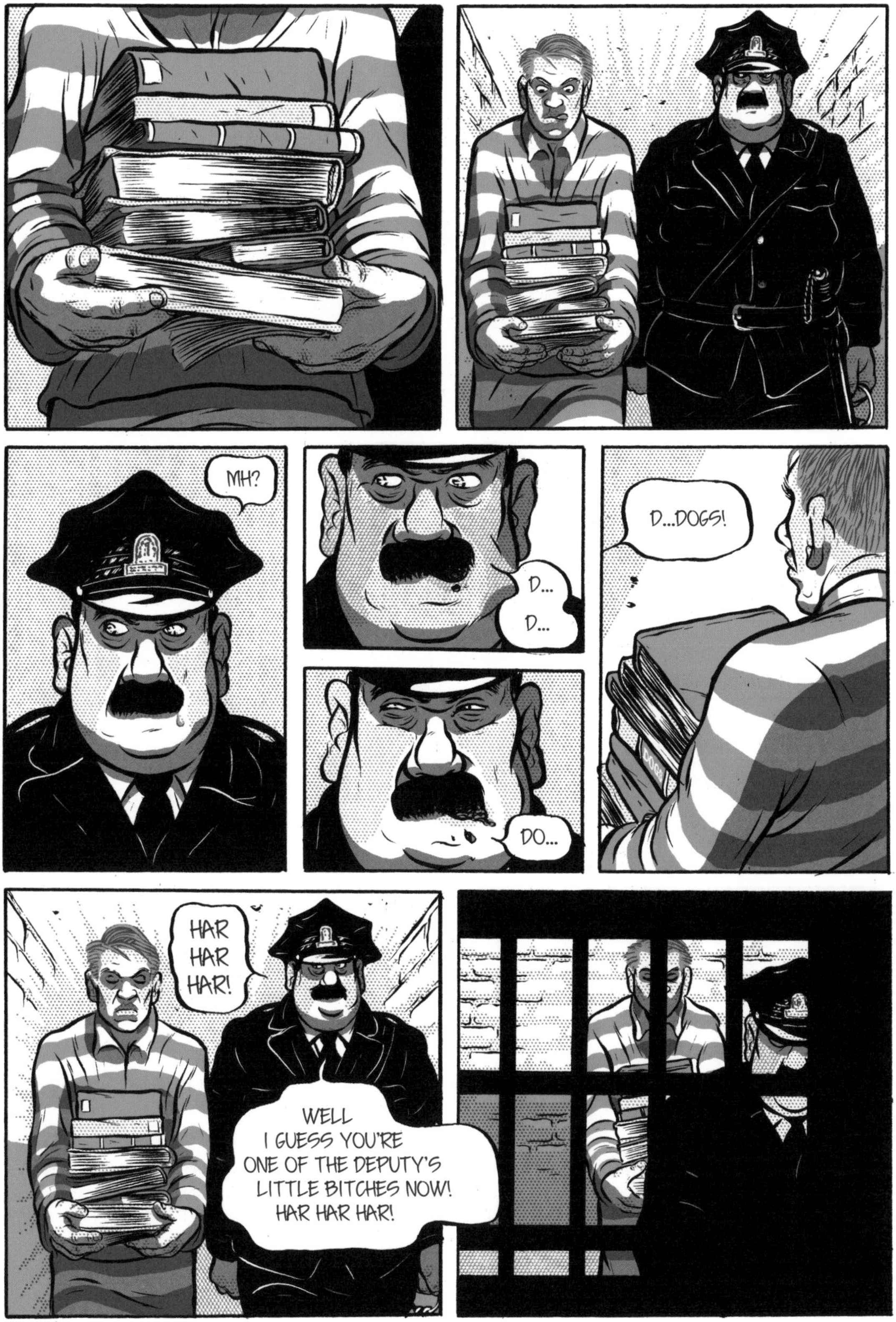
MH?
D...
D...
D...DOGS!
DO...
DOGS
HAR
HAR
HAR!
WELL
I GUESS YOU'RE
ONE OF THE DEPUTY'S
LITTLE BITCHES NOW!
HAR HAR HAR!

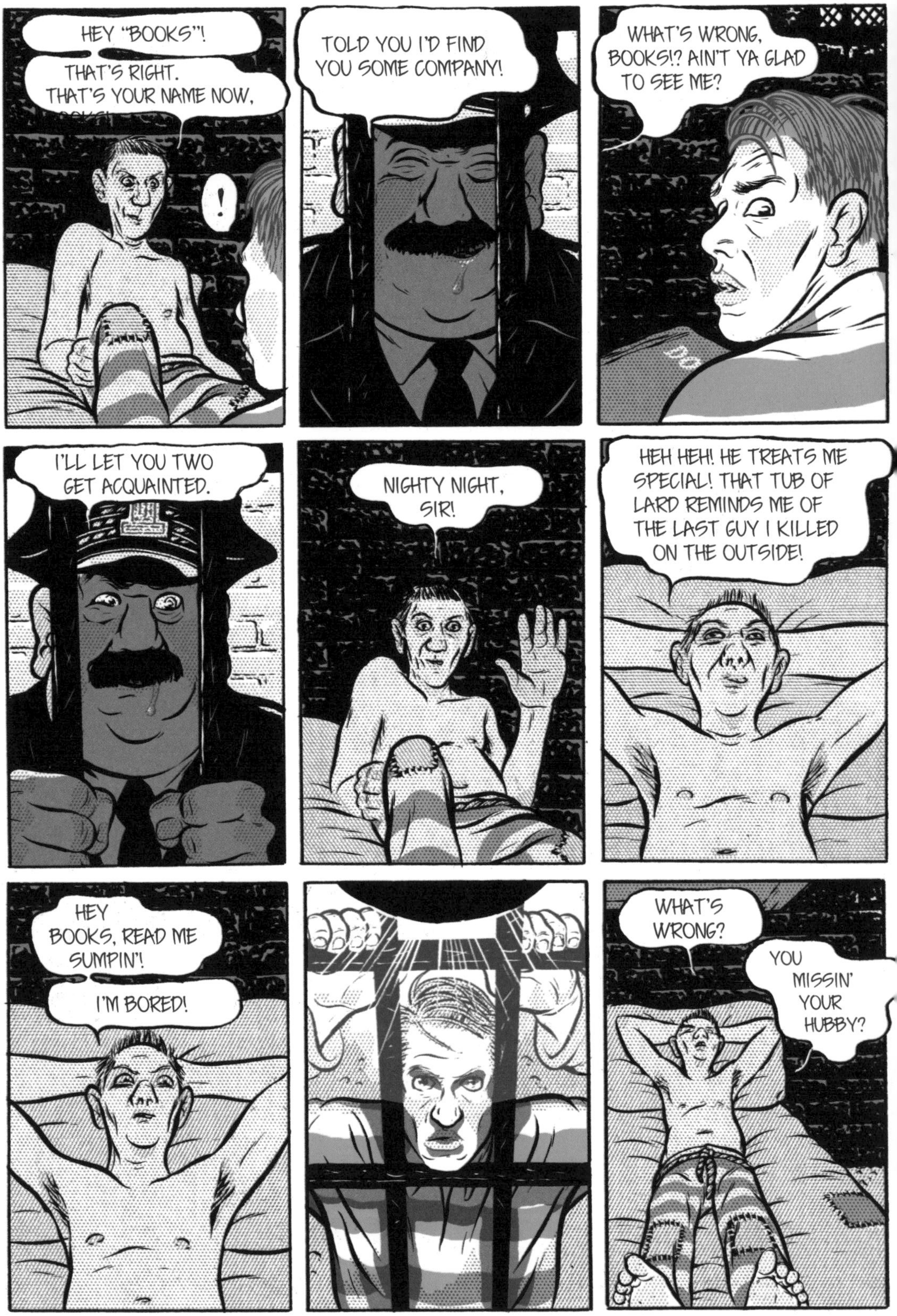
HEY "BOOKS"!
THAT'S RIGHT. THAT'S YOUR NAME NOW,
!
TOLD YOU I'D FIND YOU SOME COMPANY!
WHAT'S WRONG, BOOKS!? AIN'T YA GLAD TO SEE ME?
I'LL LET YOU TWO GET ACQUAINTED.
NIGHTY NIGHT, SIR!
HEH HEH! HE TREATS ME SPECIAL! THAT TUB OF LARD REMINDS ME OF THE LAST GUY I KILLED ON THE OUTSIDE!
HEY BOOKS, READ ME SUMPIN'!
I'M BORED!
WHAT'S WRONG?
YOU MISSIN' YOUR HUBBY?

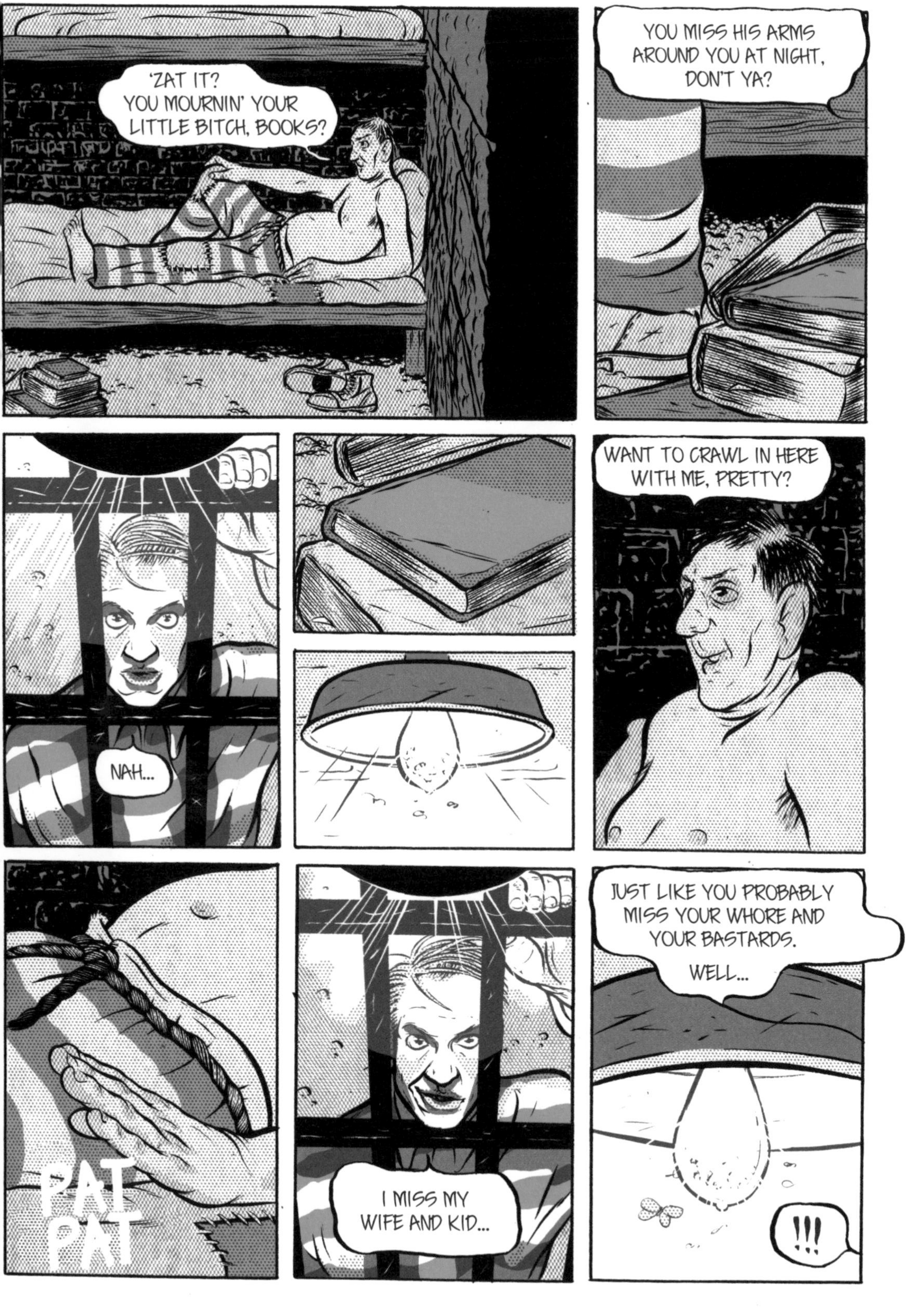

'ZAT IT?
YOU MOURNIN' YOUR LITTLE BITCH, BOOKS?
YOU MISS HIS ARMS AROUND YOU AT NIGHT, DON'T YA?
NAH...
WANT TO CRAWL IN HERE WITH ME, PRETTY?
PAT PAT
I MISS MY WIFE AND KID...
JUST LIKE YOU PROBABLY MISS YOUR WHORE AND YOUR BASTARDS.
WELL...
!!!

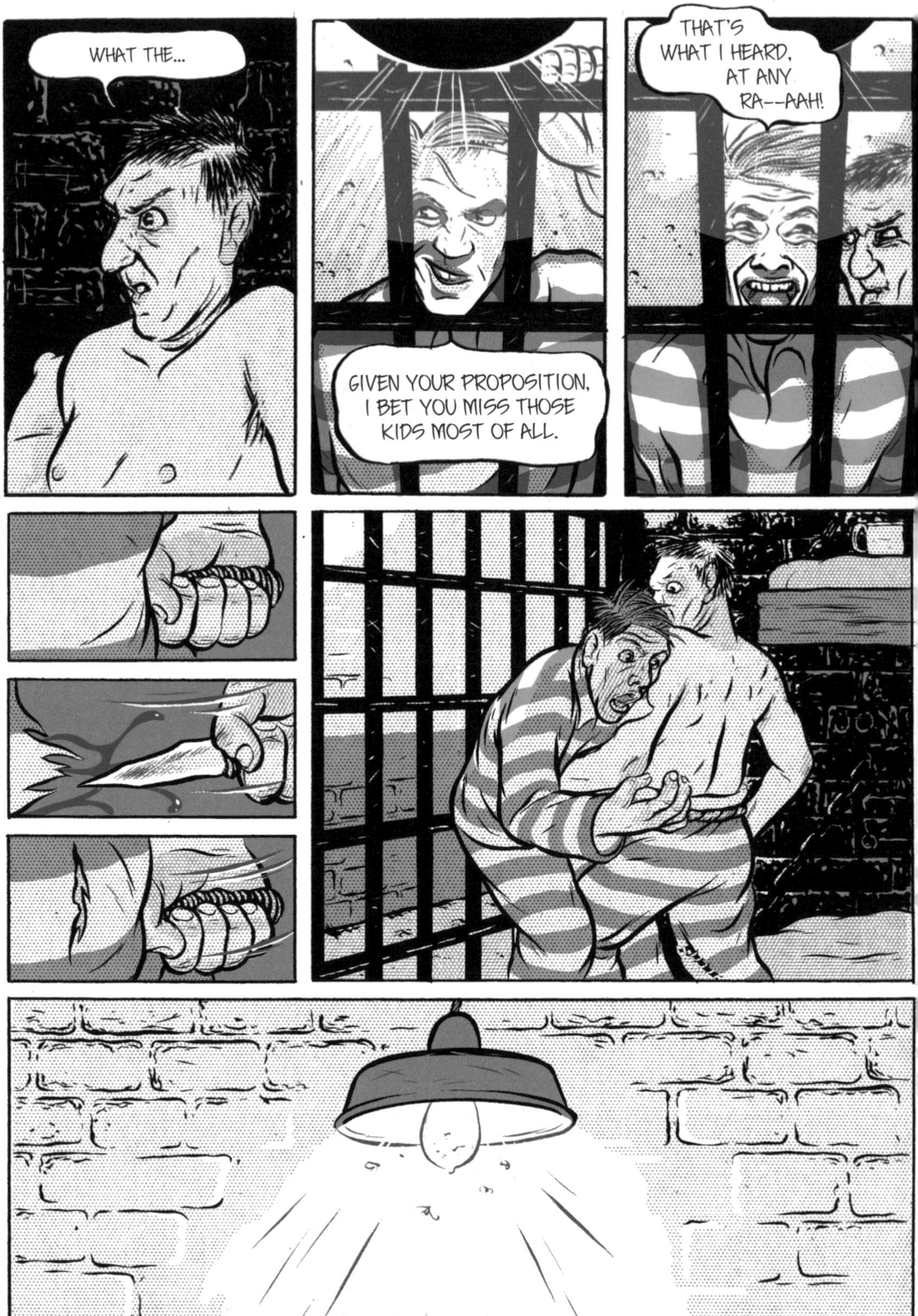
WHAT THE...
GIVEN YOUR PROPOSITION, I BET YOU MISS THOSE KIDS MOST OF ALL.
THAT'S WHAT I HEARD, AT ANY RA--AAH!

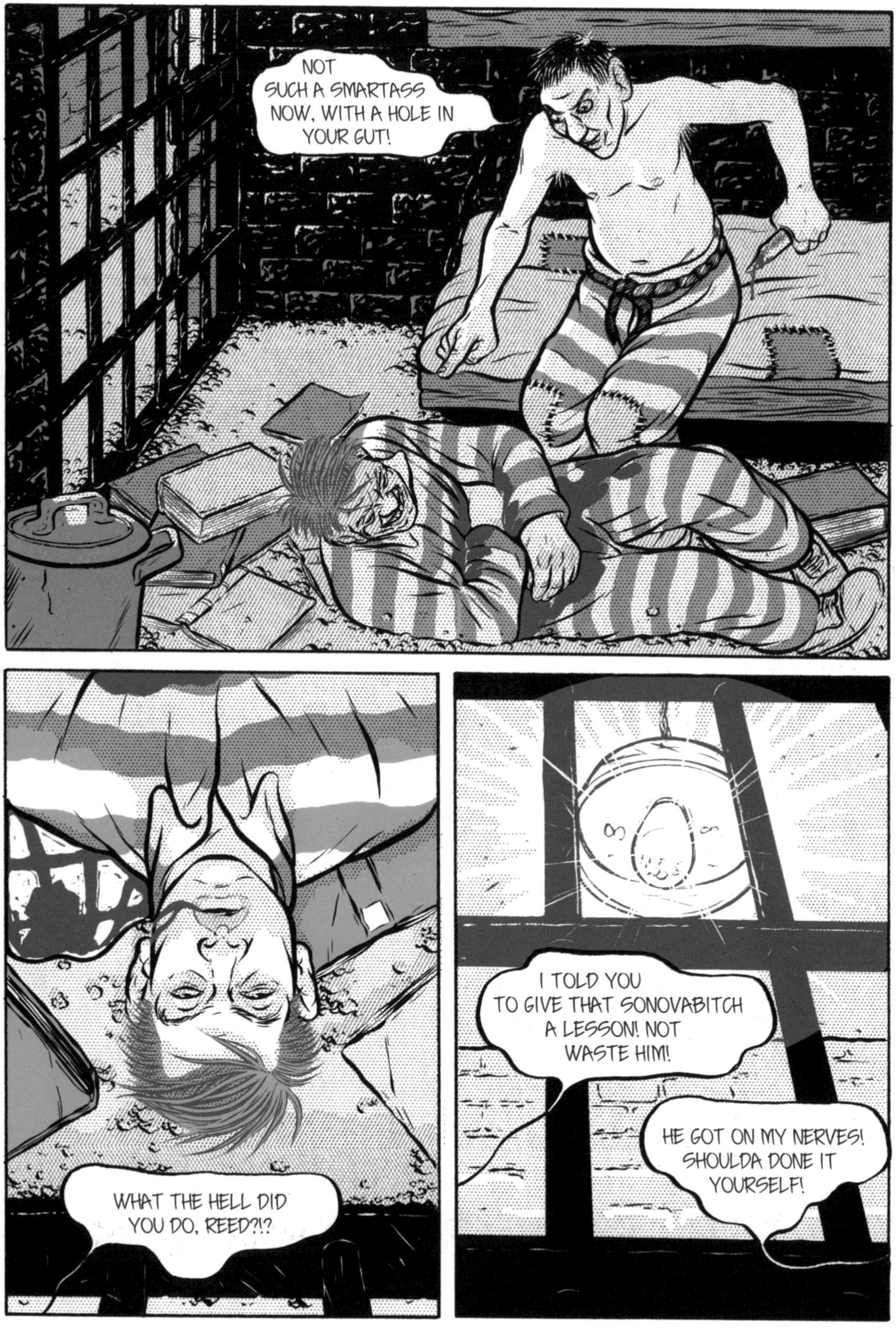
NOT SUCH A SMARTASS NOW, WITH A HOLE IN YOUR GUT!
WHAT THE HELL DID YOU DO, REED?!?
I TOLD YOU TO GIVE THAT SONOVABITCH A LESSON! NOT WASTE HIM!
HE GOT ON MY NERVES! SHOULDA DONE IT YOURSELF!

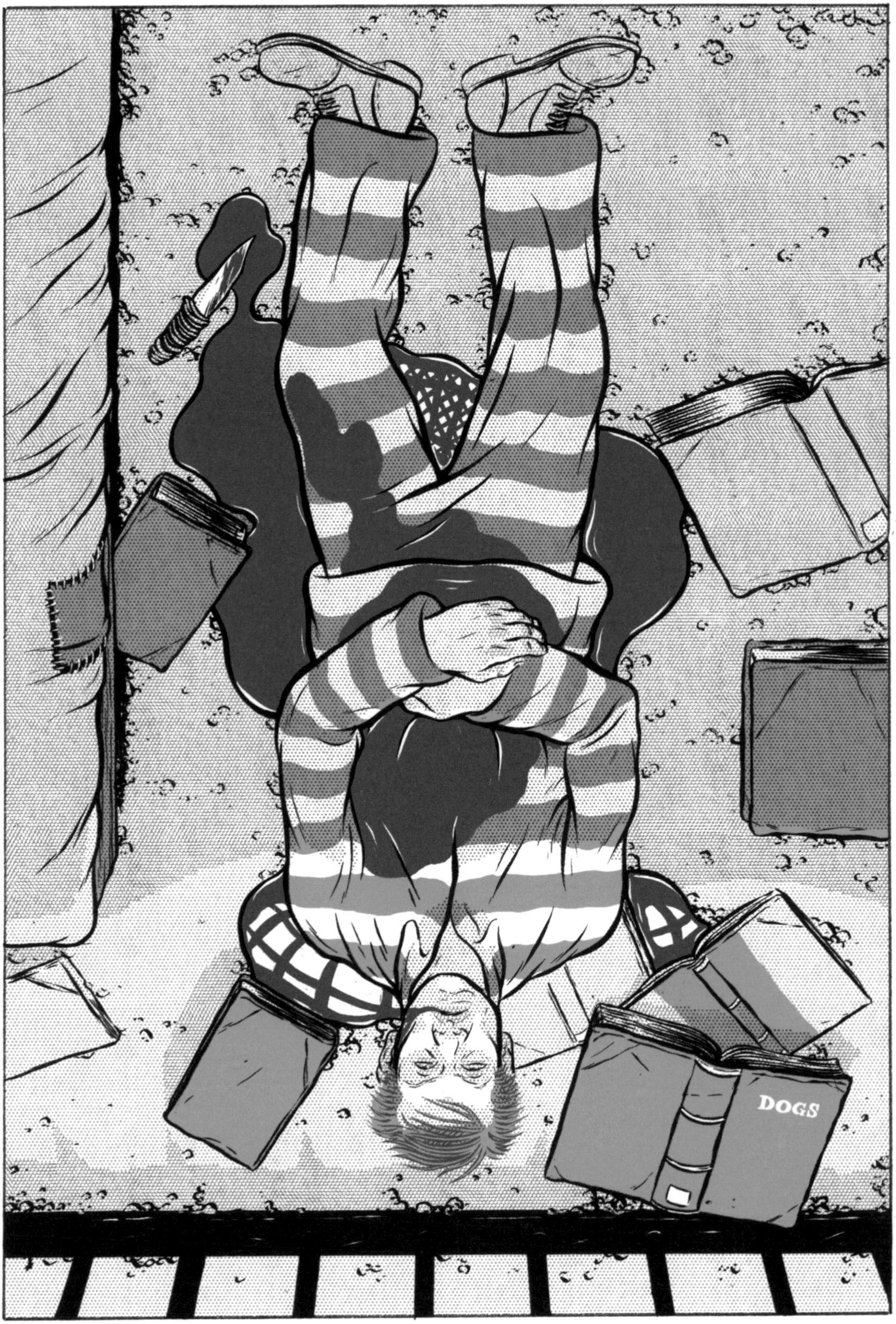
DOGS

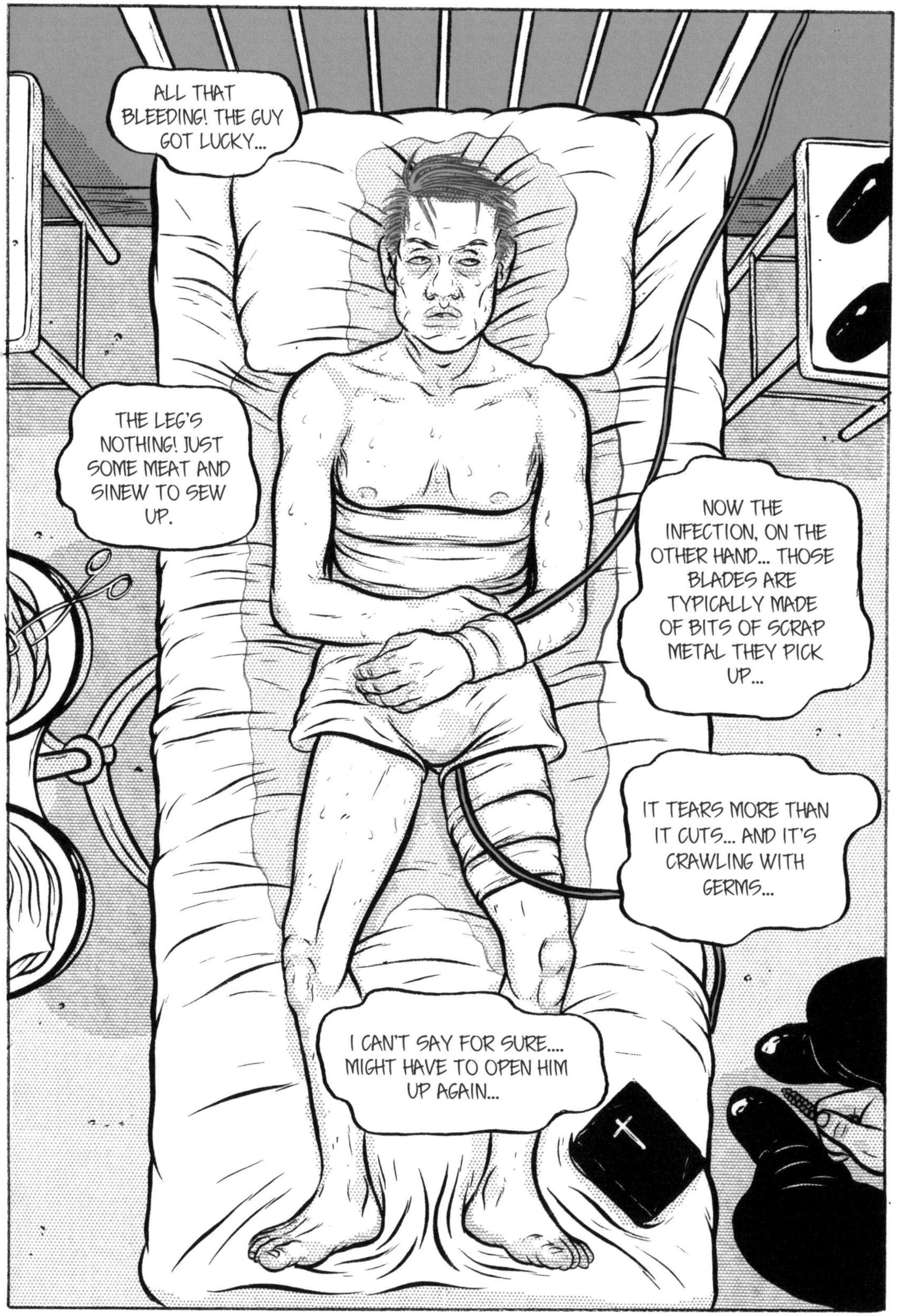
ALL THAT BLEEDING! THE GUY GOT LUCKY...
THE LEG'S NOTHING! JUST SOME MEAT AND SINEW TO SEW UP.
NOW THE INFECTION, ON THE OTHER HAND... THOSE BLADES ARE TYPICALLY MADE OF BITS OF SCRAP METAL THEY PICK UP...
IT TEARS MORE THAN IT CUTS... AND IT'S CRAWLING WITH GERMS...
I CAN'T SAY FOR SURE.... MIGHT HAVE TO OPEN HIM UP AGAIN...

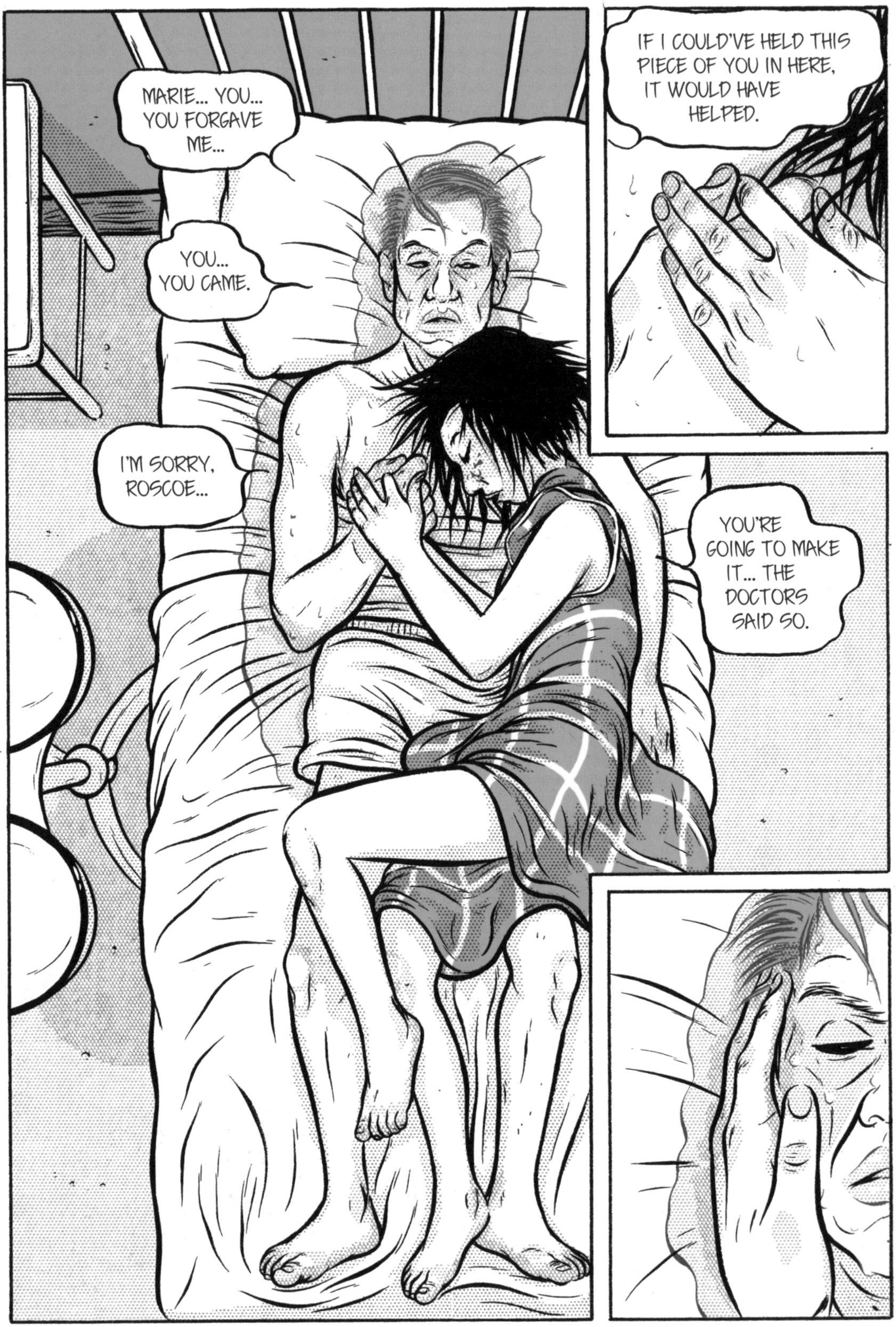
MARIE... YOU... YOU FORGAVE ME...
YOU... YOU CAME.
I'M SORRY, ROSCOE...
IF I COULD'VE HELD THIS PIECE OF YOU IN HERE, IT WOULD HAVE HELPED.
YOU'RE GOING TO MAKE IT... THE DOCTORS SAID SO.

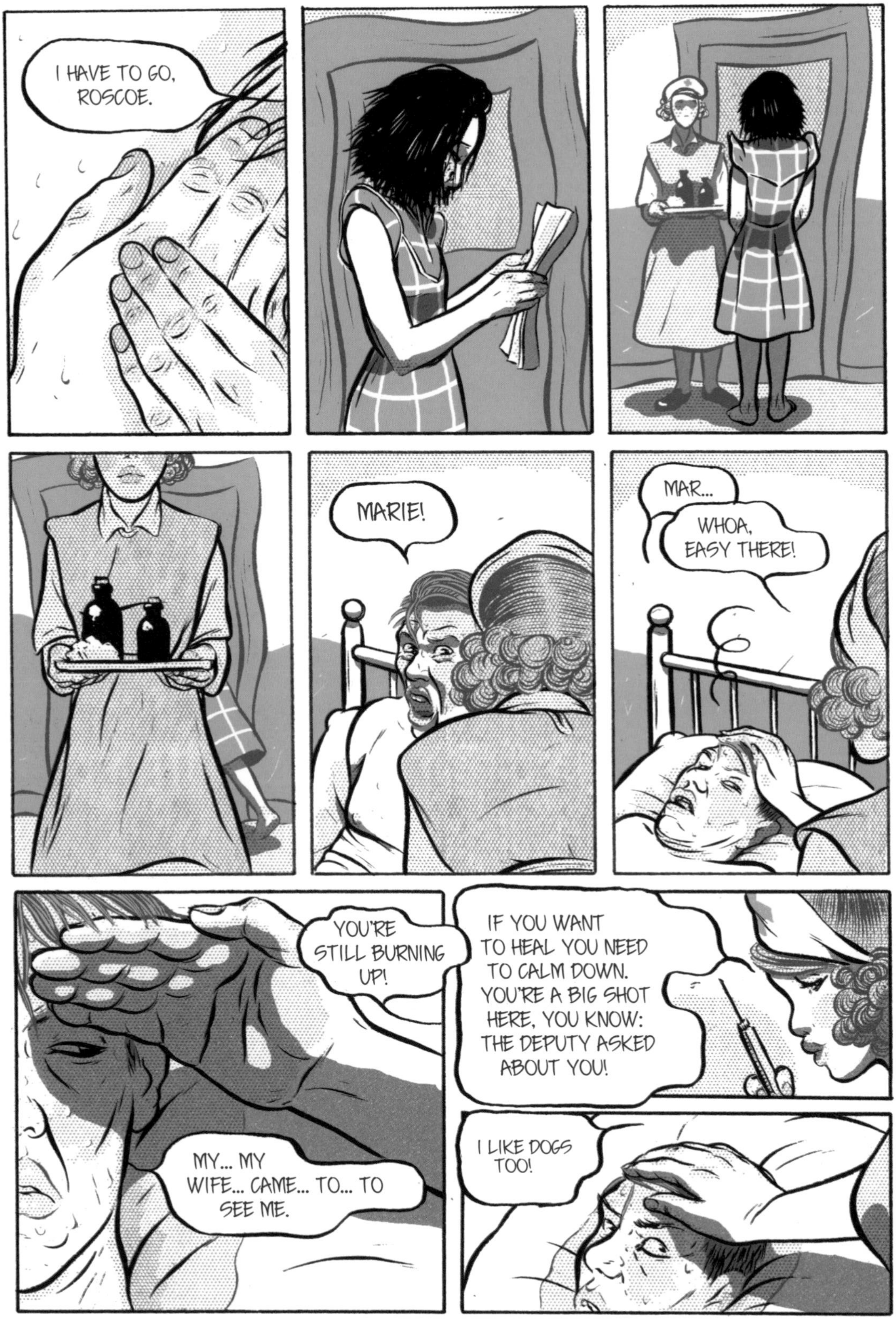
I HAVE TO GO, ROSCOE.
MARIE!
MAR...
WHOA, EASY THERE!
YOU'RE STILL BURNING UP!
MY... MY WIFE... CAME... TO... TO SEE ME.
IF YOU WANT TO HEAL YOU NEED TO CALM DOWN. YOU'RE A BIG SHOT HERE, YOU KNOW: THE DEPUTY ASKED ABOUT YOU!
I LIKE DOGS TOO!

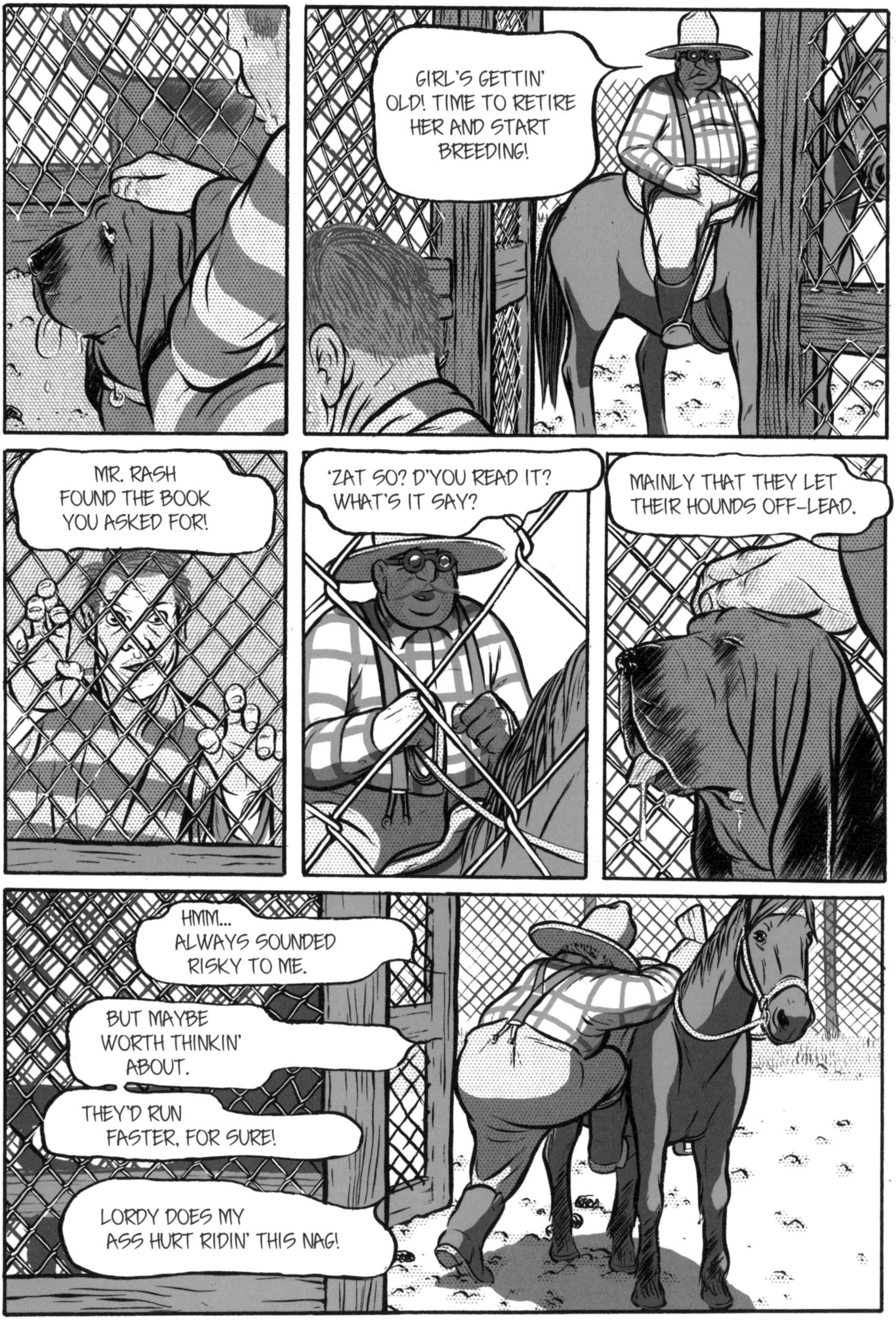
GIRL'S GETTIN' OLD! TIME TO RETIRE HER AND START BREEDING!
MR. RASH FOUND THE BOOK YOU ASKED FOR!
'ZAT SO? D'YOU READ IT? WHAT'S IT SAY?
MAINLY THAT THEY LET THEIR HOUNDS OFF-LEAD.
HMM... ALWAYS SOUNDED RISKY TO ME.
BUT MAYBE WORTH THINKIN' ABOUT.
THEY'D RUN FASTER, FOR SURE!
LORDY DOES MY ASS HURT RIDIN' THIS NAG!

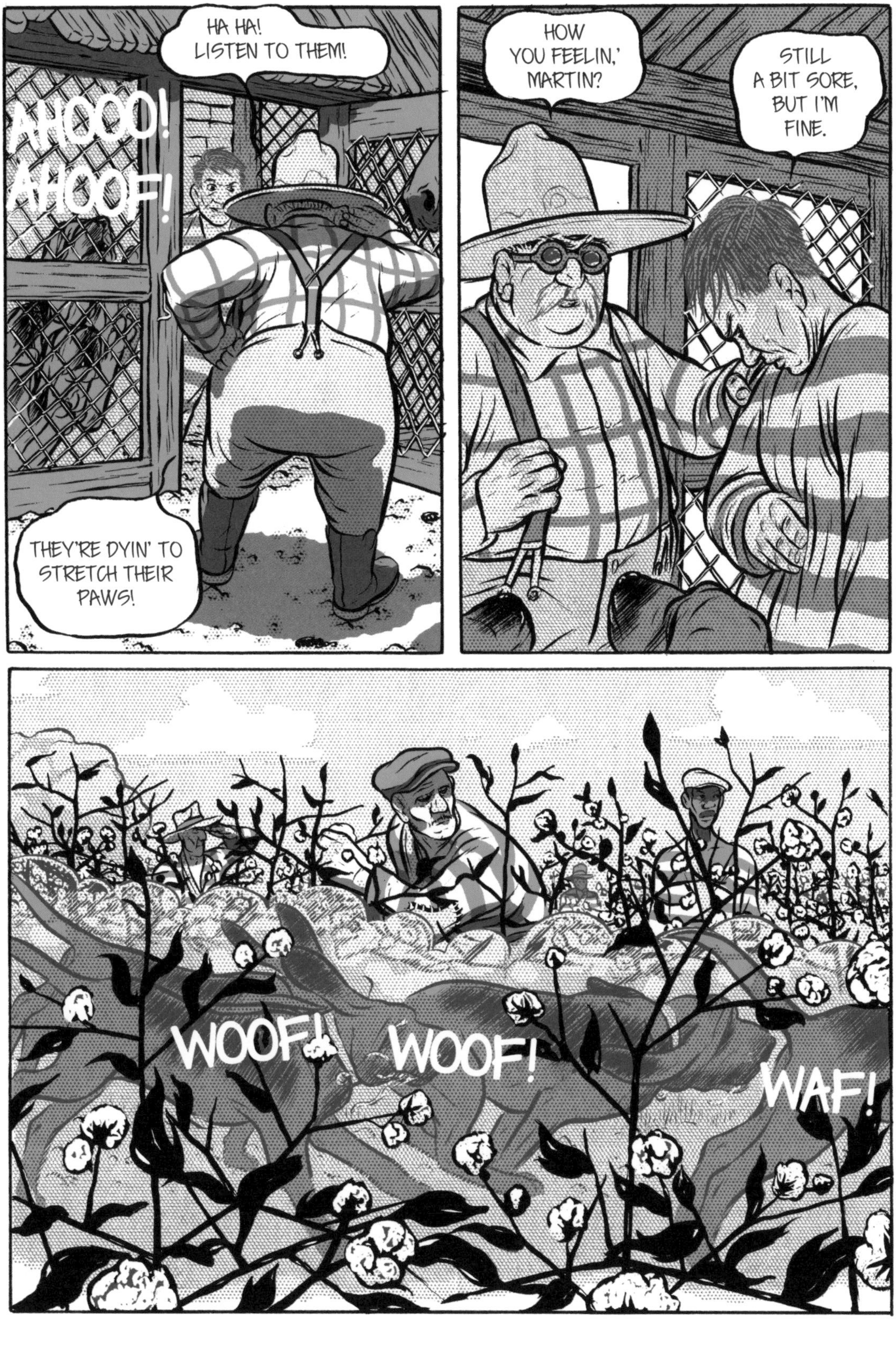
HA HA!
LISTEN TO THEM!
AHOOO!
AHOOF!
THEY'RE DYIN' TO STRETCH THEIR PAWS!
HOW YOU FEELIN,' MARTIN?
STILL A BIT SORE, BUT I'M FINE.
WOOF!
WOOF!
WAF!

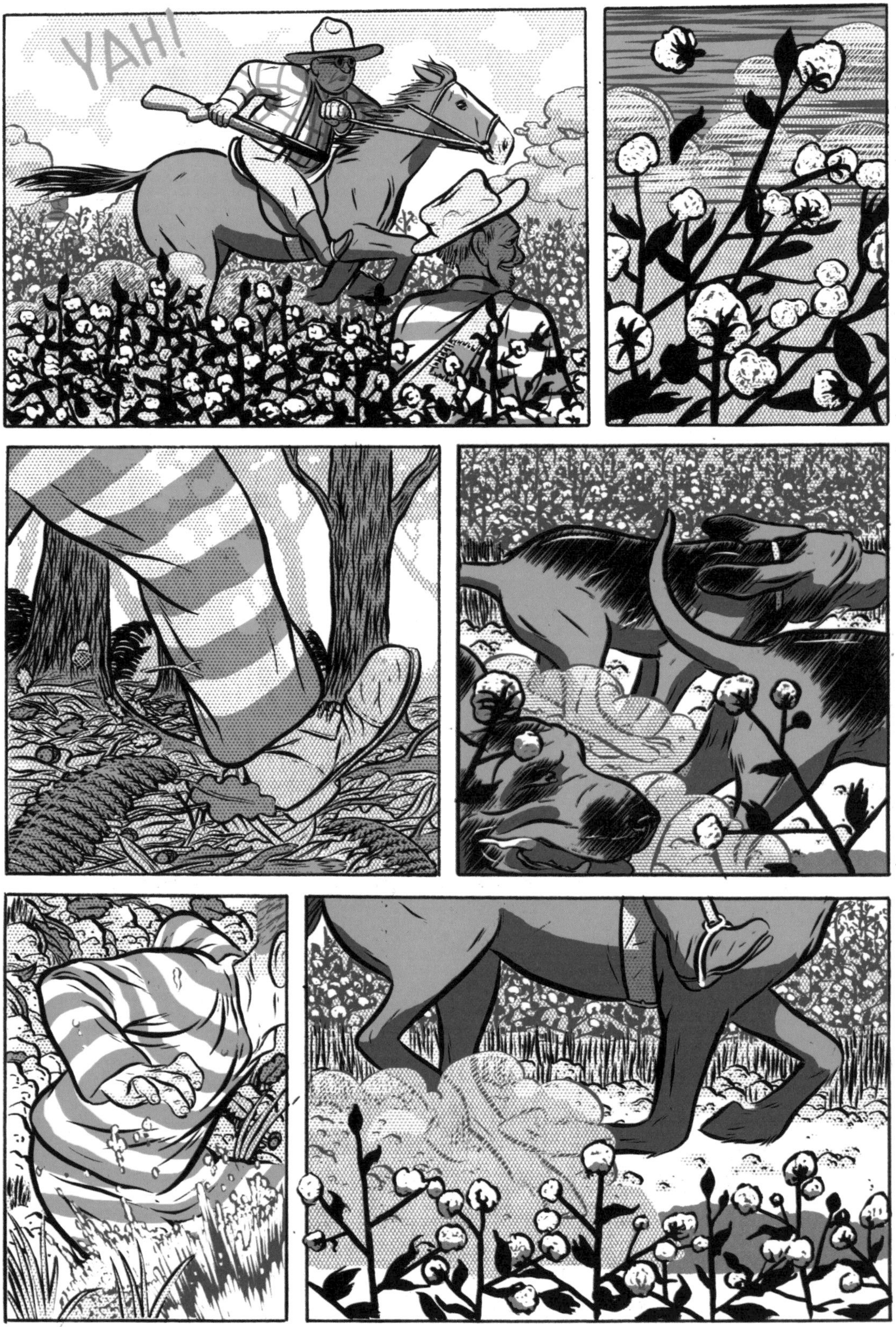
YAH!

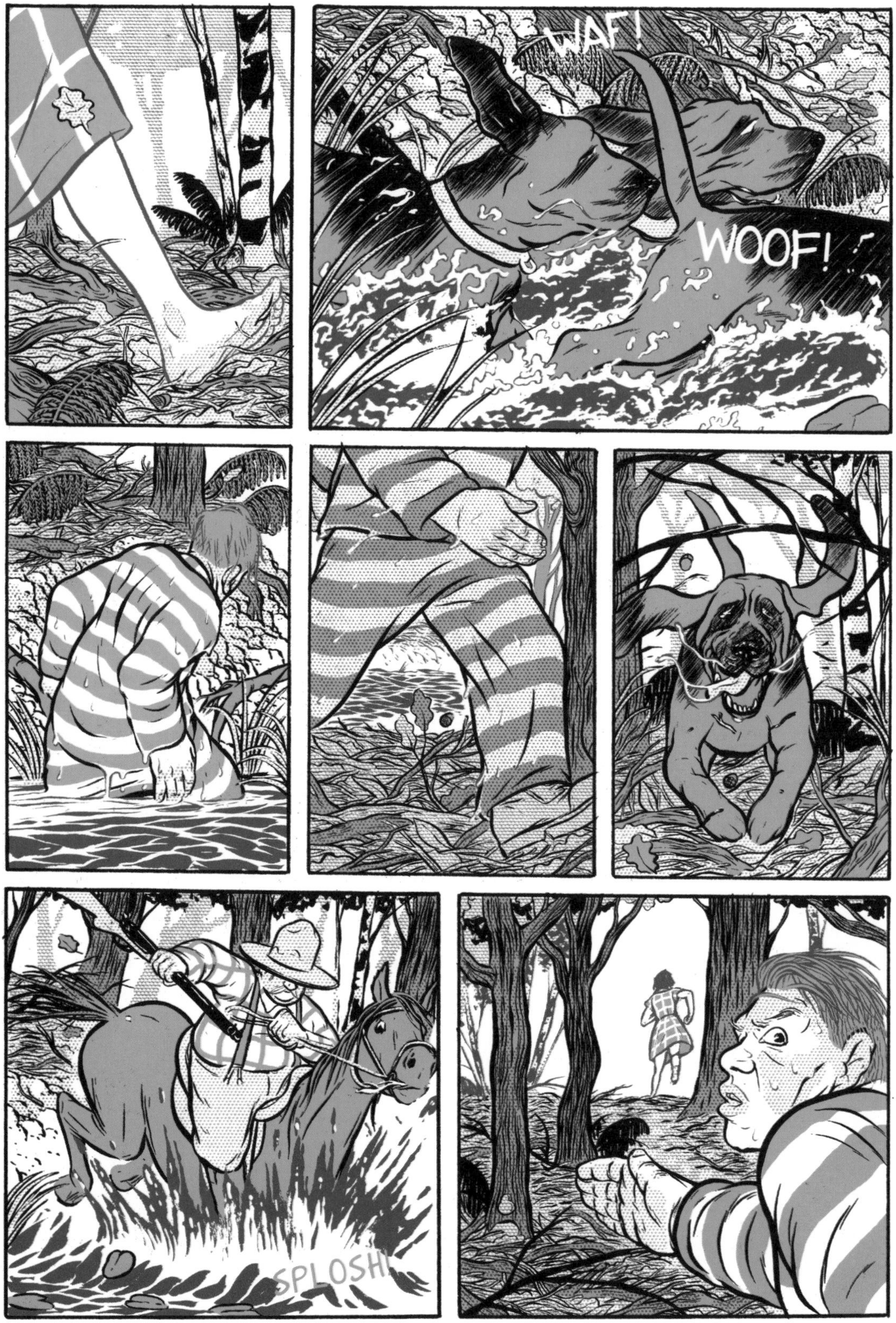
WAF!
WOOF!
SPLOSH!

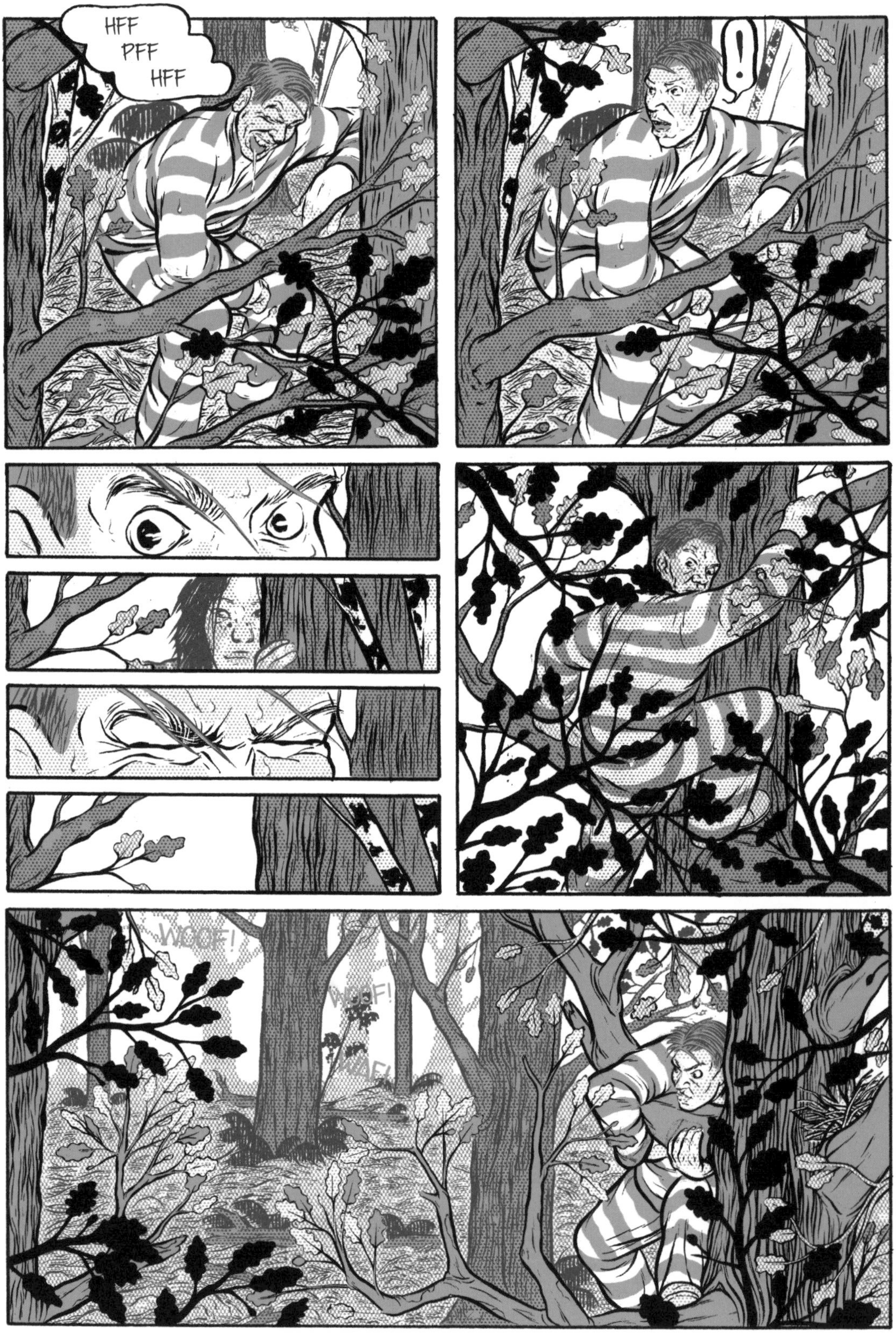
HFF
PFF
HFF
!
WOOF!
WOOF!

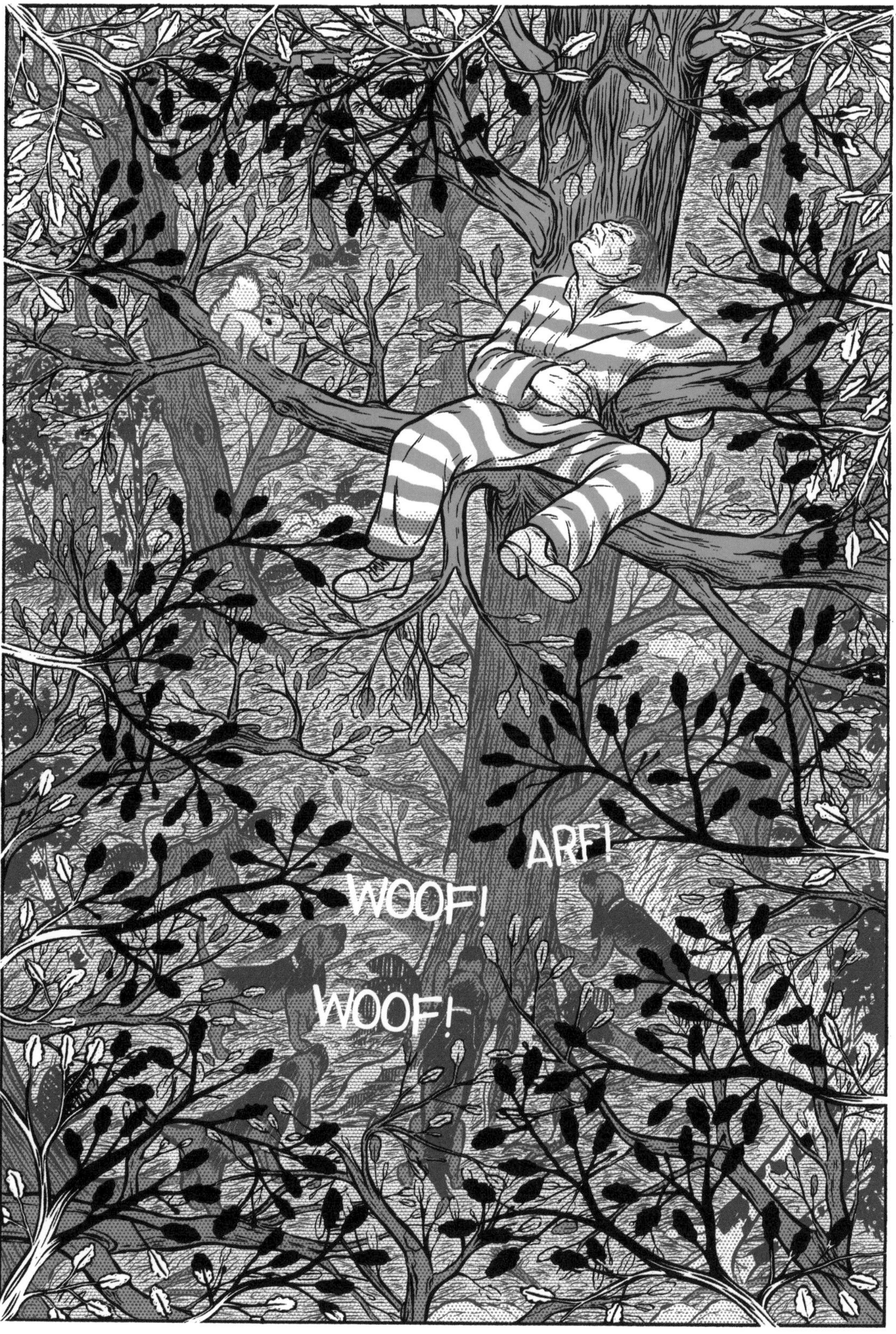
ARF!
WOOF!
WOOF!

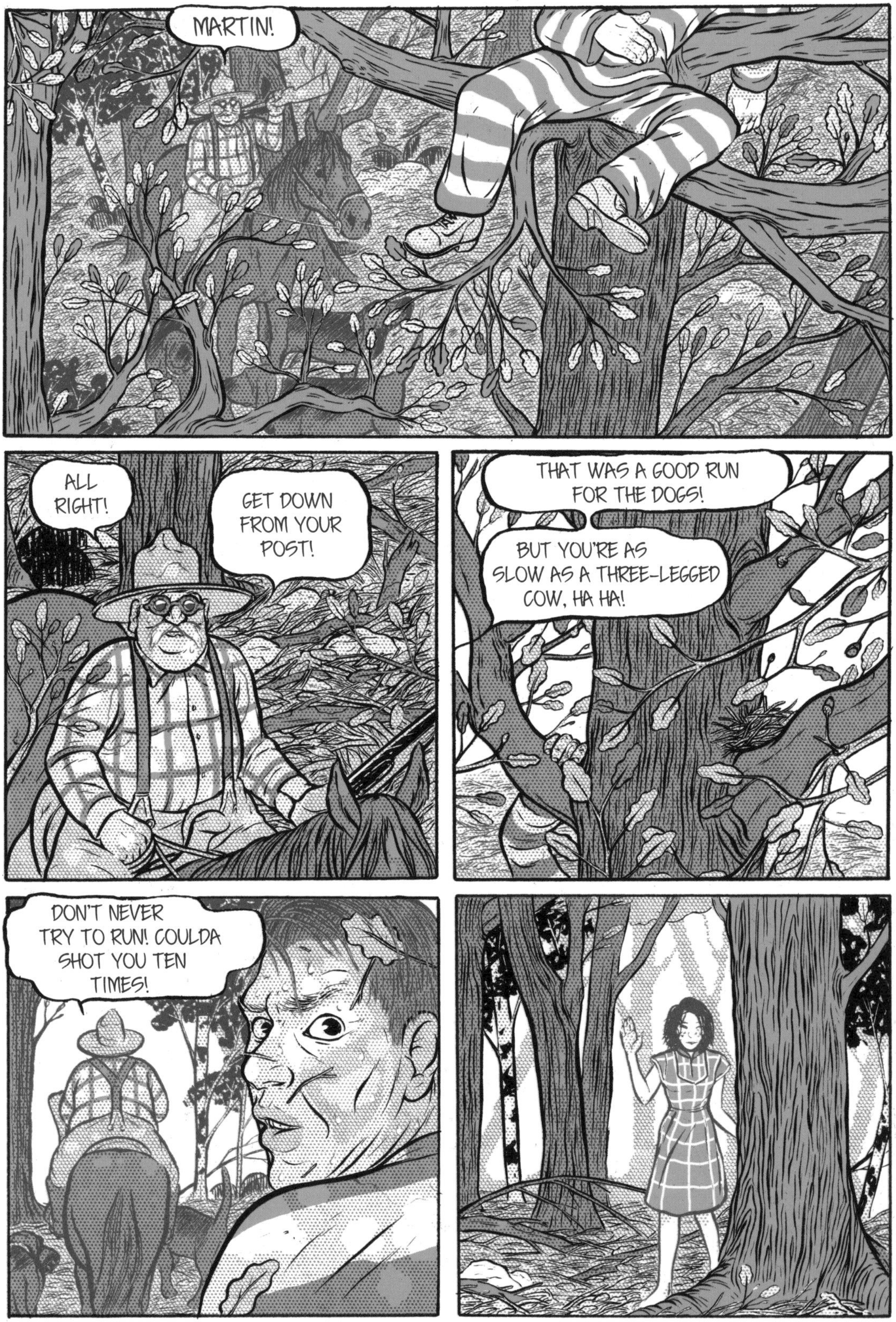
MARTIN!
ALL RIGHT!
GET DOWN FROM YOUR POST!
THAT WAS A GOOD RUN FOR THE DOGS!
BUT YOU'RE AS SLOW AS A THREE-LEGGED COW, HA HA!
DON'T NEVER TRY TO RUN! COULDA SHOT YOU TEN TIMES!

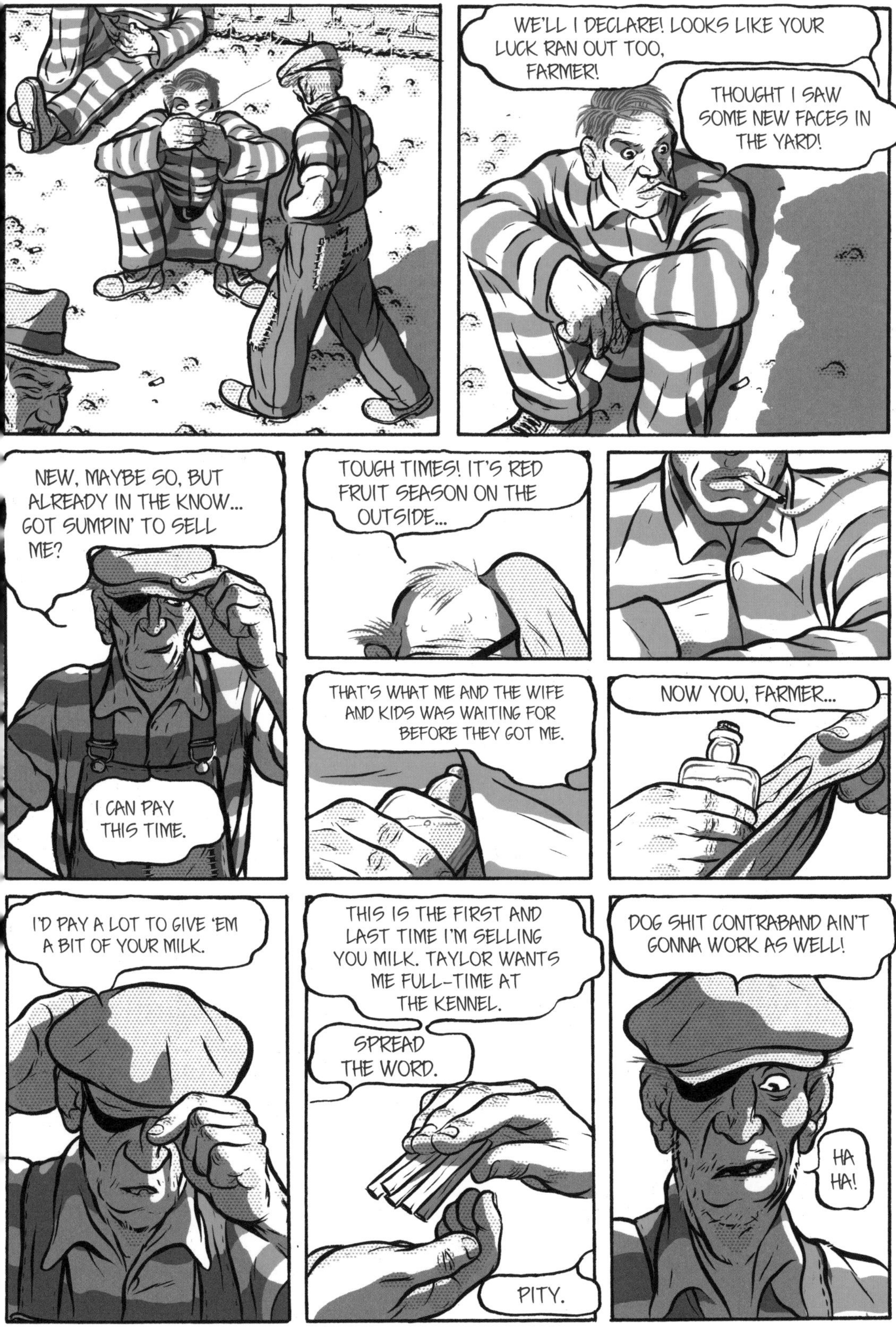
WE'LL I DECLARE! LOOKS LIKE YOUR LUCK RAN OUT TOO, FARMER!
THOUGHT I SAW SOME NEW FACES IN THE YARD!
NEW, MAYBE SO, BUT ALREADY IN THE KNOW... GOT SUMPIN' TO SELL ME?
I CAN PAY THIS TIME.
TOUGH TIMES! IT'S RED FRUIT SEASON ON THE OUTSIDE...
THAT'S WHAT ME AND THE WIFE AND KIDS WAS WAITING FOR BEFORE THEY GOT ME.
NOW YOU, FARMER...
I'D PAY A LOT TO GIVE 'EM A BIT OF YOUR MILK.
THIS IS THE FIRST AND LAST TIME I'M SELLING YOU MILK. TAYLOR WANTS ME FULL-TIME AT THE KENNEL.
SPREAD THE WORD.
PITY.
DOG SHIT CONTRABAND AIN'T GONNA WORK AS WELL!
HA HA!

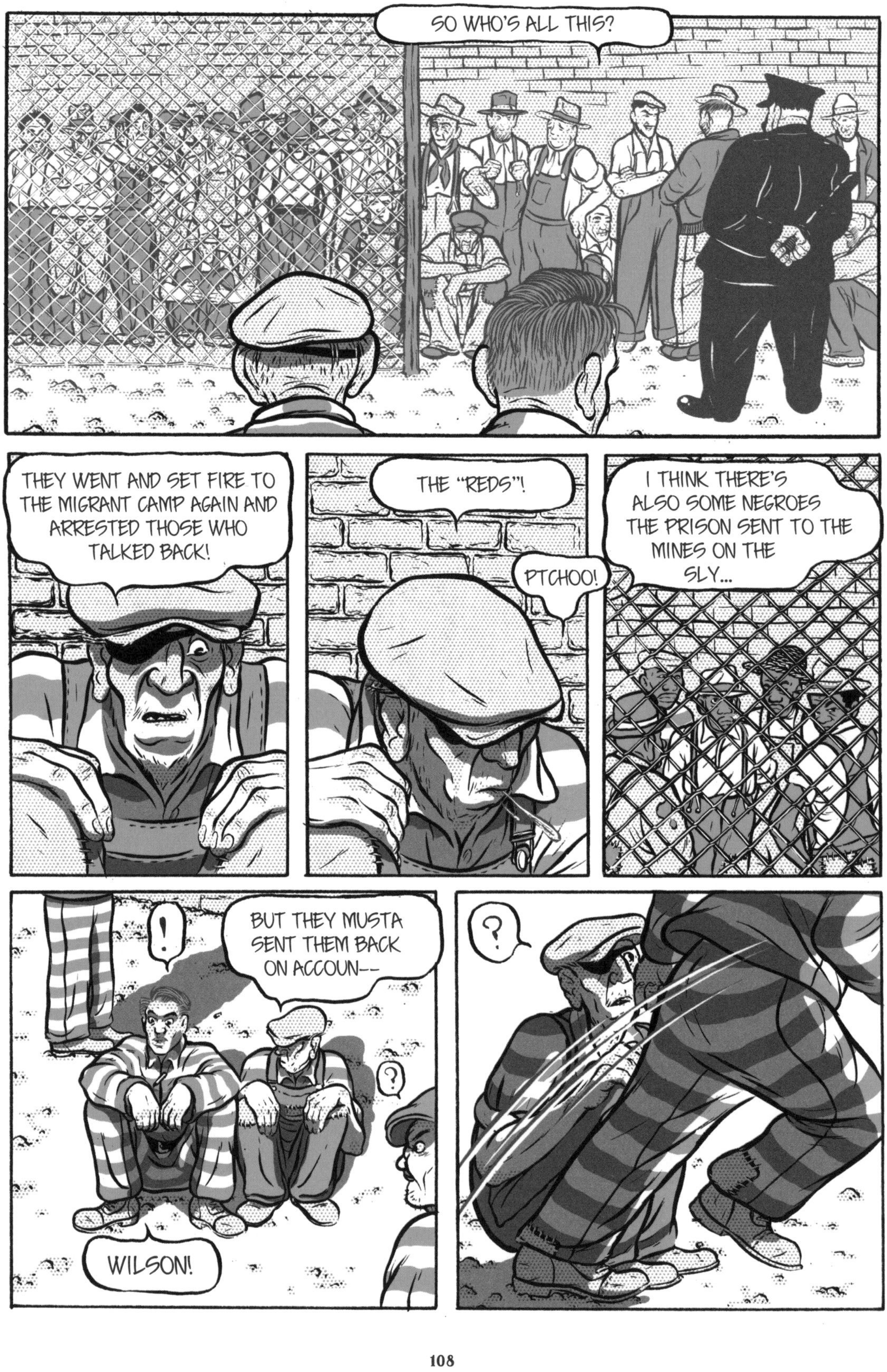
SO WHO'S ALL THIS?
THEY WENT AND SET FIRE TO THE MIGRANT CAMP AGAIN AND ARRESTED THOSE WHO TALKED BACK!
THE "REDS"!
PTCHOO!
I THINK THERE'S ALSO SOME NEGROES THE PRISON SENT TO THE MINES ON THE SLY...
!
BUT THEY MUSTA SENT THEM BACK ON ACCOUN--
?
WILSON!
?

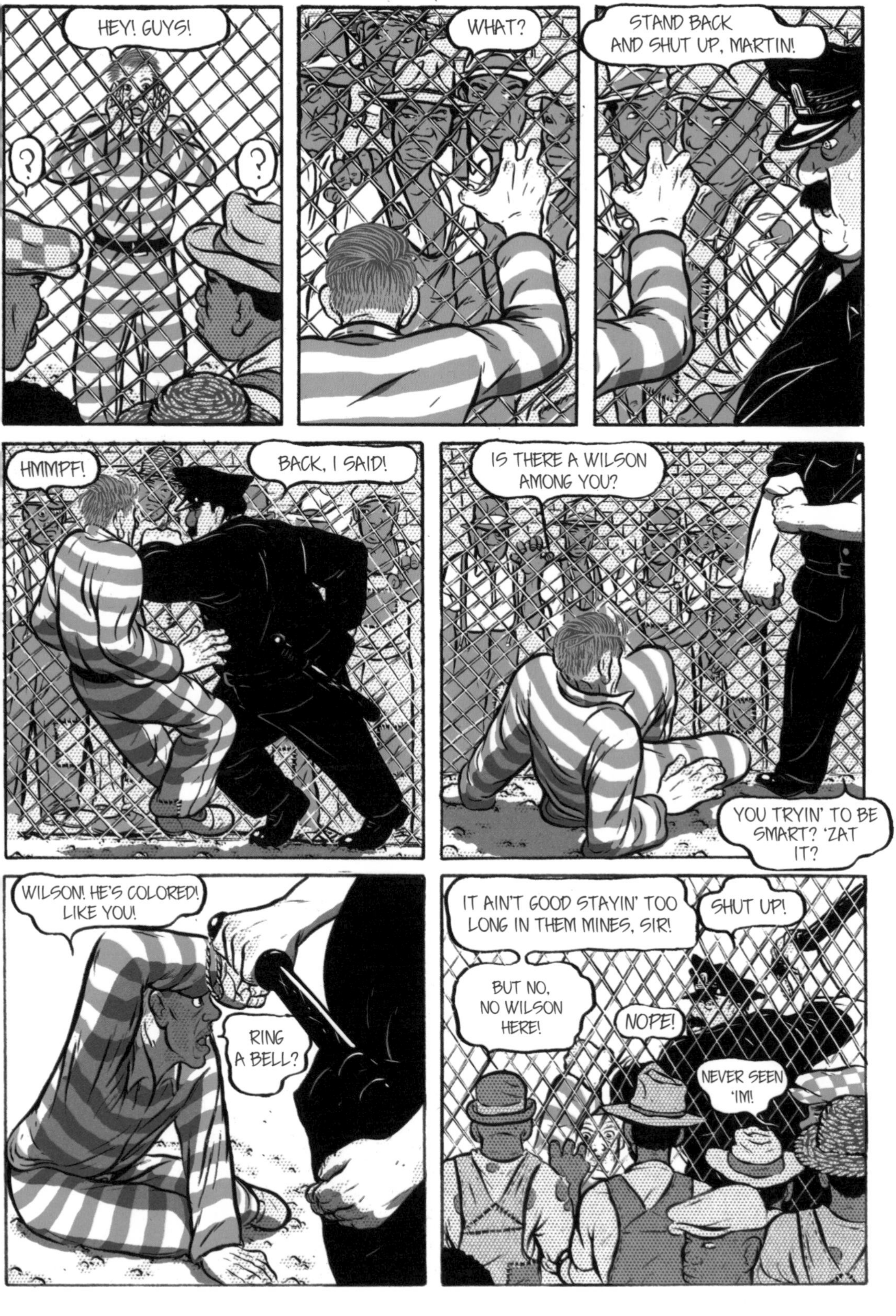
HEY! GUYS!
?
?
WHAT?
STAND BACK
AND SHUT UP, MARTIN!
HMMPF!
BACK, I SAID!
IS THERE A WILSON
AMONG YOU?
YOU TRYIN' TO BE
SMART? 'ZAT
IT?
WILSON! HE'S COLORED!
LIKE YOU!
RING
A BELL?
IT AIN'T GOOD STAYIN' TOO
LONG IN THEM MINES, SIR!
SHUT UP!
BUT NO,
NO WILSON
HERE!
NOPE!
NEVER SEEN
'IM!

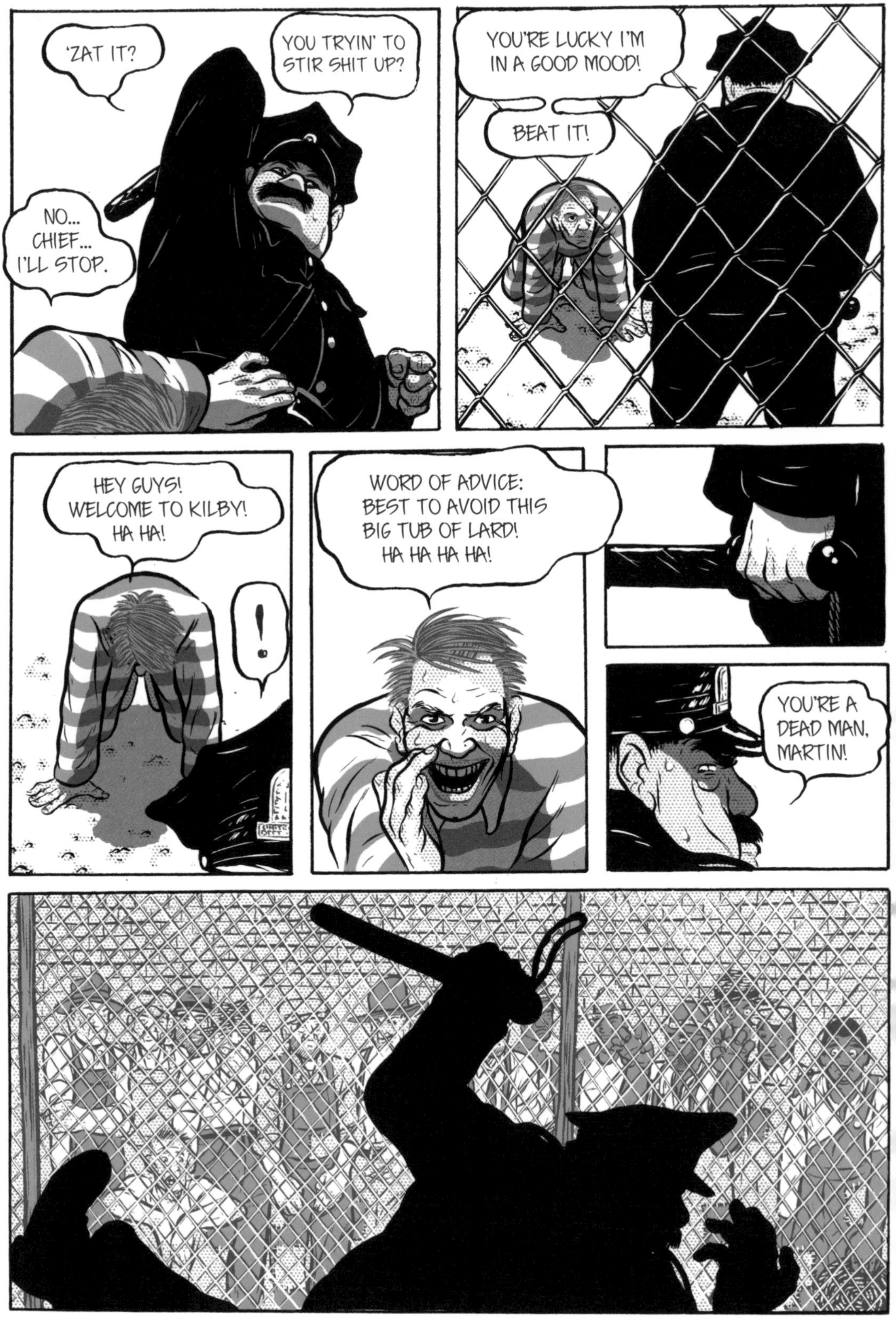
'ZAT IT?
YOU TRYIN' TO STIR SHIT UP?
NO... CHIEF... I'LL STOP.
YOU'RE LUCKY I'M IN A GOOD MOOD!
BEAT IT!
HEY GUYS! WELCOME TO KILBY! HA HA!
!
WORD OF ADVICE: BEST TO AVOID THIS BIG TUB OF LARD! HA HA HA HA!
YOU'RE A DEAD MAN, MARTIN!

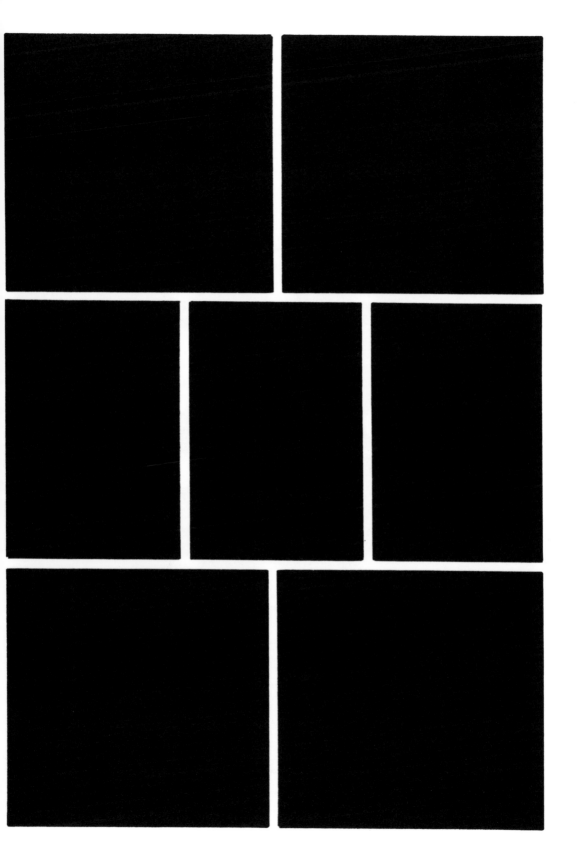

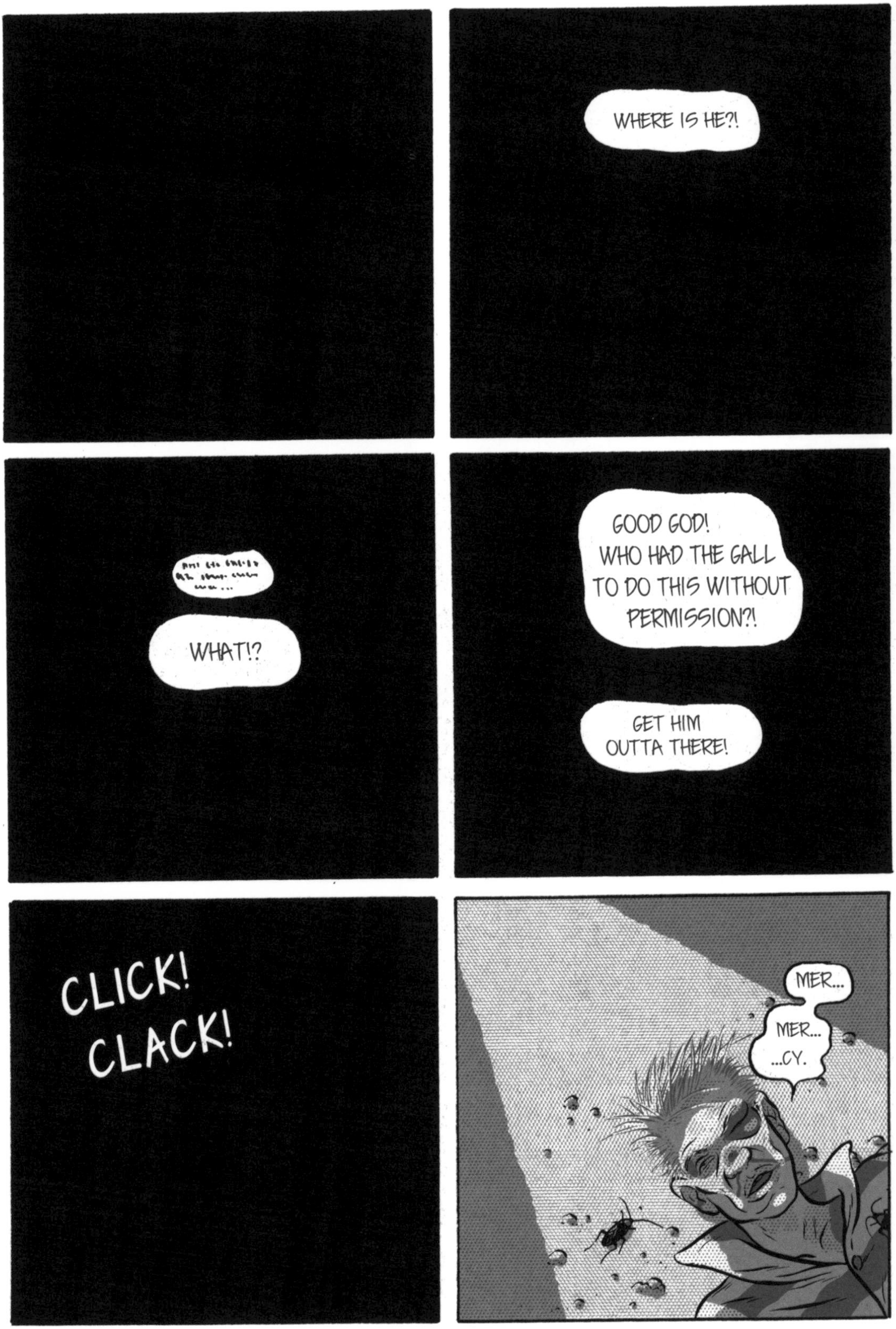
WHERE IS HE?!
WHAT!?
GOOD GOD! WHO HAD THE GALL TO DO THIS WITHOUT PERMISSION?!
GET HIM OUTTA THERE!
CLICK! CLACK!
MER...
MER... ...CY.

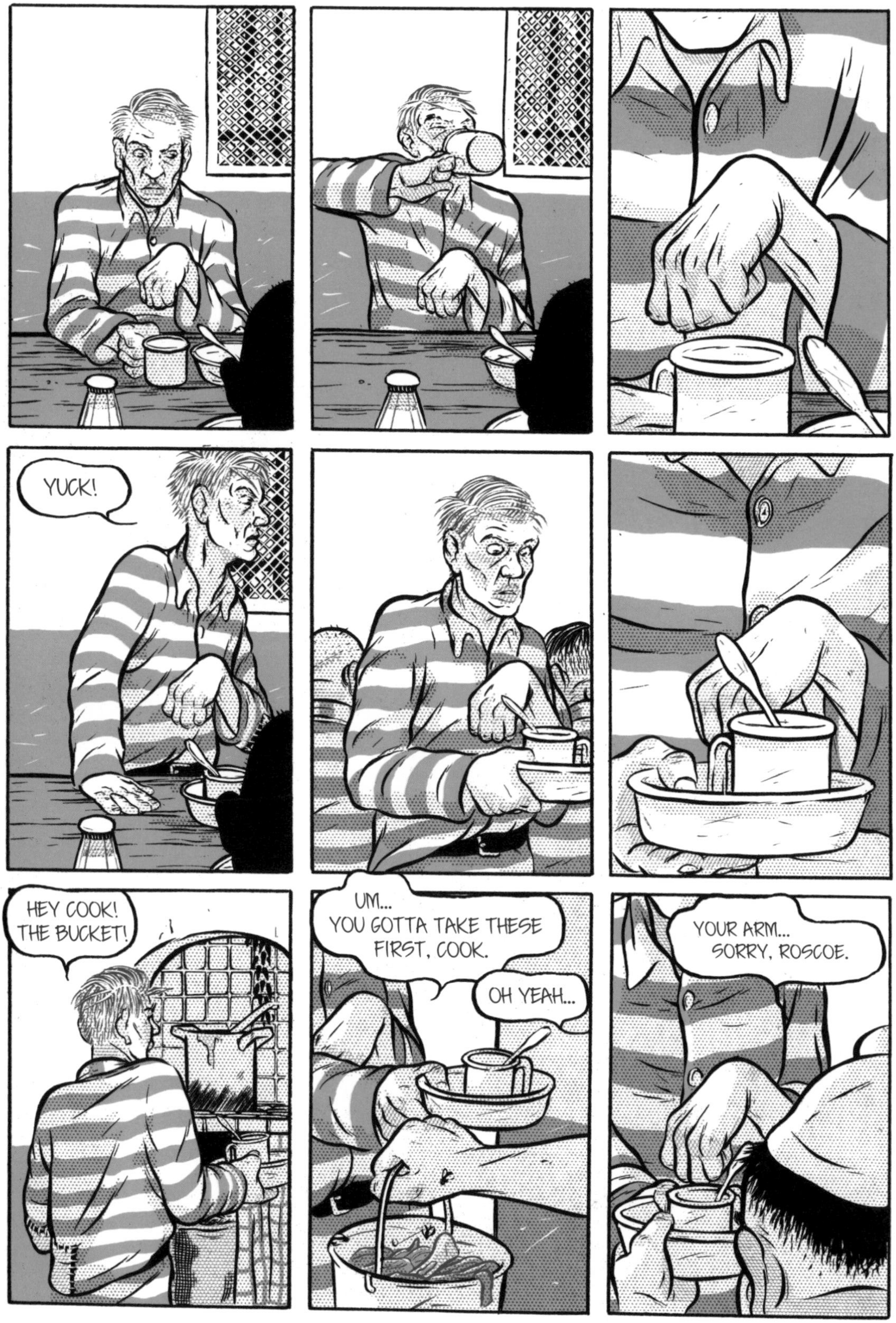
YUCK!
HEY COOK! THE BUCKET!
UM... YOU GOTTA TAKE THESE FIRST, COOK.
OH YEAH...
YOUR ARM... SORRY, ROSCOE.

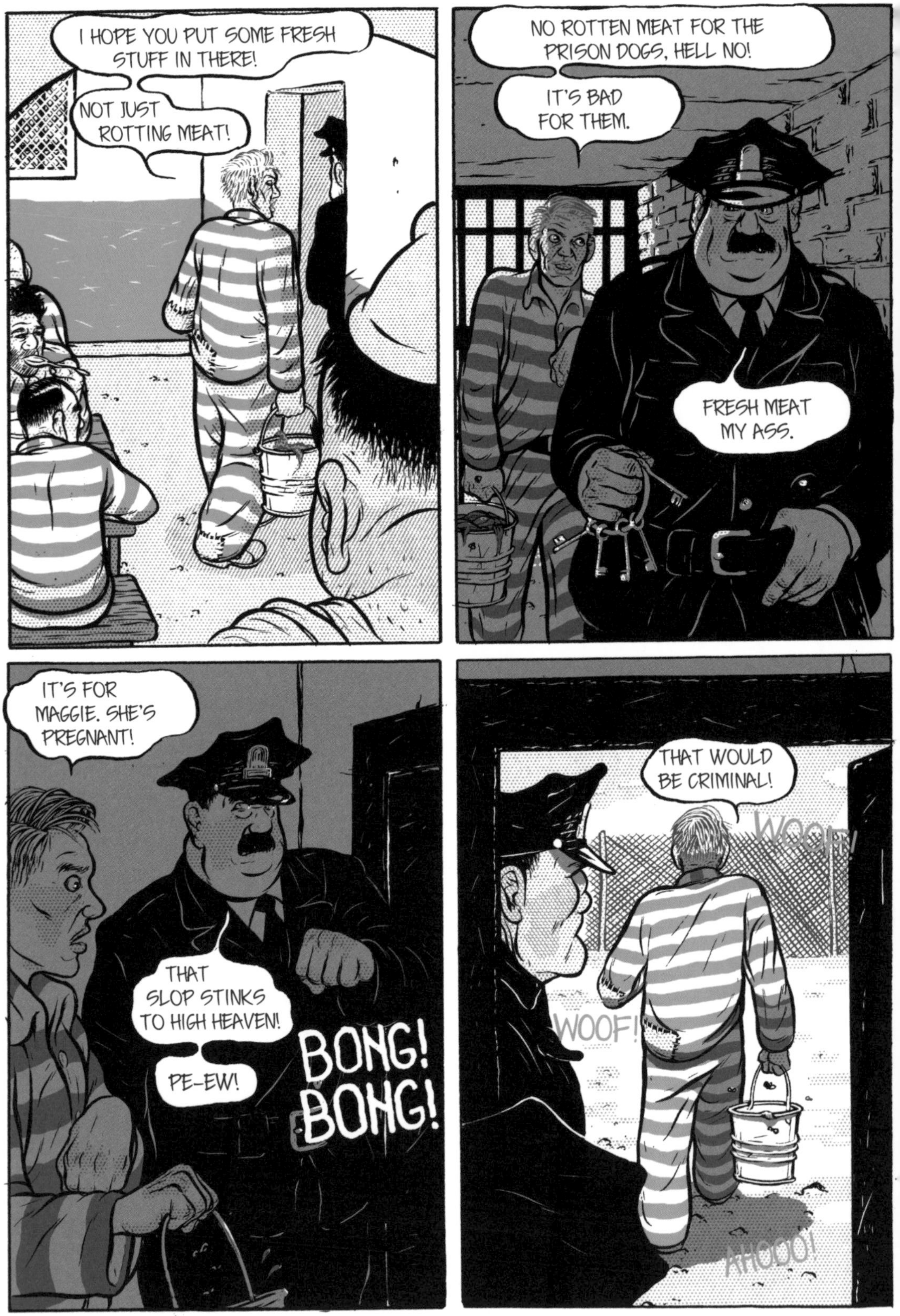
I HOPE YOU PUT SOME FRESH STUFF IN THERE!
NOT JUST ROTTING MEAT!
NO ROTTEN MEAT FOR THE PRISON DOGS, HELL NO!
IT'S BAD FOR THEM.
FRESH MEAT MY ASS.
IT'S FOR MAGGIE. SHE'S PREGNANT!
THAT SLOP STINKS TO HIGH HEAVEN!
PE-EW!
BONG! BONG!
THAT WOULD BE CRIMINAL!
WOOF!
WOOF!
AHOOO!

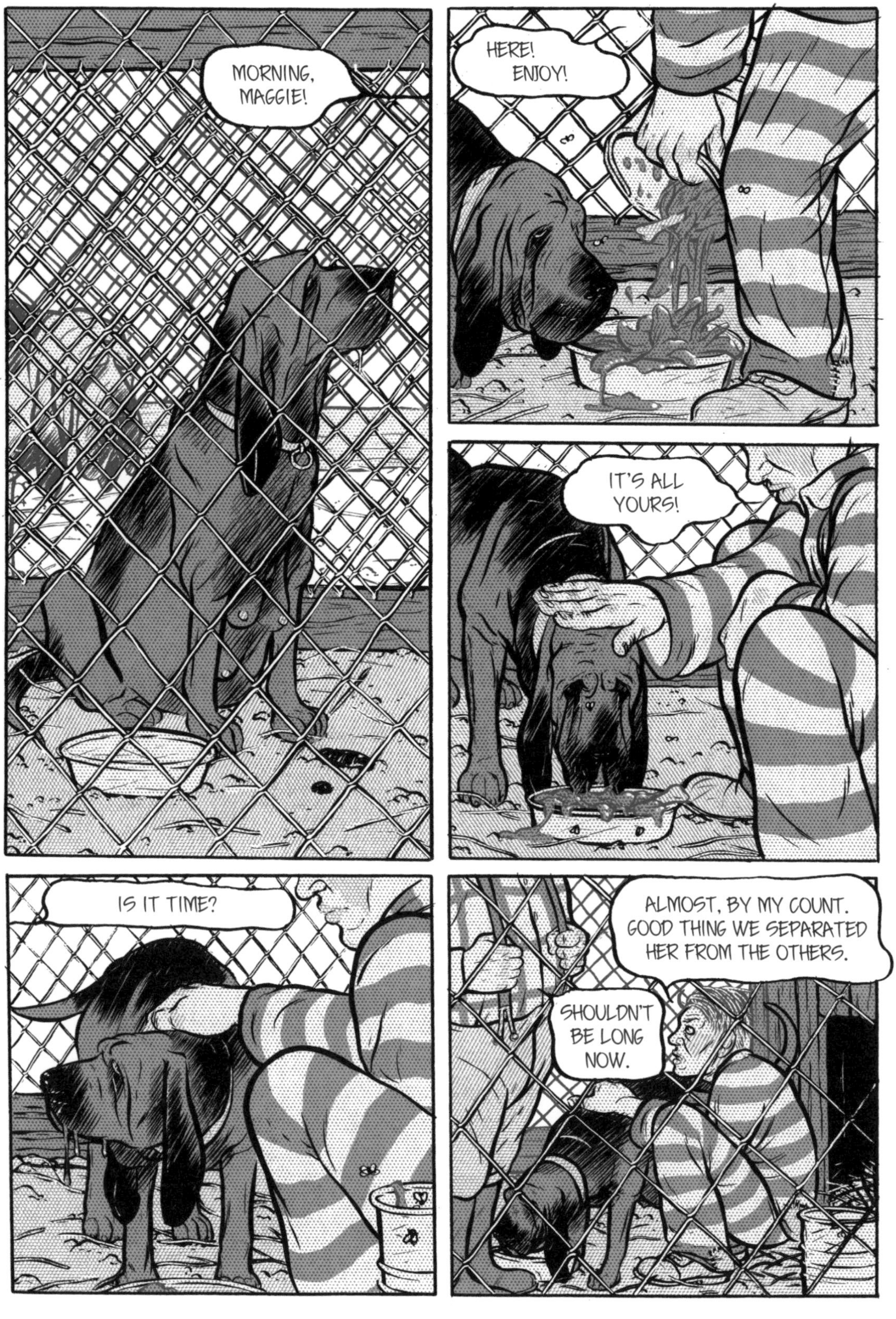
MORNING, MAGGIE!
HERE! ENJOY!
IT'S ALL YOURS!
IS IT TIME?
ALMOST, BY MY COUNT. GOOD THING WE SEPARATED HER FROM THE OTHERS.
SHOULDN'T BE LONG NOW.

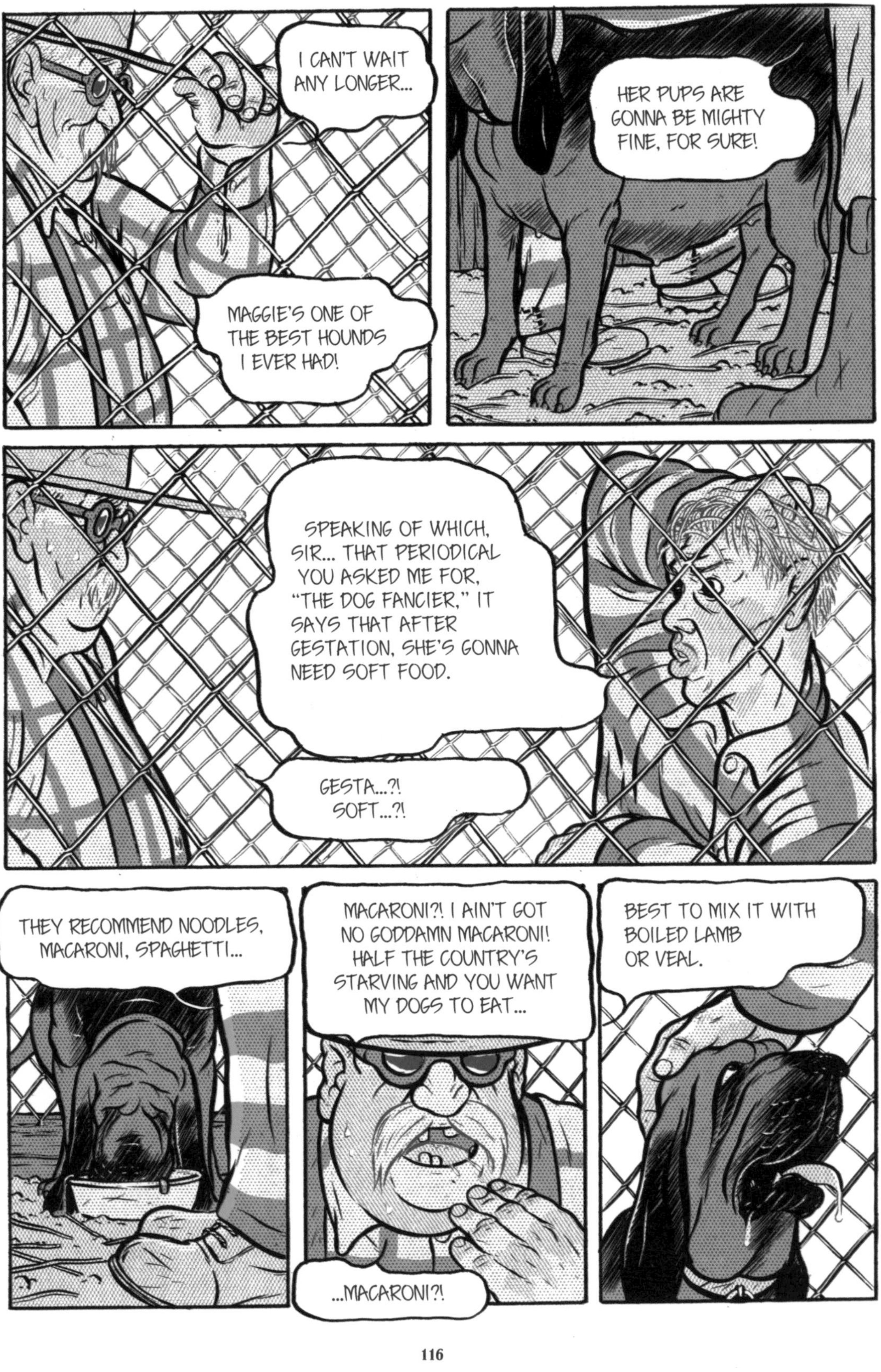
I CAN'T WAIT ANY LONGER...
MAGGIE'S ONE OF THE BEST HOUNDS I EVER HAD!
HER PUPS ARE GONNA BE MIGHTY FINE, FOR SURE!
SPEAKING OF WHICH, SIR... THAT PERIODICAL YOU ASKED ME FOR, "THE DOG FANCIER," IT SAYS THAT AFTER GESTATION, SHE'S GONNA NEED SOFT FOOD.
GESTA...?! SOFT...?!
THEY RECOMMEND NOODLES, MACARONI, SPAGHETTI...
MACARONI?! I AIN'T GOT NO GODDAMN MACARONI! HALF THE COUNTRY'S STARVING AND YOU WANT MY DOGS TO EAT...
...MACARONI?!
BEST TO MIX IT WITH BOILED LAMB OR VEAL.

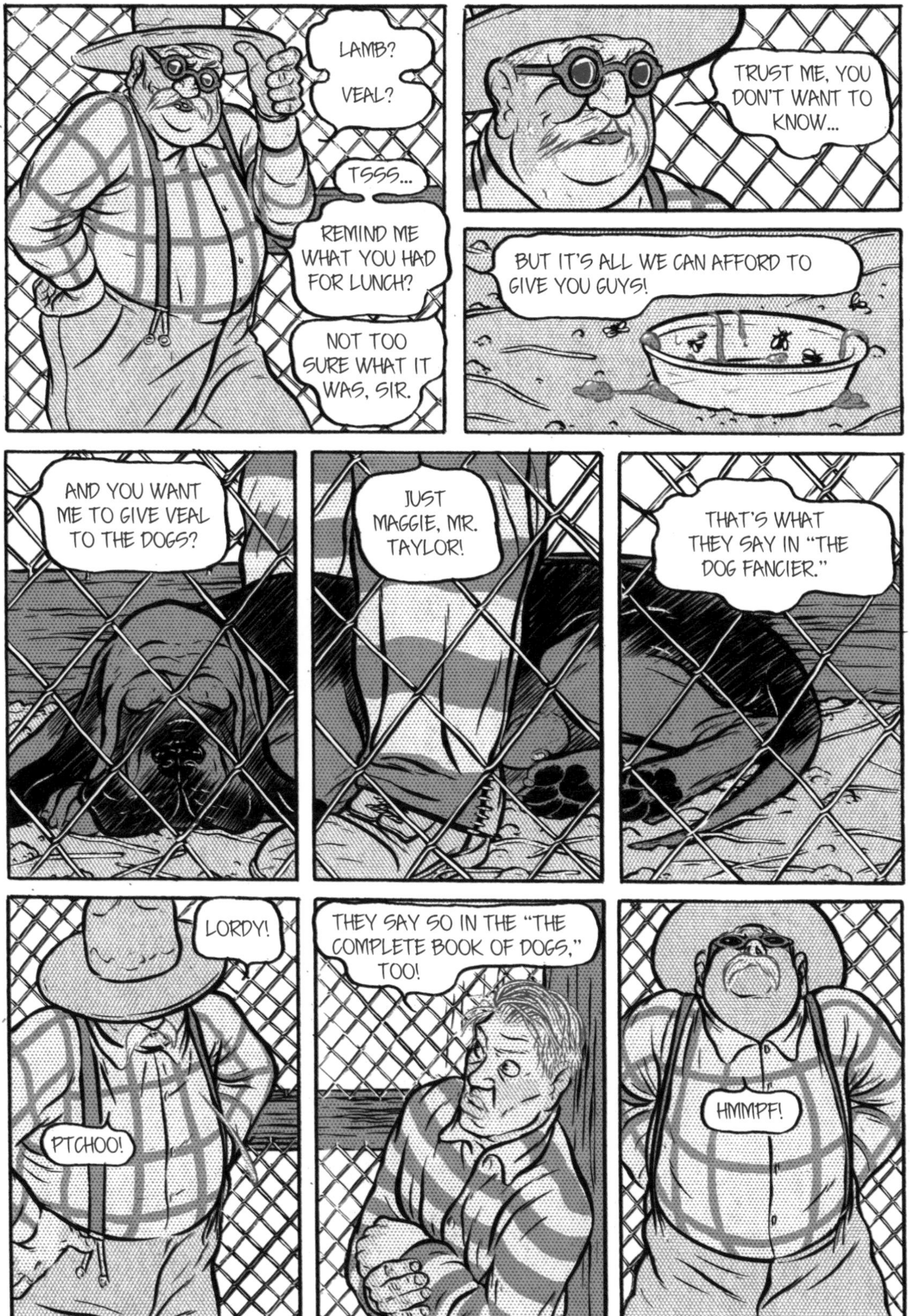
LAMB?
VEAL?
TSSS...
REMIND ME WHAT YOU HAD FOR LUNCH?
NOT TOO SURE WHAT IT WAS, SIR.
TRUST ME, YOU DON'T WANT TO KNOW...
BUT IT'S ALL WE CAN AFFORD TO GIVE YOU GUYS!
AND YOU WANT ME TO GIVE VEAL TO THE DOGS?
JUST MAGGIE, MR. TAYLOR!
THAT'S WHAT THEY SAY IN "THE DOG FANCIER."
LORDY!
PTCHOO!
THEY SAY SO IN THE "THE COMPLETE BOOK OF DOGS," TOO!
HMMPF!

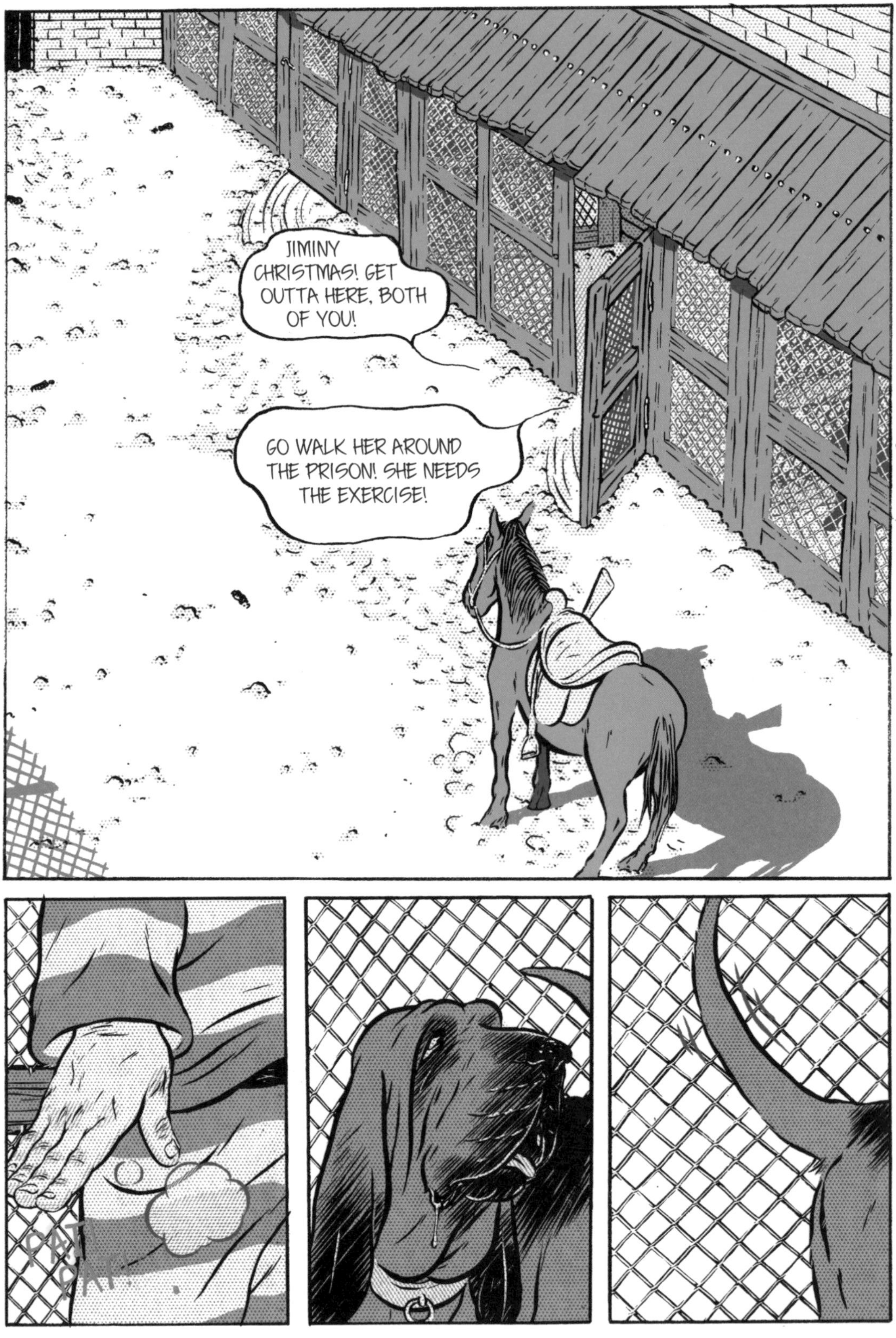
JIMINY CHRISTMAS! GET OUTTA HERE, BOTH OF YOU!
GO WALK HER AROUND THE PRISON! SHE NEEDS THE EXERCISE!
PAT PAT!

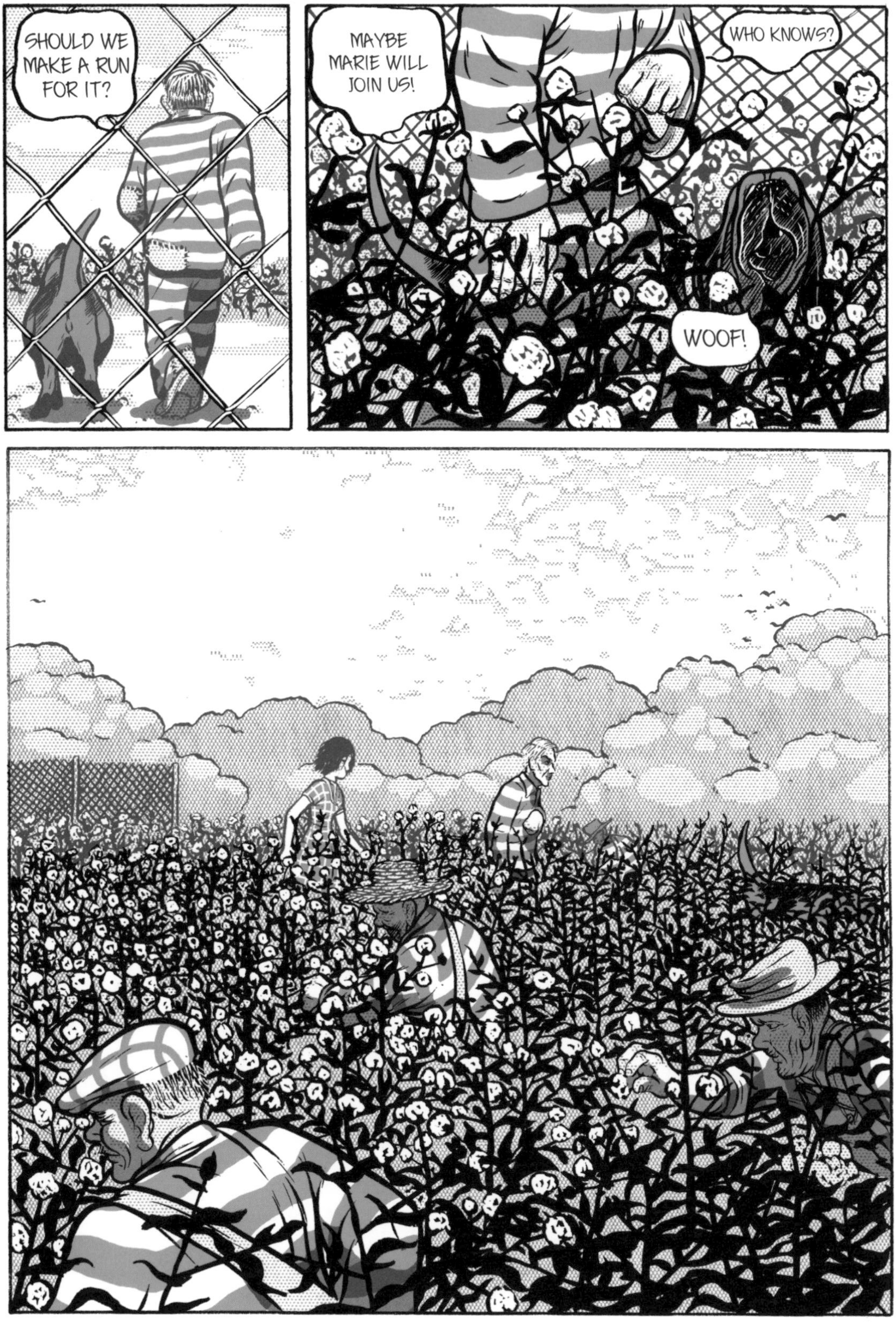
SHOULD WE MAKE A RUN FOR IT?
MAYBE MARIE WILL JOIN US!
WHO KNOWS?
WOOF!

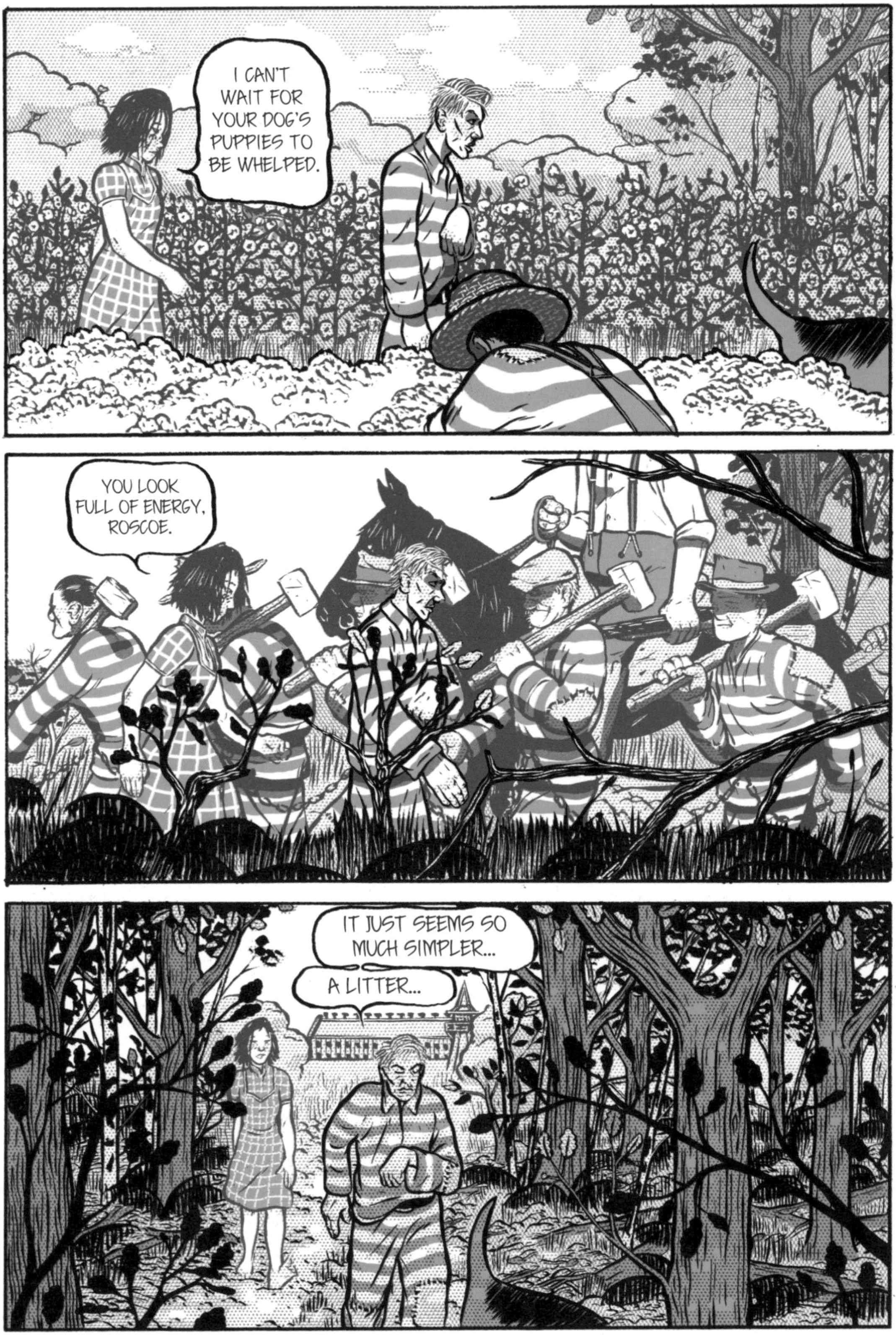
I CAN'T WAIT FOR YOUR DOG'S PUPPIES TO BE WHELPED.
YOU LOOK FULL OF ENERGY, ROSCOE.
IT JUST SEEMS SO MUCH SIMPLER...
A LITTER...

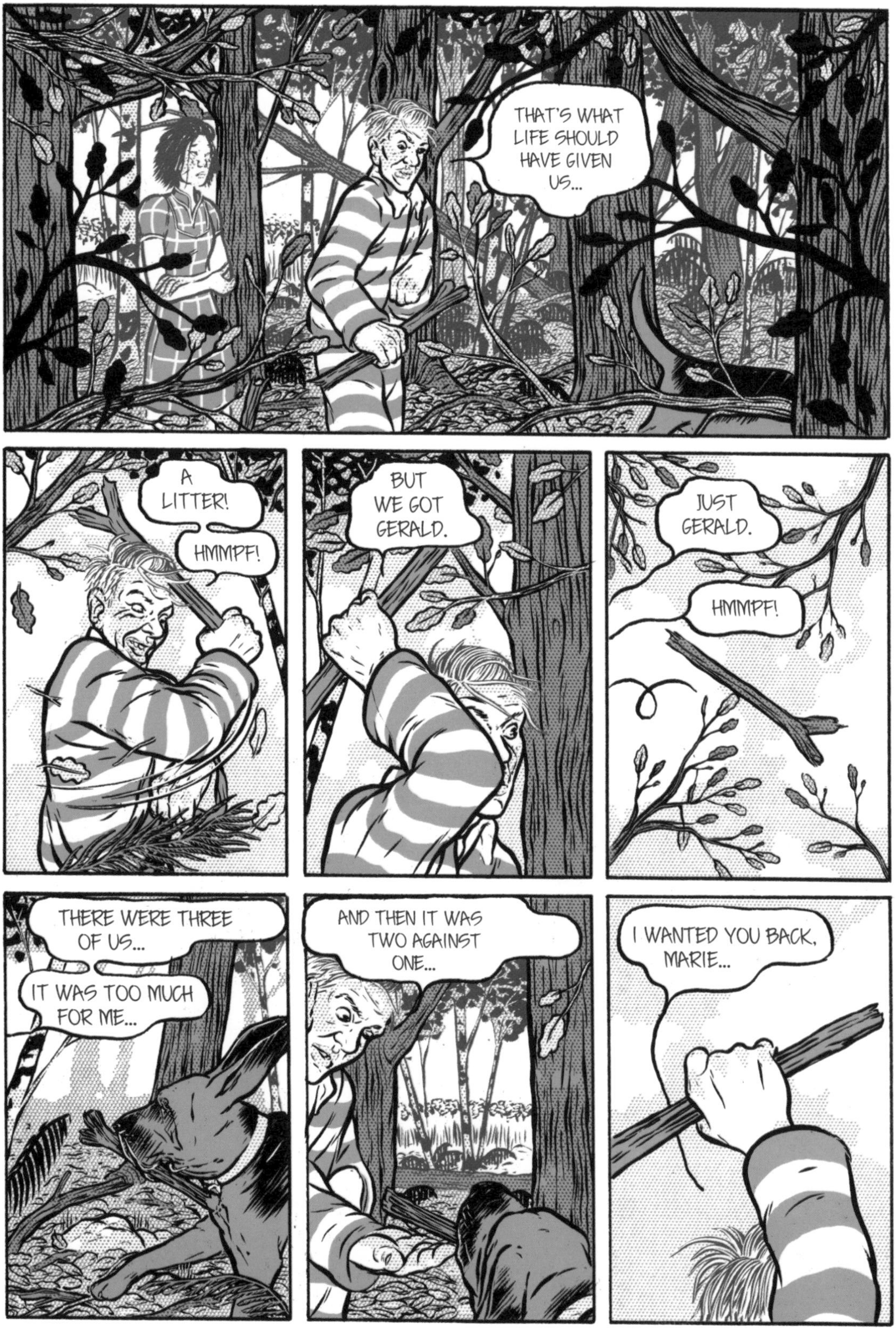
THAT'S WHAT LIFE SHOULD HAVE GIVEN US...
A LITTER!
HMMPF!
BUT WE GOT GERALD.
JUST GERALD.
HMMPF!
THERE WERE THREE OF US...
IT WAS TOO MUCH FOR ME...
AND THEN IT WAS TWO AGAINST ONE...
I WANTED YOU BACK, MARIE...

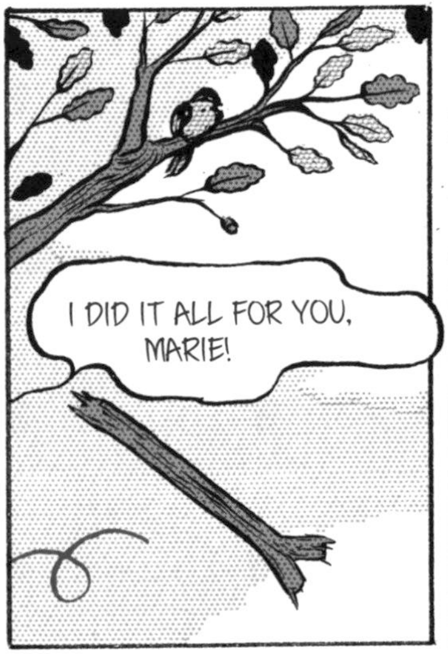
I DID IT ALL FOR YOU, MARIE!

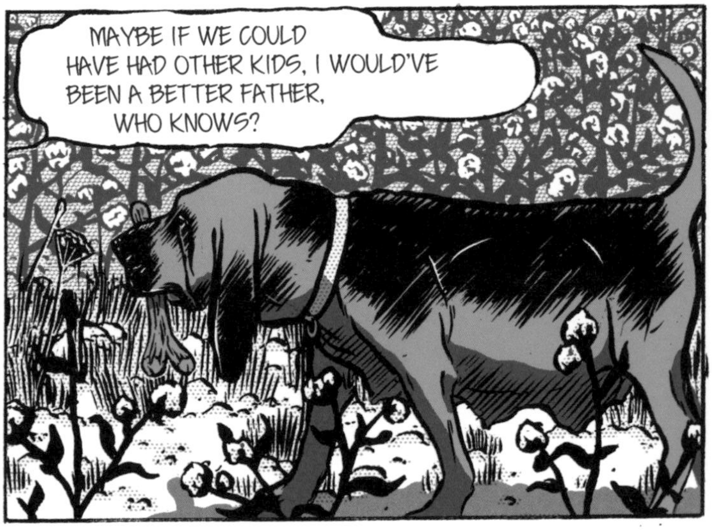
MAYBE IF WE COULD HAVE HAD OTHER KIDS, I WOULD'VE BEEN A BETTER FATHER, WHO KNOWS?

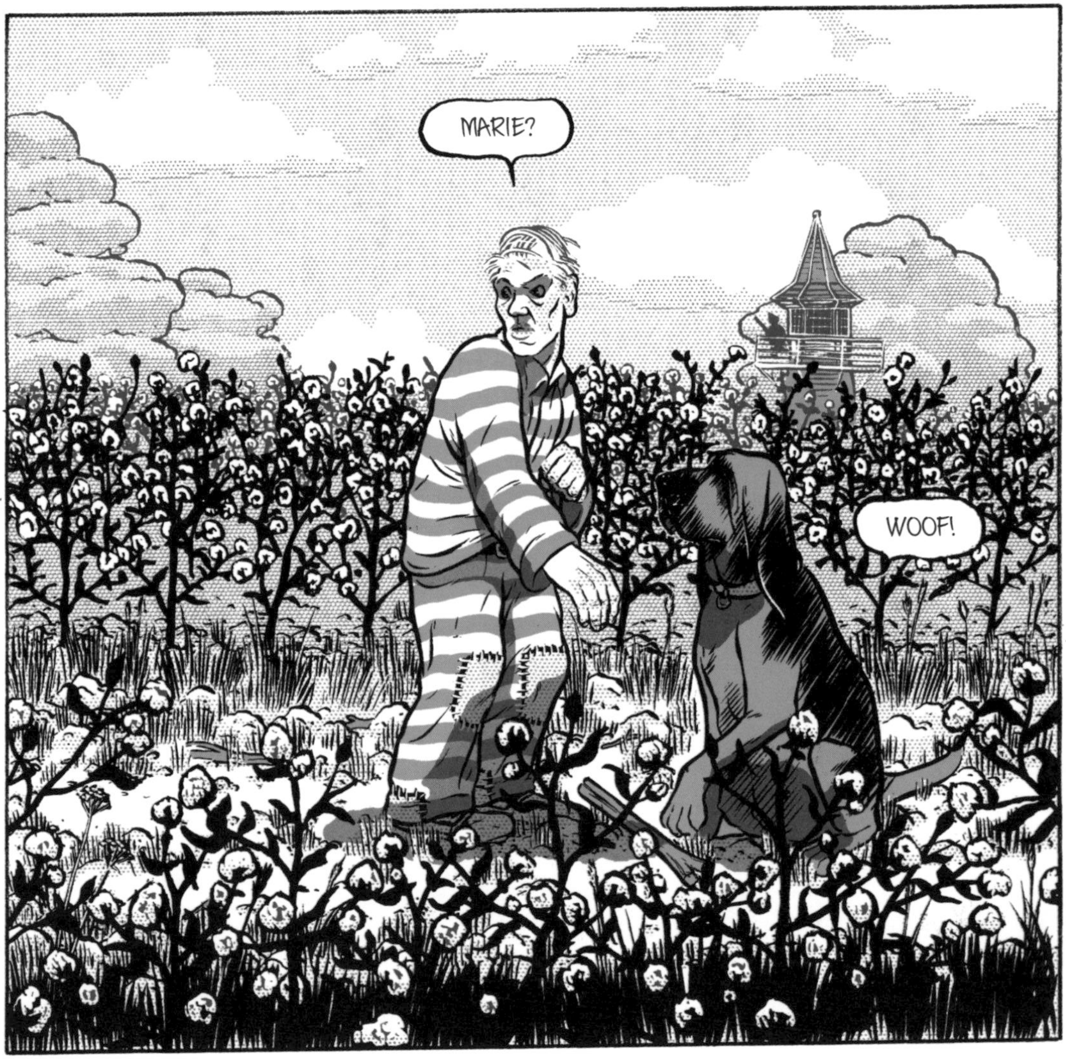
MARIE?
WOOF!

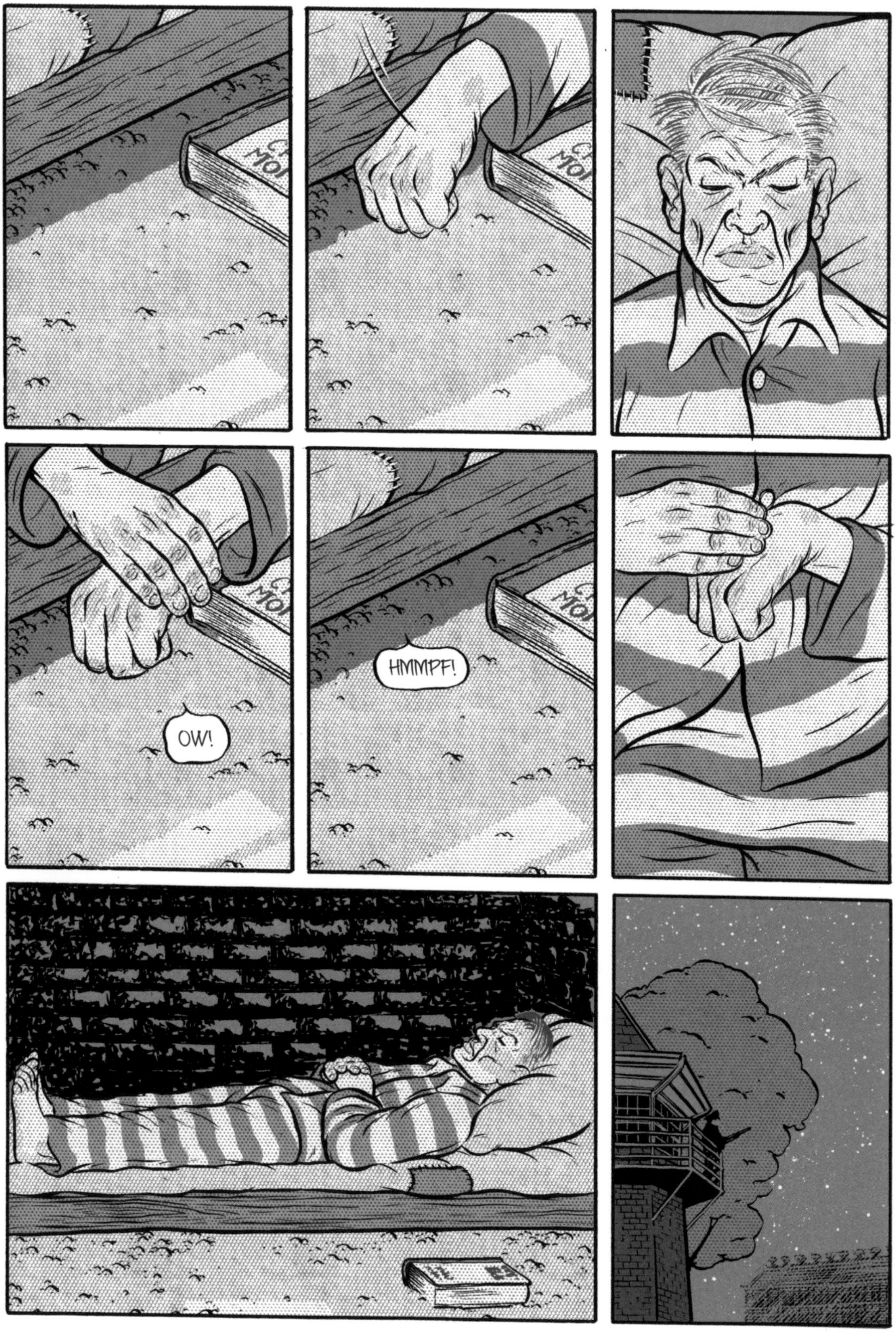
OW!
HMMPF!

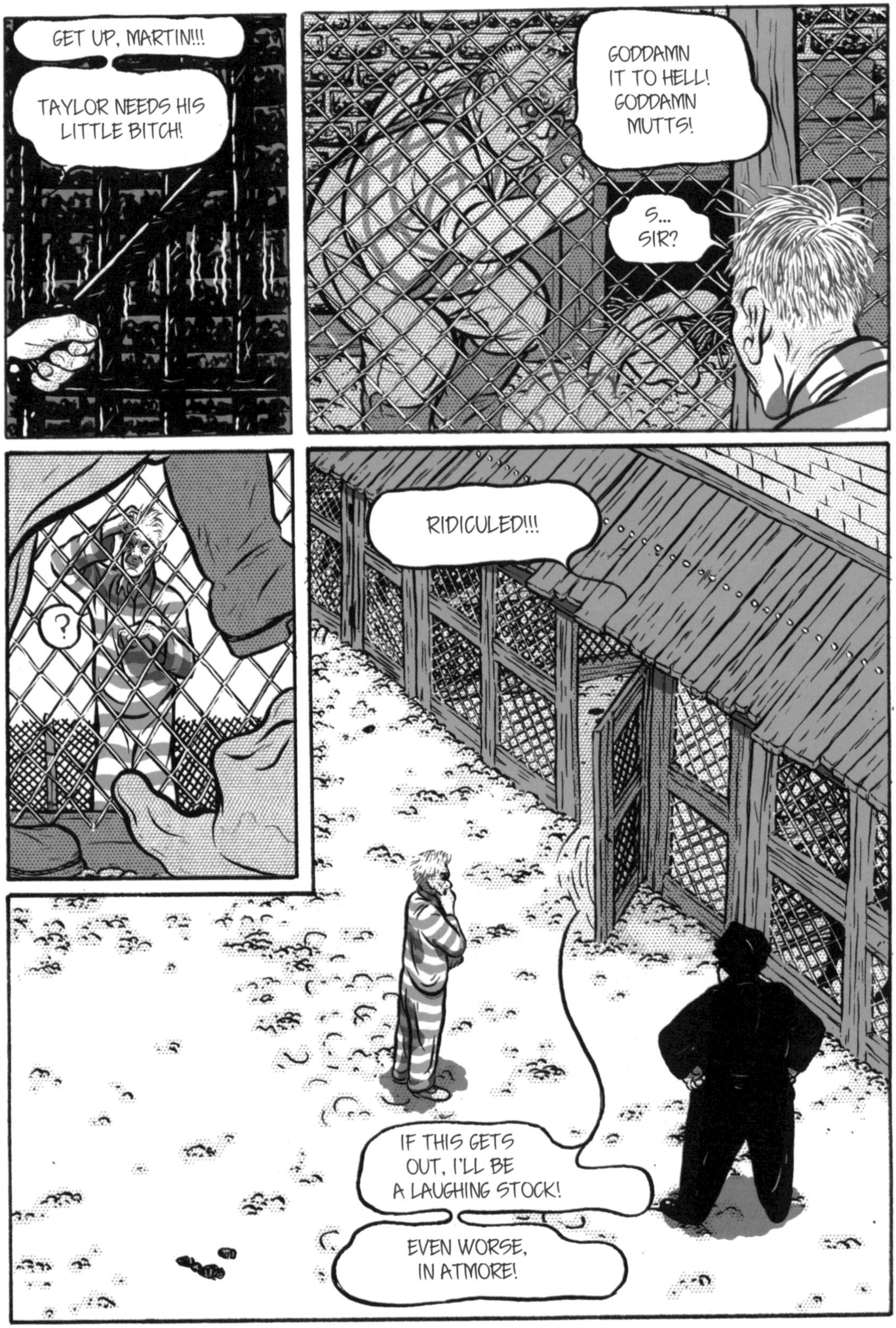
GET UP, MARTIN!!!
TAYLOR NEEDS HIS LITTLE BITCH!
GODDAMN IT TO HELL! GODDAMN MUTTS!
S... SIR?
?
RIDICULED!!!
IF THIS GETS OUT, I'LL BE A LAUGHING STOCK!
EVEN WORSE, IN ATMORE!

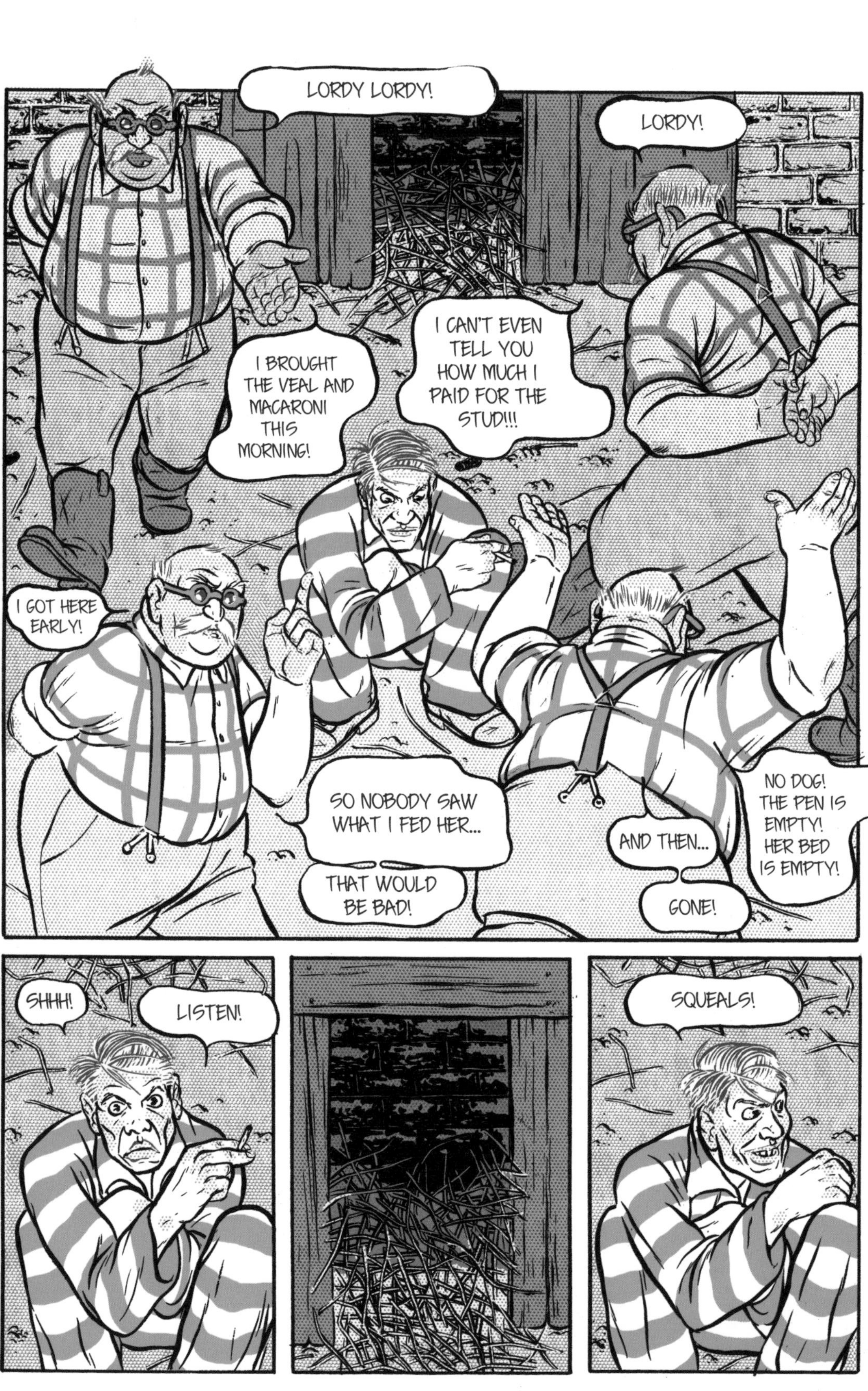
LORDY LORDY!
LORDY!
I BROUGHT THE VEAL AND MACARONI THIS MORNING!
I CAN'T EVEN TELL YOU HOW MUCH I PAID FOR THE STUD!!!
I GOT HERE EARLY!
SO NOBODY SAW WHAT I FED HER...
THAT WOULD BE BAD!
AND THEN...
GONE!
NO DOG! THE PEN IS EMPTY! HER BED IS EMPTY!
SHHH!
LISTEN!
SQUEALS!

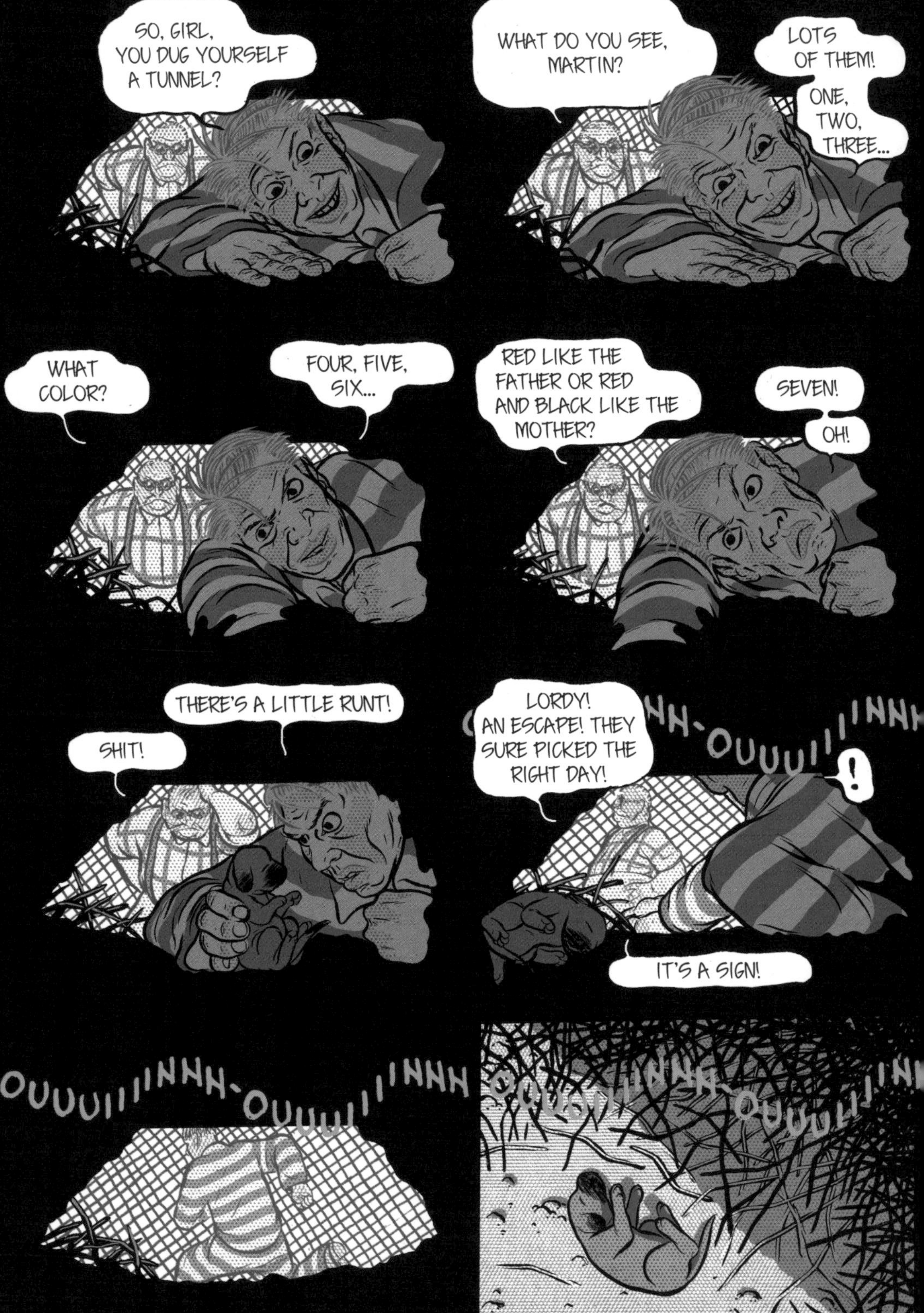
SO, GIRL, YOU DUG YOURSELF A TUNNEL?
WHAT DO YOU SEE, MARTIN?
LOTS OF THEM!
ONE, TWO, THREE...
WHAT COLOR?
FOUR, FIVE, SIX...
RED LIKE THE FATHER OR RED AND BLACK LIKE THE MOTHER?
SEVEN!
OH!
THERE'S A LITTLE RUNT!
SHIT!
LORDY! AN ESCAPE! THEY SURE PICKED THE RIGHT DAY!
!
IT'S A SIGN!
OUUUI'''NNH-OUUUI'''NNH

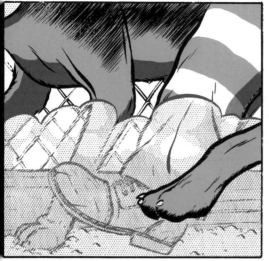

APPARENTLY, TWO GUYS WERE MISSING AT ROLL CALL!

A NEW GUY AND REED.

REED...

AIN'T THAT THE SCUM THAT STABBED YOU?

YEP.

OK, LISTEN UP GUYS!

THE TRAIL STARTS ON THE CORNFIELD! TAKE THE DOGS AND GO! I'M GETTING MY HORSE!

ARF!

AHOO!

ARF!

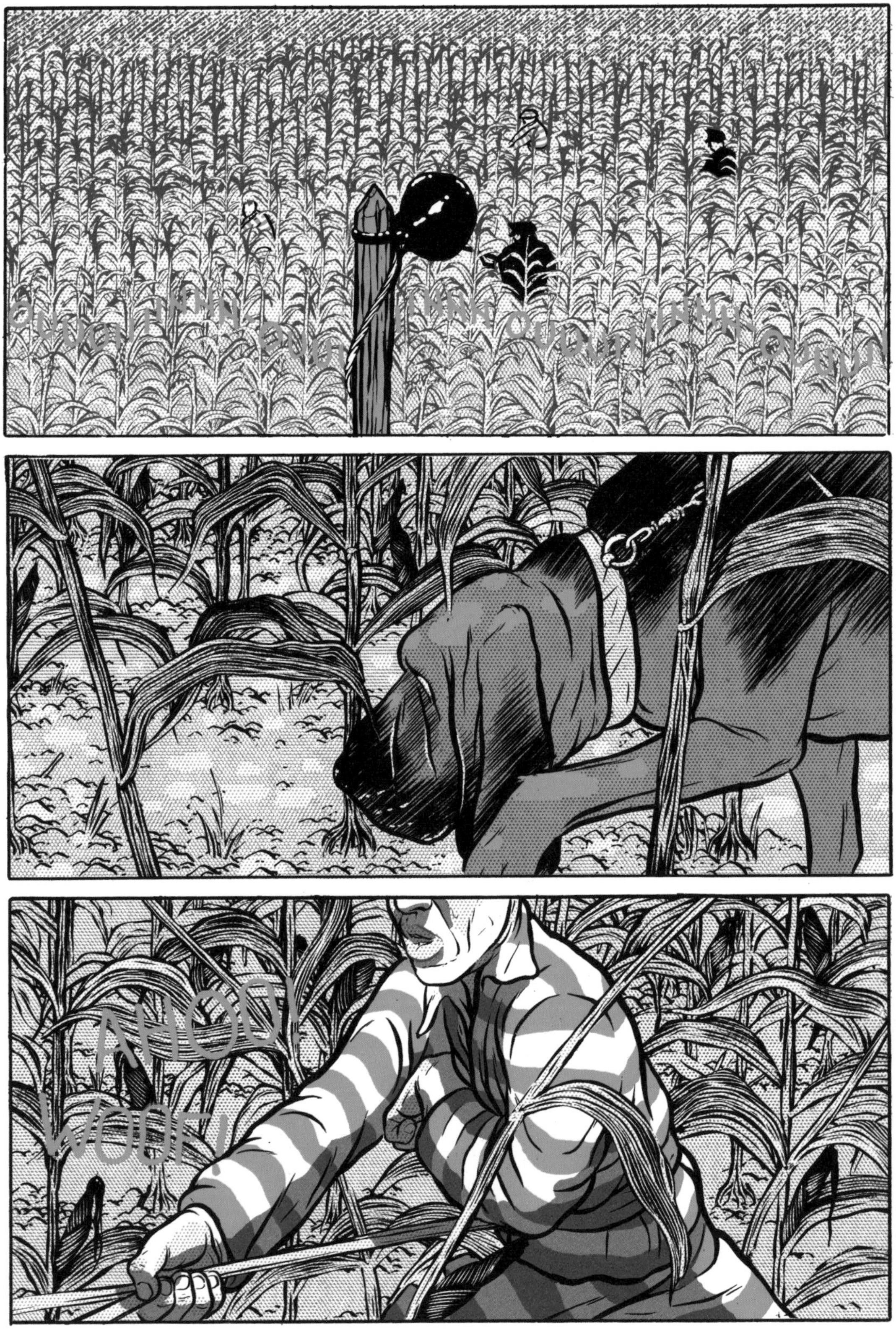
AHOO!
WOOF!

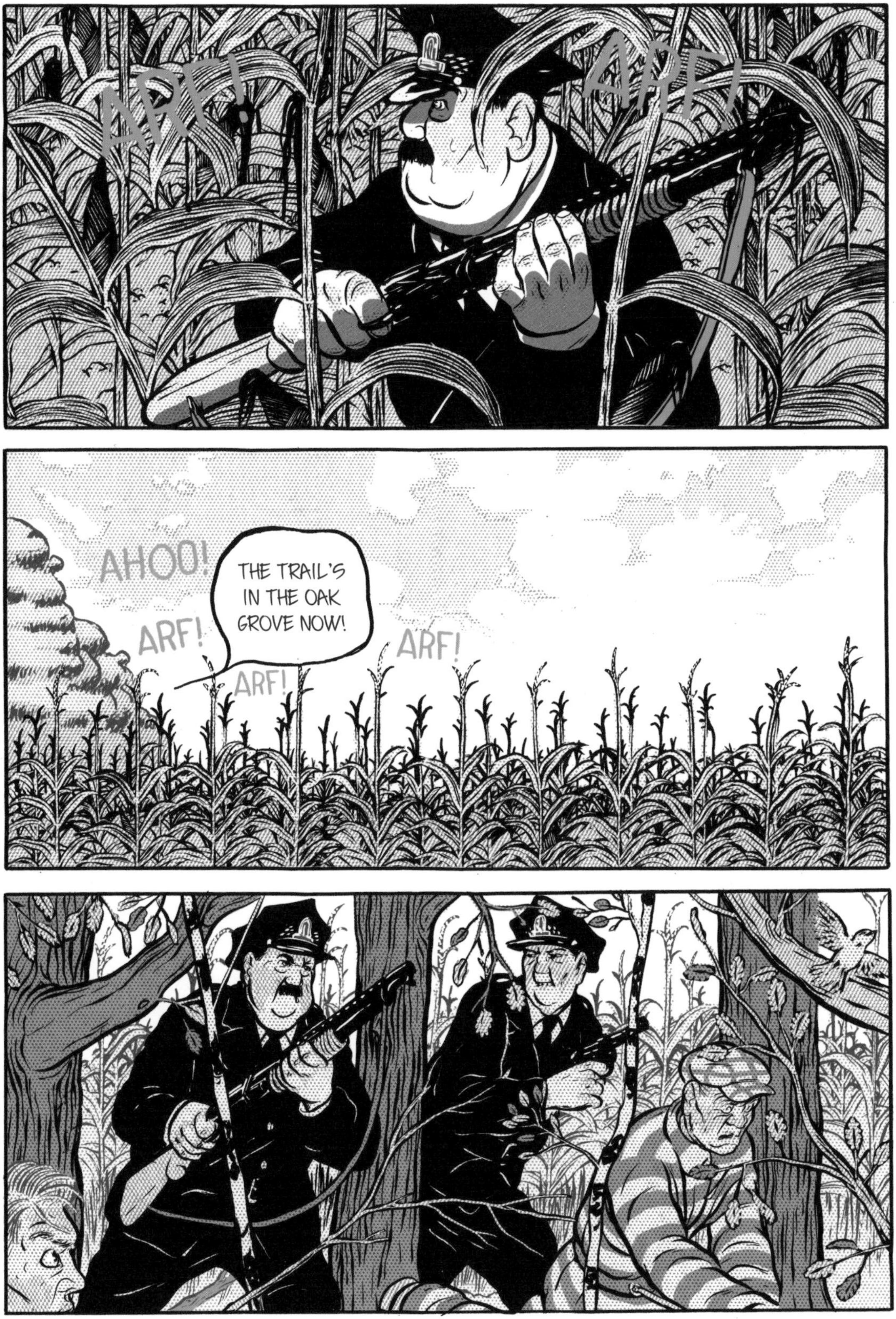
ARF!
ARF!
AHOO!
ARF!
THE TRAIL'S IN THE OAK GROVE NOW!
ARF!
ARF!

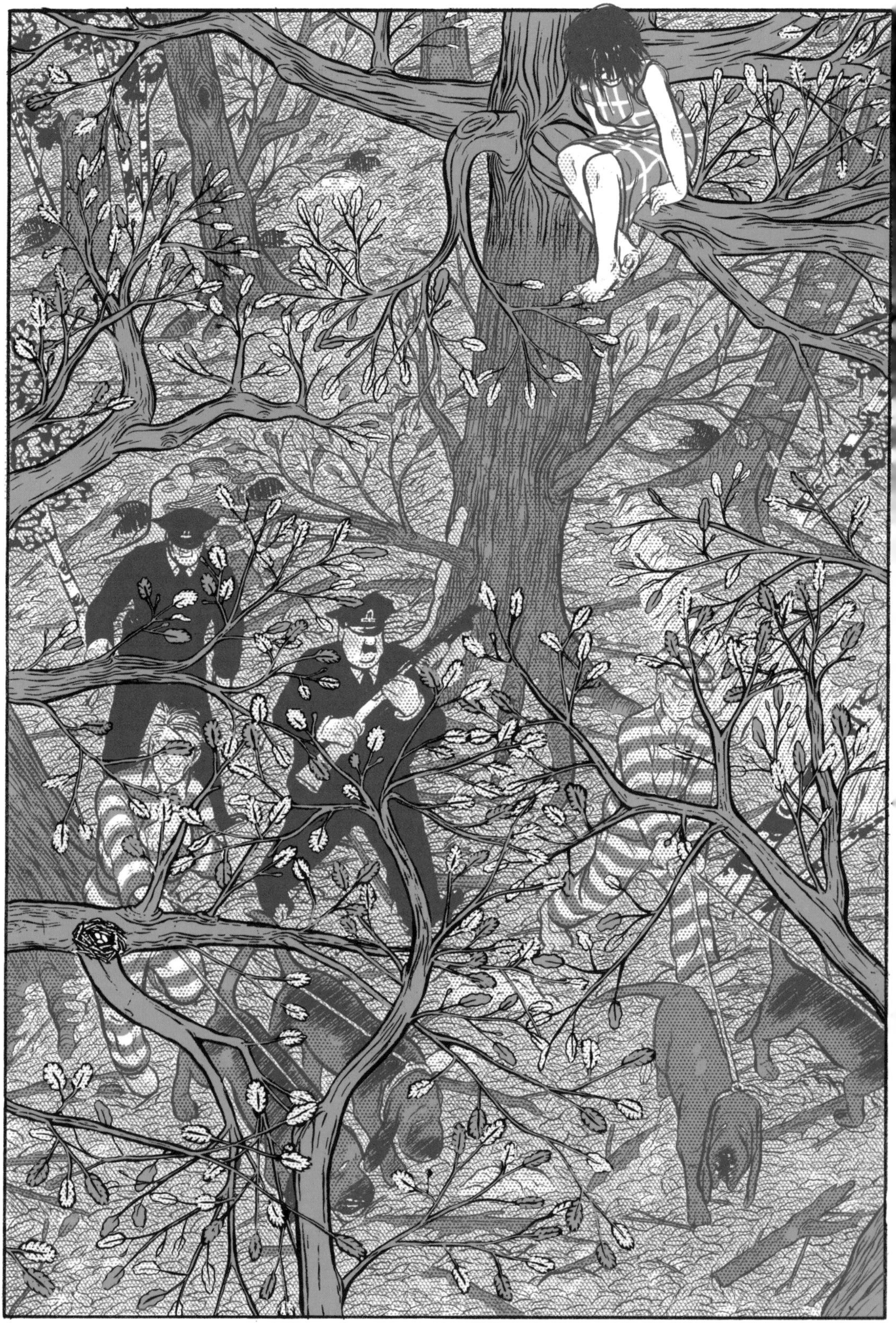

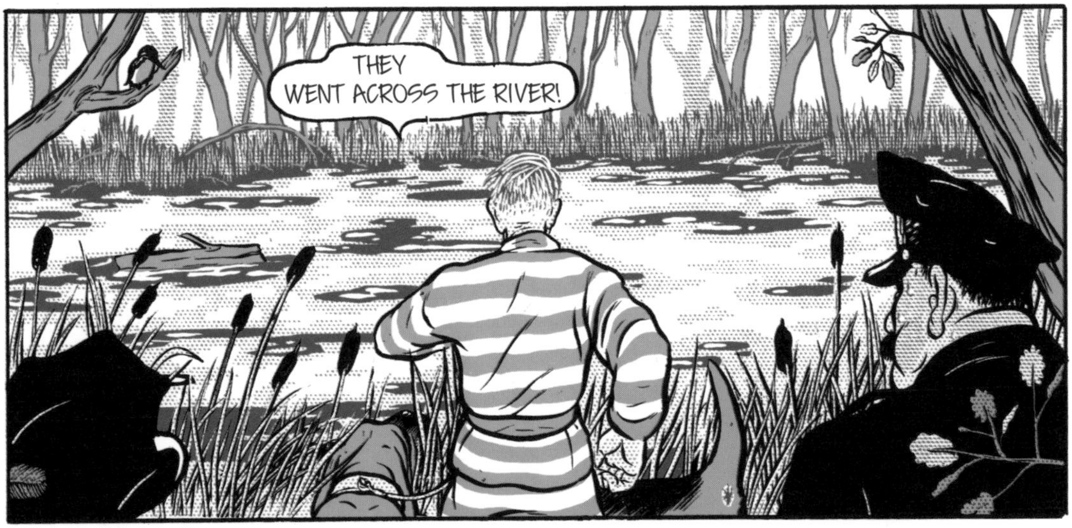
THEY WENT ACROSS THE RIVER!

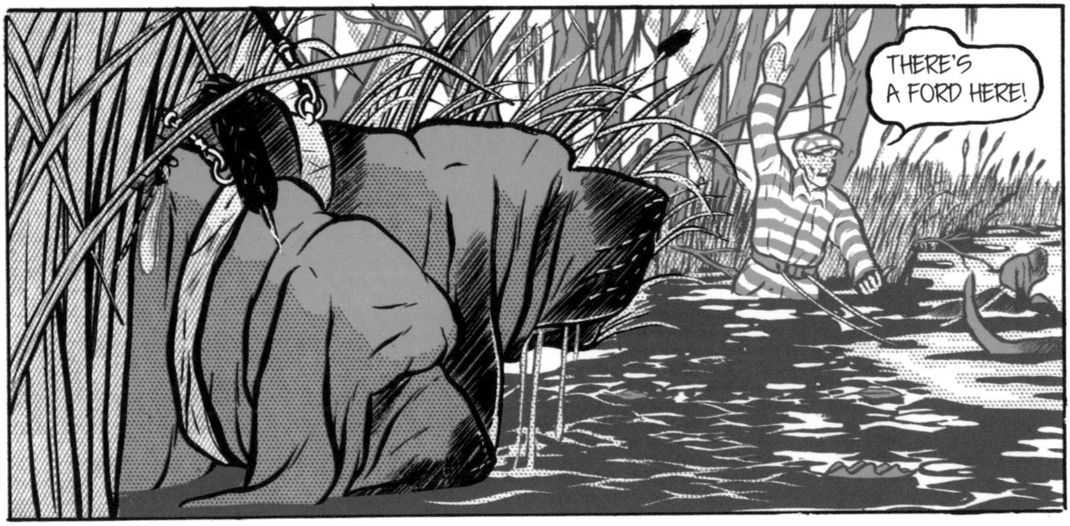
THERE'S A FORD HERE!

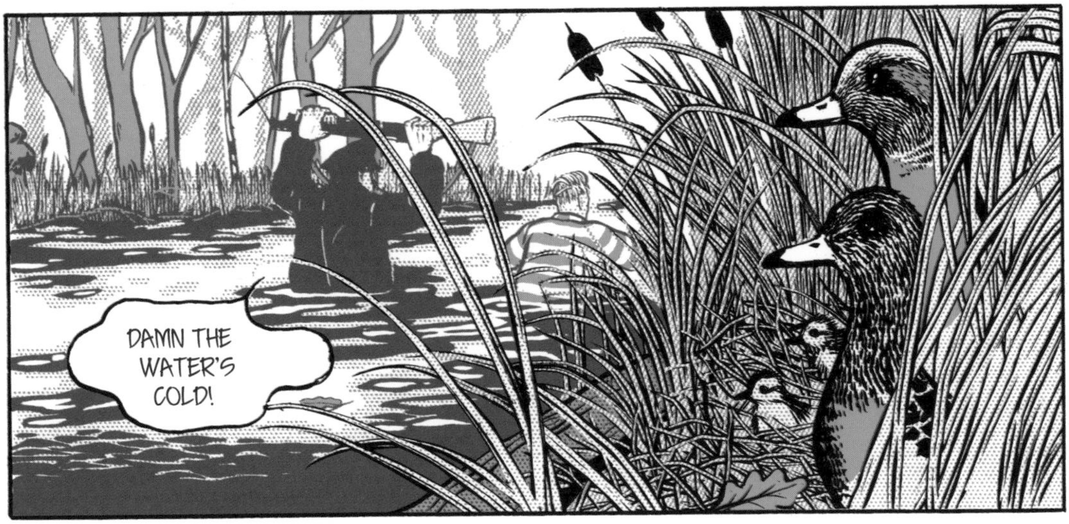
DAMN THE WATER'S COLD!

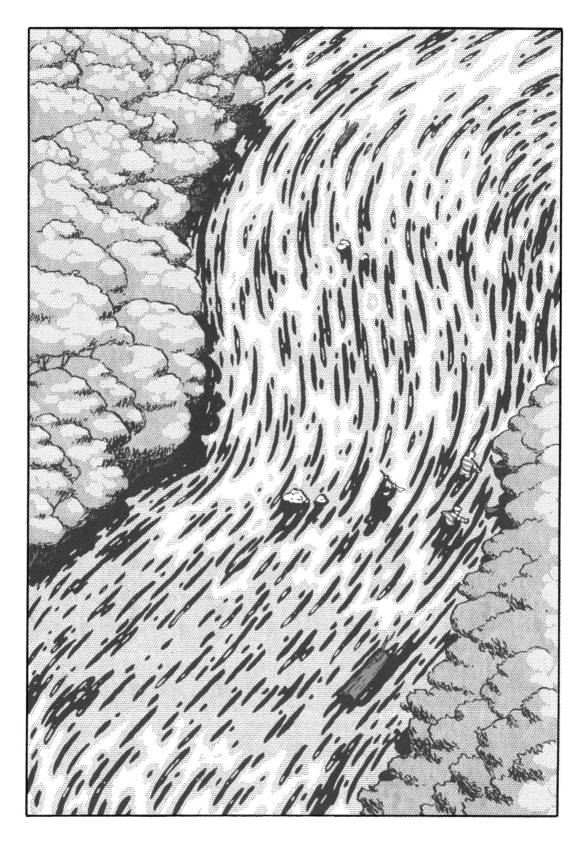

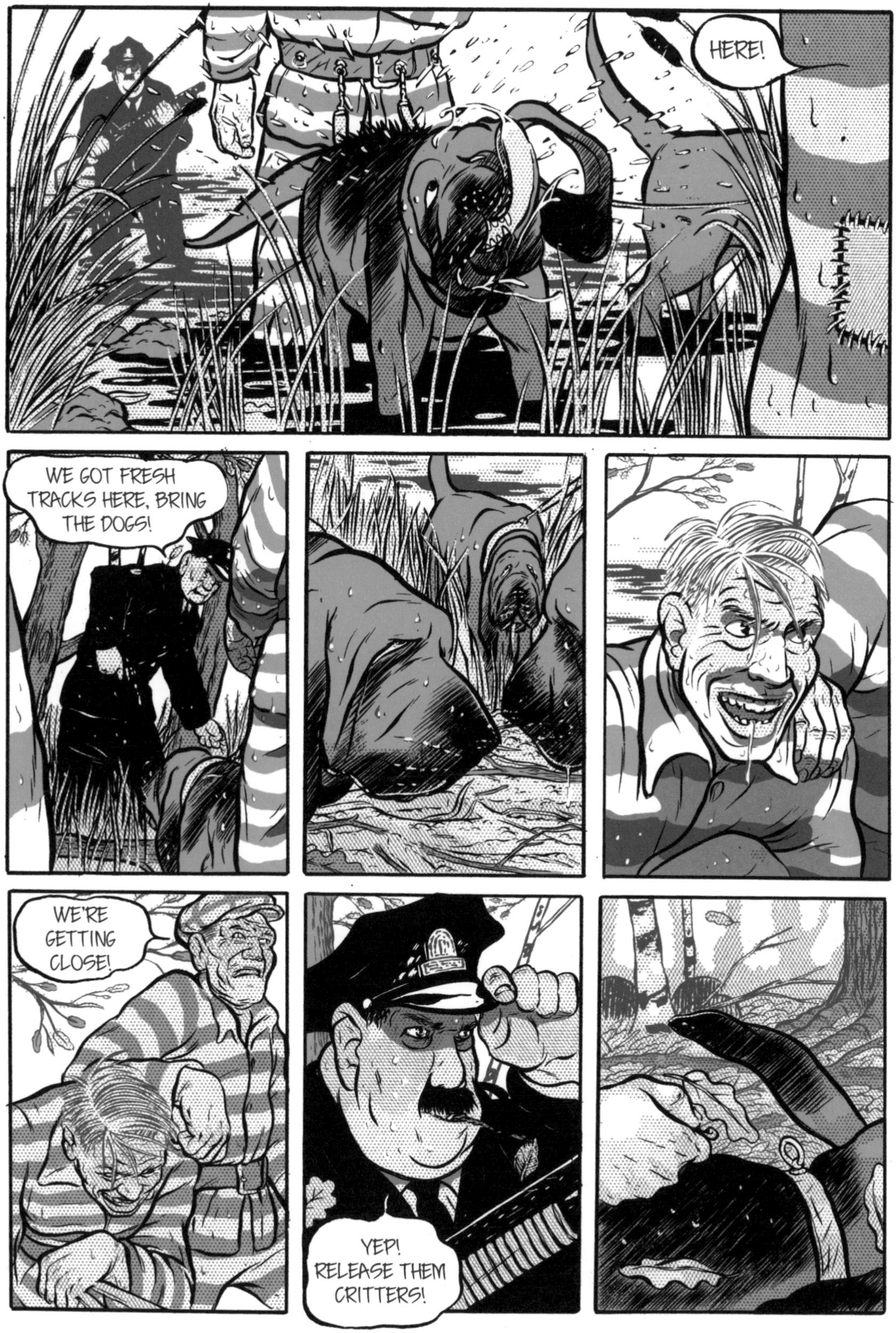
HERE!
WE GOT FRESH TRACKS HERE, BRING THE DOGS!
WE'RE GETTING CLOSE!
YEP! RELEASE THEM CRITTERS!

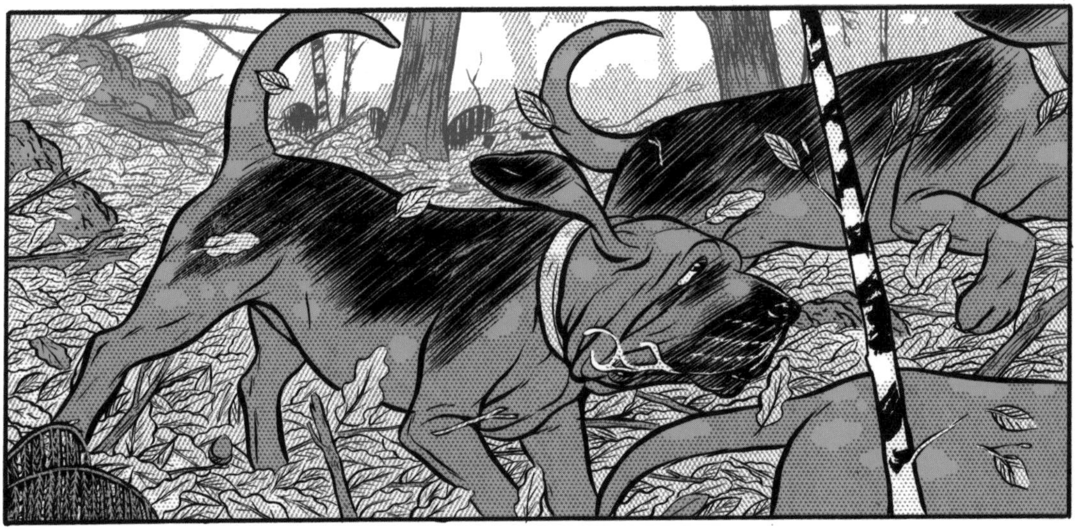

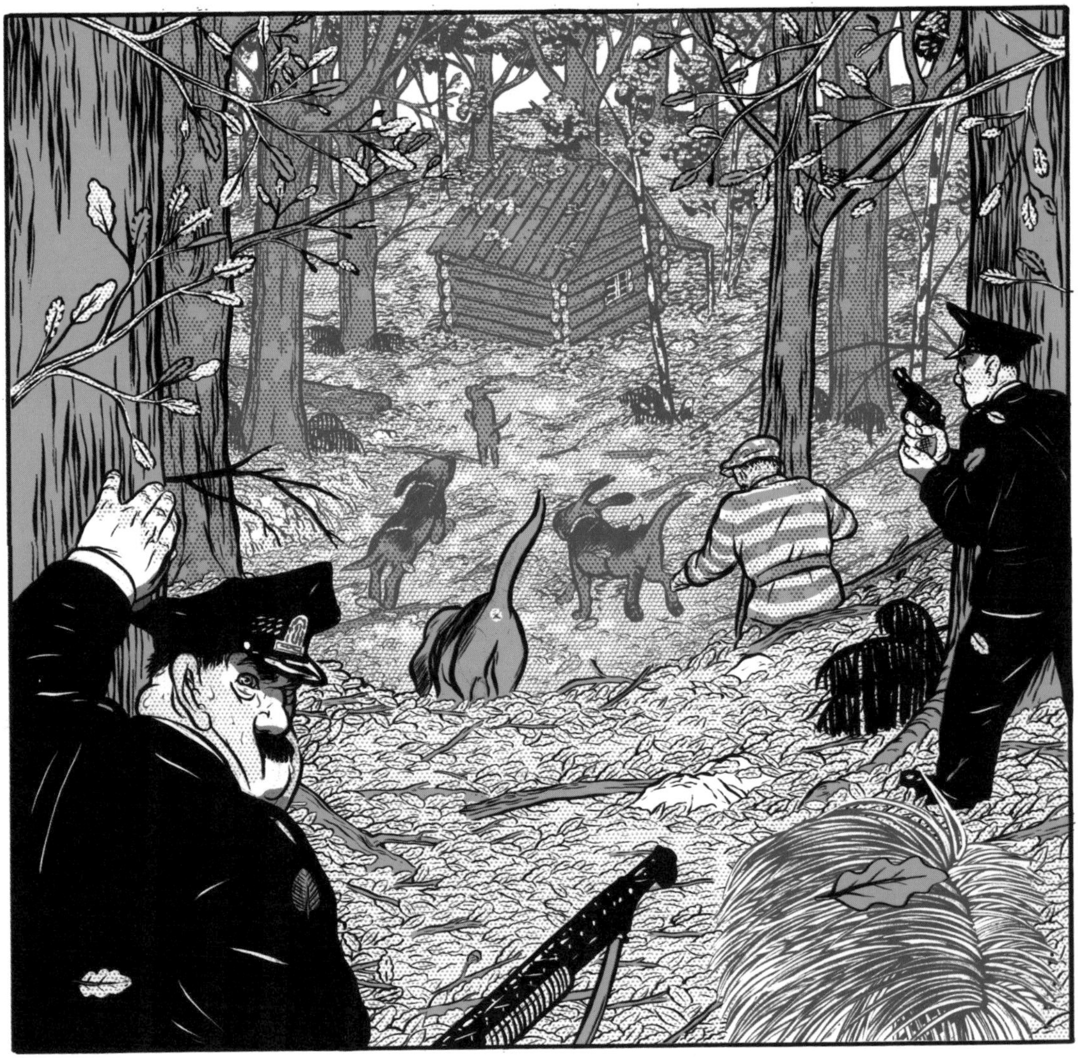

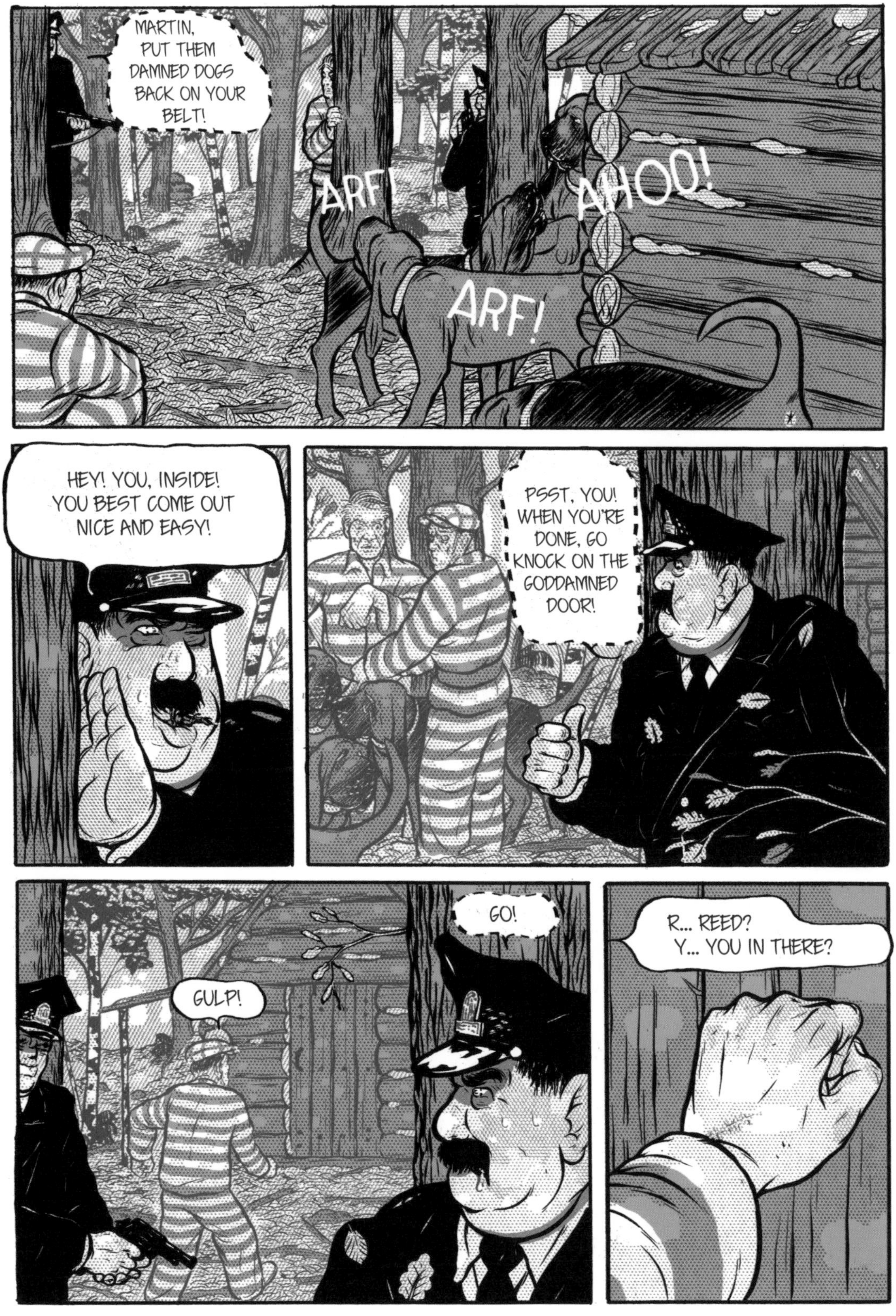
MARTIN, PUT THEM DAMNED DOGS BACK ON YOUR BELT!
ARF!
AHOO!
ARF!
HEY! YOU, INSIDE! YOU BEST COME OUT NICE AND EASY!
PSST, YOU! WHEN YOU'RE DONE, GO KNOCK ON THE GODDAMNED DOOR!
GO!
GULP!
R... REED? Y... YOU IN THERE?

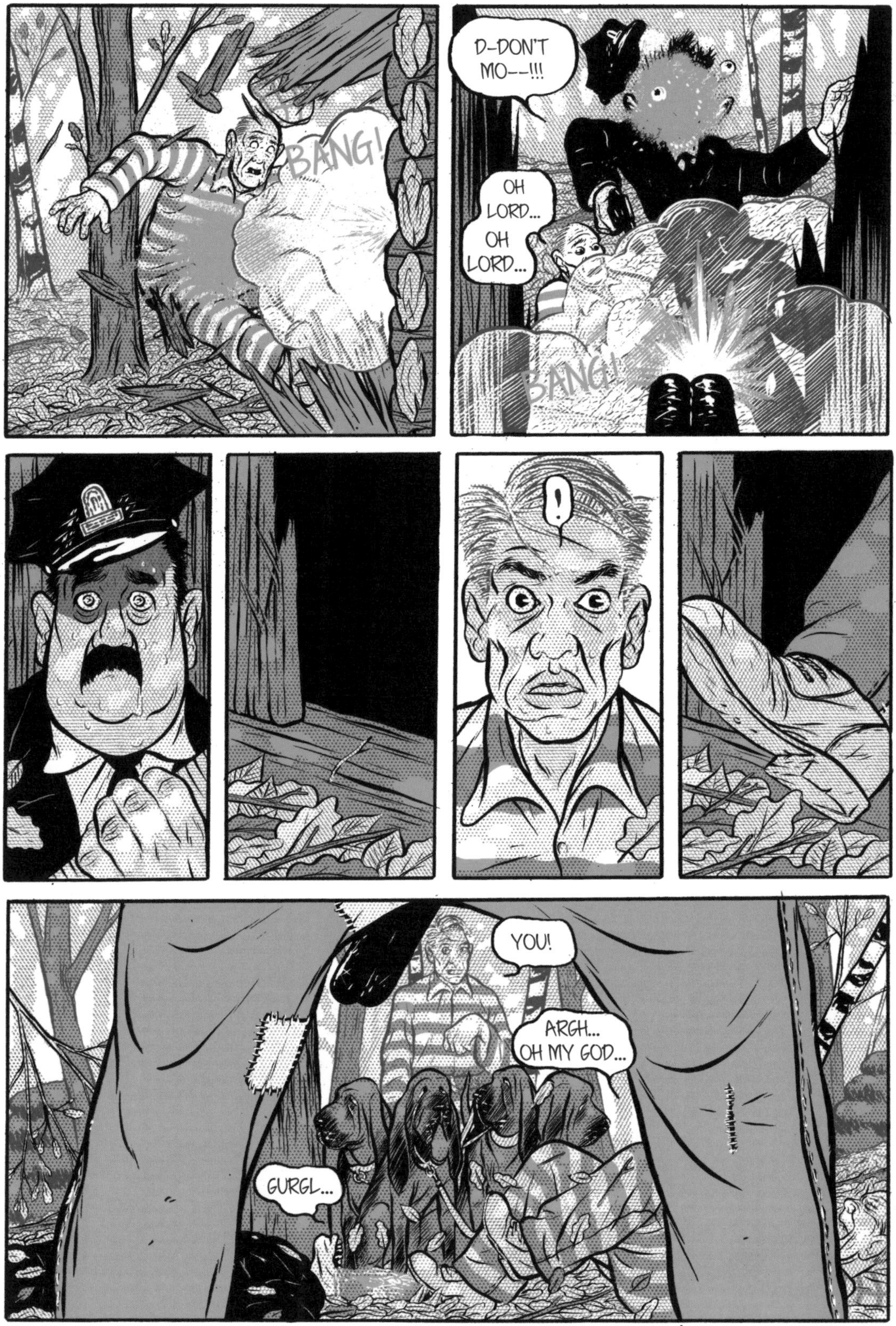
BANG!
D-DON'T MO--!!!
OH LORD... OH LORD...
BANG!
!
YOU!
ARGH... OH MY GOD...
GURGL...

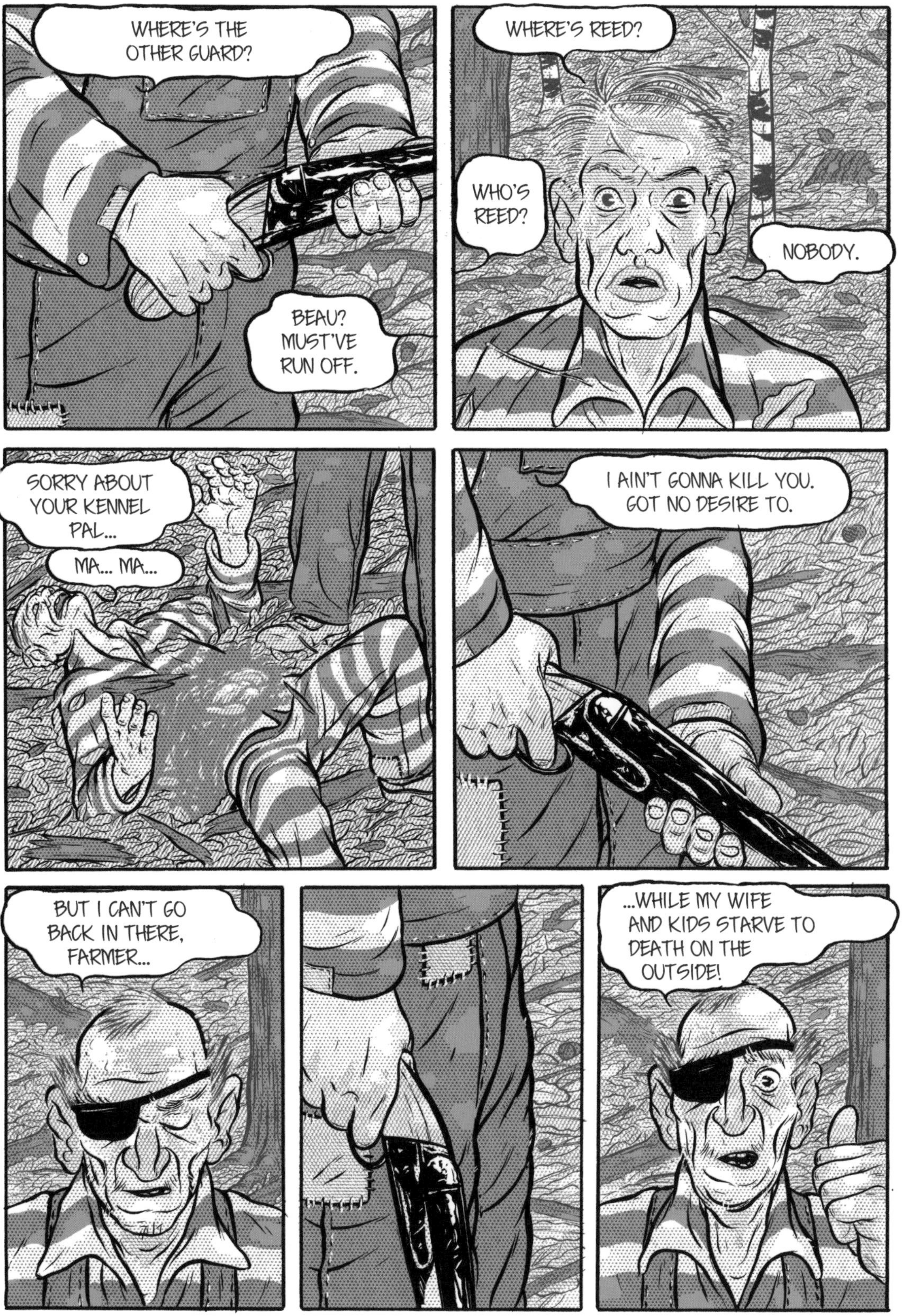
WHERE'S THE OTHER GUARD?
BEAU? MUST'VE RUN OFF.
WHERE'S REED?
WHO'S REED?
NOBODY.
SORRY ABOUT YOUR KENNEL PAL...
MA... MA...
I AIN'T GONNA KILL YOU. GOT NO DESIRE TO.
BUT I CAN'T GO BACK IN THERE, FARMER...
...WHILE MY WIFE AND KIDS STARVE TO DEATH ON THE OUTSIDE!

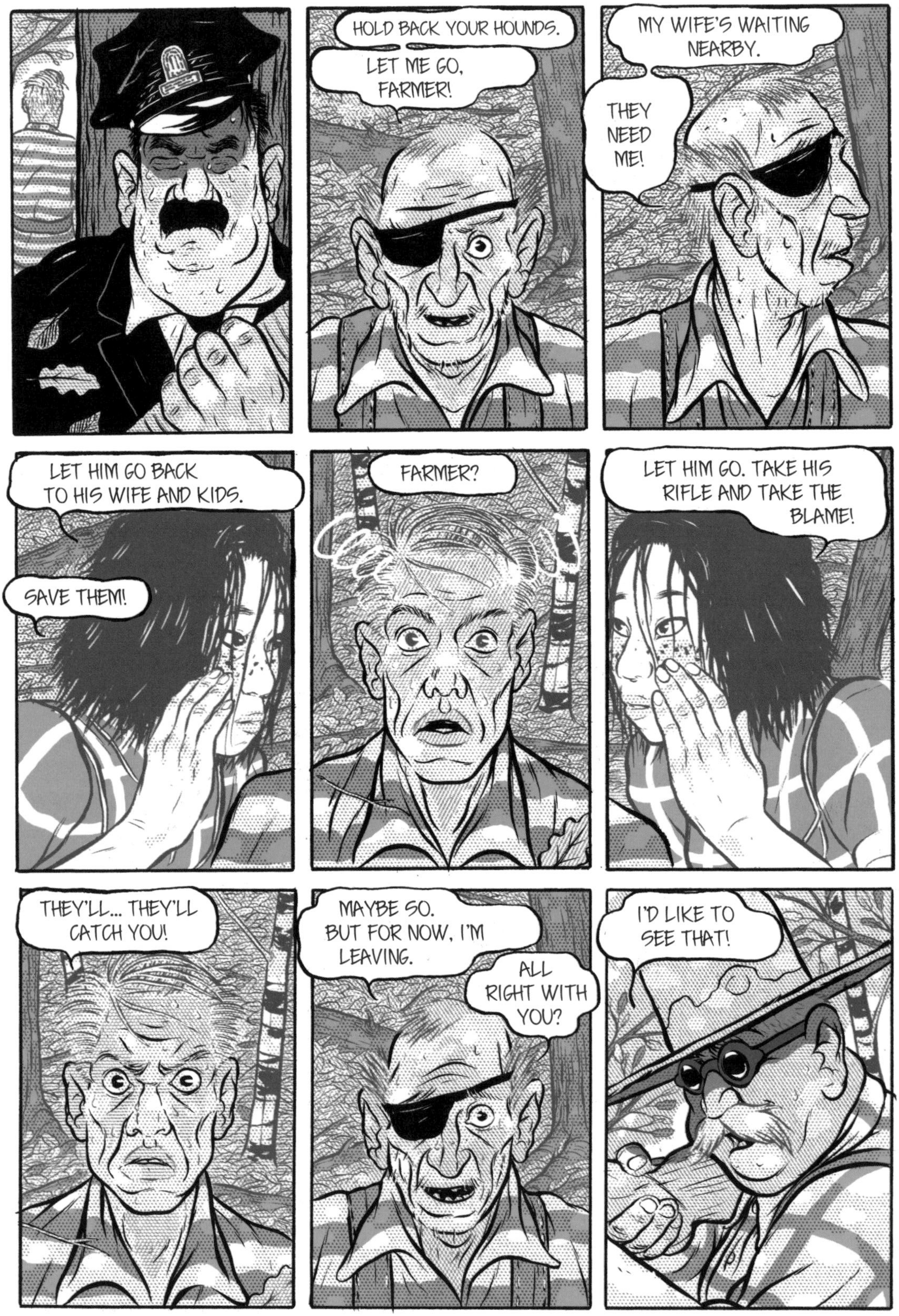
HOLD BACK YOUR HOUNDS.
LET ME GO, FARMER!
MY WIFE'S WAITING NEARBY.
THEY NEED ME!
LET HIM GO BACK TO HIS WIFE AND KIDS.
SAVE THEM!
FARMER?
LET HIM GO. TAKE HIS RIFLE AND TAKE THE BLAME!
THEY'LL... THEY'LL CATCH YOU!
MAYBE SO. BUT FOR NOW, I'M LEAVING.
ALL RIGHT WITH YOU?
I'D LIKE TO SEE THAT!

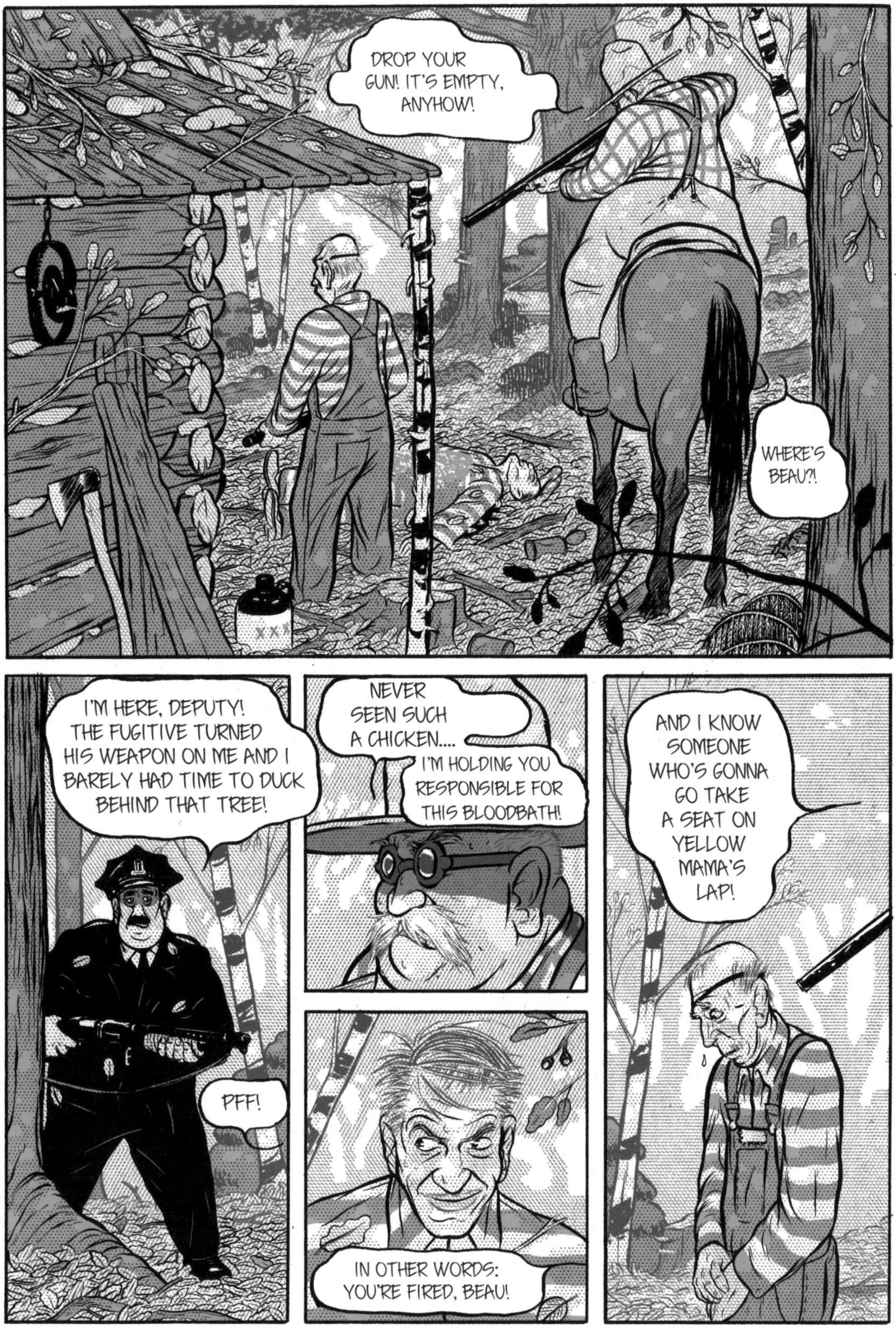
DROP YOUR GUN! IT'S EMPTY, ANYHOW!
WHERE'S BEAU?!
I'M HERE, DEPUTY! THE FUGITIVE TURNED HIS WEAPON ON ME AND I BARELY HAD TIME TO DUCK BEHIND THAT TREE!
PFF!
NEVER SEEN SUCH A CHICKEN....
I'M HOLDING YOU RESPONSIBLE FOR THIS BLOODBATH!
IN OTHER WORDS: YOU'RE FIRED, BEAU!
AND I KNOW SOMEONE WHO'S GONNA GO TAKE A SEAT ON YELLOW MAMA'S LAP!

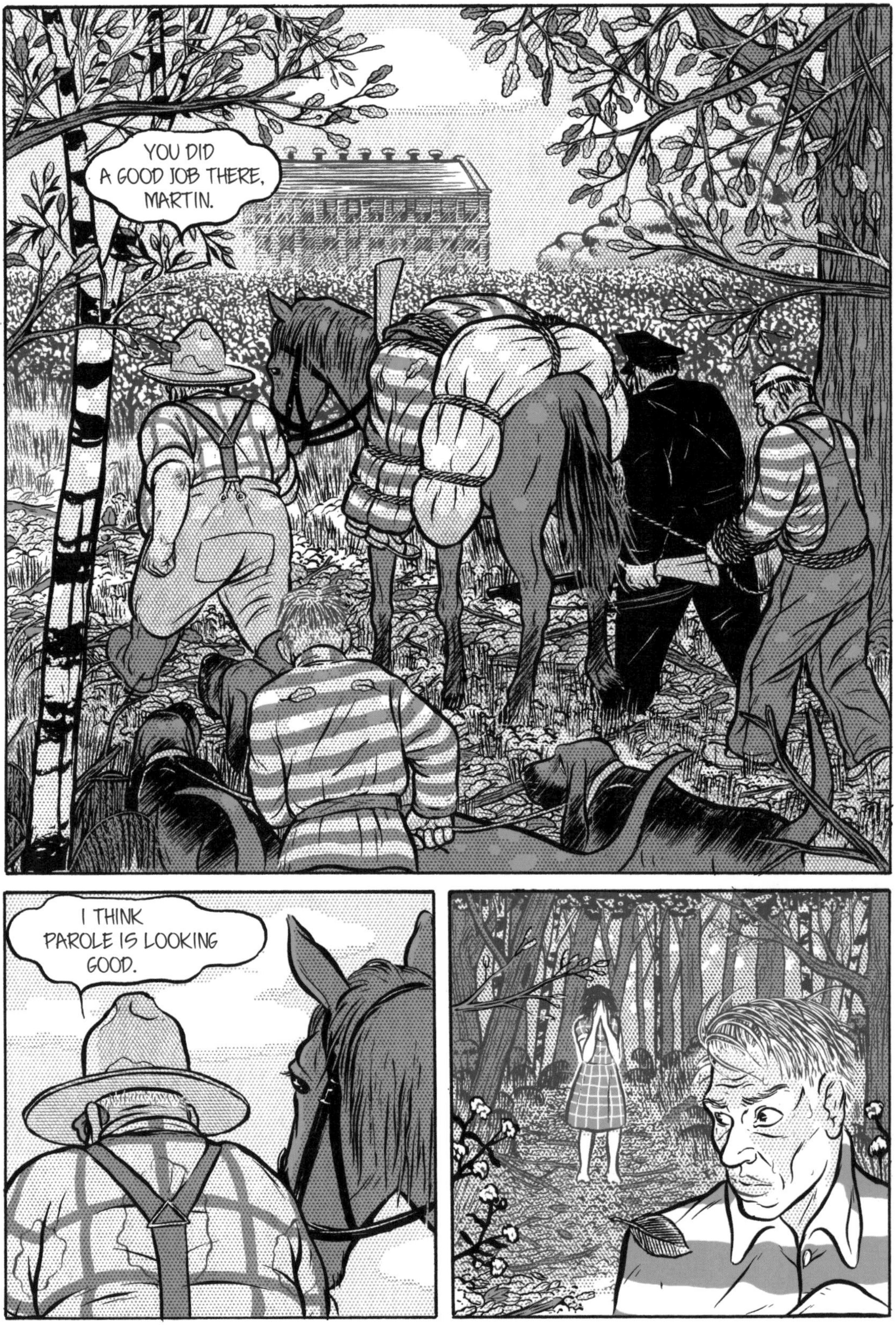
YOU DID A GOOD JOB THERE, MARTIN.
I THINK PAROLE IS LOOKING GOOD.

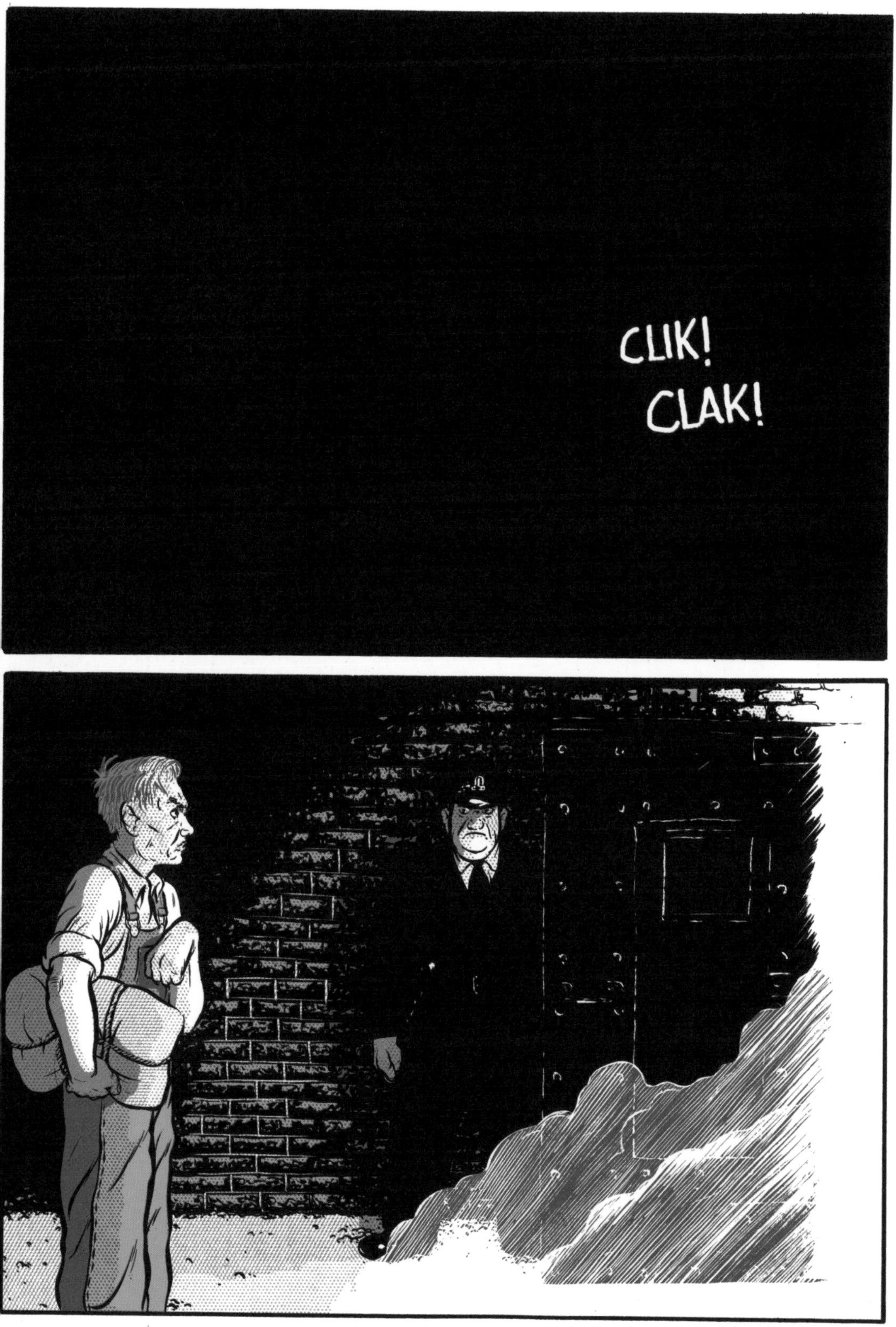
CLIK!
CLAK!

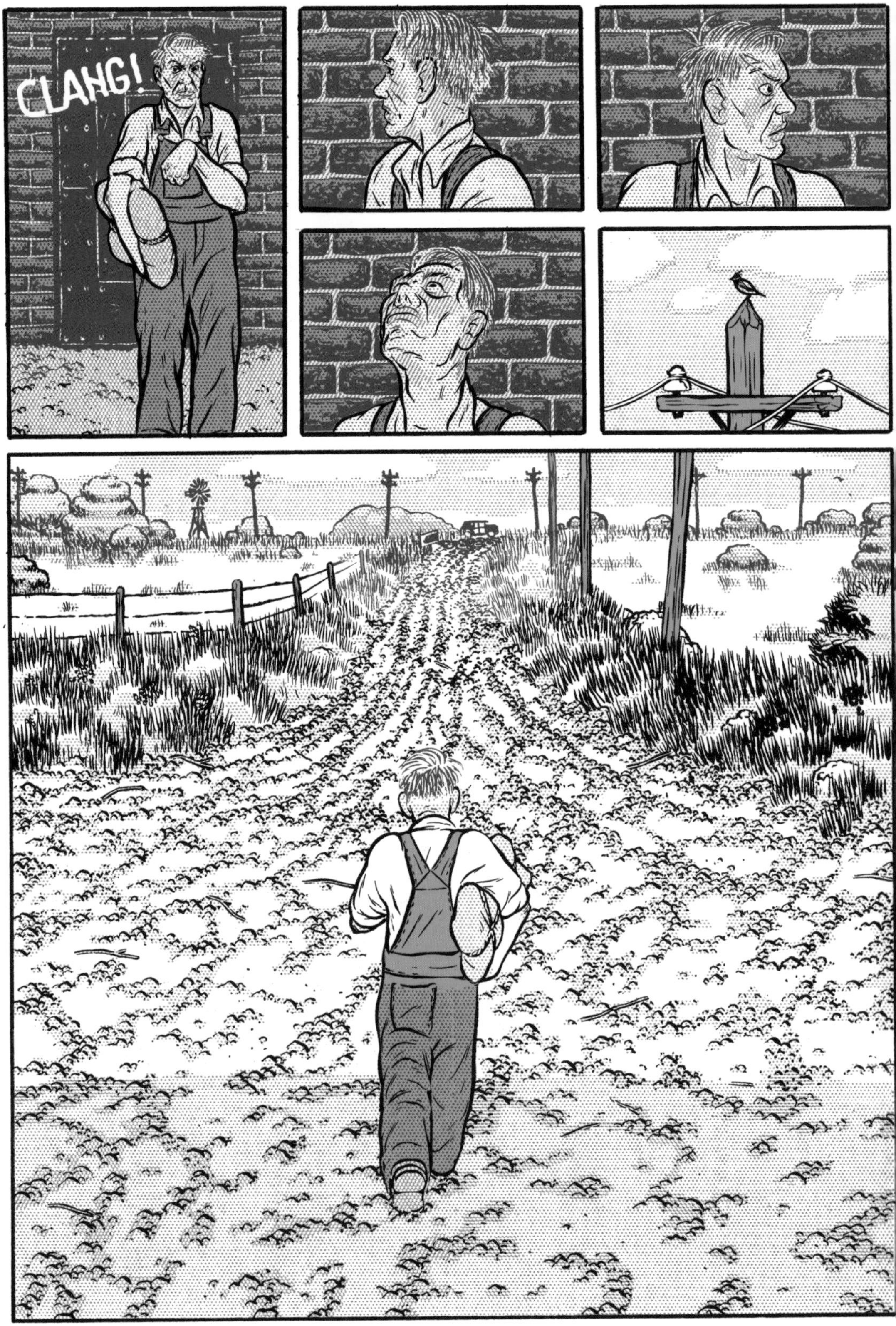
CLANG!

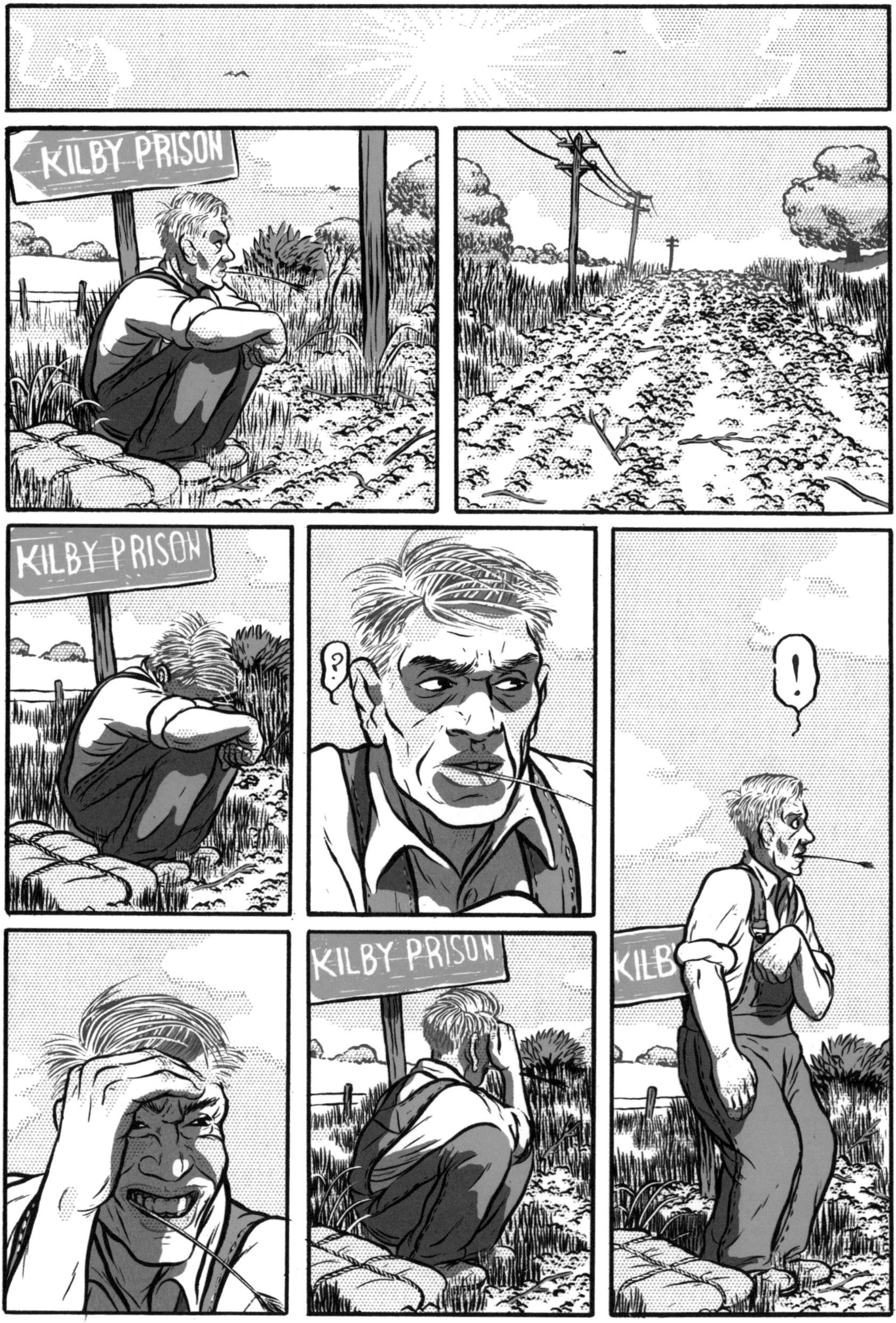
KILBY PRISON
KILBY PRISON
?
!
KILBY PRISON
KILB

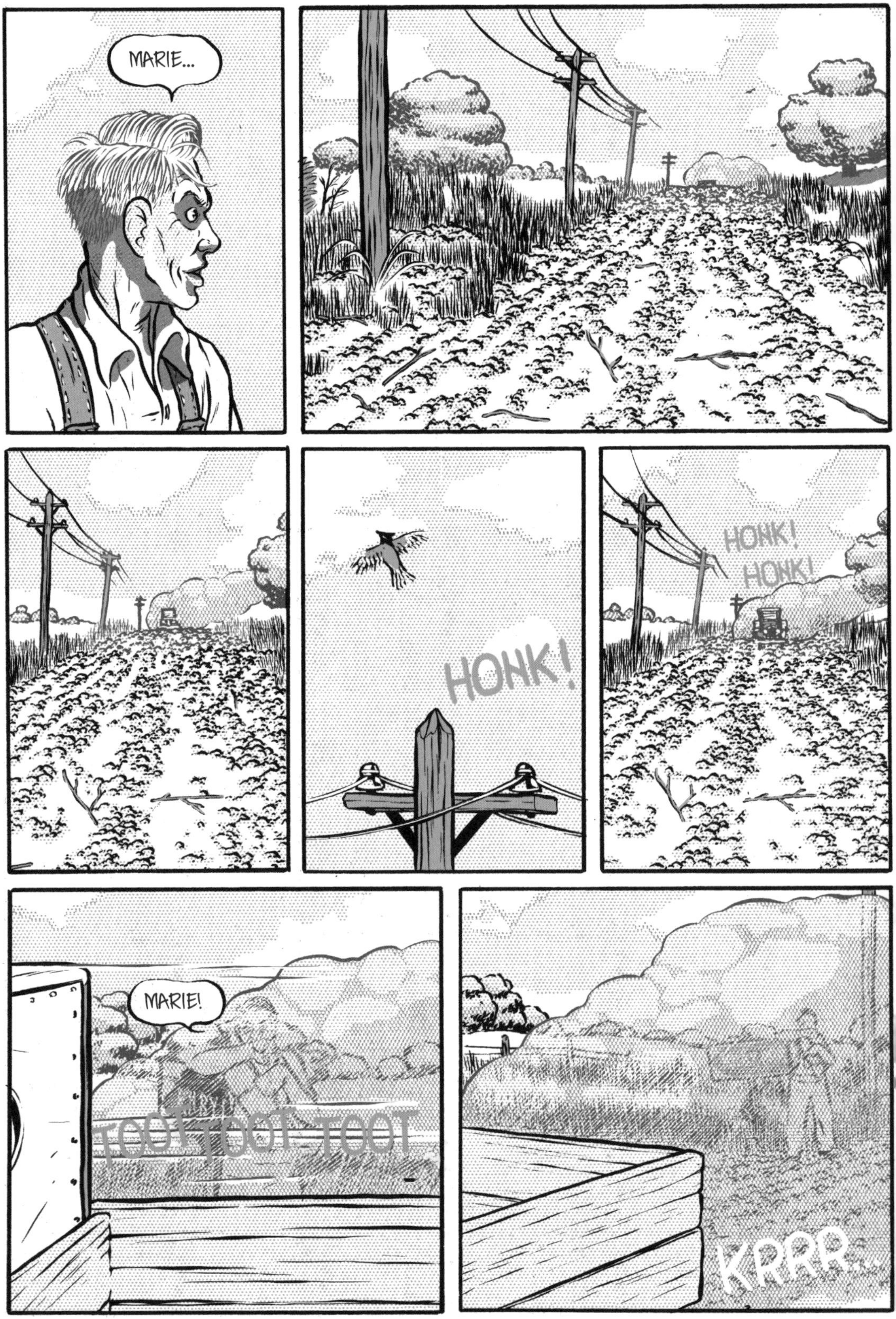
MARIE...
HONK!
HONK!
HONK!
MARIE!
TOOT TOOT TOOT
KRRR..

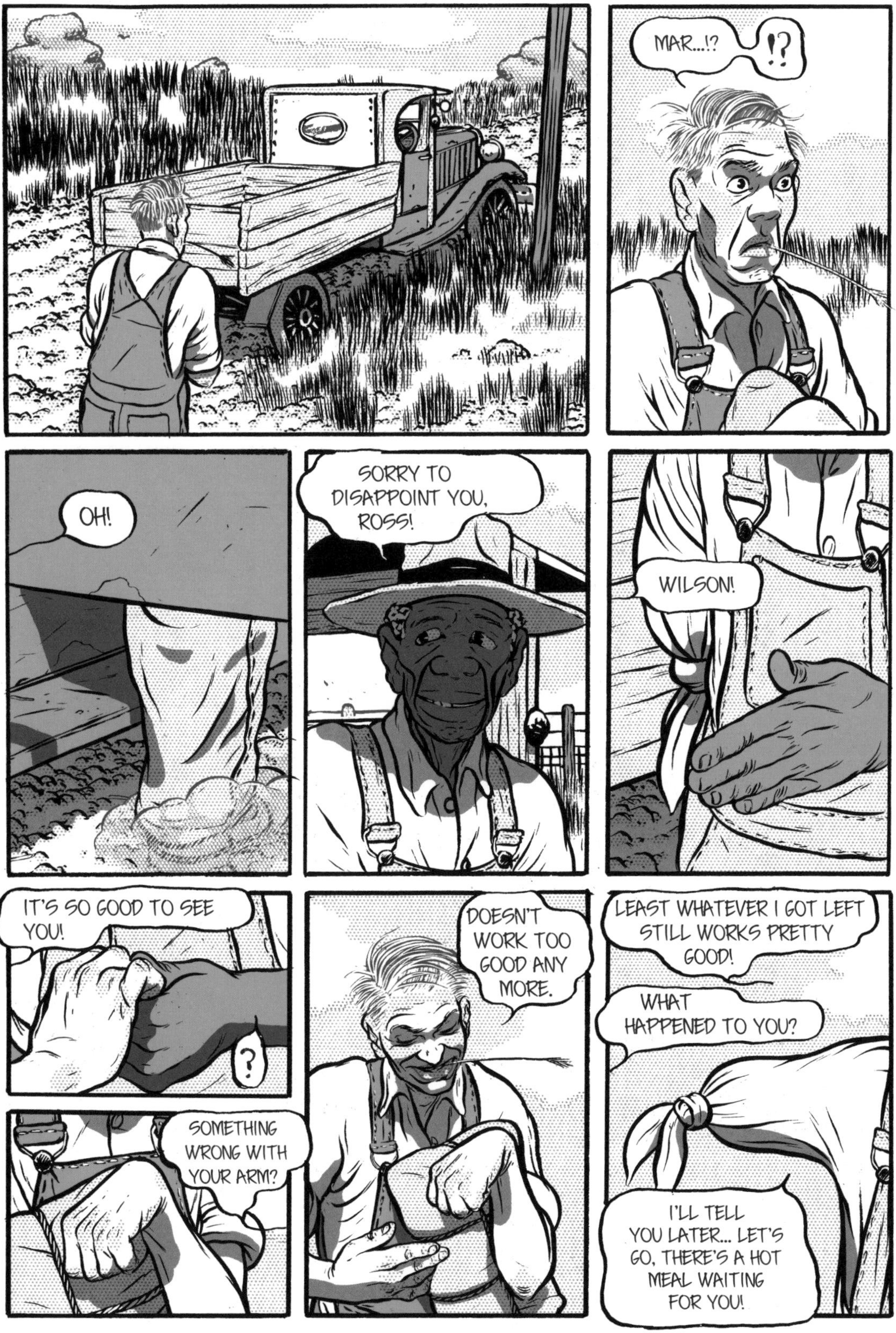
MAR...!?
!?
OH!
SORRY TO DISAPPOINT YOU, ROSS!
WILSON!
IT'S SO GOOD TO SEE YOU!
?
SOMETHING WRONG WITH YOUR ARM?
DOESN'T WORK TOO GOOD ANY MORE.
LEAST WHATEVER I GOT LEFT STILL WORKS PRETTY GOOD!
WHAT HAPPENED TO YOU?
I'LL TELL YOU LATER... LET'S GO, THERE'S A HOT MEAL WAITING FOR YOU!

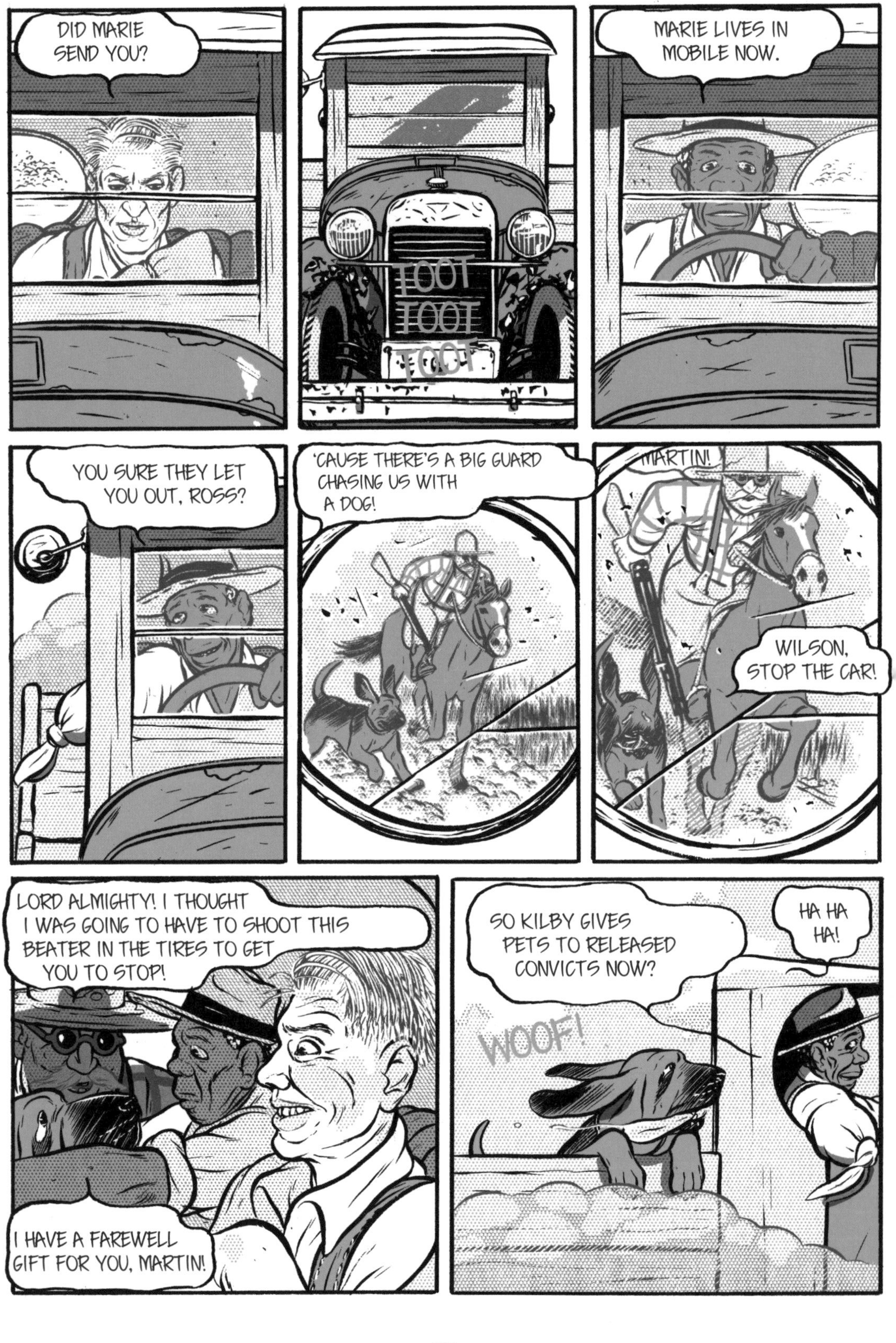
DID MARIE SEND YOU?
TOOT TOOT TOOT
MARIE LIVES IN MOBILE NOW.
YOU SURE THEY LET YOU OUT, ROSS?
'CAUSE THERE'S A BIG GUARD CHASING US WITH A DOG!
MARTIN!
WILSON, STOP THE CAR!
LORD ALMIGHTY! I THOUGHT I WAS GOING TO HAVE TO SHOOT THIS BEATER IN THE TIRES TO GET YOU TO STOP!
I HAVE A FAREWELL GIFT FOR YOU, MARTIN!
SO KILBY GIVES PETS TO RELEASED CONVICTS NOW?
HA HA HA!
WOOF!

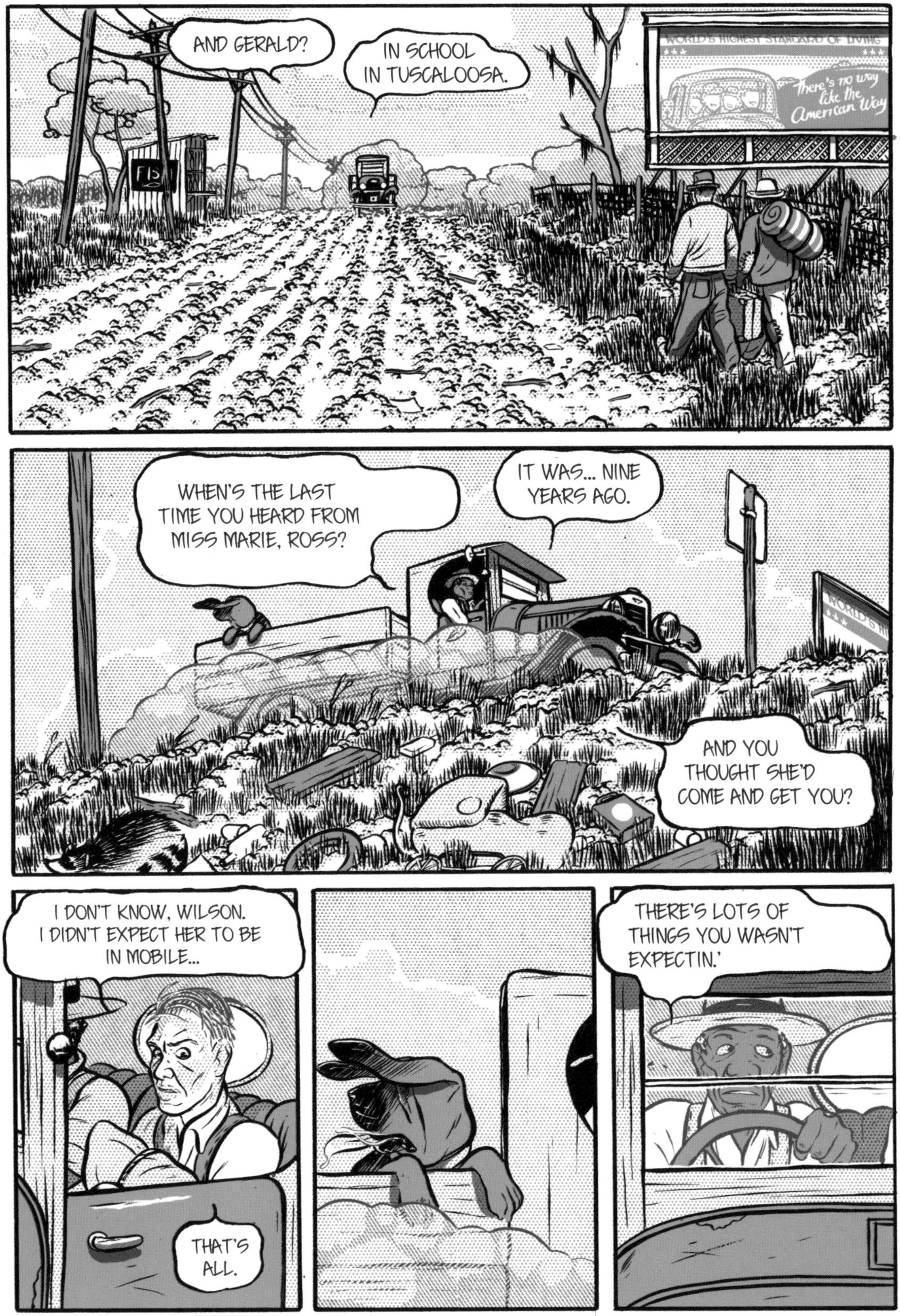
AND GERALD?
IN SCHOOL IN TUSCALOOSA.
WORLD'S HIGHEST STANDARD OF LIVING
There's no way like the American Way
WORLD'S HIGHEST STANDARD OF LIVING
WHEN'S THE LAST TIME YOU HEARD FROM MISS MARIE, ROSS?
IT WAS... NINE YEARS AGO.
AND YOU THOUGHT SHE'D COME AND GET YOU?
I DON'T KNOW, WILSON. I DIDN'T EXPECT HER TO BE IN MOBILE...
THAT'S ALL.
THERE'S LOTS OF THINGS YOU WASN'T EXPECTIN.'

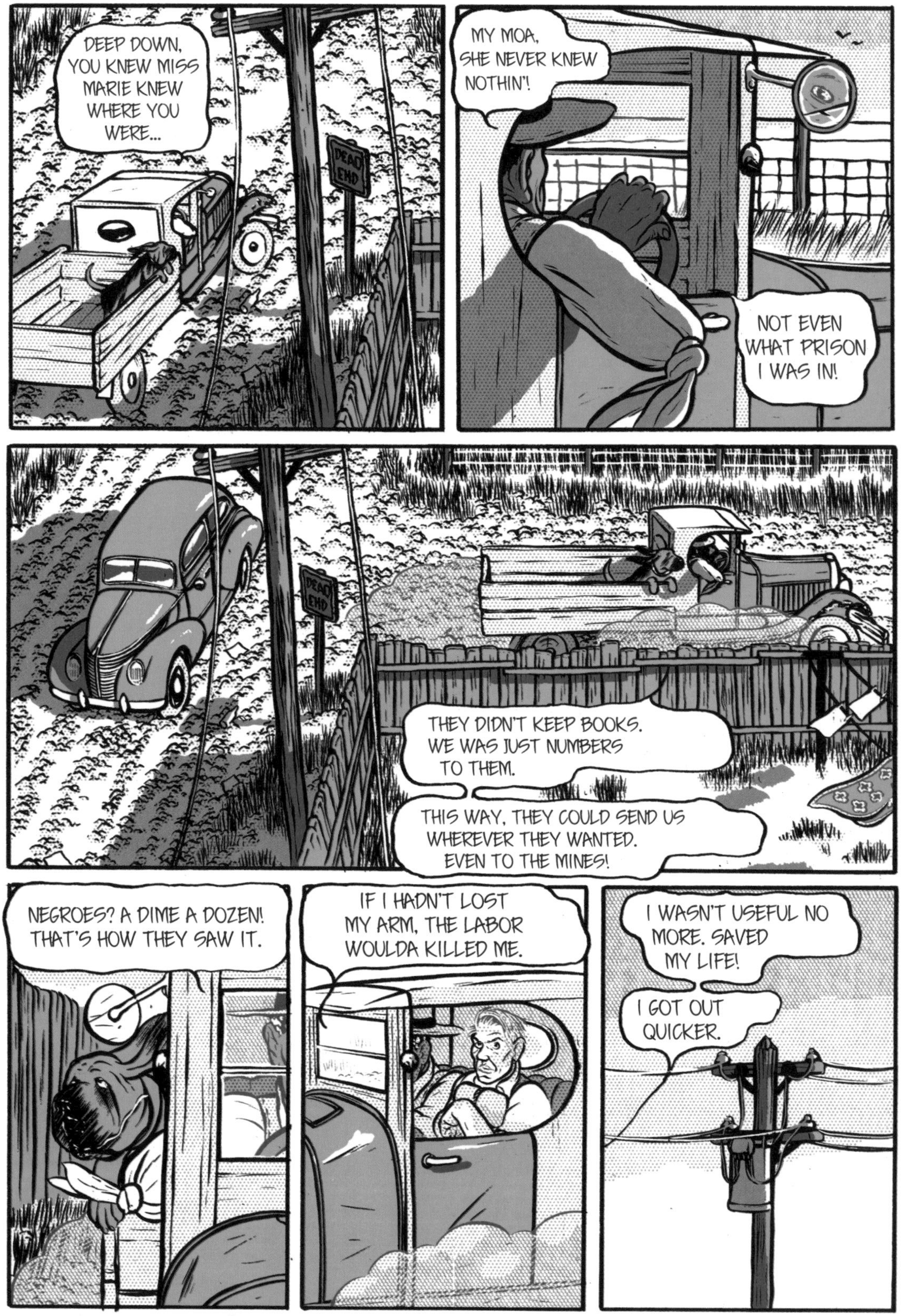
DEEP DOWN, YOU KNEW MISS MARIE KNEW WHERE YOU WERE...
DEAD END
MY MOA, SHE NEVER KNEW NOTHIN'!
NOT EVEN WHAT PRISON I WAS IN!
DEAD END
THEY DIDN'T KEEP BOOKS. WE WAS JUST NUMBERS TO THEM.
THIS WAY, THEY COULD SEND US WHEREVER THEY WANTED. EVEN TO THE MINES!
NEGROES? A DIME A DOZEN! THAT'S HOW THEY SAW IT.
IF I HADN'T LOST MY ARM, THE LABOR WOULDA KILLED ME.
I WASN'T USEFUL NO MORE. SAVED MY LIFE!
I GOT OUT QUICKER.

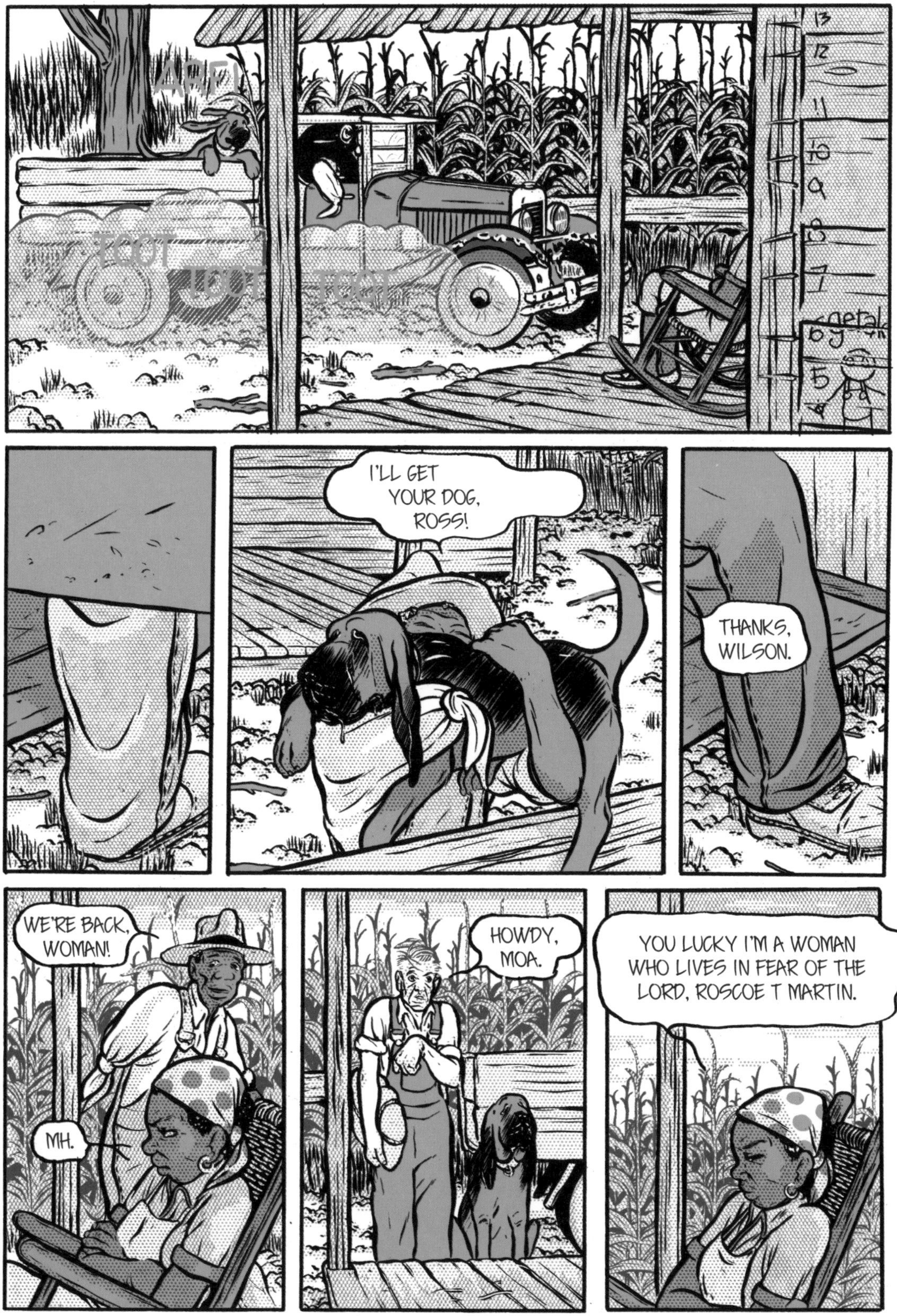
ARF!
TOOT
TOOT
TOOT
I'LL GET YOUR DOG, ROSS!
THANKS, WILSON.
WE'RE BACK, WOMAN!
MH.
HOWDY, MOA.
YOU LUCKY I'M A WOMAN WHO LIVES IN FEAR OF THE LORD, ROSCOE T MARTIN.

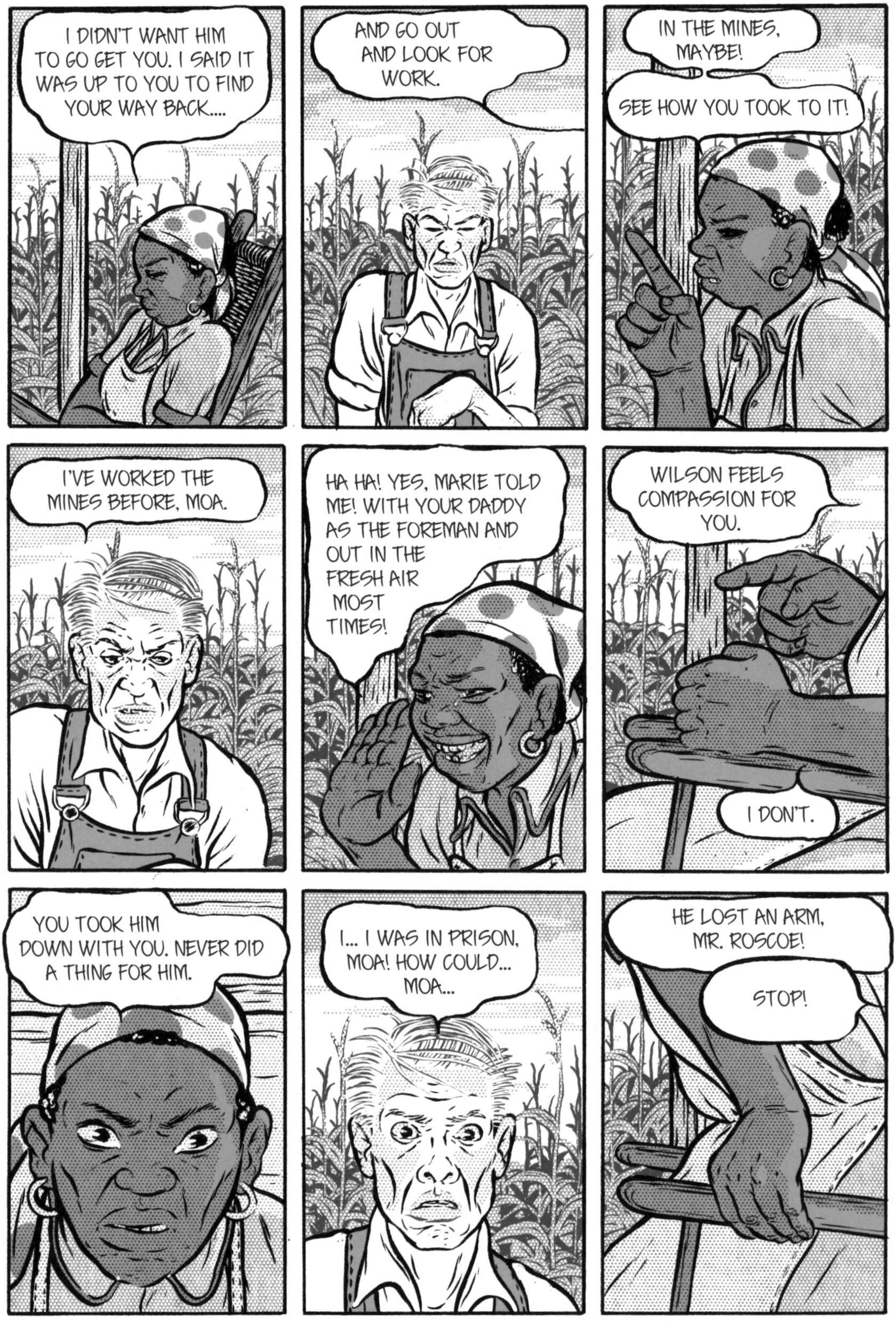
I DIDN'T WANT HIM TO GO GET YOU. I SAID IT WAS UP TO YOU TO FIND YOUR WAY BACK....
AND GO OUT AND LOOK FOR WORK.
IN THE MINES, MAYBE!
SEE HOW YOU TOOK TO IT!
I'VE WORKED THE MINES BEFORE, MOA.
HA HA! YES, MARIE TOLD ME! WITH YOUR DADDY AS THE FOREMAN AND OUT IN THE FRESH AIR MOST TIMES!
WILSON FEELS COMPASSION FOR YOU.
I DON'T.
YOU TOOK HIM DOWN WITH YOU. NEVER DID A THING FOR HIM.
I... I WAS IN PRISON, MOA! HOW COULD... MOA...
HE LOST AN ARM, MR. ROSCOE!
STOP!

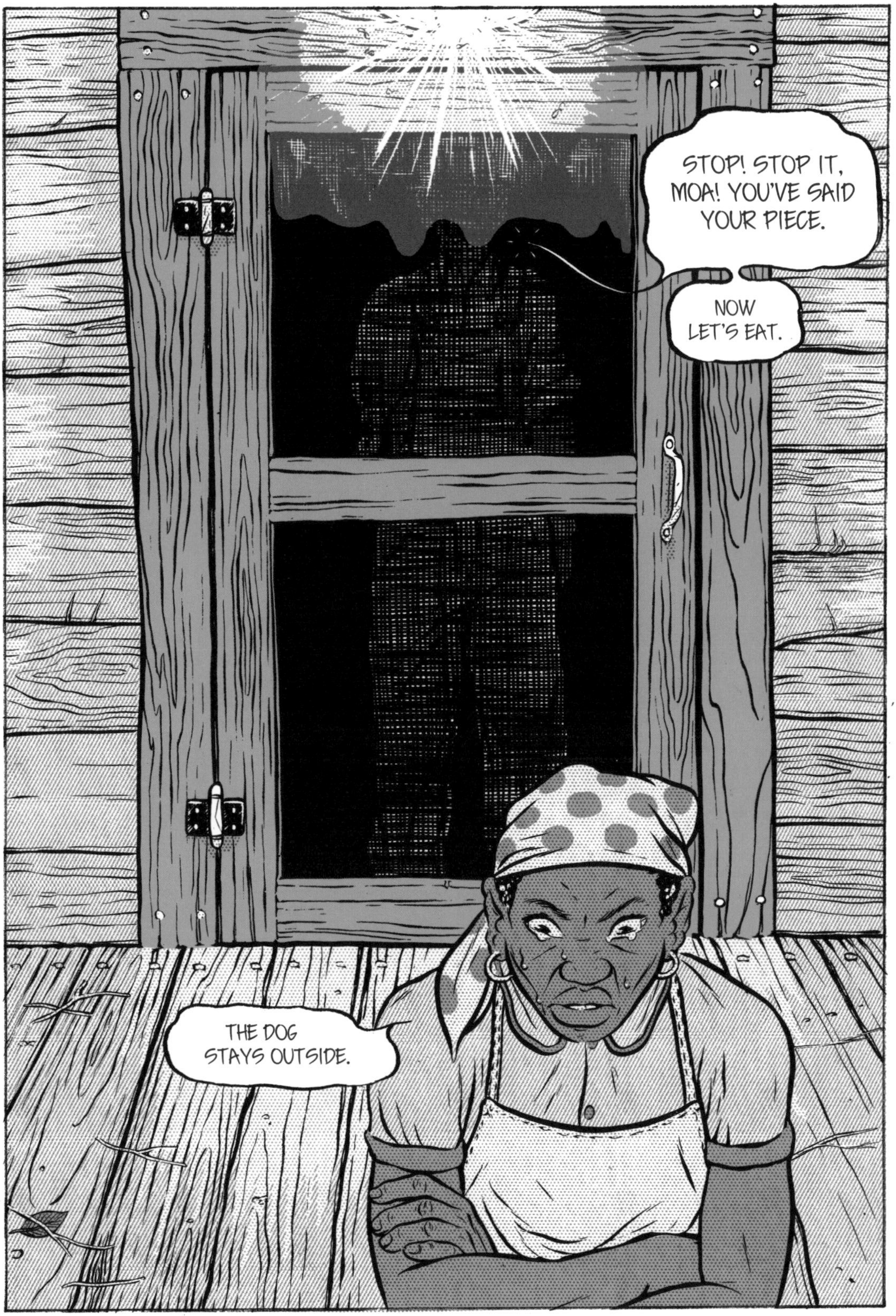
STOP! STOP IT, MOA! YOU'VE SAID YOUR PIECE.
NOW LET'S EAT.
THE DOG STAYS OUTSIDE.

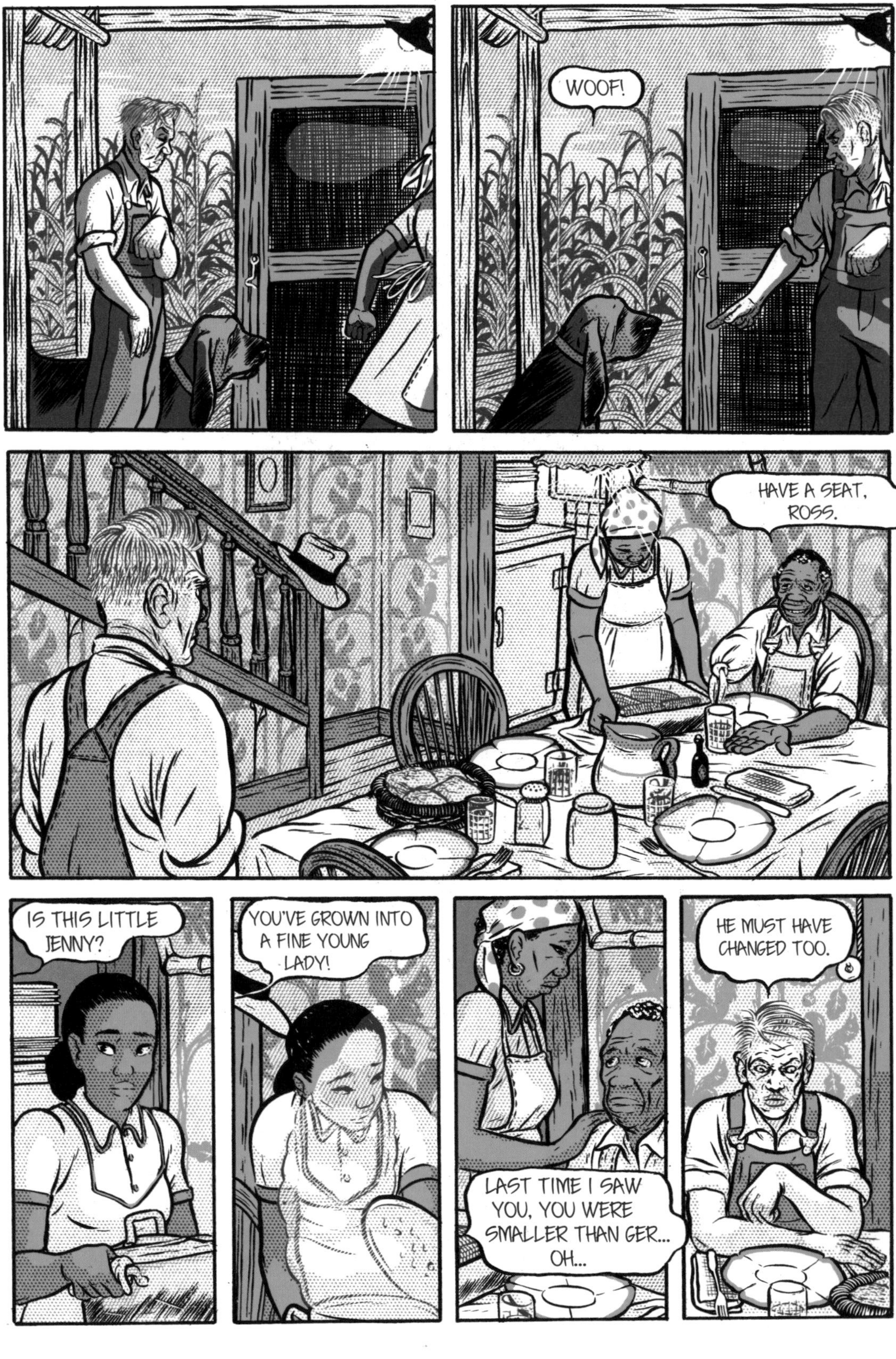
WOOF!
HAVE A SEAT, ROSS.
IS THIS LITTLE JENNY?
YOU'VE GROWN INTO A FINE YOUNG LADY!
LAST TIME I SAW YOU, YOU WERE SMALLER THAN GER... OH...
HE MUST HAVE CHANGED TOO.

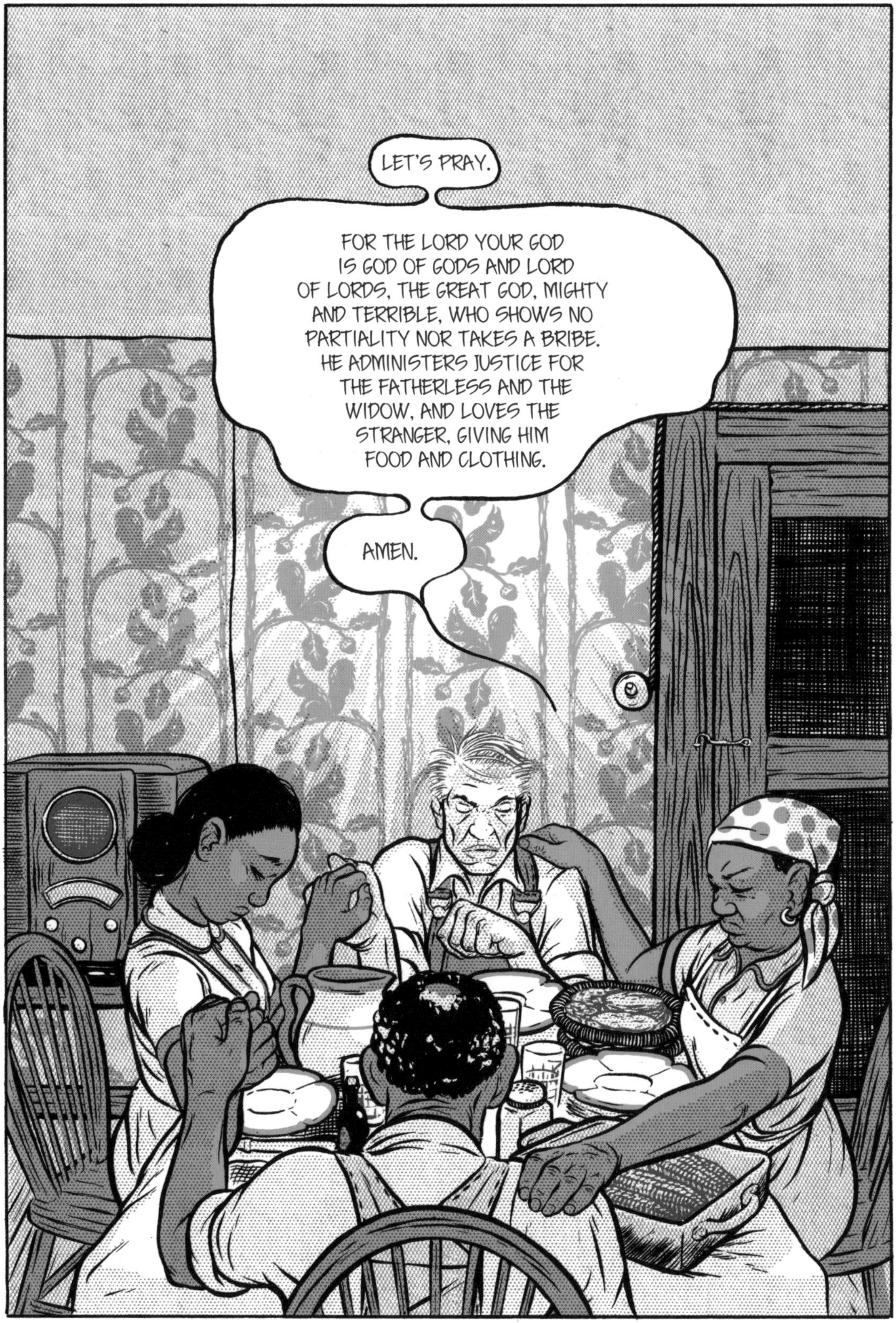
LET'S PRAY.
FOR THE LORD YOUR GOD IS GOD OF GODS AND LORD OF LORDS, THE GREAT GOD, MIGHTY AND TERRIBLE, WHO SHOWS NO PARTIALITY NOR TAKES A BRIBE. HE ADMINISTERS JUSTICE FOR THE FATHERLESS AND THE WIDOW, AND LOVES THE STRANGER, GIVING HIM FOOD AND CLOTHING.
AMEN.

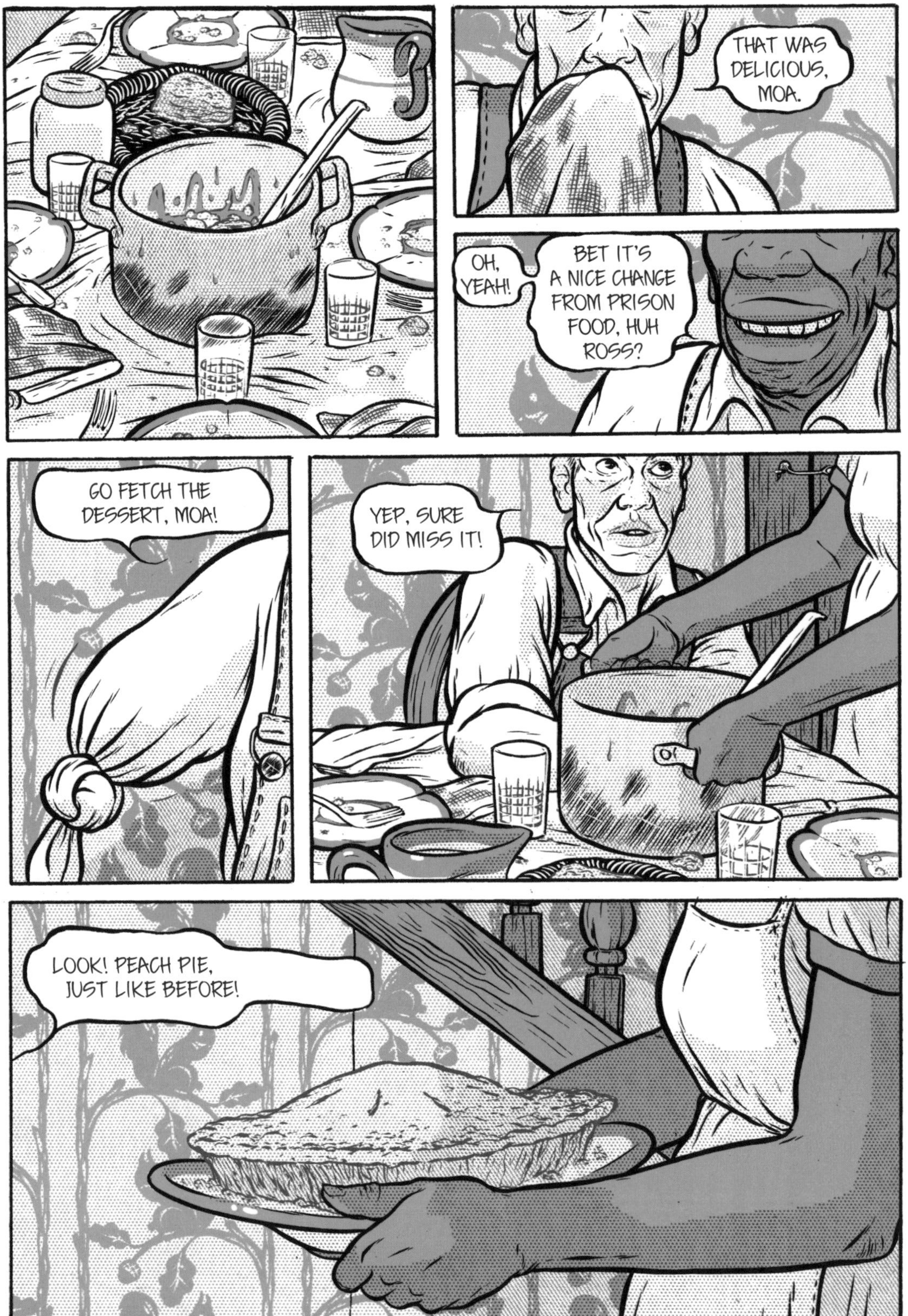
THAT WAS DELICIOUS, MOA.
OH, YEAH!
BET IT'S A NICE CHANGE FROM PRISON FOOD, HUH ROSS?
GO FETCH THE DESSERT, MOA!
YEP, SURE DID MISS IT!
LOOK! PEACH PIE, JUST LIKE BEFORE!

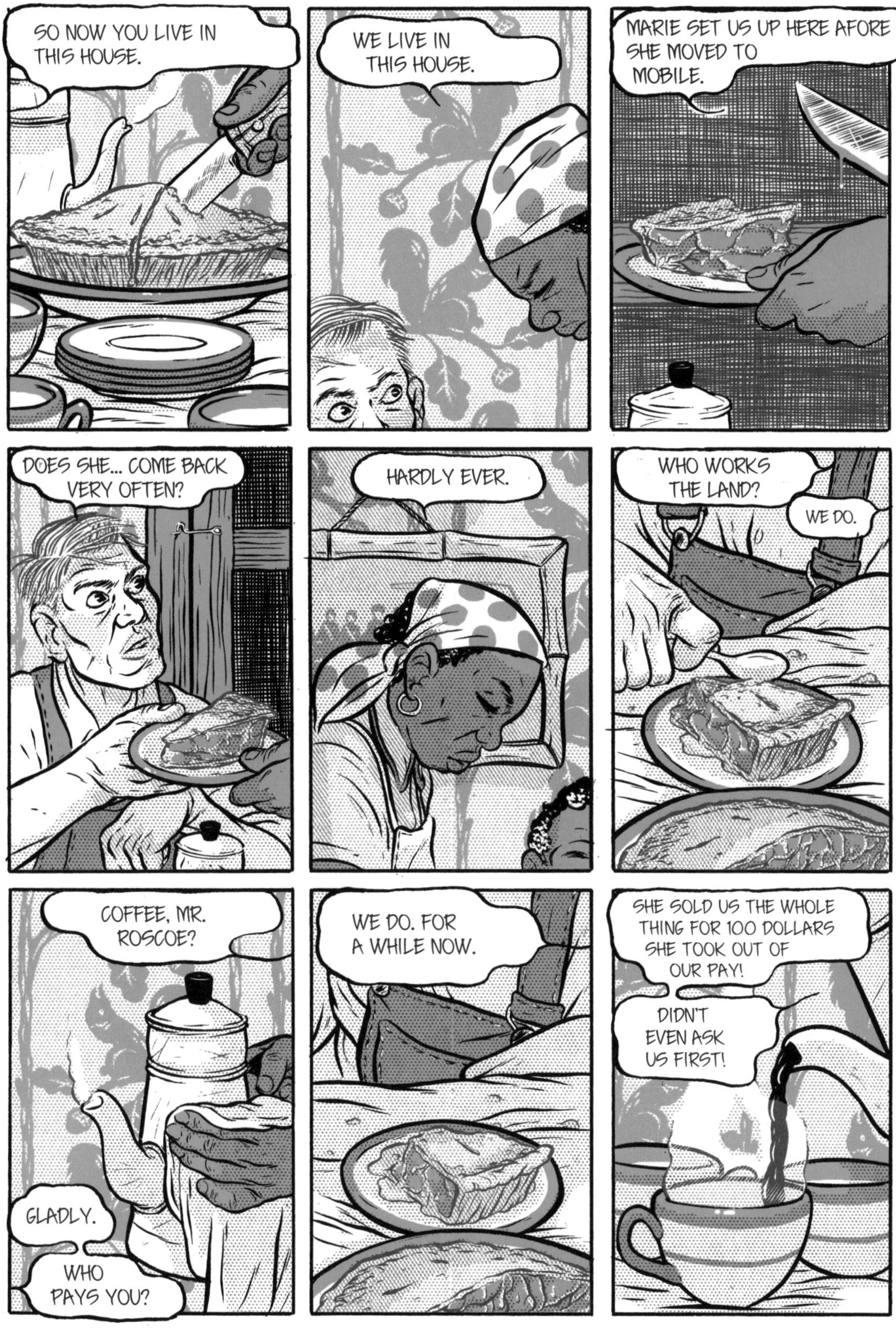
SO NOW YOU LIVE IN THIS HOUSE.
WE LIVE IN THIS HOUSE.
MARIE SET US UP HERE AFORE SHE MOVED TO MOBILE.
DOES SHE... COME BACK VERY OFTEN?
HARDLY EVER.
WHO WORKS THE LAND?
WE DO.
COFFEE, MR. ROSCOE?
GLADLY.
WHO PAYS YOU?
WE DO. FOR A WHILE NOW.
SHE SOLD US THE WHOLE THING FOR 100 DOLLARS SHE TOOK OUT OF OUR PAY!
DIDN'T EVEN ASK US FIRST!

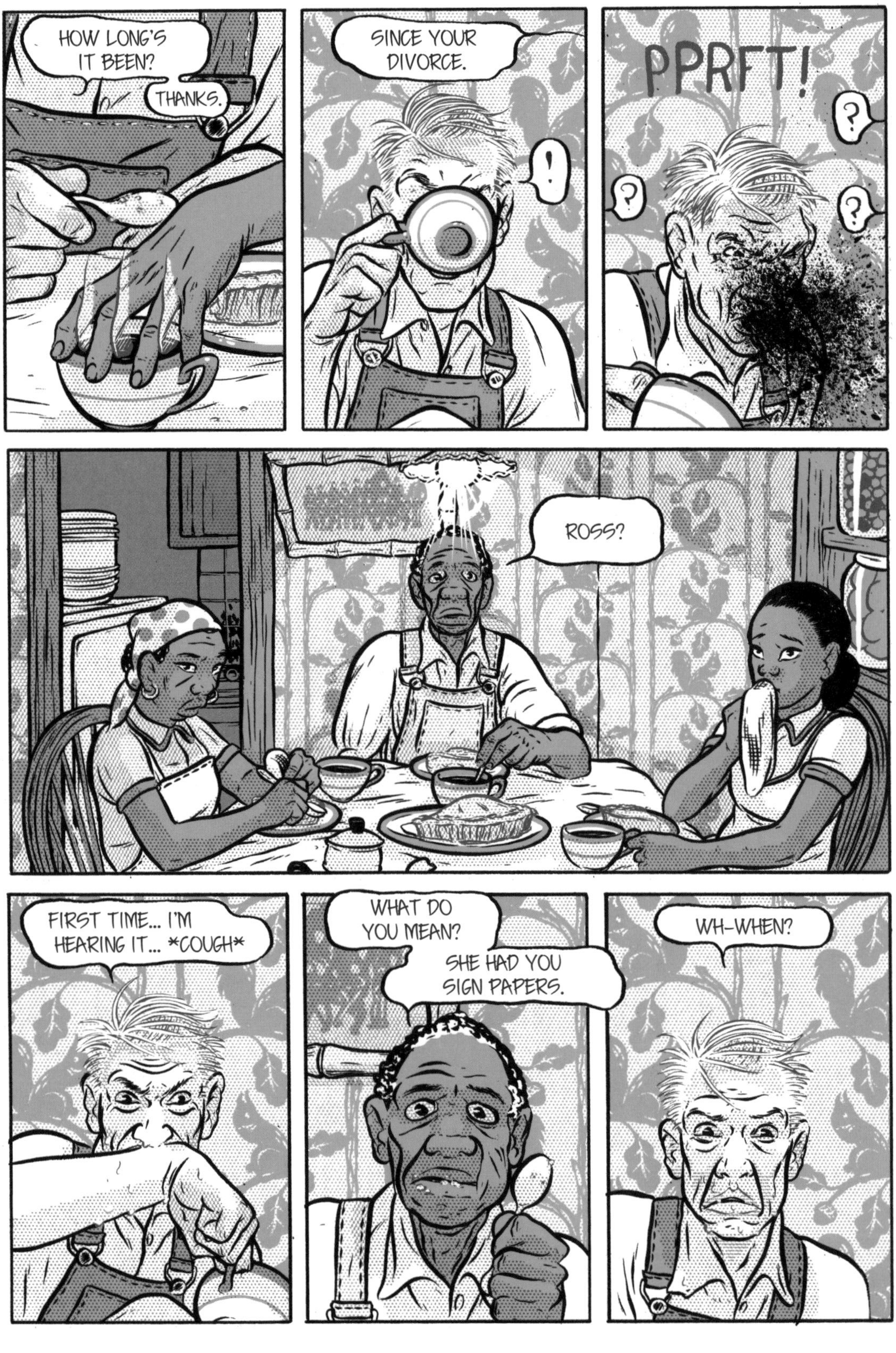
HOW LONG'S IT BEEN?
THANKS.
SINCE YOUR DIVORCE.
!
PPRFT!
?
?
?
ROSS?
FIRST TIME... I'M HEARING IT... *COUGH*
WHAT DO YOU MEAN?
SHE HAD YOU SIGN PAPERS.
WH-WHEN?

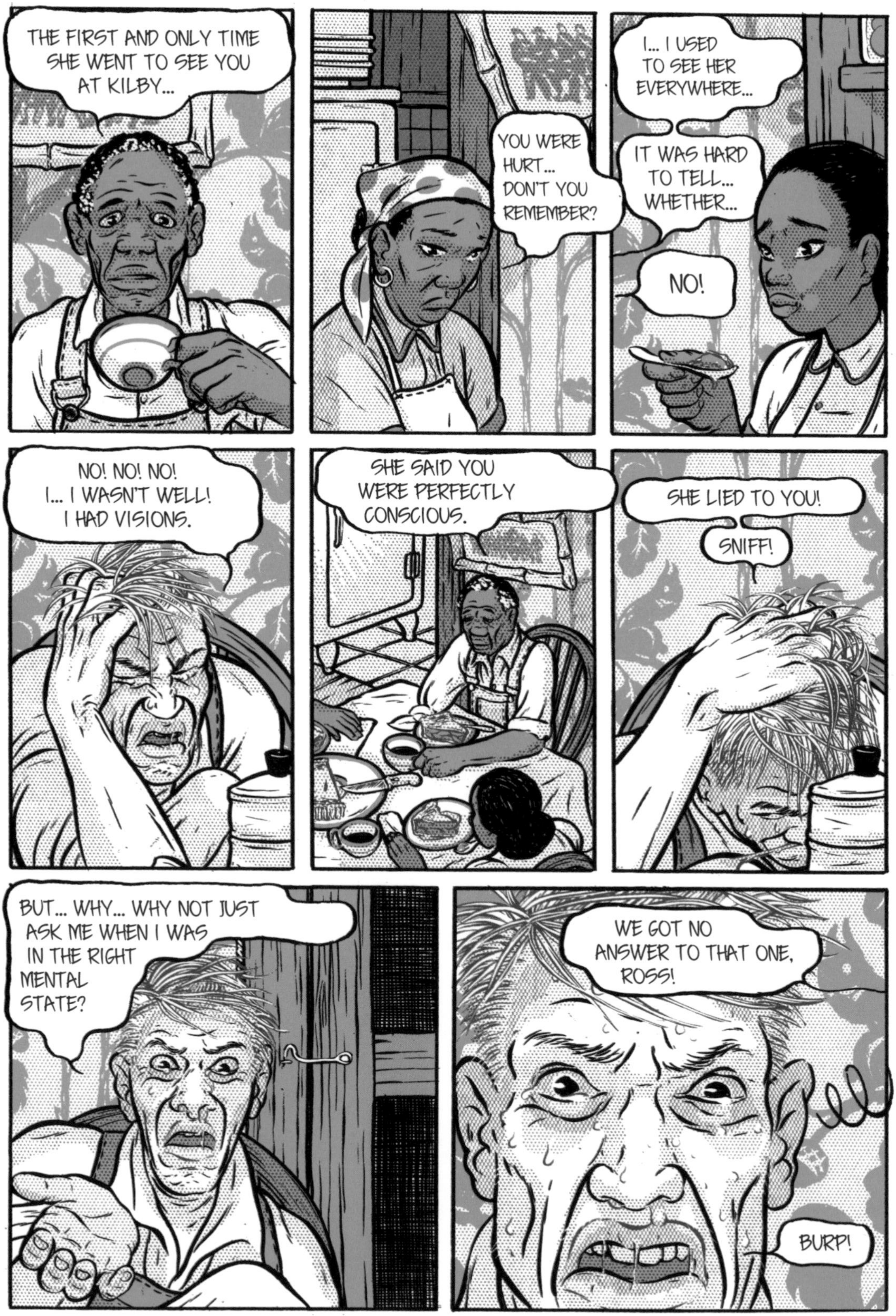
THE FIRST AND ONLY TIME SHE WENT TO SEE YOU AT KILBY...
YOU WERE HURT... DON'T YOU REMEMBER?
I... I USED TO SEE HER EVERYWHERE...
IT WAS HARD TO TELL... WHETHER...
NO!
NO! NO! NO! I... I WASN'T WELL! I HAD VISIONS.
SHE SAID YOU WERE PERFECTLY CONSCIOUS.
SHE LIED TO YOU!
SNIFF!
BUT... WHY... WHY NOT JUST ASK ME WHEN I WAS IN THE RIGHT MENTAL STATE?
WE GOT NO ANSWER TO THAT ONE, ROSS!
BURP!

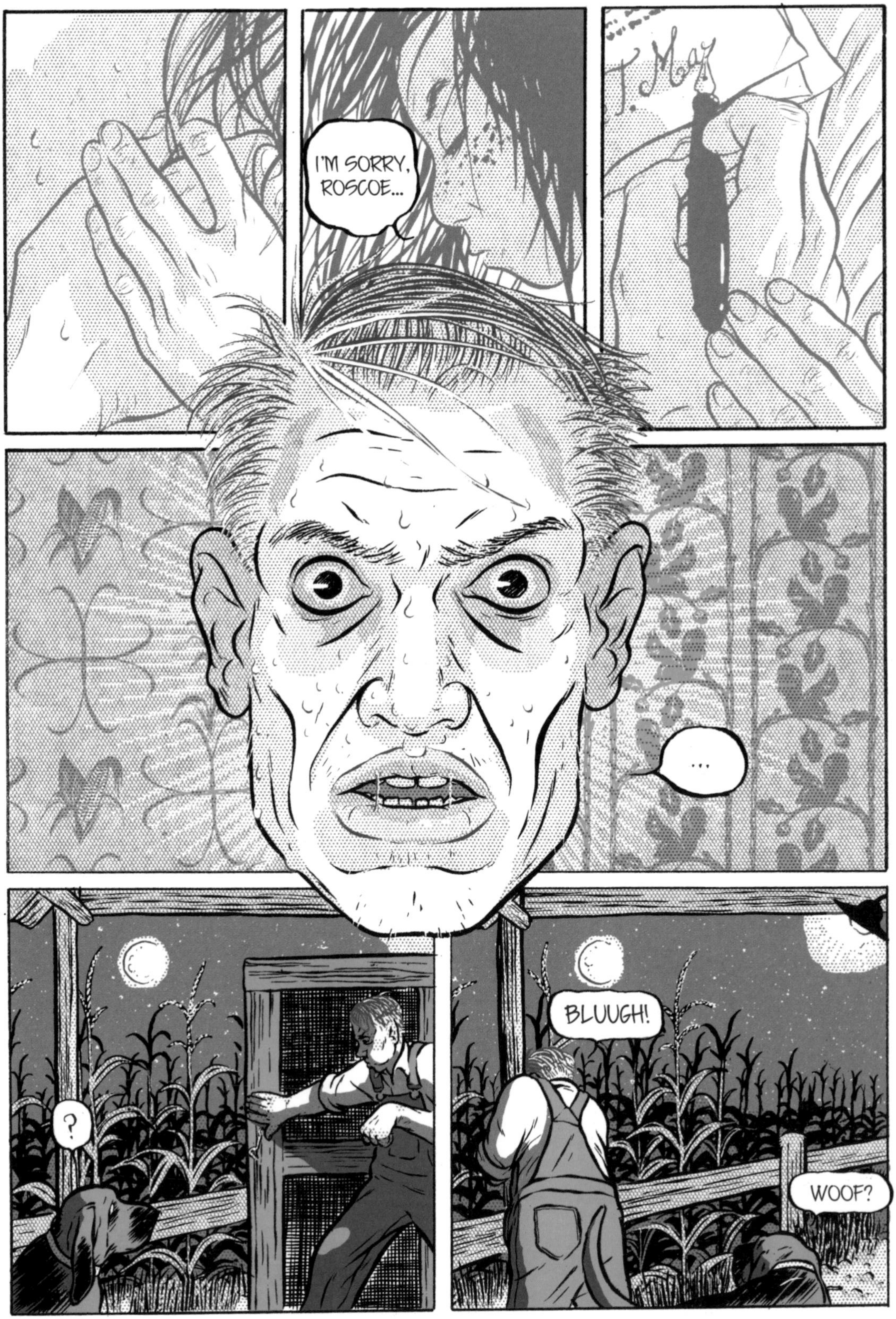
I'M SORRY, ROSCOE...
...
?
BLUUGH!
WOOF?

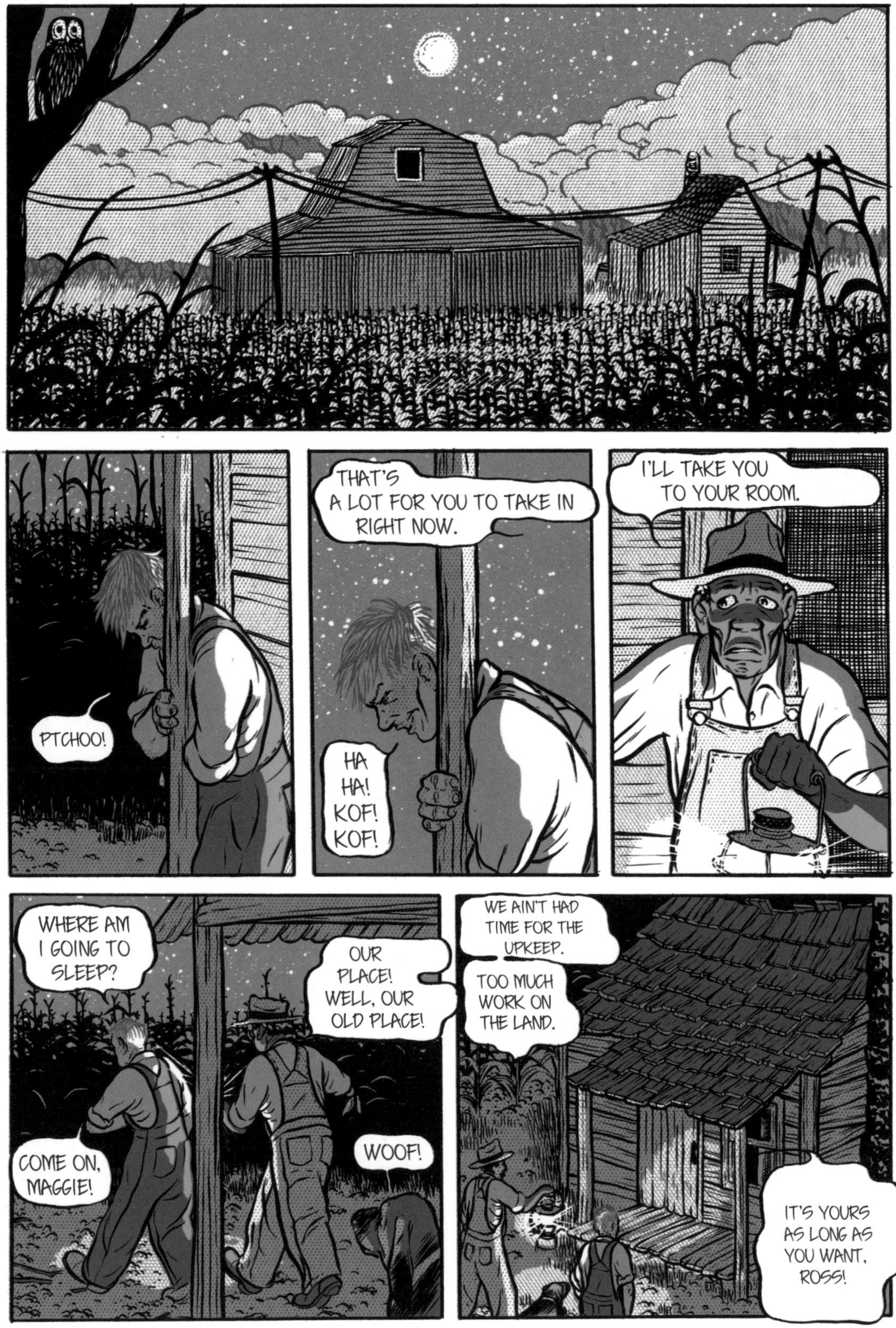
PTCHOO!
THAT'S A LOT FOR YOU TO TAKE IN RIGHT NOW.
HA HA! KOF! KOF!
I'LL TAKE YOU TO YOUR ROOM.
WHERE AM I GOING TO SLEEP?
OUR PLACE! WELL, OUR OLD PLACE!
COME ON, MAGGIE!
WOOF!
WE AIN'T HAD TIME FOR THE UPKEEP.
TOO MUCH WORK ON THE LAND.
IT'S YOURS AS LONG AS YOU WANT, ROSS!

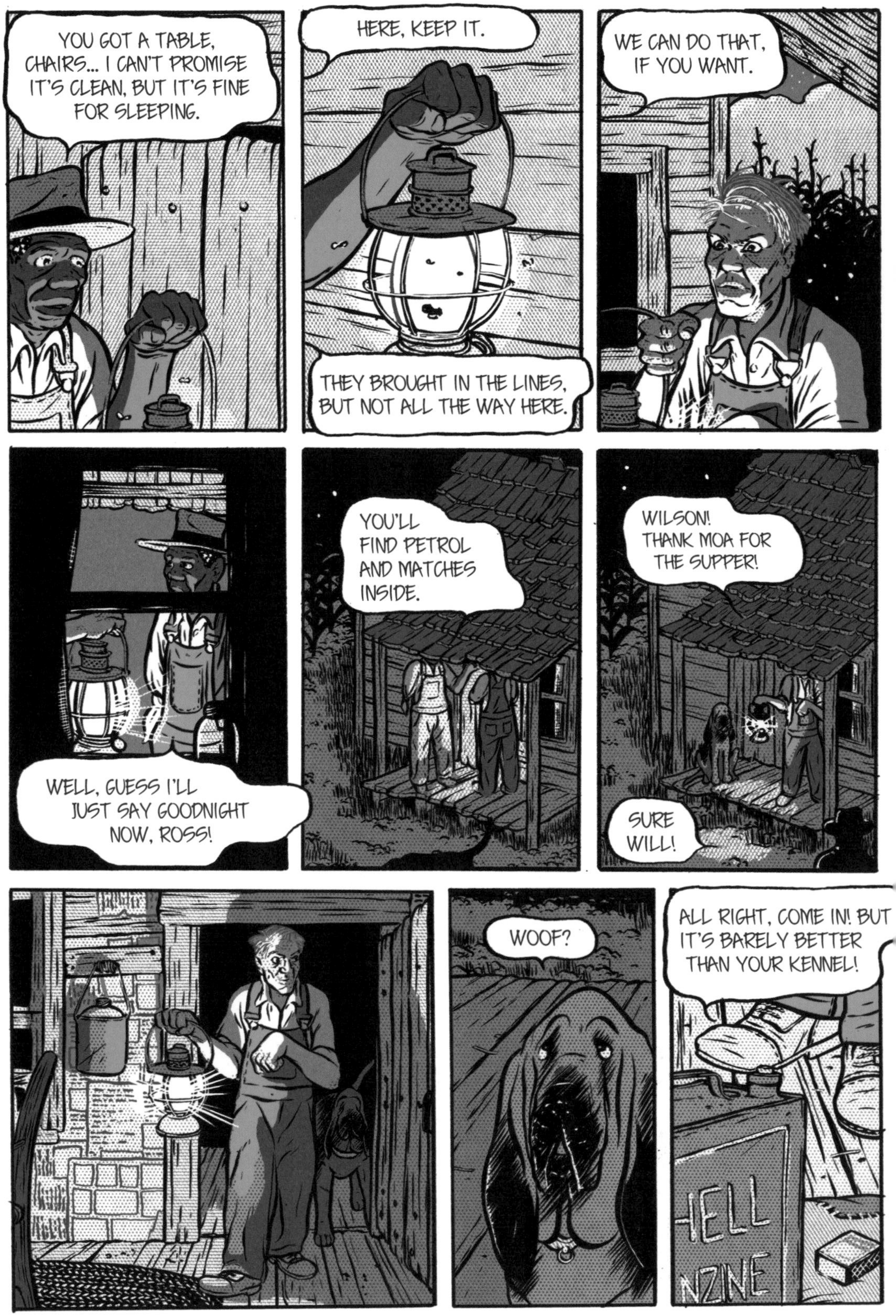
YOU GOT A TABLE, CHAIRS... I CAN'T PROMISE IT'S CLEAN, BUT IT'S FINE FOR SLEEPING.
HERE, KEEP IT.
THEY BROUGHT IN THE LINES, BUT NOT ALL THE WAY HERE.
WE CAN DO THAT, IF YOU WANT.
WELL, GUESS I'LL JUST SAY GOODNIGHT NOW, ROSS!
YOU'LL FIND PETROL AND MATCHES INSIDE.
WILSON! THANK MOA FOR THE SUPPER!
SURE WILL!
WOOF?
ALL RIGHT, COME IN! BUT IT'S BARELY BETTER THAN YOUR KENNEL!
HELL
NZINE

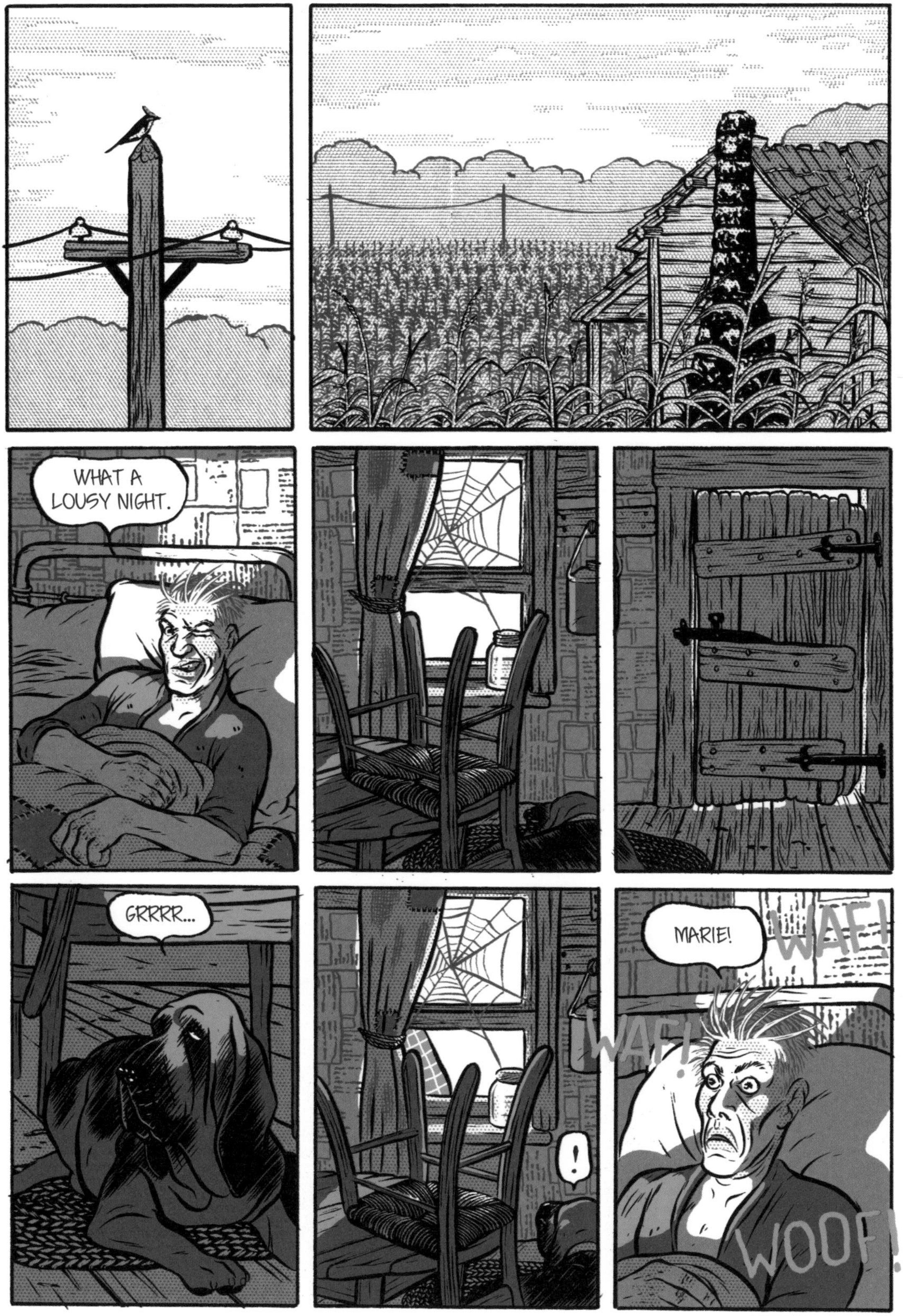
WHAT A LOUSY NIGHT.
GRRRR...
!
MARIE!
WAF!
WAF!
WOOF!

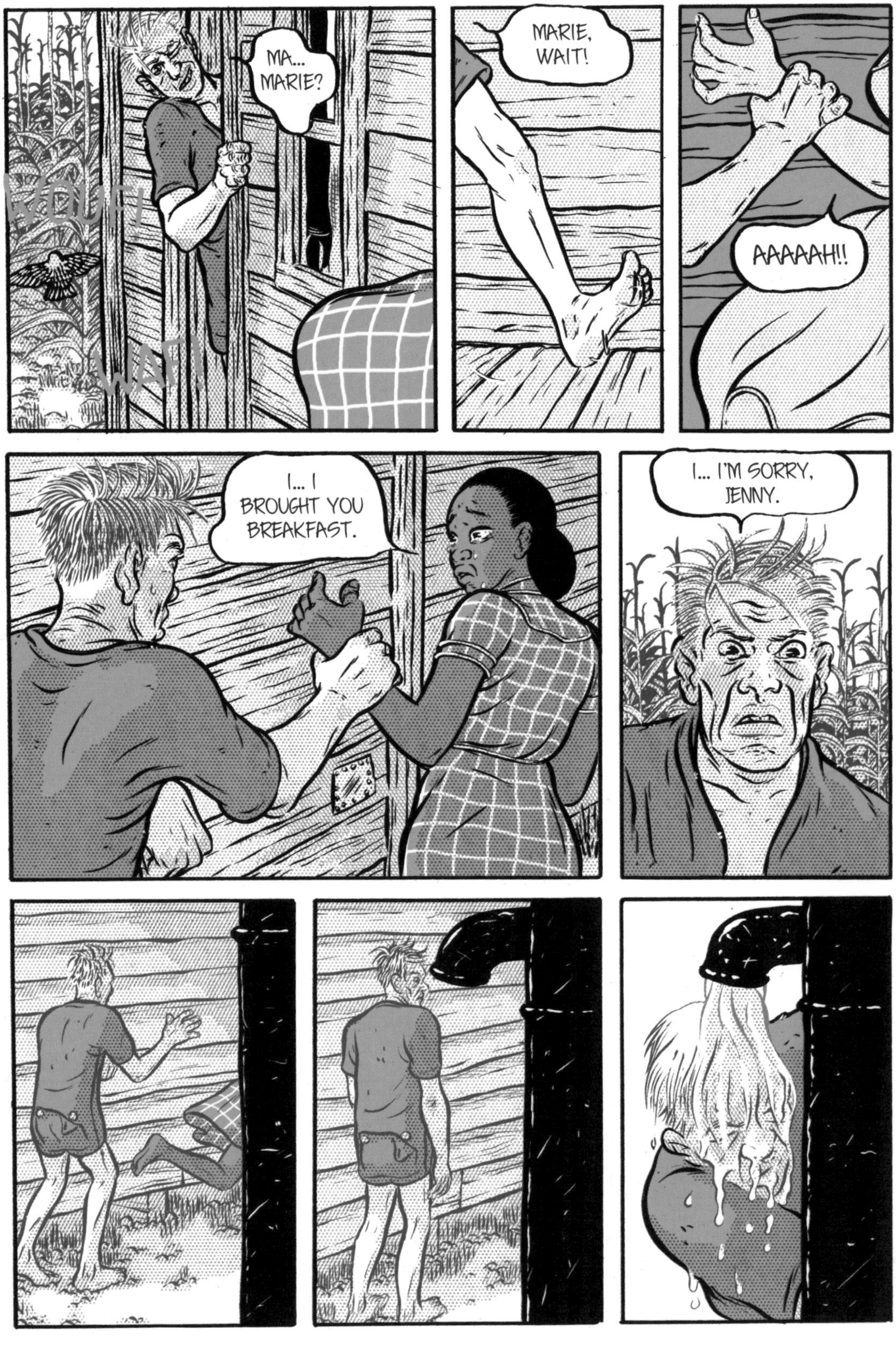
MA...
MARIE?
WOUF!
WAF!
MARIE,
WAIT!
AAAAAH!!
I... I
BROUGHT YOU
BREAKFAST.
I... I'M SORRY,
JENNY.

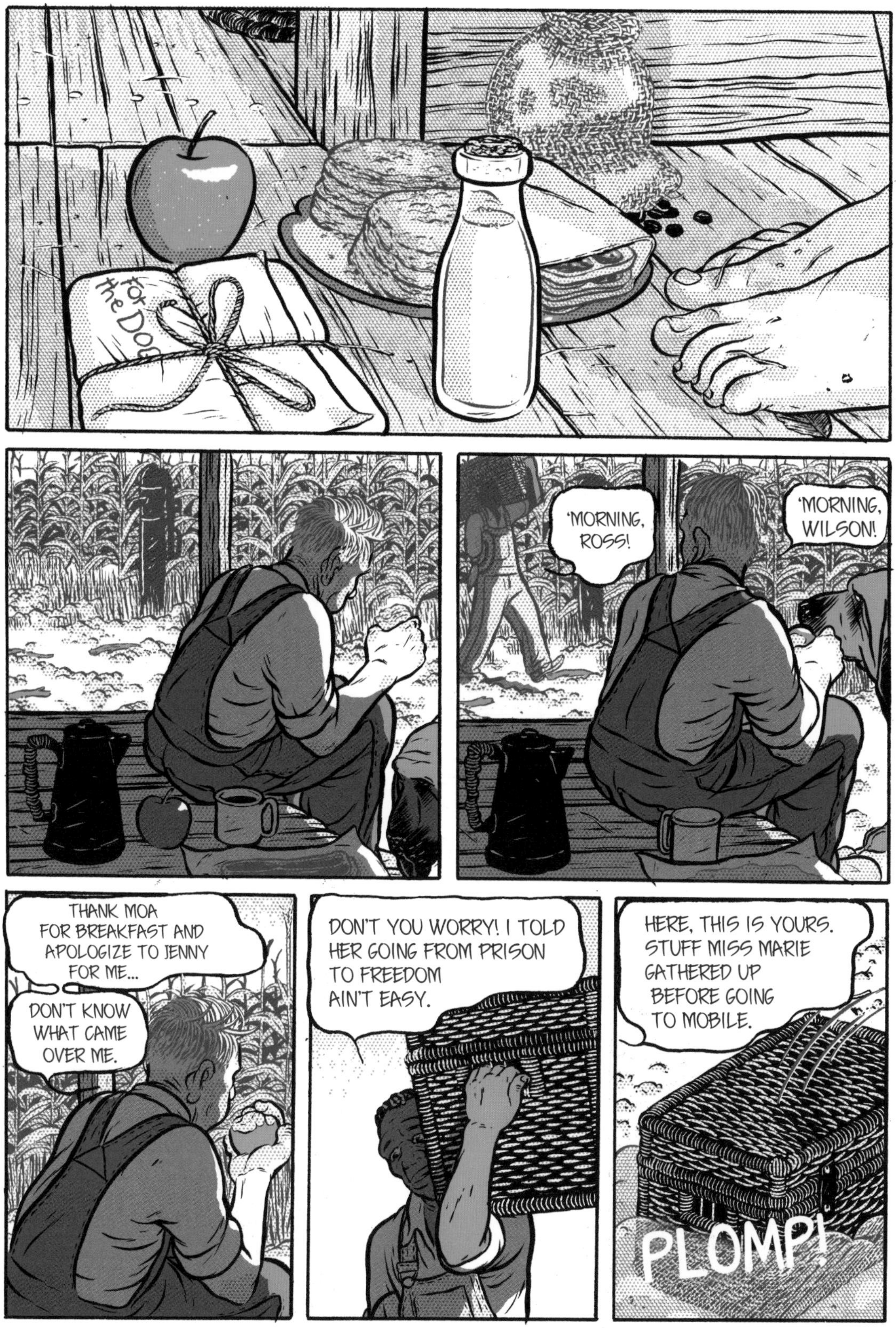
For the Dog
'MORNING, ROSS!
'MORNING, WILSON!
THANK MOA FOR BREAKFAST AND APOLOGIZE TO JENNY FOR ME...
DON'T KNOW WHAT CAME OVER ME.
DON'T YOU WORRY! I TOLD HER GOING FROM PRISON TO FREEDOM AIN'T EASY.
HERE, THIS IS YOURS. STUFF MISS MARIE GATHERED UP BEFORE GOING TO MOBILE.
PLOMP!

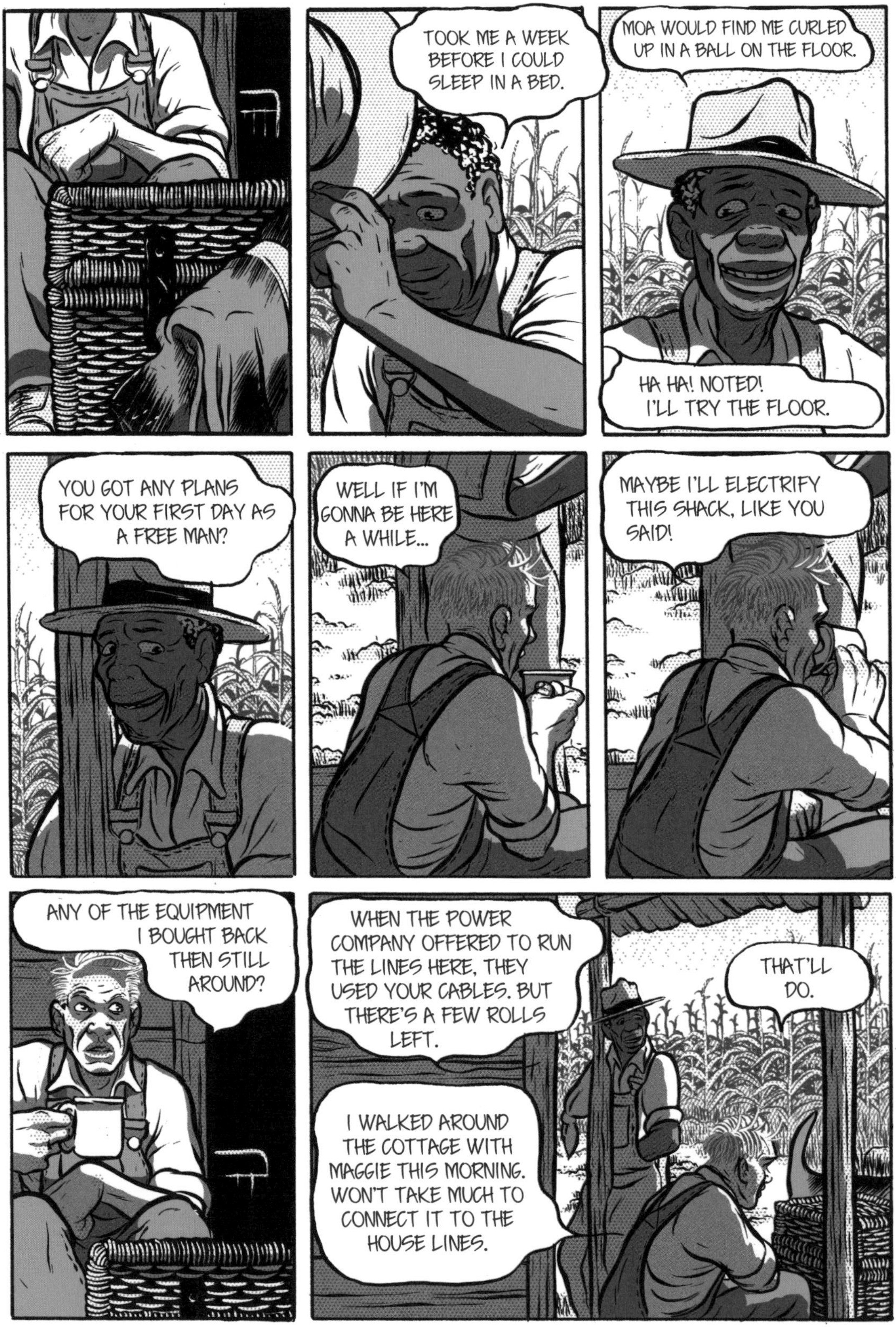
TOOK ME A WEEK BEFORE I COULD SLEEP IN A BED.
MOA WOULD FIND ME CURLED UP IN A BALL ON THE FLOOR.
HA HA! NOTED! I'LL TRY THE FLOOR.
YOU GOT ANY PLANS FOR YOUR FIRST DAY AS A FREE MAN?
WELL IF I'M GONNA BE HERE A WHILE...
MAYBE I'LL ELECTRIFY THIS SHACK, LIKE YOU SAID!
ANY OF THE EQUIPMENT I BOUGHT BACK THEN STILL AROUND?
WHEN THE POWER COMPANY OFFERED TO RUN THE LINES HERE, THEY USED YOUR CABLES. BUT THERE'S A FEW ROLLS LEFT.
I WALKED AROUND THE COTTAGE WITH MAGGIE THIS MORNING. WON'T TAKE MUCH TO CONNECT IT TO THE HOUSE LINES.
THAT'LL DO.

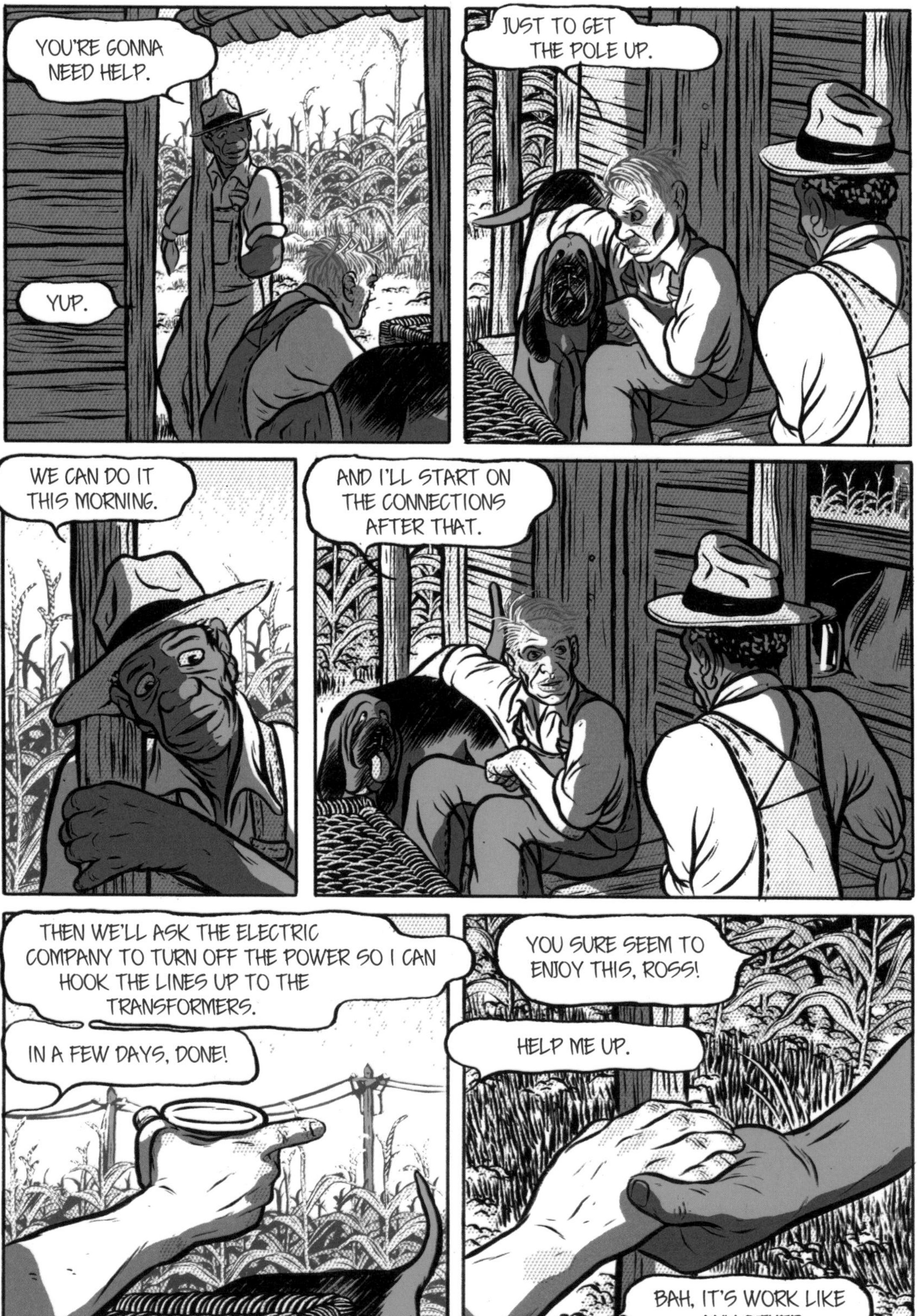
YOU'RE GONNA NEED HELP.
YUP.
JUST TO GET THE POLE UP.
WE CAN DO IT THIS MORNING.
AND I'LL START ON THE CONNECTIONS AFTER THAT.
THEN WE'LL ASK THE ELECTRIC COMPANY TO TURN OFF THE POWER SO I CAN HOOK THE LINES UP TO THE TRANSFORMERS.
IN A FEW DAYS, DONE!
YOU SURE SEEM TO ENJOY THIS, ROSS!
HELP ME UP.
BAH, IT'S WORK LIKE ANY OTHER.

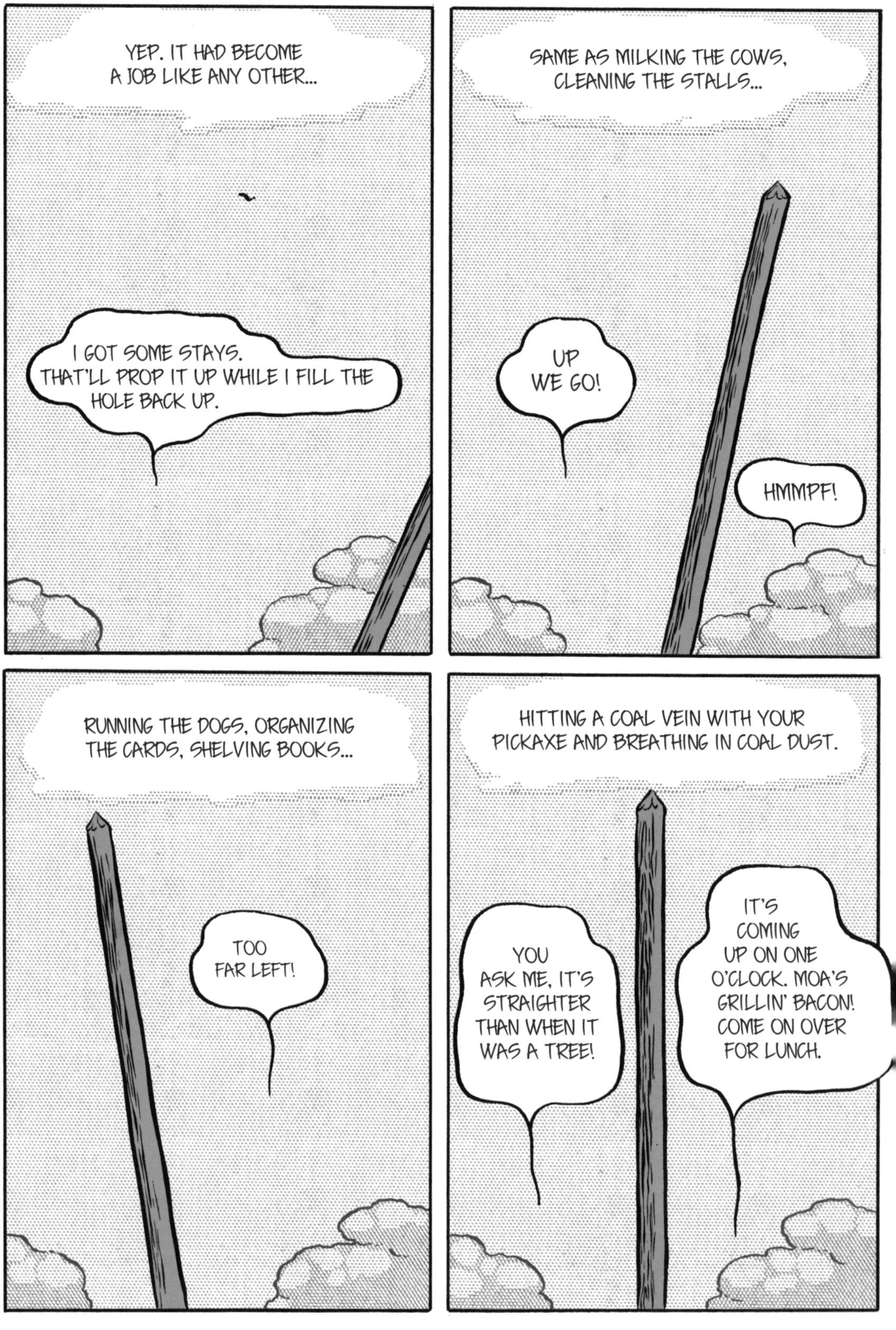
YEP. IT HAD BECOME A JOB LIKE ANY OTHER...
I GOT SOME STAYS. THAT'LL PROP IT UP WHILE I FILL THE HOLE BACK UP.
SAME AS MILKING THE COWS, CLEANING THE STALLS...
UP WE GO!
HMMPF!
RUNNING THE DOGS, ORGANIZING THE CARDS, SHELVING BOOKS...
TOO FAR LEFT!
HITTING A COAL VEIN WITH YOUR PICKAXE AND BREATHING IN COAL DUST.
YOU ASK ME, IT'S STRAIGHTER THAN WHEN IT WAS A TREE!
IT'S COMING UP ON ONE O'CLOCK. MOA'S GRILLIN' BACON! COME ON OVER FOR LUNCH.

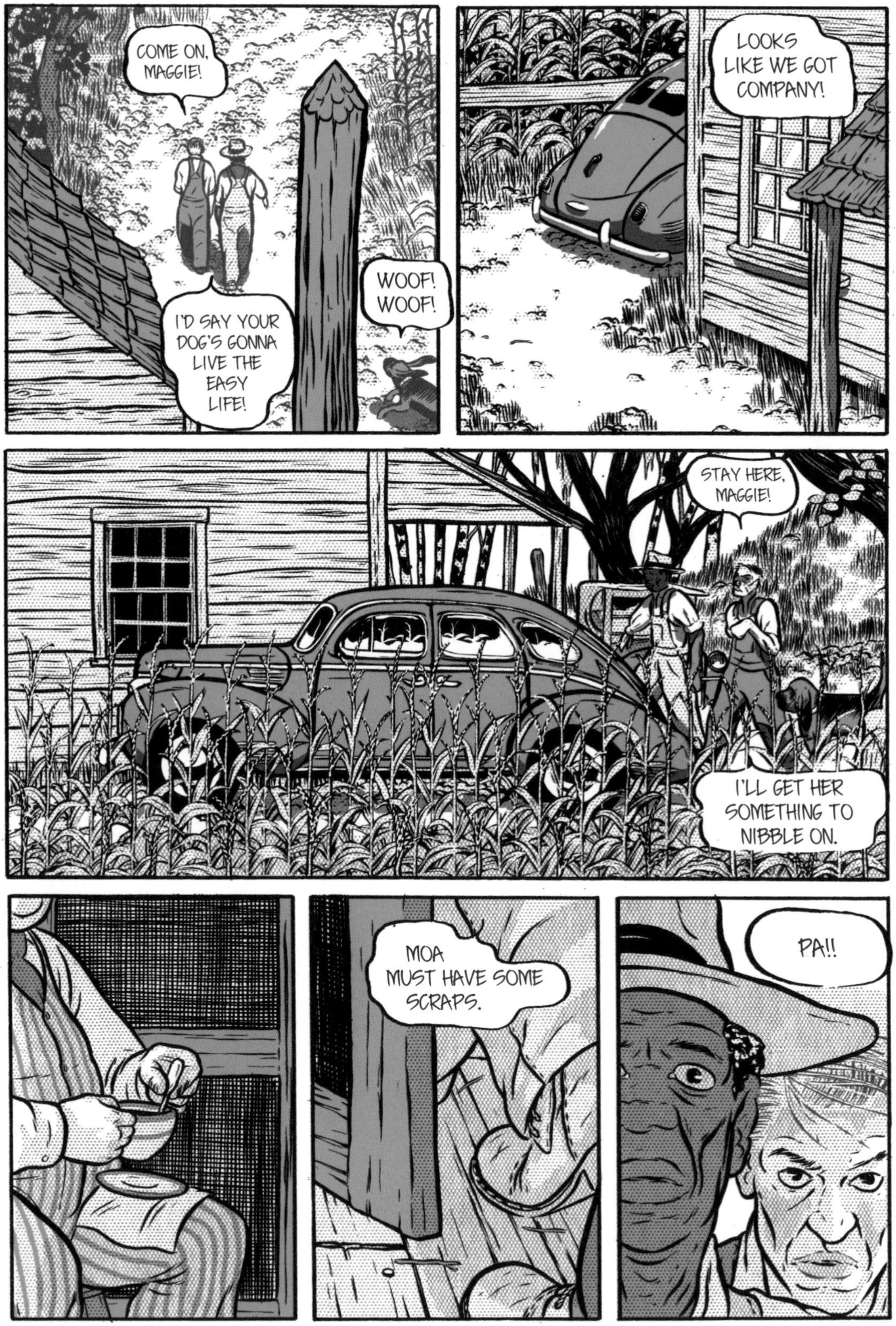
COME ON, MAGGIE!
I'D SAY YOUR DOG'S GONNA LIVE THE EASY LIFE!
WOOF! WOOF!
LOOKS LIKE WE GOT COMPANY!
STAY HERE, MAGGIE!
I'LL GET HER SOMETHING TO NIBBLE ON.
MOA MUST HAVE SOME SCRAPS.
PA!!

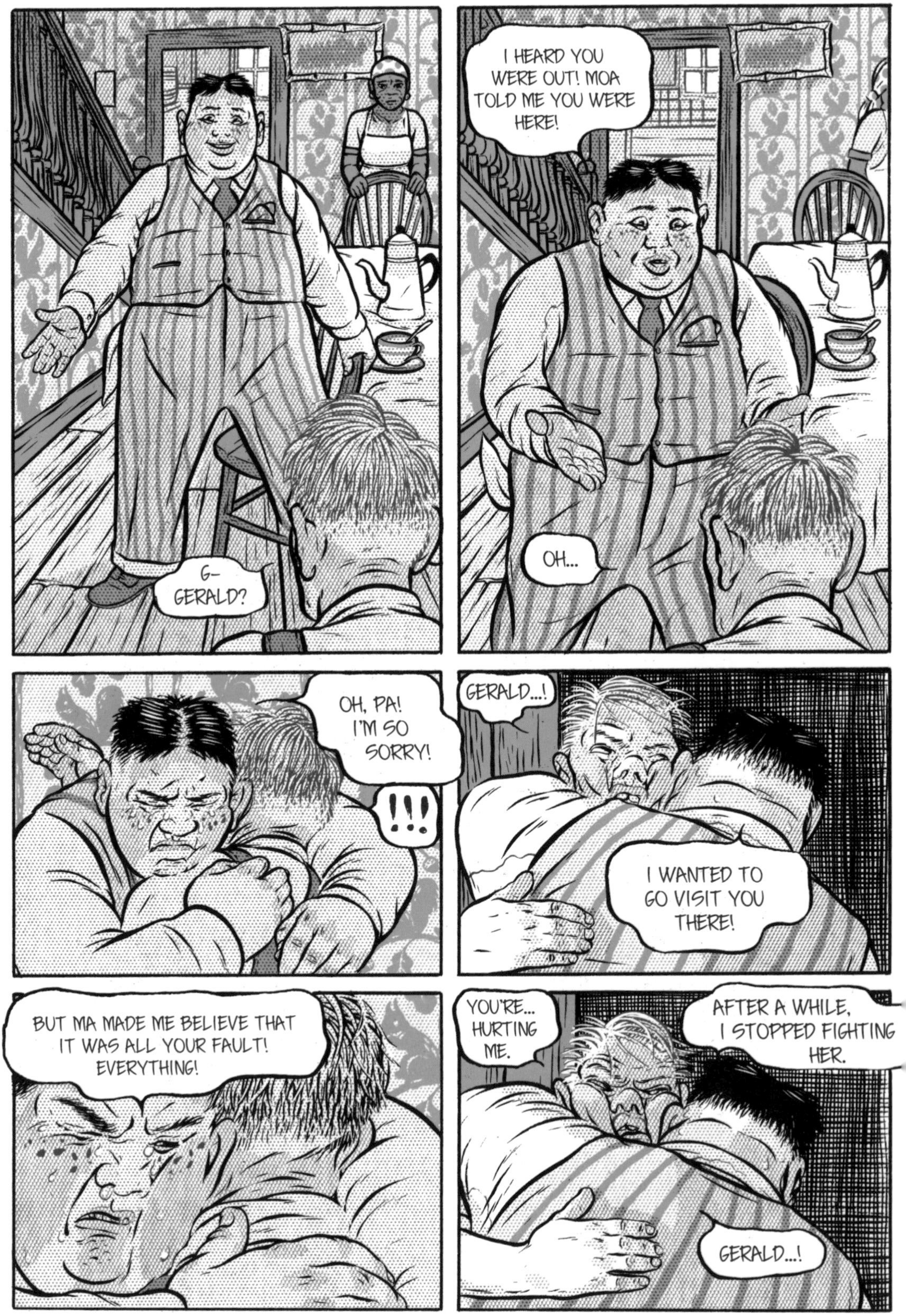

G- GERALD?
I HEARD YOU WERE OUT! MOA TOLD ME YOU WERE HERE!
OH...
OH, PA! I'M SO SORRY!
!!!
GERALD...!
I WANTED TO GO VISIT YOU THERE!
BUT MA MADE ME BELIEVE THAT IT WAS ALL YOUR FAULT! EVERYTHING!
YOU'RE... HURTING ME.
AFTER A WHILE, I STOPPED FIGHTING HER.
GERALD...!

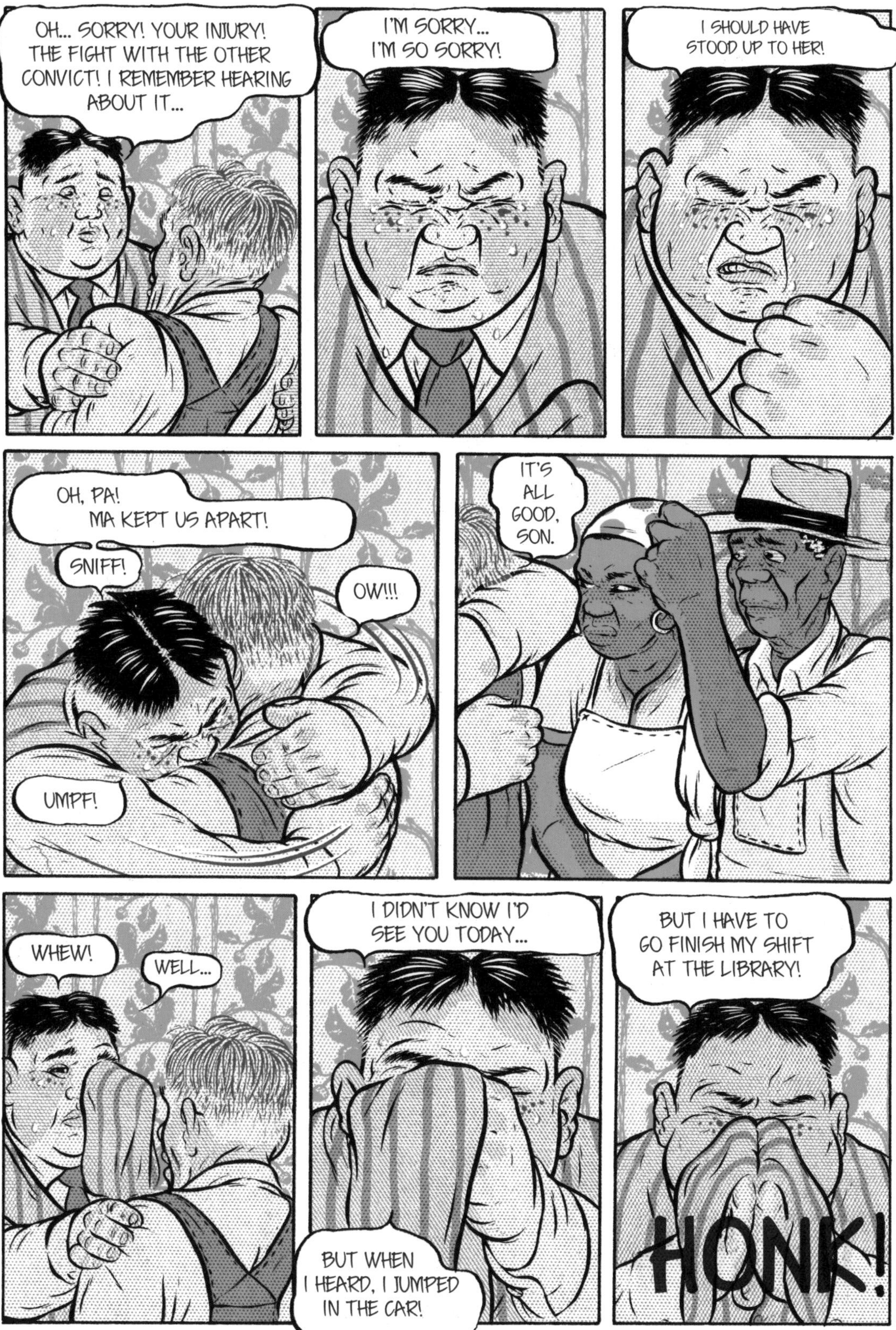
OH... SORRY! YOUR INJURY! THE FIGHT WITH THE OTHER CONVICT! I REMEMBER HEARING ABOUT IT...
I'M SORRY... I'M SO SORRY!
I SHOULD HAVE STOOD UP TO HER!
OH, PA! MA KEPT US APART!
SNIFF!
OW!!!
UMPF!
IT'S ALL GOOD, SON.
WHEW!
WELL...
I DIDN'T KNOW I'D SEE YOU TODAY...
BUT WHEN I HEARD, I JUMPED IN THE CAR!
BUT I HAVE TO GO FINISH MY SHIFT AT THE LIBRARY!
HONK!

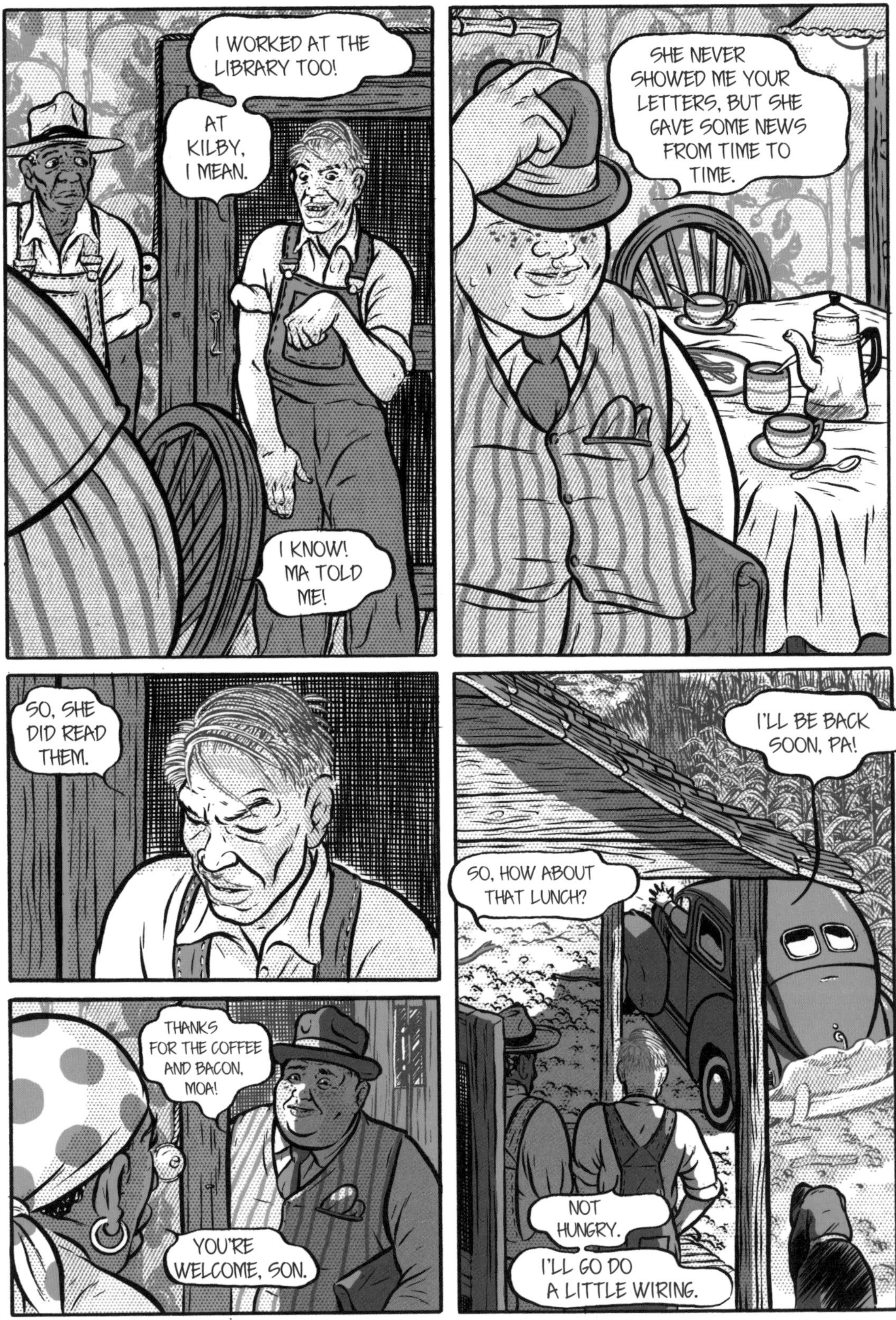
I WORKED AT THE LIBRARY TOO!
AT KILBY, I MEAN.
I KNOW! MA TOLD ME!
SHE NEVER SHOWED ME YOUR LETTERS, BUT SHE GAVE SOME NEWS FROM TIME TO TIME.
SO, SHE DID READ THEM.
THANKS FOR THE COFFEE AND BACON, MOA!
YOU'RE WELCOME, SON.
I'LL BE BACK SOON, PA!
SO, HOW ABOUT THAT LUNCH?
NOT HUNGRY.
I'LL GO DO A LITTLE WIRING.

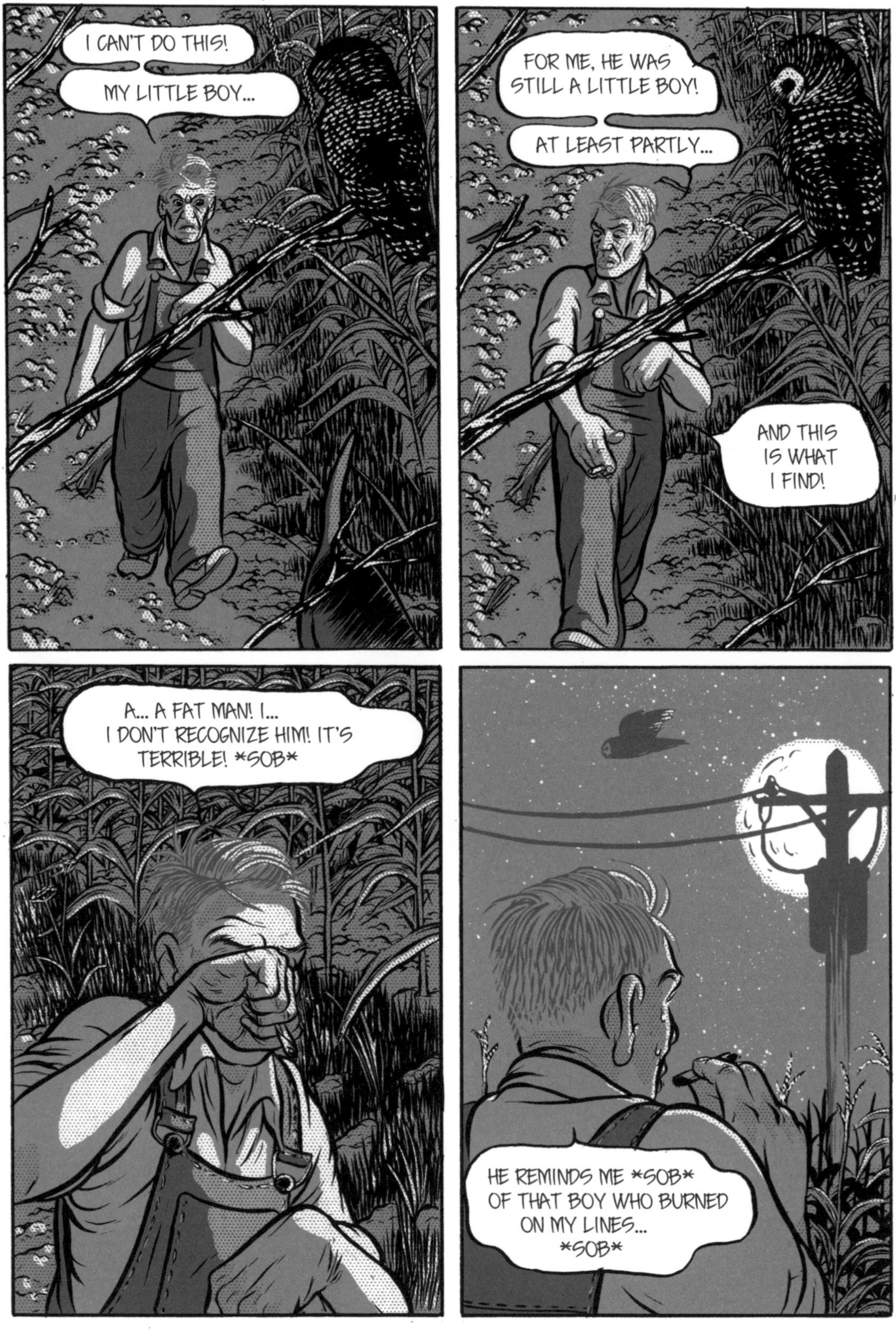
I CAN'T DO THIS!
MY LITTLE BOY...
FOR ME, HE WAS STILL A LITTLE BOY!
AT LEAST PARTLY...
AND THIS IS WHAT I FIND!
A... A FAT MAN! I... I DON'T RECOGNIZE HIM! IT'S TERRIBLE! *SOB*
HE REMINDS ME *SOB* OF THAT BOY WHO BURNED ON MY LINES... *SOB*

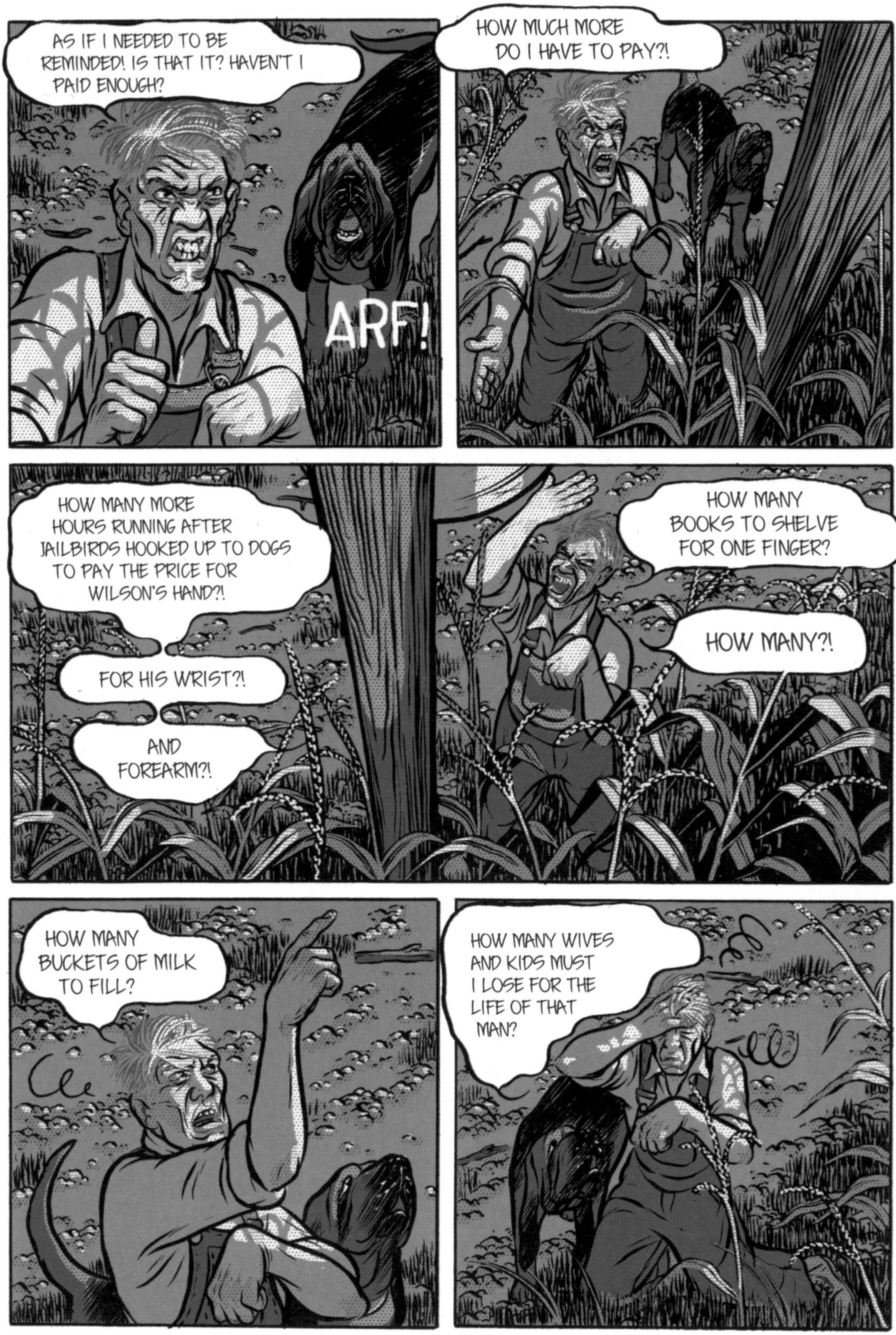
AS IF I NEEDED TO BE REMINDED! IS THAT IT? HAVEN'T I PAID ENOUGH?
ARF!
HOW MUCH MORE DO I HAVE TO PAY?!
HOW MANY MORE HOURS RUNNING AFTER JAILBIRDS HOOKED UP TO DOGS TO PAY THE PRICE FOR WILSON'S HAND?!
FOR HIS WRIST?!
AND FOREARM?!
HOW MANY BOOKS TO SHELVE FOR ONE FINGER?
HOW MANY?!
HOW MANY BUCKETS OF MILK TO FILL?
HOW MANY WIVES AND KIDS MUST I LOSE FOR THE LIFE OF THAT MAN?

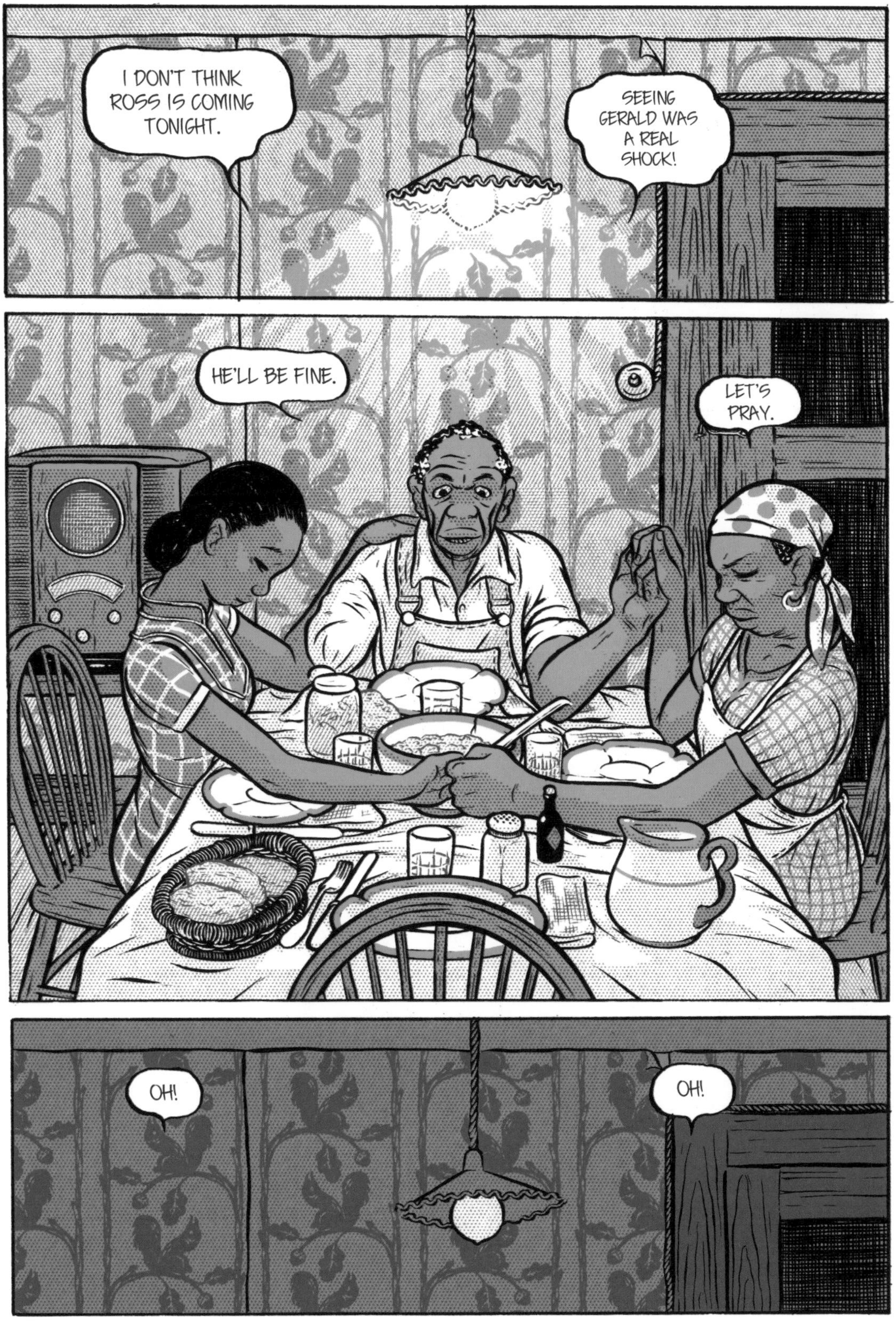
I DON'T THINK ROSS IS COMING TONIGHT.
SEEING GERALD WAS A REAL SHOCK!
HE'LL BE FINE.
LET'S PRAY.
OH!
OH!

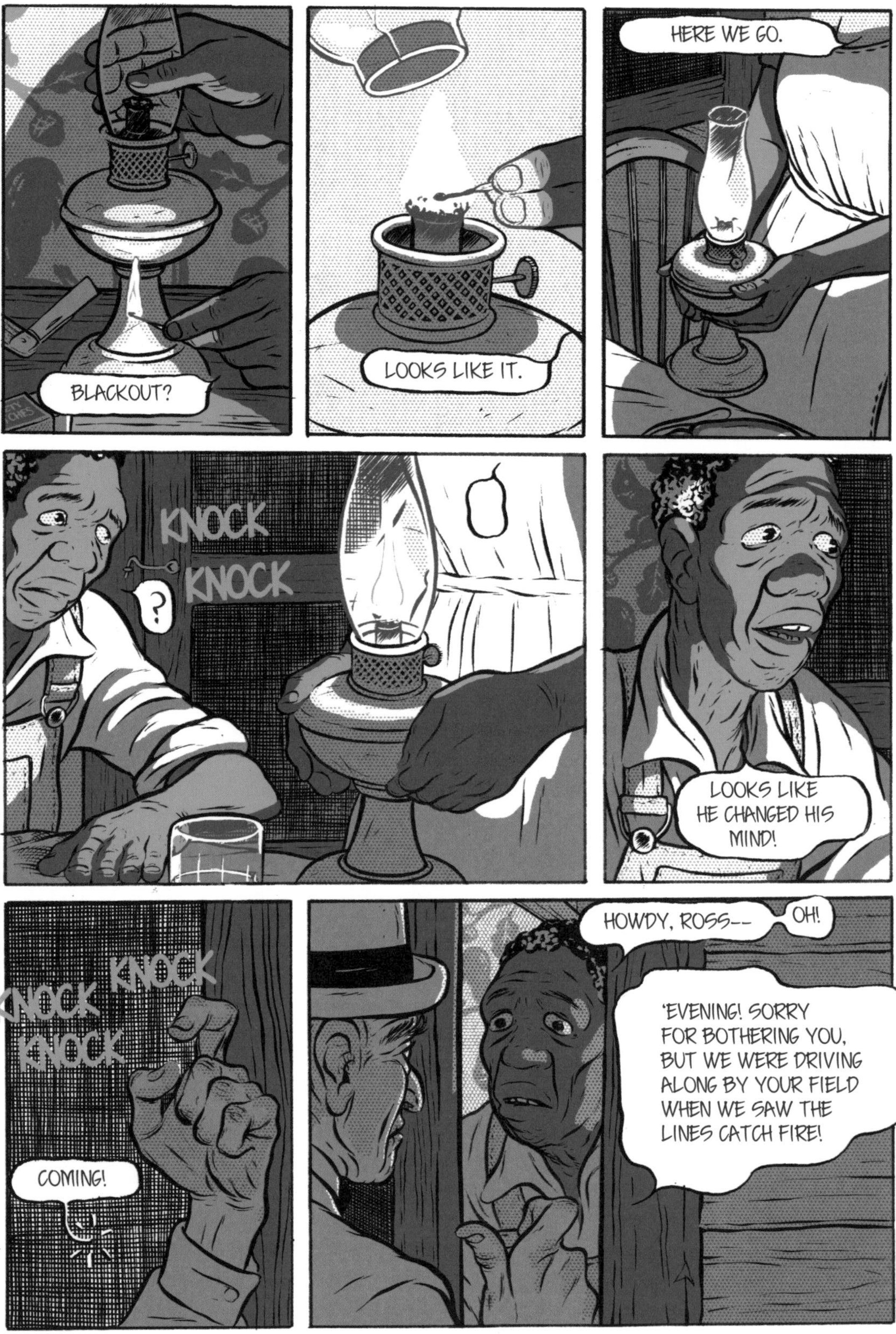
BLACKOUT?
LOOKS LIKE IT.
HERE WE GO.
KNOCK
KNOCK
?
LOOKS LIKE HE CHANGED HIS MIND!
KNOCK
KNOCK
KNOCK
COMING!
HOWDY, ROSS--
OH!
'EVENING! SORRY FOR BOTHERING YOU, BUT WE WERE DRIVING ALONG BY YOUR FIELD WHEN WE SAW THE LINES CATCH FIRE!

THE LINES CAUGHT...
SNIFF

SNIFF
SNIFF

SNIFF
THAT... THAT SMELL!

WILSON!

I KNOW IT!

HEY!

SAME AS 15 YEARS AGO...

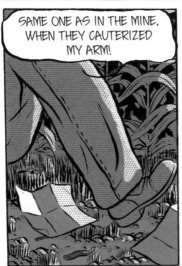

SAME ONE AS IN THE MINE, WHEN THEY CAUTERIZED MY ARM!

SAME ONE AS WHEN THEY TURN THE CHAIR ON IN PRISON, I BET!

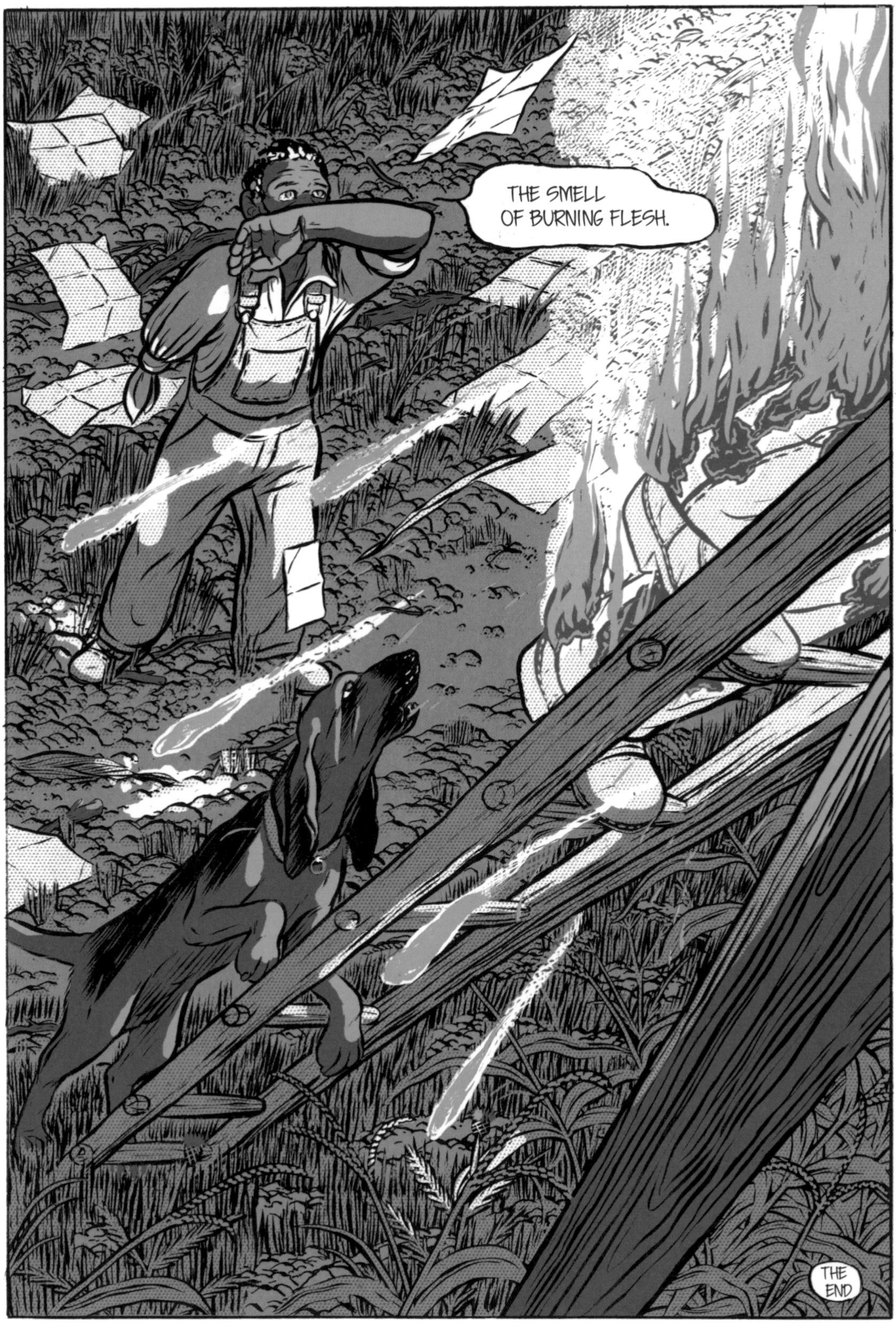
THE SMELL OF BURNING FLESH.
THE END